Queen L

Queen Live

A Concert Documentary *by Greg Brooks*

OMNIBUS PRESS

Copyright © 1995 Omnibus Press
(A Division of Book Sales Limited)

Edited by Chris Charlesworth.
Cover & book designed by Michael Bell Design.
Picture research by Nikki Russell.

ISBN 0.7119.4814.3
Order No. OP47752

Exclusive Distributors:
Book Sales Limited
8/9 Frith Street, London W1V 5TZ, UK.

Music Sales Corporation
257 Park Avenue South, New York, NY 10010, USA.

Music Sales Pty Limited
120 Rothschild Avenue, Rosebery, NSW 2018, Australia.

To the Music Trade only:
Music Sales Limited
8/9 Frith Street, London W1V 5TZ, UK.

Queen Live

Photo credits: Richard E. Aaron / Star File: 28B,
53B, 60T&B; Andrew Catlin / SIN: 176; Dagmar / Star File:
22T, 62T; Bob Gruen / Star File: 71; London Features
International: front cover insets, 8, 10, 12B, 13, 14, 16B,
18T&B, 21B, 31, 33, 38, 39, 41B, 42B, 45B, 46, 47, 57, 69,
75, 76B, 84T, 85, 87, 92, 95, 106, 109B, 111, 112, 124, 127,
134, 139B, 141T, 143, 144T&B, 145, 148, 149T, 151, 176;
Jeff Mayer / Star File: 28T, 44B, 73 L, 120; Karla Merrifield /
Star File: 34, 35, 56, 63T; Johnny Olsen / Retna: front cover
main; Pictorial Press: 17, 48T&B, 52B, 68T, 72, 73R, 80,
81, 88, 105, 116; Barry Plummer: front cover inset, back
cover main & insets, 14B, 42T, 44T, 51, 55, 58, 59 L&R,
62B, 63B, 64, 66, 68B, 83, 86, 90T&B, 91, 93T&C, 103,
107, 108, 109T, 110B, 113, 119, 123, 138; Neal Preston /
Retna: 12T, 93B, 96, 104, 117, 150B; Chuck Pulin /
Star File: 43, 50; Michael Putland / Retna: 15, 19, 23, 24,
32B, 70; Duncan Raban / All Action: 141B, 142 L; Steve
Rapport / Retna: 129, 133; Relay: front & back cover
insets, 20, 21T, 22B, 26, 27T, 27B, 32T, 37, 45T, 49T&B,
52T, 53T, 54, 61, 67, 74, 76T, 77, 78, 84B, 97, 98, 99, 110T,
132, 136, 139T, 150T; Rex Features: 16T, 22B, 23, 29,
36, 40, 41T, 65T&B, 89, 100, 121, 131, 135, 140, 142R,
146, 147T, 149B, 152, 153, 154, 155T&B, 156T&B, 157;
Justin Thomas / All Action: 128, 130, 137R; Vinnie
Zuffante / Star File: 137 L.

Printed and bound in Singapore.

A catalogue record for this book is available from the
British Library.

A Concert Documentary

Introduction

As one the world's most innovative and exciting live acts, Queen were expected to tour frequently, which they did, and compared to most bands there is a generous quantity of live recordings and videos on the market. Three live albums and seven videos is significant concert representation by any standards, but few come even remotely close to capturing the true emotion, atmosphere and sheer power that Queen generated in concert. Fans and collectors regard the album output, especially, as far from sufficient. Most are only too aware of the wealth of material known to exist within the band's own archive and which still awaits proper release.

Although many fans regard 'Live Killers' (issued in 1979) to be the best concert representation so far released, even that has a number of curious omissions ('Somebody To Love', 'If You Can't Beat Them', 'Fat Bottomed Girls', 'It's Late'). At the time of it's release it even met with criticism from within the band. Indeed, two of them made public their contempt for it, as well as for live albums generally. I have always regarded the various criticisms aimed at 'Live Killers' as unfair. In my opinion it is by far the most exciting and complete record of a tour yet to have been made officially available. I say officially because many great shows (too numerous to list) have emerged via unofficial channels, but still await a proper home video release.

Having sifted my way through many hours of concert material from the 'Live Killers' period (Europe 1979), it is clear that the album is a far better representation of events than its two successors ever were, and the less said about 'Live Magic' the better. The versions of 'Don't Stop Me Now', 'Spread Your Wings', 'Love Of My Life', 'Now I'm Here', 'Dreamer's Ball', ''39' and Roger's blistering 'I'm In Love With My Car', were in my view never surpassed at any other venue on that tour.

It is perhaps ironic that despite so few recordings being available to fans, there does exist (in Queen's archive) a huge volume of material that warrants release. Shows known to exist on video include Hammersmith Odeon (1975), Hyde Park (1976), Earls Court (1977), Houston, Texas (1977), Paris (1979), Brazil and Argentina (1981), Milton Keynes and Frankfurt (1982), Japan (1985), not to mention the much acclaimed Live Aid performance. None of these concerts have ever seen the light of day (legitimately), and none it seems are likely to - in the foreseeable future at least. The Hammersmith Odeon and Milton Keynes shows came very close to being issued on home video at one point, but both projects were ultimately shelved.

The response from fans to EMI's release of the 'Rare Live' video compilation in 1989 was less than enthusiastic. Although the idea was sound enough, the end result was not. At best it was disappointing and at worst wholly inadequate. Despite some slick editing, the snippets of shows do Queen's live performances little justice, chopping and changing randomly from one concert to another. Watching this video is like watching a television drama while someone flicks through the other channels.

Fortunately or unfortunately - depending on which side of the music industry fence your sympathies lie - bootleggers were almost always at Queen shows. They have ensured over the years that shows which would otherwise have been enjoyed only by those present at the time are available (in part at least) for everyone to experience. Such unauthorised items are illegal and responsible for colossal losses in revenue each year within the music industry. They can also be the source of great disappointment to fans, as many offer notoriously poor sound quality. Some are so bad as to be completely inaudible. Despite vast numbers having been seized over the years, many continue to flood the market. Collectors are well advised to exercise caution before buying.

While bootlegs are frowned upon by the music industry as a whole, they are the only means by which fans can gain access to material which would otherwise be unavailable to them. In Queen's case bootlegging was inevitable. The shortage of officially sanctioned concert product gave collectors little choice other than to resort to unofficial alternatives. Though I do not for one minute condone bootlegs, I also make no apology for the numerous references to them in this book. Without them, this project would have been impossible. Furthermore, had I only the official issues from which to refer, the end result would have lacked details which are the very essence and heart of the Queen live show. A huge wealth of information is available from bootlegs. The performance is heard in all it's glory, warts and all, unedited, and exactly as it happened. The listener hears the concert (or most of it) as it was supposed to sound, and did sound, to the audience then present, not a polished studio interpretation.

Queen never repeated the same evening's entertainment on two nights running. Although the basic track listing of a show could remain the same from one night to the next, the delivery and manner in which it was executed could differ enormously, and frequently did. The same song could very well be performed in a number of different ways, depending on numerous factors: the atmosphere within each venue, the mood within the band and, especially, the rapport between Freddie and the audience.

A large proportion of the show set lists which follow have been compiled using information sent to me by fellow collectors over a sixteen year period. As most of them originate from an assortment of bootleg recordings - which are notorious for offering only an edited account of the show they represent, and very rarely a complete one - it is likely that some lists, especially early ones, are marginally incomplete or appear in slightly the wrong sequence.

In most cases I was able to cross reference any list which appeared implausible or incomplete, and make the appropriate amendments. However, since there is no definitive Queen concert list to consult, nor anything remotely like it, and given that many shows have not one single bootleg relating to them, it was occasionally necessary to offer instead the most likely set list. In those instances, details from shows of a similar period which are known to be accurate were used to compile a very close approximation as to the set Queen performed, or to fill in any missing gaps.

Despite having access to over four hundred separate fan and collectors lists from all around the world, I typically encountered the same shows time and time again. While details relating to one show, gained from several different sources, can precisely determine most of the true set list of a given performance, at the same time, few recordings offer a full show. An educated guess at the entire set is all that can therefore be offered.

In some cases collectors who submitted lists were unaware that some examples they forwarded contained false or misleading information. This was not deliberate. Great numbers of bootlegs do not feature the material they purport to, or they include music recorded from another performance entirely. Such tapes are usually put together to exploit new or unsuspecting collectors. The inclusion of one or two rare songs that were not actually performed on a specific night are used to inspire additional sales of a bootleg, sales which would otherwise not have occurred. In extreme cases, material from several shows is strung together and issued as an enigmatic, atypical recording. Freddie and Brian's between song conversation is cunningly excised to make the ploy almost impossible to detect. For this reason, it can be dangerous to rely too heavily upon some information, no matter how credible the source is.

To confuse the issue yet further, Queen often performed an identical set on two or three consecutive nights, but not always in the same sequence. A song which was not performed in its usual allotted position, will appear to be misplaced on the collectors set list. An illustration of this is the legendary Christmas Eve show of 1975. Because the band inadvertently missed out 'Seven Seas Of Rhye' during the main set, they instead fitted it in after 'In The Lap Of The Gods', at the end of the show. The bootleg sleeve note details would seem to be inaccurate, especially when compared to other listings of the period, but are in fact correct.

There is no foolproof method to determine which lists are accurate, and which are unreliable. While the majority of set list information hereafter is entirely accurate, I do not claim that to be the case in every instance. Where possible the data has been cross referenced six or seven times. Although the band maintained a policy of recording almost every show they ever performed (directly from the mixing desk), it was impossible to access that information.

In conclusion, I should point out that while some tours (or legs thereof) have huge bootleg representation, others have absolutely none. This factor accounts for the general imbalance of information throughout these pages. I apologise in advance, therefore, for the many entries which appear with little or no accompanying text. It was entirely unavoidable.

Greg Brooks - August 1995

Queen Live

Preface

In a career which spanned three decades, Queen inspired innumerable articles, books and television and radio interviews. Every aspect of their history has been explored in one form or another; every fact, figure, quote, misquote and anecdote used and re-used time and time again, in biographies, newspaper articles and documentaries. As most information on the band was exhausted years ago, predicting the content of each new publication — even before the first page has been turned — has become absurdly simple.

Despite an extensive library of printed matter, very little has actually been written which focuses specifically on Queen's live performances. It was partly for this reason that I decided to compile this book. What began as a project purely for my own use quickly snowballed into what most people around me regard as a book — though I prefer to call it a Live Study. Although I had anticipated the project would occupy some considerable time, I did not envisage it taking six years to complete.

In undertaking a project such as this, there is a danger of going into too much detail and bordering on monotonous or boring. It is immensely difficult to know exactly where to draw the line between that which is relevant and interesting information, and that which is unnecessary and tedious. I apologise in advance should any of the following text fall into the latter category. I must add, however, that in my experience nothing related to Queen, however trivial it might seem, is ever considered boring by the typical fan.

I hope, if nothing else, that this book offers an insight into what made Queen such extraordinary concert showmen. It is an avenue of Queen's career which has for too long been overlooked, yet which was such a fundamental part of the band's evolution, as much a part of Queen as 'Bohemian Rhapsody' and black nail varnish.

Queen Live

Acknowledgements

I am indebted to many individuals who were kind
enough to assist me with background and cross reference
information for this book. Almost without exception,
everyone I contacted responded with material which
was used in one form or another. I am extremely grateful
to each and every one. I offer sincere thanks to the
following:

Paul Bird (for additional sleeve illustrations), Ron
Wheeler, Keith Lambert, John Jemmett, Tom Crossland,
Jeanette Lea, Becky Wellam, Paul Lynas, Andy Armitage,
Colin Naylor, Dylan Taylor, Martin Latham, Angela
Brown, Steve Jesson, John (Bendy) Pett, Paul Barrett,
Carole Smith, Mike Phillips, Neil French, Colin
Humphries, David Parr, Paul Ryan, Mike Salter, Bunny,
Jan Sharpe and Nick (Bailey Boy) Bailey. Special thanks
are extended to Ernst H. Larson (in Norway), Antonio
Henrique Seligman (Brazil), Frank Hazenberg (Holland),
Celia Diego Alvarez (Spain), Inma Pacheco Jimena (Spain),
Justin Leiter (USA), Grenville Madison (USA),
L. Mattending (Canada), Giancarlo Calo (Italy), Oliver
Tamminga (Germany), Kim Thomson (South Africa)
and my good friends George & Shalva Kokochashvili,
in the Republic of Georgia. Thanks also to Thomas
Ross, Trevor Horswell and Darren Mundy who submitted
artwork which could not be included in this book.

Very special thanks to Jim Jenkins. His ability to date
photographs of the band, and in many cases determine
specifically which song they were performing at the
time, never ceased to amaze me. His stockpile of Queen
related anecdotes is second to none, as is his band
knowledge. Very special thanks to Bob Harris, Arthur
Hardy (for invaluable guidance and encouragement
right from day one), Andy Broad (for bringing Queen
to my attention in the first instance), Beverley Ludlow,
Vanessa Florey, BB, Greg (Teraitch) Hardy (for nothing
in particular), Iain Wright (for restoring my computer
back to a usable state, after I had rendered it useless).
And most especially my mother Rosemary, whose
wallpaper and paint work was regularly destroyed
by my many Queen posters.

And to Jan Holmes – the light at the end of the tunnel.

Most of us take the gift of sight for granted, but a
letter I received in response to material for this project
pointed out that those without it are faced with
difficulties which really should not exist in the 1990's.
Perhaps at some point in the near future, all Queen
related reading matter will be made available in Braille.
Perhaps this book will be the first. Many thanks to
Patricia Sanders (in The Netherlands). Your kind words
were greatly appreciated. I take your point.

A proportion of incidental information in this book
was extracted from Queen Fan Club magazines. Since its
formation in 1974 – when it consisted of a one page
A4 news update – the Fan Club has gone from strength
to strength and is now established as the largest
independent Information Service of its kind in Britain.
Sincere thanks are extended to all the individuals
responsible for keeping the fans informed all these years,
but most especially the present Secretary Jacky Smith,
who has for the past thirteen years laboured tirelessly
on our behalf. Her efforts have resulted in fans all around
the world being allowed access (wherever possible) to
information and Queen related product, which would
otherwise have been unavailable.

For information on how to join the
Official Queen Fan Club, contact Jacky or Val at:
Offical International Queen Fan Club
The Old Bakehouse, 16a Barnes High Street, Barnes,
London SW13, England.
Telephone: 0181-392 2800.

For details of the
Princes Of The Universe Fanzine contact:
Neil French, 7 Chandlers Drive, Erith, Kent, DA8 1LL.

In addition to the above, the frequently published
Queen Fan Newsletter can be obtained by contacting:
David Parr, 128 St. Thomas Road, Preston, Lancashire,
PR1 6AY.

This book is dedicated to the memory of Louise
Blake and Phil Cross (Bruce) – a constant source of
inspiration, wherever they may be.

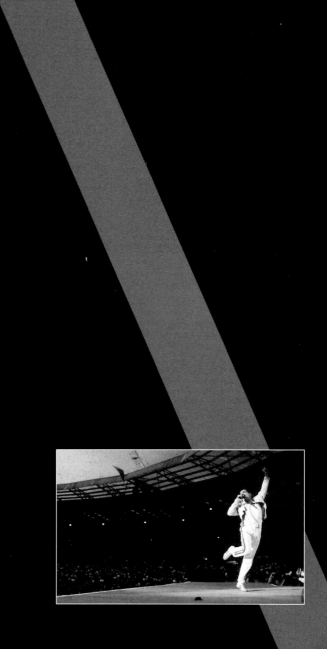

Foreword

If this reads as if I'm writing for the Queen Fan Club Magazine I make no apologies. My regard for the band stems entirely from their attitude towards those they identified as most important – their fans.

The warmth that exists between Queen and their followers is unique, and nothing better illustrates this than the atmosphere at their live concerts – the subject of this immaculately researched book.

I was fortunate to introduce the band on stage on two key occasions, at *The Old Grey Whistle Test Christmas Special* at Hammersmith Odeon in 1975, and at Hyde Park the following year.

Walking out on stage at Hyde Park was unbelievable. One hundred and twenty thousand fans stretched from the front of the stage to the very perimeters of London's largest green space. The show was utterly spectacular.

Christmas 1975 was a more intimate occasion. Television lighting requirements dictated that most of the audience were bathed in yellow light, and from the side of the stage I had a clear view of the audience and their reaction to the show. The expression of sheer joy on the faces of those fans, the affection and warmth with which they sang every word of every song, is something I remember as if it was yesterday.

Of course, the band were aware of this adoration, but to their great credit they never manipulated or exploited it. They always gave their best and treated their fans with courtesy and respect. And it was great fun. Freddie's showmanship was straight out of Hollywood, their musical ability stunning.

I loved them live and as a fan Queen have treated me extremely well.

Bob Harris - *May 1995*

A Concert Documentary

June 27
City Hall, Truro, Cornwall

July 12
Imperial College, London

July 25
PJ's Club, Truro, Cornwall

August 23
Imperial College, London

September 4
Swiss Cottage Private School, London

October 16
College of Estates Management Hall,
London

October 30
College of Technology, St Helens,
Merseyside

October 31
Cavern Club, Liverpool

November 14
Balls Park College, Hertford,
Hertfordshire

December 5
Shoreditch College, Egham, Surrey

December 18
College of Technology, St Helens,
Merseyside

December 19
Congregational Church Hall, St Helens,
Merseyside

Queen's very first live performances were regarded at the time not so much as concerts, but as informal gatherings of friends, fellow students and college acquaintances. Unlike conventional shows, tickets were distributed only to individuals who could be relied upon for constructive critical feedback.

One performance saw the band billed not as Queen, but Smile – a throwback to the Tim Staffell, Roger Taylor and Brian May pre-Queen group, which disbanded some time earlier. Freddie's suggestion for group name was used for the first time on the second show, on July 12. Thereafter, of course, it never changed.

It was not until February 1971, after three bassists had been tried and found wanting, that John Deacon joined the band. The first, Mike Grose, left in early August 1970 to pursue other avenues, although he had become bored by then. His departure was amicable. As Queen had a gig pencilled in for August 23, a replacement was required urgently, and it came in the form of Barry Mitchell, who remained with them for six months. His last performances were on January 8 and 9, when Queen played alongside Genesis as support to Kevin Ayres and The Whole World Band. The next bassist lasted only two performances before being sacked for stealing the centre stage position at the show on February 20, when Queen were supporting Yes.

By late February, it must have seemed very unlikely that a compatible bassist existed. Salvation came when

Brian, Roger and their friend John Harris met John Deacon at a disco. John auditioned at Imperial College and was hastily recruited, thus completing the quartet who would ultimately remain together three months short of twenty-one years.

Brian: "It was a question of not being able to find the right man at the beginning, we tried a few people. Deacy was just a natural really. We thought he was a spectacular bass player. We were really pleased."

Four months of intensive rehearsals followed before the new line-up was ready to perform their first shows in July. The gigs were typically attended by sixty or seventy people, and provide Queen with an opportunity to gauge valuable audience reaction and comment. The invitation for one of the shows asks guests to attend "a good time with good music, from a band who desperately need an opinion."

Precise details regarding the material that Queen performed during this period are sketchy. Very little is documented and even less has been made available to fans. They played a combination of their own compositions and covers of other artists' material, as Smile had done at their shows, and these covers included material by Buddy Holly, James Brown, The Everly Brothers, The Yardbirds and The Rolling Stones, all of whom had been major musical influences on them, especially – in Brian's case – Eric Clapton. Indeed,

has never surfaced on any subsequent Queen album. It seems unlikely that the track was ever recorded. If it does exist in the vaults, it is uncatalogued.

The track 'Shag Out', which occasionally appears on collectors' lists, is not actually a song in itself, but a segment from 'Hangman'. At some stage a short guitar/drum extract (without vocals) was issued on a bootleg, and it is likely that the bootleggers invented the title 'Shag Out'.

With the emergence in May 1991 of Freddie's biblical 'Mad The Swine' (a track left off the début album because of a difference of opinion between Queen and Roy Thomas Baker), and the long lost re-take of 'Keep Yourself Alive' cropping up on the Hollywood Records compact disc the same year, it is evident that Queen must have recorded rather more early material, as yet unavailable, than they would have us believe.

In addition to live performances and their studies, the band rehearsed in the Imperial College lecture theatre three or four times a week. Brian was evidently regarded as a trustworthy student by the college management who allowed him to use the facilities. It was during this period that Queen began to assemble a small team to assist with concert preparation, lighting and sound. John Harris was one of the first, and he would ultimately remain with Queen for many years. In 1975 Roger dedicated 'I'm In Love With My Car' (from 'A Night At The Opera') to him. The 'Jazz' album in 1978 was also dedicated to him.

Although the group's budget would eventually allow them to employ the services of Zandra Rhodes to design their stage attire, for the time being they utilised Freddie's design training by adapting clothes and jewellery from his and Roger's stall in Kensington Market.

On September 18, 1970, Freddie and Roger closed the stall as a mark of respect to their hero Jimi Hendrix who died that day. They were devastated. That night they performed 'Voodoo Chile' in rehearsals as a mark of respect. Three weeks later the same song reached No.1 in the British charts, the only time Hendrix reached the top.

Brian would much later dedicate a solo composition to him ('Bluesbreaker' on the 1983 Star Fleet project). They also played material by Elvis Presley, Gene Vincent, Little Richard, Rick Nelson, Shirley Bassey, Bill Haley and The Spencer Davis Group. Only when a satisfactory following had been established would they introduce more of their own material.

Brian: "You can only get so far in playing to audiences who don't understand what you're doing, so we did more heavy rock'n'roll with the Queen delivery to give people something they could get hold of – get on, sock it to 'em, get off. If you go on stage and people don't know your material, you can get boring."

Although a great many cover versions featured in the set (most commonly: 'Jailhouse Rock', 'Be Bop A Lula', 'Shake Rattle And Roll', 'Stupid Cupid', 'Bama Lama Bama Loo' and 'Big Spender'), the band also included two original songs and segments of experimental material that had worked best during rehearsals.

One original began life as an old Freddie Mercury pre-Queen group track called 'Lover', and developed into what is now titled 'Liar'. Another song, which they used to open shows, was called 'Stone Cold Crazy', and would surface much later on the 'Sheer Heart Attack' album credited to all four members of the band, the first time

this occurred. Because the track underwent so many changes during its development, no-one could recall who actually wrote which parts.

The band experimented with early versions of tracks that would turn up on the first two albums, and some which were rejected. In addition to well-known songs like 'Keep Yourself Alive' and 'Doing All Right' (a song written by Brian May and Tim Staffell, and actually recorded by Smile), they frequently performed a little-known song called 'Hangman'. This featured only in very early concerts (up to 1975), and

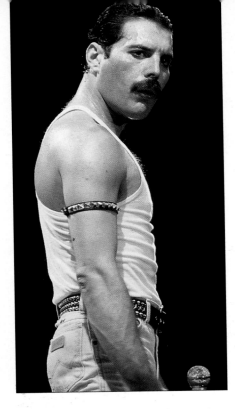

January 8
Marquee Club, London

January 9
Technical College, Ewell, Surrey

February 19
Hornsey Town Hall, London

February 20
Kingston Polytechnic, London

July 2
Surrey College, Surrey

July 11
Imperial College, London

July 17
The Garden, Penzance, Cornwall

July 19
Rugby Club, Hayle, Cornwall

July 24
Young Farmers' Club, Wadebridge, Cornwall

July 29
The Garden, Penzance, Cornwall

July 31
City Hall, Truro, Cornwall

August 2
Rugby Club, Hayle, Cornwall

August 9
Driftwood Spars, St Agnes, Cornwall

August 12
Tregye Hotel, Truro, Cornwall

August 14
NCO's Mess, RAF Culdrose, Truro, Cornwall

August 17
City Hall, Truro, Cornwall

August 21
Carnon Downs Festival, Tregye, Cornwall

October 6
Imperial College, London

December 9
Swimming Baths, Epsom, Surrey

December 31
Rugby Club, Twickenham, London

The band spent the first half of 1971 continuing college studies, rehearsals and performances. Although Queen's reputation was beginning to grow, they were unwilling to commit themselves entirely to the band, rehearsing as and when all four members were available at the same time. Although Freddie and Roger had their hearts set on a rock career, for Brian and John Queen was still a venture that occupied free time between studies. It would take the 'Queen II' album, in Brian's case, and 'Sheer Heart Attack', in John's, before all four would become sold on the idea that a rock band could be their full-time occupation from which a proper living could be earned.

In mid-July 1971 the band embarked on a two-month tour of Cornwall, which Roger had arranged through his various contacts in the area; hence the band were frequently billed as "Roger Taylor and Queen". The tour concluded on August 21 at the Tregye Country Club, near Truro, their first outdoor performance. Queen were the penultimate act to appear on a nine group bill headed by Arthur Brown's Kingdom Come, and Hawkwind.

In an attempt to attract more interest and additional bookings, in September Brian arranged a show at Imperial College. Though most of the invited agency-related audience attends, no bookings are forthcoming. A somewhat disillusioned Queen found themselves in need of a boost in morale.

Their break came when a friend of Brian's, who was working for Pye Studios, mentioned that his company was seeking a group to test out and demonstrate the facilities of their new Wembley-based recording studio. Days later Queen were at De Lane Lea Studios putting the equipment through its paces. In return for their time, the band were permitted to record demonstration tapes with which they subsequently approached record companies.

It is at De Lane Lea that the band were seen by producers John Anthony and Roy Thomas Baker, who subsequently recommended them to Trident Studios co-owners Barry and Norman Sheffield. Although Anthony remembers Brian and Roger from Smile's recording days, it is a 'Keep Yourself Alive' recital which impresses him and his colleague.

From October 6 until the end of the year, Queen played mostly college gigs, utilising a repertoire that remained a combination of cover versions and self-written material. A typical set of the time would be; 'Liar', 'Son & Daughter', 'Doing All Right', 'Hangman', 'Stone Cold Crazy', 'Keep Yourself Alive' and 'Jailhouse Rock'. The rock'n'roll covers were performed as encores. 'See What A Fool I've Been' was performed as a second encore, but only infrequently.

'Liar' would occasionally change position, to conclude the show.

'Son & Daughter' was a considerably accelerated rendering to that which would later appear on the début album.

Like 'Son & Daughter', Queen performed 'Keep Yourself Alive' in a somewhat accelerated form to that which would eventually kick off the eponymously titled début album.

The song underwent copious changes before it took on the form which was recorded and issued as the first single (in July 1973). A fascinating insight into one of the versions emerged in 1991 when a four-minute so-called "Long Lost Re-Take" was added as a bonus track to the Hollywood Records 'Queen' compact disc. A short sleeve note from Brian reads: "This is a complete re-make of 'Keep Yourself Alive'. This version never surfaced anywhere. It contains many new ideas and quirks, as well as reproductions of some of the old ones."

Early live performances of 'Keep Yourself Alive' incorporated examples of crowd participation, of which Freddie was to become a master. As the concert repertoire grew, so too did opportunities for him to manipulate, and converse with, the audience.

17

By no means a frequent supplement to the set was the enigmatic 'See What A Fool I've Been' which never appeared on any studio album and was for a long period only available as flipside to 'Seven Seas Of Rhye'. When it was performed live it usually featured late in the set, or as an encore. Although Brian May is credited as composer, there is some confusion as to whether it is an original or a cover of an old song. Smile vocalist Tim Staffell has gone on record as saying 'See What A Fool I've Been' is an old blues number that he first heard on a Sonny Terry & Brownie McGhee album.

If 'Liar' did not conclude the show, Queen would close instead with 'Jailhouse Rock', 'Stupid Cupid' or 'Bama Lama Bama Loo'. A typical show would span between forty and fifty minutes. In contrast, the shows which the band performed on their final tour, in 1986, frequently ran to four times that.

1971 concluded with a New Year's Eve performance at the London Rugby Club.

January 28
Bedford College, London

March 10
King's College Hospital, London

March 24
Forest Hill Hospital, London

November 6
The Pheasantry Club, London

December 20
The Marquee Club, London

Surprisingly, Queen performed only five shows in 1972. This was due to academic studies, personal commitments and lengthy negotiations with the Sheffield brothers (Norman and Barry), who would ultimately sign the band to their Trident Audio Productions Company later in the year.

Prior to Trident's interest, Queen spent much of early 1972 unsuccessfully approaching other record companies with the demonstration tapes they had recorded at De Lane Lea Studios.

The tapes were produced by Louis Austin and contained versions of 'Keep Yourself Alive', 'Liar', 'Jesus' and 'The Night Comes Down'. The quality of the last one was such that it was eventually used for the début album, hence the album's only production credit to Louis Austin.

The first show of the year at Bedford College, on January 28, was organised by John. Only six people attended and John later cited it as one of the most embarrassing experiences of his life.

The four remaining gigs were all London based. The Forest Hill show was attended by Barry Sheffield, who until then had only heard Queen's demo tape, and was taking up John Anthony's recommendation to see them live before committing his company to a deal. Sheffield realised Anthony's claims were not exaggerated, and Queen finally sign to Trident in November, a move they would ultimately live to regret.

The band had previously been approached by Chrysalis Records, but they declined this offer on the grounds that the advance was insufficient. With hindsight, Queen would have avoided many subsequent legal and financial problems if they'd gone with Chrysalis.

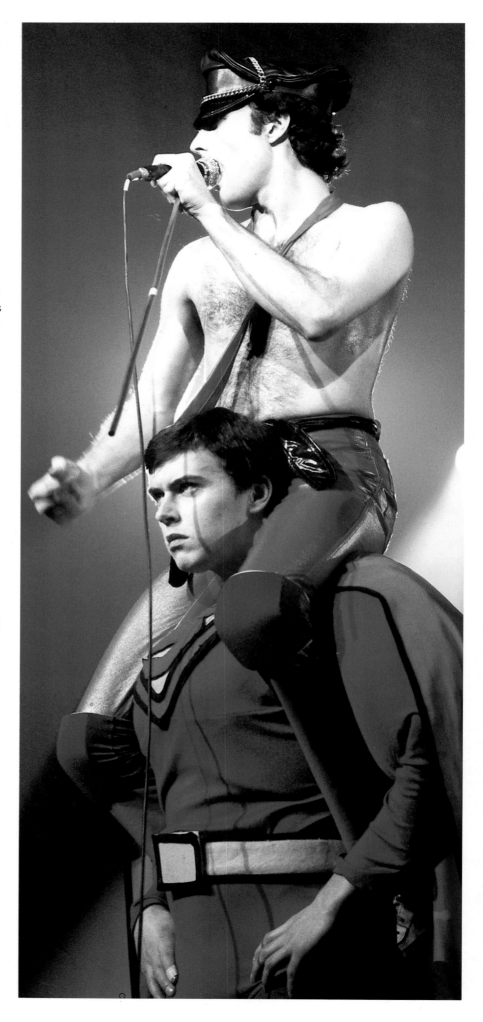

Queen recorded their début album at Trident Studios, in St Anne's Court, Soho, which was owned by their management company. The drawback was that they could only record in 'downtime', periods when the studios were not required by regular paying customers, or when the room became unexpectedly available. The irregular nature of the sessions did little to inspire confidence within the band.

Brian May: "They would call us up and say David Bowie's finished a few hours early, so you've got from 3.00 am to 7.00 am when the cleaners come in, to do a bit – if you want to come in now boys. A lot of it was done that way. There were a few full days, but mainly bits and pieces."

Mike Stone (début album's engineer): "That first album was completely different to anything else I had been doing. The remixes took ages and ages, and the band all seemed such perfectionists that every little squeak had to be just right. It was quite nerve-racking working with a born superstar on the first major work I had engineered."

There were problems at the Pheasantry Club gig in Chelsea on November 6 when the PA system arrived at the venue only an hour

before they are due on stage. John Deacon and John Harris desperately scrambled around to wire everything up in time. Consequently the performance was marred by technical problems.

Norman Sheffield: "It was a disastrous gig. Four great players – the talent within the four was absolutely totally apparent to me. But as a unit it was pretty scruffy."

By late November, the tiresome recording sessions for the début album had at last concluded. Despite the unusual recording schedule, both the band and record company were pleased with the final product. Queen wasted no time in starting work on the second album.

On November 1 the band had signed a recording contract with Trident, committing all material recorded up to that point, and a number thereafter, to the company. In return Trident would negotiate the best available distribution deal on their behalf. Eventually, in March 1973, a deal with EMI is secured.

A cassette bootleg recording, which has come to light recently, appears at first glance to originate from the show at the Marquee Club in London, on December 20, 1972, and is therefore the earliest example of a Queen bootleg to have surfaced. On closer inspection, however, it is more likely to be a compilation of live material taken from numerous other recordings. The tape contains no Freddie between-song-patter, which is suspicious. However, the versions of 'Ogre Battle' and 'Hangman' are sufficiently musically sparse to suggest otherwise. 'Ogre Battle' contains gaps and pauses unheard in any other versions.

February 5

Langham 1 Studio, London

My Fairy King / Keep Yourself Alive / Doing All Right / Liar

Queen attended Langham 1 Studio, in London, to record their first session for the BBC. The session is organised by Trident. Bernie Andrews produces the session with John Etchells as engineer. A significant proportion of the material committed to tape is somewhat different from that already recorded for the début album, which was not due for release until five months later.

Because of limited production time, which would normally have seen additional layers of percussion, guitar and vocal harmonies added to the mix, 'My Fairy King' emerges somewhat less fussy than the album cut. The lead and backing vocals are much clearer and Freddie's subtle piano parts are more defined. While 'Keep Yourself Alive' and the Smile track 'Doing All Right' are reproduced almost note for note from the album versions, 'Liar' contains vocal ad-libs from Freddie which are not on the album. As you might expect, the album version is the better of the two.

For an entirely alternative approach to 'Liar', 1991's Hollywood Records compact disc (HR 61064 2) again offers the definitive example. Remixed by John Luongo and Gary Hellman, a six and a half minute interpretation offers a heavily guitar-oriented version, and brings previously less dominant incidental instruments such as tambourine and maracas much higher up in the mix. The bongo drum accompaniment is a nice touch, too.

The session was broadcast ten days after recording, on John Peel's Radio One show, as part of the *Sounds Of The Seventies* series.

Although originally booked for only one session, Queen would return on five further occasions. To date only two of the sessions have emerged officially (Sessions 1 and 3), released as 'Queen At The Beeb' in December 1989. Despite the album's sleeve note advice to the contrary, bootleg copies of most tracks have been relatively easy to access for years.

Queen recorded twenty-four tracks in all for the BBC:

Session 1

My Fairy King / Keep Yourself Alive / Doing All Right / Liar

Session 2

See What A Fool I've Been / Liar / Son & Daughter / Keep Yourself Alive

Session 3

Ogre Battle / Great King Rat / Modern Times Rock'n'Roll / Son & Daughter

Session 4

Modern Times Rock'n'Roll / The March Of The Black Queen / Nevermore / White Queen

Session 5

Now I'm Here / Stone Cold Crazy / Flick Of The Wrist / Tenement Funster

Session 6

Spread Your Wings / It's Late / My Melancholy Blues / We Will Rock You (Audience handclapping added later)

There is some confusion about which studio Queen used to record the first session. I can clarify that the location definitely was Langham 1 Studio, and not Maida Vale. Ken Norman's *The Complete BBC Sessions*, which details every session ever recorded for the BBC provided conclusive evidence.

April 9

Marquee Club, Wardour Street, London

Father To Son / Son & Daughter / Doing All Right / Hangman / Stone Cold Crazy / Keep Yourself Alive / Liar / Jailhouse Rock / Encore: Be Bop A Lula

'Father To Son' begins the show, and 'Liar' instead concludes it.

This show is set up as a showcase event for Elektra executive Jack Holtzman who may sign the band, but first wants to see them perform live.

Queen's newly appointed publicist, Tony Brainsby, asks his assistant John Bagnall to attend this concert. He later recalls: "It really was the embryonic Queen stage act that night. I remember going backstage afterwards and seeing Freddie slumped in their dressing room, physically shattered by the act. What I remember most clearly is that as he was changing, I saw that his legs were absolutely black with bruises, and he explained that that was where he had been slapping his thighs with a tambourine during different numbers. I think that was the first time I ever had a real awareness of how much physical pain and effort could go into such a stage performance."

July 6

Queen's début single 'Keep Yourself Alive' is issued in the UK. Paired with 'Son & Daughter', it fails to chart. Both tracks are Brian May compositions.

When Queen are told that the song failed to chart because it "takes too long to happen" (a reference to the intro), they decide that the follow-up single will, if nothing else, feature an introduction that cannot be ignored.

Brian: "We said, 'Right, in the next one we're gonna put everything into the first ten seconds'. So we did that. You can hear in 'Seven Seas Of Rhye' the piano thing, then you hear these monstrous guitar swoops come in, and then you get this big crunch and the beat starts. So everything has happened in the first eight seconds of the record. We said if this doesn't get them — nothing will."

July 13

Queen Mary College, Basingstoke, Hampshire

Father To Son / Son & Daughter / Ogre Battle / Doing All Right / Hangman / Stone Cold Crazy / Keep Yourself Alive / Liar / Jailhouse Rock / Encore: Be Bop A Lula

EMI release Queen's eponymously titled début album in the UK on the same day, and Freddie tells the audience about it during the show. He also expresses irritation at its delay, which was caused by minor printing errors on the sleeve notes which Queen insisted be rectified. An accurate note which does appear reads: "Representing at last something of what Queen music has been over the last three years."

The American release did not follow until September 4, where despite considerable promotional backing, it only reached No.83. It fared rather better at home, climbing to No.24.

As will become evident, each new Queen album brought a significant

volume of material which was never included in the live shows of the time. Although much new material would have converted well to the stage environment had it been given the opportunity, in most cases it was never even tried. Many of the omissions are inexplicable. The début album was no exception. Although 'Seven Seas Of Rhye' was absent from the show — it was not finished in time for the début album, and later appeared (in full) on 'Queen II' — Brian May's 'The Night Comes Down' should have been an obvious choice for their concert repertoire, especially since Queen invariably began their show just before or just after darkness had fallen. Many fans regard this track as one of the album high points, yet it was never featured in any show.

The most glaring absentees however are Freddie's elaborate 'My Fairy King', and the album's penultimate track 'Jesus', which epitomises the early Queen sound with stunning guitar work from Brian. Another song from the period with a biblical theme was Freddie's 'Mad The Swine' which was originally written and recorded for the début album (and produced by Queen and Roy Thomas Baker) but ultimately dropped when band and producer could not agree on the percussion sound. Why the track

was not issued instead as a B-side, as was 'See What A Fool I've Been', remains unexplained.

The three excised songs are but the first in a catalogue of fifty-eight album tracks which were — for whatever reason — never performed in a Queen live performance. While there will always be a proportion of material on every album which is overlooked for concerts, some of Queen's selections seem rather strange. Similarly, some of that which was played seemed equally unlikely.

July 24

'Keep Yourself Alive' is featured on the BBC's *Old Grey Whistle Test*. Since producer Mike Appleton has only an anonymous white label test pressing of the début album in his office, he is unaware of the identity of the artist. He nevertheless commissions appropriate footage from the BBC archives to accompany it, an unusual piece of animated election campaign film used by President Franklin Roosevelt. Having seen the broadcast, staff at both Trident and EMI call the BBC to inform them of the identity of the group.

July 25

Langham 1 Studio, London

See What A Fool I've Been / Liar / Son & Daughter / Keep Yourself Alive

Queen record their second session for the BBC. As with the first, Queen decide which material they will record. The session is produced by Jeff Griffin and Chris Lycett, and engineered by John Etchells. Three of the tracks are transmitted on August 13, and 'Keep Yourself Alive' on September 24, on the Bob Harris show, again as part of the *Sounds Of The Seventies* series.

They record further versions of 'Liar' and 'Keep Yourself Alive' as they had in February, and a fresh rendering of 'Son & Daughter'. Though Brian's 'See What A Fool I've Been' was not included on the album, and only appeared as flipside to 'Seven Seas Of Rhye', it did feature in the live set of the time, and was therefore a logical choice for this session.

Langham 1 Studio, the venue for Queen's first four BBC sessions, was only intended to be a temporary recording location while the Maida Vale Studio underwent refurbishment. However, it remained in almost constant use right up until 1981.

August

The band return to Trident Studios to begin work on "Queen II". This time they record under proper conditions, and not in downtime. Many new techniques are tried, most of which were too time consuming to be attempted at previous sessions. The entire album is recorded in August.

September 13
Golders Green Hippodrome, London

Procession / Father To Son / Son & Daughter / Ogre Battle / Hangman / Stone Cold Crazy / Keep Yourself Alive / Liar / See What A Fool I've Been / Encore Medley: Jailhouse Rock; Stupid Cupid; Bama Lama Bama Loo; Jailhouse Rock (Reprise)

The show now opens with a pre-recorded passage of music just recorded for the second album. It was the very first time that a tape had been used in any live concert. Brian's eerie and somewhat medieval sounding 'Procession' would begin as the house lights suddenly dimmed. The band, meanwhile, made their way in darkness to their respective stage positions, in time for Freddie's opening words of the show: "A word in your ear, from father to son".

'Father To Son' contains numerous guitar solos from Brian which would be absent from the "Queen II" cut. No time is wasted on introductions between songs and Freddie moves straight into Brian's début album tale of teenage insurrection, 'Son & Daughter'. Although the album version of this song includes the line: "the world expects a man to buckle down and shovel shit", in concert, Freddie would instead sing: "A woman expects a man to buckle down and shovel it".

To give the song a fresh slant, Freddie would often sing alternative lyrics, and for this reason, some of the early live recordings sound almost like demo versions. It is quite evident that 'Son & Daughter' underwent numerous changes along the way, and the version performed here, and in subsequent concerts, contains what are essentially the origins of the 'Brighton Rock' guitar solo.

Most bootlegs of this show contain 'See What A Fool' at this point in the set, but it was actually played much later in the show.

Next up was the somewhat frantic 'Ogre Battle', whose lyrics became indecipherable in the concert environment. 'Liar' begins with a drum solo introduction from Roger, before Brian and John join him, and the song quickly builds up to the opening vocals. Unlike the studio version of 'Keep Yourself Alive', the live renditions of the time commenced with a drum solo,

instead of guitar chords from Brian. It also featured an occasional mid-song drum solo, in which Roger would demonstrate that every part of his kit was there for a reason, and not just for ostentation. The rock'n'roll medley here is a classic example of Queen's early delivery and style.

This show was recorded by the BBC for an *In Concert* broadcast, and a one hour edit was transmitted the following month, on October 20, on Radio One. The transmission yielded many bootleg recordings, most commonly 'Queen On The Green'. Originally available on vinyl, it now circulates only in audio cassette form. Because so few first or second generation tapes exist, contemporary purchases are usually disappointing. New collectors are unwittingly buying a copy of a copy, of yet another copy (as is so often the case), hence the appalling sound quality. The chances of locating good quality copies now are remote.

October 13
Bad Godesburg, Frankfurt

Procession / Father To Son / Son & Daughter / Ogre Battle / Hangman / Stone Cold Crazy / Keep Yourself Alive / Liar / See What A Fool I've Been / Encore Medley: Jailhouse Rock; Stupid Cupid; Big Spender; Bama Lama Bama Loo; Jailhouse Rock (Reprise)

This was Queen's very first concert outside the United Kingdom.

Like most of Queen's early concert material, 'Liar' was performed rather differently from the version which had been recorded for the début album issued three months earlier. There was no typical version as such; instead the band played variations around the same theme, rather like Brian often did during 'Brighton Rock'. Early versions of 'Liar' were essentially whatever had worked best during rehearsals. No two live recordings of the song from this period are identical. In later concerts the track would retain a similar structure.

For 'Ogre Battle' Freddie would invariably invite the audience to accompany him to the battlefield, and so began the mythological tale of 'Ogre men inside two-way mirror mountains'. The song was one of Queen's busiest

to vinyl, and live versions were equally boisterous. Unfortunately no decent bootlegs have materialised from this era, and although some recordings do exist they are closely guarded by the band members.

Only segments of this show seem to have survived on bootleg recordings. Two examples have the first three tracks missing. If the recording which currently circulates is indeed from this show — which is questionable — then it is worth acquiring. The medley sequence is outstanding, especially 'Big Spender' and 'Bama Lama'.

October 14
Le Blow Up Club, Luxembourg

Procession / Father To Son / Son & Daughter / Ogre Battle / Hangman / Stone Cold Crazy / Keep Yourself Alive / Liar / See What A Fool I've Been / Encore Medley: Jailhouse Rock; Stupid Cupid; Bama Lama Bama Loo; Jailhouse Rock (Reprise)

This show was to be broadcast as a Radio Luxembourg *In Concert* special, but the recording equipment failed, and nothing was recorded.

October 20
Paris Theatre, London

This show was apparently recorded by Radio One for an *In Concert* broadcast. Because no good quality bootlegs from it have ever appeared, it is unlikely that it was ever transmitted. The programme was supposedly aired at some point late in October.

A recording from this show does exist, but the poor sound quality suggests it was made by a member of the audience.

October 26
Imperial College, London

Procession / Father To Son / Son & Daughter / Ogre Battle / Hangman / Stone Cold Crazy / Keep Yourself Alive / Liar / See What A Fool I've Been / Encore Medley: Jailhouse Rock; Shake Rattle And Roll; Stupid Cupid; Bama Lama Bama Loo; Jailhouse Rock (Reprise) / 2nd Encore: Big Spender

This show was attended by EMI's Paul Watts who was anxious to see his company's latest signing: "It was simply amazing. Their stage performance was superb, as was their music, and the rapport they built up with the audience was fantastic."

November 2
Imperial College, London

Procession / Father To Son / Son & Daughter / Ogre Battle / Hangman / Stone Cold Crazy / Keep Yourself Alive / Liar / See What A Fool I've Been / Encore Medley: Jailhouse Rock; Stupid Cupid; Bama Lama Bama Loo; Jailhouse Rock (Reprise)

Queen perform this concert as a last minute rehearsal for the tour due to begin in ten days' time. The sell-out show is attended by a host of music journalists, one of whom, Rosemary Horride, later writes: "The atmosphere in the hall was electric, the kids were with Queen all the way. The group were musically

very good, their stage presence was excellent and when you consider that the material was all their own, it was a remarkable performance. It was obvious how hard the band have worked at entertaining, by the tremendous rapport that was established."

Such complimentary reviews would prove to be the exception rather than the rule. From that moment on most reviews highlighted only the low points of the show, and blatantly ignored the good. While a less than satisfactory performance always guaranteed a poor review, a faultless one rarely inspired the opposite.

In subsequent years, the British press would take exception to Queen's reluctance to give interviews, especially during the period leading up to Freddie's death. This reluctance stemmed from the poor reviews they received during Queen's formative years. Misquote after misquote, and copious exaggerated "darlings" and "dears" typically dominated any band-related article. In an American interview in the week preceding the Freddie Tribute Concert, in April 1992, Brian would later confirm this point, commenting that the British press were particularly troublesome, which was why they often closed ranks against the fourth estate.

1973 UK TOUR

In November, Queen embarked on a five week, 25 show, tour of England and Scotland, as support act to Mott The Hoople. The tour opened in Leeds and concluded in Peterborough. The performances at Cheltenham College, Liverpool University and Liverpool Top Rank were not part of the Mott Tour, and featured Queen only, with no other act.

Mott were at the time enjoying chart success with 'All The Way From Memphis', and would later see their follow-up single 'Roll Away The Stone' peak at No. 8. With big sellers like

'Honaloochie Boogie' and the David Bowie produced 'All The Young Dudes' already under their belt, they were a force to be reckoned with. Supporting them would be no easy task.

November 12
Town Hall, Leeds

Procession / Father To Son / Son & Daughter / Ogre Battle / Hangman / Great King Rat / Medley: Jailhouse Rock; Shake Rattle And Roll / Keep Yourself Alive / Liar / Encore: Big Spender / Modern Times Rock'n'Roll

'Stone Cold Crazy' is not performed on this tour.

Although the bootleg from this concert supposedly includes two tracks recorded at the pre-show soundcheck ('Hangman' and 'Liar'), there really is no way of confirming it. At one time there were only a handful of recordings in circulation with soundcheck material included, then suddenly, almost overnight, there emerged a whole series of them. It seems likely that the bootleggers had simply found another opportunity to tempt collectors into buying more spurious items.

November 13
St Georges, Blackburn, Lancashire

November 15
Gaumont, Worcester

Procession / Father To Son / Son & Daughter / Ogre Battle / Great King Rat / Medley: Jailhouse Rock; Shake Rattle And Roll; Stupid Cupid; Jailhouse Rock (Reprise) / Keep Yourself Alive / Liar / Encore: Big Spender / Bama Lama Bama Loo

November 16
University, Lancaster

Procession / Father To Son / Son & Daughter / Ogre Battle / Great King Rat / Medley: Jailhouse Rock; Shake Rattle And Roll; Stupid Cupid; Be Bop A Lula; Jailhouse Rock (Reprise) / Keep Yourself Alive / Liar / Encore: Big Spender / Modern Times Rock'n'Roll

November 17
Stadium, Liverpool

Procession / Father To Son / Son & Daughter / Hangman / Ogre Battle / Great King Rat / Medley: Jailhouse Rock; Tutti Frutti; Shake Rattle And Roll; Stupid Cupid; Jailhouse Rock (Reprise) / Keep Yourself Alive / Liar / Encore: Big Spender / Modern Times Rock'n'Roll

November 18
Victoria Hall, Hanley, Staffordshire

November 19
Civic, Wolverhampton

Queen played a similar set to that at Lancaster University, but with 'See What A Fool I've Been' included. It is unclear exactly where in the set this song was performed. Two collectors' lists from different sources offer conflicting advice, one after 'Ogre Battle', the other as the very last song. Though it would appear the song featured only rarely in the set, it is a fair bet that it was played more often than has been documented.

November 20
New Theatre, Oxford

Procession / Father To Son / Son & Daughter / Ogre Battle / Hangman / Great King Rat / Medley: Jailhouse Rock; Shake Rattle And Roll; Stupid Cupid; Be Bop A Lula; Jailhouse Rock (Reprise) / Keep Yourself Alive / Liar / Encore: Big Spender

Some of the original vinyl bootleg recordings of this show include an extremely poor quality pre-show sound check. Likewise, subsequent audio tapes contain even worse copies of it. On close examination, however, almost all can be exposed as fraudulent. They actually consist of snippets of material edited together from numerous other shows of the period.

As a general rule, a typical Queen set of the time would rarely last longer than 45 minutes. Any recording which exceeds that running time is therefore clearly fraudulent. Bootlegs which appear to offer every conceivable song in the Queen repertoire, as well as half a dozen rock-'n'roll medley numbers, should be regarded as dubious.

November 21
Guildhall, Preston, Lancashire

Procession / Father To Son / Son & Daughter / Ogre Battle / Great King Rat / Medley: Jailhouse Rock; Shake Rattle And Roll; Stupid Cupid; Jailhouse Rock (Reprise) / Keep Yourself Alive / Liar / Encore: Big Spender / Bama Lama Bama Loo

November 22
City Hall, Newcastle-Upon-Tyne

November 23
Apollo Theatre, Glasgow

Procession / Father To Son / Son & Daughter / Ogre Battle / Great King Rat / Medley: Jailhouse Rock; Shake Rattle And Roll; Stupid Cupid; Jailhouse Rock (Reprise) / Keep Yourself Alive / Liar / Encore: Big Spender / Bama Lama Bama Loo

John Bagnall later recalled a conversation he had with Roger, after this performance: "I remember talking to Roger that night and saying that it had gone so well that I had the feeling they were going to happen now, and him saying to me: 'I really feel we're going to make it now. I really feel it's going to happen'."

November 25
Caley Cinema, Edinburgh

November 26
Opera House, Manchester

Procession / Father To Son / Son & Daughter / Ogre Battle / Hangman / Great King Rat / Medley: Jailhouse Rock; Shake Rattle And Roll; Stupid Cupid; Jailhouse Rock (Reprise) / Keep Yourself Alive / Liar / Encore: Big Spender / Modern Times Rock'n'Roll

The content of the 'Rock'n'Roll medley' differed enormously from one evening to the next, dependent on various factors – Freddie's rapport with the audience, the atmosphere inside the venue, and general mood within the band. Material performed most frequently was Elvis Presley's 'Jailhouse Rock', Little Richard's 'Bama Lama Bama Loo', Gene Vincent's 'Be Bop A Lula', Bill Haley's 'Shake Rattle And Roll' and less frequent renditions of 'Big Spender' and 'Stupid Cupid'.

November 27
Town Hall, Birmingham

Procession / Father To Son / Son & Daughter / Ogre Battle / See What A Fool I've Been / Great King Rat / Medley: Jailhouse Rock; Shake Rattle And Roll; Stupid

Cupid; Jailhouse Rock (Reprise) / Keep Yourself Alive / Liar / Encore: Big Spender / Bama Lama Bama Loo

Freddie's mid-song chat during this period was somewhat more reserved and subdued than most fans now recall. He wasn't always so full of confidence, and sounded extremely young:

"Good evening. We're called Queen. It's nice to be in Birmingham, there's so many of you, it's lovely. We'll do a number from our album now - it's called 'Son & Daughter'..."

"As you've probably gathered, this is the first time we're playing Birmingham, and you're very nice – that's nice (nervous laugh), that's right. We're gonna do one from our second album, it's called... ("Can we have a bit more in the monitors?")... 'Ogre Battle'..."

"Thank you... that's nice. I can just see people all round me, and there's a few out there... oi (he shouts to them), how you doing out there? You seem a bit quiet (laughs again). Anyway we'd like to play a little snootchie woochie one, it's called 'Hangman' – that's right, you're enjoying yourself, so is everybody else, I see..."

"Some time ago we had a single out, written by Brian here, I don't know if you've heard of it, I don't know if you bought it, it's called 'Keep Yourself Alive'."

November 28
Brangwyn Hall, Swansea

An inspired American critic of the time wrote: "A singular and lightly stylised pot-pourri of heavy metal, rococo and English vaudeville themes, soldered together with explosions, dry ice, strobes, spots and a workshop full of technological tricks."

November 29
Colston Hall, Bristol

Procession / Father To Son / Son & Daughter / Ogre Battle / Hangman / Great King Rat / Medley: Jailhouse Rock; Shake Rattle And Roll; Stupid Cupid; Jailhouse Rock (Reprise) / Keep Yourself Alive / Liar / Encore: Big Spender / Bama Lama Bama Loo

During the show Freddie says: "Err, we feel pleased that you're a nice mild audience. Er, we'd like to carry on with a number now, it's from our first album, it's called 'Son & Daughter'." Following a

blistering 'Brighton Rock' type guitar solo, complete with delays and echoes, and an additional verse of "A woman expects a man to buckle down and shovel it", not recorded on the album cut, but always added in concert, the band move on to the battlefield again, and the 'Queen II' side two opening track 'Ogre Battle'. Roger terminates the song with a scream, and Freddie remarks simply; 'Wicked!'

Freddie hesitates for a moment and then initiates the next song: "Okay, this is gonna be one of our slow ones. It's a real hip-swinger, we do it from time to time. We thought we'd put it in especially for you – as you're a nice audience, yes. It's called 'Hangman'." And so begins a song which sounds like a mish-mash of various Queen material from the time, all mixed together. While Freddie, as always, sings the main vocal, Roger and Brian combine to provide backing on the "hang that rope from the highest tree" parts, and main chorus. This is a rare and exciting insight into a song which has never been released.

"Now, a long time ago we had a little single out, I don't know whether you heard it? It's called 'Keep Yourself... Alive'." Towards the end of the song – in keeping with the studio version – Roger asks: "Do you think you're better ev'ry day?". "No, I just think I'm two steps nearer to my grave," Freddie sings back. John then plays a bass line bridge, and everyone unites for the main concluding verses.

During the main chorus of 'Liar' John even adds some rare vocal backing. This is a technically complex composition, but it still converted well to the live situation, building into a powerful crescendo of driving drums, bass and lead guitar.

Having given Brian his cue, the band crash into a breathtaking rendition of 'Jailhouse Rock'. A few seconds of 'Shake Rattle' and 'Stupid Cupid' follow before 'Jailhouse' is reprised and Brian strums the instantly recognisable opening chords of 'Big Spender'. Little Richard's 'Bama Lama Bama Loo' concludes the show with lyrics borrowed from "Tutti Frutti". This was the shape of things to come.

Some bootlegs purporting to originate from this performance boast the inclusion of the pre-show sound-check, but it is clear that a large audience is present which would not be the case at a soundcheck. The tapes are still worth locating, though, if only for a stunning recital of 'Father To Son' – even if Freddie's slightly amended words do not make complete sense. This version also features some wonderful bass guitar work from John. On some bootlegs John's backing can easily be overlooked, but it's impossible to do so here.

November 30
Winter Gardens, Bournemouth

December 1
Kursaal, Southend, Essex

Having already performed their usual warm-up spot, Queen returned to the stage later (minus John Deacon) to join Mott The Hoople, and contribute backing vocals to 'All The Young Dudes'.

It has not been possible to track down a recording (in any format) of this show, from either Mott The Hoople or Queen collectors.

December 2
Central, Chatham, Kent

December 3
Langham 1 Studio, London

Ogre Battle / Great King Rat / Modern Times Rock'n'Roll / Son & Daughter

Queen record their third BBC session. Bernie Andrews and Mike Franks produce it, and Nick Griffiths engineers. Like all the sessions (except the final one), it is broadcast as part of the Radio One series *Sounds Of The Seventies*, three days later on John Peel's programme.

The last four tracks of 1989's 'Queen At The Beeb' CD (BOJCD 001), offered this session legitimately for the first time. A sequel looks likely to emerge in the near future. Perhaps a double album comprising all the remaining sixteen tracks could at least be considered.

Compared to the album versions of this material, the BBC sessions offer a minimum of production and, as a result, have a different kind of charm and atmosphere to the studio cuts. Furthermore, Roger Taylor's 'Modern Times Rock'n'Roll' appears here in a greatly improved form from that on the album version. The novel "It's not that I'm bright, Just happy-go-lucky" line – not present on the album – adds to its appeal.

December 6
Cheltenham College, Cheltenham

December 7
Shaftesbury Hall, London

Procession / Father To Son / Son & Daughter / Ogre Battle / Hangman / Great King Rat / Medley: Jailhouse Rock; Shake Rattle And Roll; Stupid Cupid; Jailhouse Rock (Reprise) / Keep Yourself Alive / Liar / Encore: Big Spender / Bama Lama Bama Loo

December 8
University, Liverpool

December 14
Hammersmith Odeon, London

Procession / Father To Son / Son & Daughter / Ogre Battle / Hangman / Great King Rat / Medley: Jailhouse Rock; Shake Rattle And Roll; Stupid Cupid / Keep Yourself Alive / Liar / Encore Medley: Big Spender / Bama Lama Bama Loo / 2nd Encore: Modern Times Rock'n'Roll

Queen and Mott The Hoople play two shows at this venue on the same day. When the first Mott performance overruns, Queen's set is shortened to compensate.

In attendance for this show - the last London (home town) gig of the year - and Queen's biggest audience up until that point (3,500), are Brian's parents.

Harold May would later recall: "We had seats down the front and we'd never been to a concert like that before. I suppose at our age we must have looked a little out of place. Anyway, there was a young man sitting in front

---

of me who suddenly turned round and said 'Who's dad are you then?' He was an out-and-out Mott The Hoople fan, but when I explained that Brian was my son, he handed me his programme and asked me to sign it. 'Don't be silly, I'm just a humble civil servant', I said, but he insisted and then asked me to put 'Brian May's dad' in brackets, after it."

December 15
University, Leicester

December 21
County Hall, Taunton, Somerset

December 22
Town Hall, Peterborough

Procession / Father To Son / Son & Daughter / Ogre Battle / Hangman / Great King Rat / Medley: Jailhouse Rock; Shake Rattle And Roll; Stupid Cupid; Jailhouse Rock (Reprise) / Keep Yourself Alive / Liar / Encore: Big Spender / Bama Lama Bama Loo

This was the last show of the tour. Queen's support role to Mott The Hoople provided invaluable concert experience. On the whole it had been a productive and generally fruitful undertaking. The press however, painted a rather different picture of events. While Mott's reviews were for the most part complimentary, Queen did not inspire such coverage. One report read: "A chilly, gutless sound that could not project itself on stage. No one number was distinctive, except perhaps 'Liar'."

December 28
Top Rank, Liverpool

Procession / Father To Son / Son & Daughter / Ogre Battle / Hangman / Great King Rat / Medley: Jailhouse Rock; Shake Rattle And Roll; Stupid Cupid; Jailhouse Rock (Reprise) / Keep Yourself Alive / Liar / Encore: Big Spender / Bama Lama Bama Loo

The band perform their final show of the year with a Christmas concert on the same bill as 10cc who had already enjoyed their first number one in England ('Rubber Bullets'), and two other Top Ten hits. A local group called Great Day kick off the show, and Queen follow them.

The set list differs little from the shows already outlined, although it does feature a lengthy Rock'n'Roll medley.

January

The year gets off to a disastrous start when, following an injection in preparation for the Australian dates (with a dirty needle, it later transpires), Brian develops gangrene in his arm. So serious is the condition that for some time there is a possibility that he may lose his arm.

January 28

Queen fly to Melbourne to perform two shows at the annual three day Sunbury Music Festival. It is their first visit to Australia, and their first performances in a continent other than Europe.

February 2

Sunbury Music Festival, Melbourne

Procession / Father To Son / Son & Daughter / Ogre Battle / Hangman / Great King Rat / Medley: Jailhouse Rock; Shake Rattle And Roll; Stupid Cupid; Jailhouse Rock (Reprise) / Keep Yourself Alive / Liar / Encore: Big Spender / Modern Times Rock'n'Roll

Queen are introduced unsympathetically, to say the least. Brian later recalled that it went somewhere along the lines of: "Well, we've got another load of limy bastards here tonight, they're probably going to be useless, but let's give 'em something to think about." The DJ compère then pulled down his trousers and mooned at the crowd, before describing Queen as "stuck up pommies". The same DJ returned to the stage later in the show, and managed, quite blatantly, to talk the audience out of accepting an encore from Queen.

During the show the lighting rig uncharacteristically breaks down. It is later discovered that it had been sabotaged. Queen are unimpressed by their first taste of Australia. They would return there on only two more occasions.

Although Brian's arm causes him considerable discomfort, and Freddie has an ear infection, and can hardly hear anything, the show goes ahead regardless. They do not perform the second of their scheduled shows the next day, however.

When Queen arrive home after the festival, they are bemused to find a hoard of press journalists awaiting them at Heathrow. The press quickly disperse (having taken not one single photograph) when they discover that Queen are not Her Majesty the Queen, as they had expected.

February 20

When David Bowie pulls out of *Top Of The Pops*, Queen are hastily drafted in as his replacement. They record a backing tape and at Ramport Studios pre-record a film which will be used. The unscheduled performance of 'Seven Seas Of Rhye' (broadcast the next day) is their first appearance on the programme.

February 23

Queen's second single 'Seven Seas Of Rhye' is released in the UK, paired with the non-album track 'See What A Fool I've Been'. Their first chart entry, it peaks at No.10 on March 9, helped largely by the *Top Of The Pops* coverage, and the British tour dates two months earlier.

UK 1974
Queen II Tour

Following rehearsals at Ealing film studios, Queen commence their first British headlining tour. The four week tour includes 22 performances in England, Scotland and Wales, and one gig on the Isle Of Man. The tour concludes with what should have been a mid-March gig, on April 2. Nutz are the support act for all but two of the shows.

March 1

Winter Gardens, Blackpool

Procession / Father To Son / Ogre Battle / White Queen / Great King Rat / Hangman / Doing All Right / Son & Daughter / Keep Yourself Alive / Liar / Encore Medley: Jailhouse Rock; Shake Rattle And Roll; Stupid Cupid; Jailhouse Rock (Reprise) / 2nd Encore: Big Spender

On the way to the gig, the vehicle transporting the band's lighting rig equipment breaks down miles from the venue. Although jeopardised, the show eventually goes ahead, albeit slightly delayed.

'White Queen' is new to this set on this tour, and 'Stone Cold Crazy' is absent.

There is speculation that Queen also performed Brian's 'The Night Comes Down' and Freddie's 'The Fairy Fellers Masterstroke' at this show. I am unable

to confirm this. If either song did feature, it would have been the first and only time they did so – to my knowledge. I have never heard even a segment of either track on any live recording.

March 2

Friars, Aylesbury, Buckinghamshire

This show is shorter than planned because Brian's arm proves too painful to continue.

March 3

Guildhall, Plymouth

Procession / Father To Son / Ogre Battle / White Queen / Great King Rat / Hangman / Doing All Right / Son & Daughter / Keep Yourself Alive / Liar / Encore Medley: Jailhouse Rock; Shake Rattle And Roll; Stupid Cupid; Jailhouse Rock (Reprise) / 2nd Encore: Big Spender

Local band Nutz are the support act. They back-up Queen for all remaining shows on this tour.

Following the show, the audience acknowledge a memorable performance by singing verses of 'God Save The Queen'. The gesture is appreciated by the band, who eventually record an arrangement of it which is used to conclude the show, and is first used on October 30, 1974. They record a definitive version during sessions for 'A Night At The Opera' and use it to conclude the album.

March 4

Festival Hall, Paignton, Devon

Procession / Father To Son / Ogre Battle / White Queen / Great King Rat / Hangman / Doing All Right / Son & Daughter / Keep Yourself Alive / Liar / Encore Medley: Jailhouse Rock; Shake Rattle And Roll; Stupid Cupid; Jailhouse Rock (Reprise) / 2nd Encore: Big Spender / Modern Times Rock'n'Roll

'Son & Daughter' is now performed somewhat differently from previous years. It resembles more closely the album version, and features fewer improvised parts. The song remained in the set until 1978.

March 8

Locarno, Sunderland, Tyne & Wear

Queen played a similar set to March 4, but with additional medley material.

'Queen II' is released in the UK. It reaches No. 5, and a month later, No. 49 in America. The 'Deacon John' mis-credit from the first album is corrected, as John dislikes it, but the 'Nobody played synthesizers' line proudly remains.

Reviews are mixed. *Sounds*: "This album captures them in their finest hours."; *Record Mirror*: "As a whole it is dire. Freddie Mercury's voice is dressed up with multi-tracking."

As with its predecessor, the album contains numerous songs that are not featured in the live show. Both 'Someday One Day' and 'The Loser In The End' from Side 1 (White Side) are overlooked, and although Side 2 (Black Side) contains material regarded by many as the very heart of the album, half of it never receives a concert airing. 'The Fairy Feller's Masterstroke' is among the most intricate and technically complex compositions ever committed to record by Queen. This probably explains why it was disregarded, although in subsequent shows the band would attempt versions of other equally complicated material on stage, including 'The Prophet's Song', 'Bohemian Rhapsody' and 'Somebody To Love'.

'The Fairy Feller' merges effortlessly with Freddie's 'Nevermore' which in turn segues almost unnoticed into 'The March Of The Black Queen'. Though the lavish 'Black Queen' did feature in the set many times (in a much shortened form), the remaining two thirds of the medley never appeared. The penultimate track, Freddie's reflective 'Funny How Love Is' has also never been performed live.

March 9

Corn Exchange, Cambridge

Procession / Father To Son / Ogre Battle / White Queen / Great King Rat / Hangman / Doing All Right / Son & Daughter / Keep Yourself Alive / Liar / Encore Medley: Jailhouse Rock; Shake Rattle And Roll; Stupid Cupid; Jailhouse Rock (Reprise) / 2nd Encore: Big Spender / Modern Times Rock'n'Roll

'Modern Times' resembles very closely the album cut, and also features Roger (its composer) singing lead vocals.

March 10

Greyhound, Croydon

March 12
Roundhouse, Dagenham

March 14
Town Hall, Cheltenham

*Procession / Father To Son / Ogre Battle / White Queen /
Great King Rat / Hangman / Doing All Right / Son &
Daughter / Keep Yourself Alive / Liar / Encore Medley:
Jailhouse Rock; Shake Rattle And Roll; Stupid Cupid;
Jailhouse Rock (Reprise) / 2nd Encore: Big Spender /
Modern Times Rock'n'Roll*

After the show the lighting crew decide that they no longer wish to endure the tedium of assembling and disassembling the rig night after night, nor the general disharmony between themselves, and promptly quit. Trident arrange a quick replacement in the form of James Dann, thus beginning a long working relationship.

March 15
University, Glasgow
Set: as March 14

March 16
University, Stirling

*Procession / Father To Son / Ogre Battle / White
Queen / Great King Rat / Hangman / Doing All Right /
Son & Daughter / Keep Yourself Alive / Liar / Encore:
See What A Fool I've Been / 2nd Encore: Jailhouse
Rock / Stupid Cupid / 3rd Encore: Jailhouse Rock
(Reprise)*

Despite having performed a full show and three encores, the audience refuse to let the band leave. The police are called when the situation quickly escalates into a riot and two people are stabbed. Two of the crew are also hurt. Meanwhile, the four band members are locked in the kitchen backstage.

The following night's concert, at Barbarella's in Birmingham, is cancelled and rescheduled for April 2.

March 19
**Winter Gardens, Cleethorpes,
Humberside**

*Procession / Father To Son / Ogre Battle / White
Queen / Great King Rat / Hangman / Doing All Right /
Son & Daughter / Keep Yourself Alive / Liar / Encore
Medley: Jailhouse Rock; Shake Rattle And Roll; Stupid
Cupid; Jailhouse Rock (Reprise) / 2nd Encore: Big
Spender / Modern Times Rock'n'Roll*

March 20
University, Manchester

March 22
Civic Centre, Canvey Island, Essex

March 23
Links Pavilion, Cromer, Norfolk

March 24
Woods Leisure Centre, Colchester

March 26
Palace Lido, Douglas

*Procession / Father To Son / Ogre Battle / White
Queen / Great King Rat / Hangman / Doing All Right /
Son & Daughter / Keep Yourself Alive / Liar / Encore
Medley: Jailhouse Rock; Shake Rattle And Roll; Stupid
Cupid; Jailhouse Rock (Reprise) / 2nd Encore: Big
Spender / Modern Times Rock'n'Roll*

March 28
University, Aberystwyth
Set: as March 26

March 29
The Gardens, Penzance

*Procession / Father To Son / Ogre Battle / White
Queen / Great King Rat / Hangman / Doing All Right /
Son & Daughter / Keep Yourself Alive / Liar / Encore
Medley: Jailhouse Rock; Shake Rattle And Roll; Stupid
Cupid; Jailhouse Rock (Reprise) / 2nd Encore: Big
Spender / Modern Times Rock'n'Roll*

March 30
Century Ballroom, Taunton

March 31
Rainbow Theatre, London

*Procession / Father To Son / Ogre Battle / White
Queen / Great King Rat / Hangman / Doing All Right /
Son & Daughter / Keep Yourself Alive / Seven Seas Of
Rhye / Liar / Encore Medley: Jailhouse Rock; Shake Rattle
And Roll; Stupid Cupid; Jailhouse Rock (Reprise) / 2nd
Encore: Big Spender / Modern Times Rock'n'Roll*

This would have been the final concert of the tour, had it not been for the following night's rescheduled show.

During 'Liar' there is a complete power breakdown. The show grinds to an embarrassing halt, but resumes again a short while later, without further incident. The 3,500 capacity crowd are good humoured, and await the restoration of power without resorting to jeering.

Despite suggestions to the contary, this show is that which makes up the 'Sheetkickers' bootleg (aka 'Shitkickers'). Freddie's pre- 'Seven Seas Of Rhye' comment regarding it being the current single, provides conclusive proof of this.

This venue was evidently the source of much frustration for Brian over the years. "The Rainbow Theatre always gave me real problems. I suppose it was because the roof was so high, all the sound seemed to be dragged upwards and away from the amps."

April 2
Barbarella's, Birmingham

Procession / Father To Son / Ogre Battle / White Queen / Great King Rat / Hangman / Doing All Right / Son & Daughter / Keep Yourself Alive / Seven Seas Of Rhye / Liar / Encore Medley: Jailhouse Rock; Shake Rattle And Roll; Stupid Cupid; Jailhouse Rock (Reprise) / 2nd Encore: Big Spender / Modern Times Rock'n'Roll

In an end-of-tour display of high spirits, the support band's lead singer and members of the road crew remove their clothes and run across the stage during the encore. Though the audience are surprised at the spectacle, Roger is not. He had bet them a bottle of champagne that they would not do it.

April 3
Langham I Studio, London

Modern Times Rock'n'Roll / March Of The Black Queen / Nevermore / White Queen

The band return once more to Langham to record their fourth and final session at this venue for the BBC. The session is transmitted on the Bob Harris show on April 15th.

Three stand-out tracks from 'Queen II' and one from the début album are recorded. While the session immediately prior to this saw a somewhat accelerated version of Roger's 'Modern Times Rock'n'Roll' recorded, this time the pace was a

little slower. The only other significant difference between the two versions came at the song's halfway mark. On this session a whistle can be heard following the "And you know there's one thing every single body could use" line, but on the previous session an additional line of "It's not that I'm bright, just happy-go-lucky" appears. The line is also absent from the original 'Queen' version.

Other material from 'Queen II' would have been of greater interest to fans than the only slightly reworked Taylor composition, which had already been laid down in the previous session. Freddie's wonderful 'The Fairy Fellers Masterstroke' is an obvious choice, though attempting to recreate such a technically complex piece, in a relatively short time, would no doubt have proved troublesome.

USA 1974

Queen embark upon their very first North American tour, again supporting Mott The Hoople. The tour spans four weeks, and includes nineteen shows, six of which are consecutive gigs at the Uris Theater, in New York. Eighteen shows of the original schedule on this tour are cancelled.

'Queen II' is released in the US on April 9, to coincide with the beginning

of this tour. The shows help to push it to No.49 in the charts there.

April 16
Regis College, Denver, Colorado

Set: as April 2, but without 'Great King Rat', which was absent on this tour

This was Queen's first concert in America.

April 17
Memorial Hall, Kansas City, Missouri

A large proportion of the shows on this tour are made up of the rock'n' roll medley material. As Brian had explained, the band decided that playing too much of their own material was both non-productive and could be seen as self indulgent. When Queen's reputation eventually began to build, so too did the amount of self-written material in the concert repertoire.

April 18
Keil Auditorium, St. Louis, Missouri

An unimpressed American critic of the time, tediously observed: "Queen's on-stage presence was an almost laughable bizarre mish-mash of every other more successful band of their genre." Someone else wrote: "They

are doing nothing special, there are moments when they sound influenced by The Who and moments when they are nearer Zeppelin."

Nobody however, noted that the band's record sales, in both Europe and America, were steadily increasing, as was their following.

April 19
Fairgrounds Appliance Building, Oklahoma City

April 20
Mid South Coliseum, Memphis, Tennessee

Procession / Father To Son / Ogre Battle / White Queen / Hangman / Doing All Right / Son & Daughter / Keep Yourself Alive / Seven Seas Of Rhye / Liar / Encore Medley: Jailhouse Rock; Shake Rattle And Roll; Stupid Cupid; Be Bop A Lula; Jailhouse Rock (Reprise) / 2nd Encore: Big Spender / Modern Times Rock'n'Roll

April 21
St Bernard Civic Center, New Orleans, Louisiana

After this show, Brian complains that he is in pain. No specific cause can be found, and the entourage continues onwards. The full extent of the problem does not emerge until May 12.

April 26
Orpheum Theater, Boston, Massachusetts

Procession / Father To Son / Ogre Battle / White Queen / Hangman / Doing All Right / Son & Daughter / Keep Yourself Alive / Seven Seas Of Rhye / Liar / Encore Medley: Jailhouse Rock; Shake Rattle And Roll; Stupid Cupid; Jailhouse Rock (Reprise) / 2nd Encore: Big Spender / Modern Times Rock'n'Roll

April 27
Palace Theater, Providence, Rhode Island

The tour thus far is something of a triumph for Queen. Any pre-tour anxieties are soon forgotten, and the band more than live up to their 'warm-up' spot obligations. They are even considered to be as good as the headlining act by many who see them, including music journalists.

Mott The Hoople band member Griffin, described the Mott/Queen working relationship at the time: "Queen are not a sabotage band, and we have had to work with some in the past, roadies who fall over leads pulling them out by accident on purpose.

The concert itself is excellent, one of the best I have seen in ages. Queen's peculiar equipment serves them well. Lead singer Freddie Mercury parodies everybody, but has style and gets away with it."

Queen were often accused of employing peculiar or unorthodox equipment arrangements for their concerts, especially in the early days. Financial restrictions usually dictated what was and wasn't used. If a particular piece of equipment was beyond the group budget, invariably John and Brian would design and build their own version, which would be used until the cash was available.

April 28
Exposition Hall, Portland, Maine

Set: as April 26

May 1
Farm Arena, Harrisburg, Pennsylvania

Procession / Father To Son / Ogre Battle / White Queen / Hangman / Doing All Right / Son & Daughter / Keep Yourself Alive / Seven Seas Of Rhye / Liar / Encore Medley: Jailhouse Rock; Shake Rattle And Roll; Stupid Cupid; Jailhouse Rock (Reprise) / 2nd Encore: Big Spender / Modern Times Rock'n'Roll

May 2
Agricultural Hall, Allentown, Pennsylvania

May 3
King's College, Wilkes Barre, Pennsylvania

May 4
Palace Theater, Waterbury, Connecticut

Mott The Hoople On Broadway
Just Uris Theater shows.

May 7/8/9/10/11/12
Uris Theater, New York

First night: Procession / Father To Son / Ogre Battle / White Queen / Hangman / Doing All Right / Son & Daughter / Keep Yourself Alive / Seven Seas Of Rhye / Liar / Encore Medley: Big Spender; Modern Times Rock'n'Roll

Both Queen and Mott The Hoople play six consecutive nights at this venue. Other songs performed during the shows included: 'Jailhouse Rock', 'The Prophet's Song' and a brief recital of 'Good Rocking Tonight'.

Final night: Procession / Father To Son / Ogre Battle / White Queen / Doing All Right / Son & Daughter / Keep Yourself Alive / Seven Seas Of Rhye / Liar / Encore Medley: Big Spender; Modern Times Rock'n'Roll

Brian collapses after the show on May 12, and though his condition is at first thought to be a form of food poisoning, it is soon discovered that he has hepatitis. The injection Brian had prior to the Australian show in January, is almost certainly responsible. Not only is the following night's show cancelled, but Queen's entire involvement in the tour is thwarted.

Kansas are drafted in to take over as Mott The Hoople's support band. Their first show is two days later, in Boston.

Having managed to smuggle a decidedly unwell Brian aboard a London-bound air flight, a somewhat dismayed (no pun intended) and frustrated Queen fly home to re-evaluate their position. In subsequent interviews years later, Brian would admit that he spent the first weeks of his recuperation worrying that the other three might find a replacement and continue without him. As far as the remainder of Queen are concerned, however, replacing Brian was never an option.

Meanwhile, staff at Queen's American record label Elektra contact everyone who came into contact with Brian, since protective gamma globulin inoculations are necessary.

Brian: "Getting ill really turned my life upside-down. Before that I must say I had worried about things in the band and my life in general. There always seemed to be something that needed some worry. Today I don't worry nearly as much."

Throughout June and July Queen work on material for their third album, rehearsing at Rockfield Studios in Gwent. Brian's health is still far from satisfactory, but he continues as best he can, until August, when he is again rushed to hospital. This time a duodenal ulcer is detected, and an emergency operation quickly follows. Consequently, an entire North America tour scheduled for September is cancelled.

The band continue work on the album, but leave gaps for Brian to add his guitar and vocal parts later. Although most sessions take place at Rockfield Studios, they record one of the early sessions at Trident Studios on July 15.

Although Brian experiences bouts of depression during his recuperation, he spends his time at home as productively as possible. From his bed he writes the lyrics to 'Now I'm Here', the inspiration for which came from the American tour dates with Mott The Hoople – hence the line "Down in the city just Hoople'n'me."

As he lay in bed scribbling down lines of song lyrics and humming guitar riffs into his bedside tape recorder, Brian was apparently approached by Ron and Russell Mael, from Sparks, who had heard about the abandoned American tour, and wondered if Brian would consider joining their band. Brian declines the offer.

Brian's ill health steadily improves, allowing him to return to the sessions. He is extremely impressed by the material which has been recorded, and especially by Freddie's lyric writing.

By September 1974 the sessions are complete, and 'Sheer Heart Attack', released two months later, emerges as Queen's most accomplished work to date. Roger Taylor's track of the same name was written for the album, but was not finished in time to be included. Though the album retains the song's title, the track finally crops up on the sixth album 'News Of The World', in October 1977.

October 11
'Killer Queen/Flick Of The Wrist' is released in the UK. It is the first track to be taken from the 'Sheer Heart Attack' album, and is Queen's first double A-sided single issue. The coupling peaks at No.2 in the UK. The same disc is issued ten days later in America, and provides Queen with their first chart placing there, peaking at No.12.

Sheer Heart Attack Tour

Nineteen concerts at eighteen different venues conclude Queen's British shows of the year with 'Hustler' as the support act. It is Queen's second tour as the headlining act and the shows features much of the new album material.

The set now includes new material from 'Sheer Heart Attack' ('Now I'm Here', 'Killer Queen', 'Leroy Brown', 'In The Lap Of The Gods Revisited'), even though the album would not be released until November 8. Other material from the album would feature in later shows. 'White Queen' and 'Seven Seas Of Rhye' are also new, though the latter of the two is not yet performed on a regular basis.

The tour programme is a commemorative show souvenir, consisting of four pages of biographical text and discography, and a wonderful black and white photograph of an extremely youthful looking Queen in the centre pages, all housed in an orange jacket, the front of which reads: "This book is designed for your further enjoyment of the show."

The typical cost of a ticket for this tour, is £1.30.

October 30
Palace, Manchester

Procession / Now I'm Here / Ogre Battle / Father To Son / White Queen / Flick Of The Wrist / Medley: In The Lap Of The Gods; Killer Queen; The March Of The Black Queen; Bring Back That Leroy Brown / Son & Daughter / Keep Yourself Alive / Seven Seas Of Rhye / Stone Cold Crazy / Liar / In The Lap Of The Gods (Revisited) / Encore Medley: Big Spender; Modern Times Rock'n'Roll / God Save The Queen

Queen record a special version of the national anthem, and use it to conclude this show. It would later conclude almost every performance of the band's career. To the fans, it generally signifies an all-too-soon end to the evening's entertainment.

'Flick Of The Wrist' and 'Now I'm Here' are new to the set on this tour. The Latter is performed somewhat differently from the version that would later appear on the 'Sheer Heart Attack' album. It is less structured, and the band perform it in a variety of ways.

October 16
Maida Vale 4 Studio, London

Now I'm Here / Stone Cold Crazy / Flick Of The Wrist / Tenement Funster

Queen record their penultimate BBC session, broadcast on November 4, 1974, on the Bob Harris show. As the previous month had seen recording sessions for the 'Sheer Heart Attack' album, the band record slightly different versions of four tracks from it.

While 'Stone Cold Crazy' and 'Now I'm Here' are only marginally different from the album versions, Roger's vocals on 'Tenement Funster' are infinitely more aggressive, as well as significantly louder. Also, the lead and bass guitar backing is so close to that of the original, that it appears as if Roger has been recorded simply singing over the real backing track, which he

was not. Being accustomed to hearing the track segue into 'Flick Of The Wrist' on the album, when it instead fades into silence here, there is a sense of waiting for something that never arrives. The phased ending seems inappropriate.

'Flick Of The Wrist' is equally very impressive, so close to the 'Sheer Heart Attack' version, that it is only at around the two minute mark that it varies from the original. Brian's lead guitar solo after the "Don't look back. Don't look back - it's a rip-off" line is dramatically different.

Like 'Tenement Funster', 'Flick Of The Wrist' seems somehow incomplete with a phased conclusion. All in all though, the Queen/Jeff Griffin combination yielded a memorable session, and one which is long overdue for a proper compact disc release.

The band unveil a brand new lighting rig here.

October 31
Victoria Hall, Hanley, Staffordshire
Set: as October 30

Although 'White Queen' entails a very complex musical arrangement on the album, the band perform it with dramatic mood and tempo changes in concert, instead of taking the easy option with a simplified, condensed version.

November 1
Liverpool Empire, Liverpool

Procession / Now I'm Here / Ogre Battle / Father To Son / White Queen / Flick Of The Wrist / Medley: In The Lap Of The Gods; Killer Queen; The March Of The Black Queen; Bring Back That Leroy Brown / Son & Daughter / Keep Yourself Alive / Seven Seas Of Rhye / Stone Cold Crazy / Liar / In The Lap Of The Gods (Revisited) / Encore Medley: Big Spender; Modern Times Rock'n'Roll / 2nd Encore: Jailhouse Rock / God Save The Queen

As in London and Cornwall (home towns of the band and Roger Taylor respectively), Queen always enjoyed huge popularity in Liverpool. From their very earliest concerts in 1970, they had established an ever increasing number of devotees. Many were in attendance here.

An assertive, responsive audience always inspired the very best performances from Queen. This was no exception. Many fans cite the show as the best they've ever seen. A full page local newspaper review next day opened with a quote from Freddie: "People think I'm an ogre at times. Some girls hissed at me in the street...'You devil'. They think we're really nasty, but that's only on stage. Well I'm certainly not an ogre."

The same article noted that while Brian uses AC30 amplifiers on stage, as The Beatles had done in the Sixties, Queen's music was very much from the Seventies. It went on: "It is cleverly arranged, carefully timed, and delivered with maximum effort to create the greatest impact. It works on a young and receptive audience like a bombshell. Forget eight year olds screaming at the Osmonds."

The reviewer also had a sense of humour: "An atmosphere approaching bedlam is prevalent inside the Empire. Hustler have come and gone and now the audience are hungry for action. They whistle and chant and clap with all the precision of the football terraces. The ancient cry of "Wally" as is still heard in northern territories, echoes around the faded gilt décor. Jack Nelson (Queen's American Manager) is intrigued by the cry and wonders if Wally are a local group and wants to sign them – until enlightened.

"The only agro comes when Queen's entourage from London try to claim their seats near the front. 'Fuck Off' directs one youth, as PR Tony Brainsby pleads for his seat. 'All these seats are taken up by that gentleman there,' says Tony, pointing at me. Ribald laughter from the watching stalls and repeated cries of 'Ooh Gentleman!'. The seat pirates eventually relinquish their hold with dark mutterings of 'alright, but we'll see you outside'.

"Within seconds most of the audience were standing up to gaze desperately at the darkened empty stage, and there they were – shadowy figures bounding towards the waiting instruments. The lights blazed and there was evil Freddie, clad all in white, the archetypal demon jock singer, pointing and snarling: "Queen is back, what do you think of that?""

November 2
University, Leeds

Following the show, hysteria uncannily similar to March's Stirling University gig, erupts in the audience. Scuffles between fans and over zealous bouncers break out. On this occasion however, Freddie manages to calm the situation down before anything too serious can develop.

During the set, Roger's on-stage monitor fails. He attempts to signal to his roadie – but to no avail, and for the rest of the performance he is unable to hear anything he plays or sings. After the show, a somewhat irate Roger proceeds to throw a tantrum in the dressing room which results in him having to be driven to the Leeds Infirmary with a severely bruised foot.

November 3
Theatre, Coventry

Procession / Now I'm Here / Ogre Battle / Father To Son / White Queen / Flick Of The Wrist / Medley: In The Lap Of The Gods; Killer Queen; The March Of The Black Queen; Bring Back That Leroy Brown / Son & Daughter / Keep Yourself Alive / Seven Seas Of Rhye / Stone Cold Crazy / Liar / In The Lap Of The Gods (Revisited) / Encore Medley: Big Spender; Modern Times Rock'n'Roll / 2nd Encore: Jailhouse Rock / God Save The Queen

'Jailhouse Rock' now concludes nearly every show.

November 5
City Hall, Sheffield

'Leroy Brown' is new to this tour. Although it is performed in the same way as on 'Sheer Heart Attack', Freddie sings hardly any words, apparently using it as an opportunity for a rest before the more vocally demanding 'Father To Son', 'Keep Yourself Alive' and 'Liar'. Brian plays a short ukulele solo towards the end of 'Leroy Brown'.

November 6
St George's Hall, Bradford

Procession / Now I'm Here / Ogre Battle / Father To Son / White Queen / Flick Of The Wrist / Medley: In The Lap Of The Gods; Killer Queen; The March Of The Black Queen; Bring Back That Leroy Brown / Son & Daughter / Keep Yourself Alive / Seven Seas Of Rhye / Stone Cold Crazy / Liar / In The Lap Of The Gods (Revisited) / Encore Medley: Big Spender; Modern Times Rock'n'Roll / 2nd Encore: Jailhouse Rock / God Save The Queen

'Big Spender' begins to make more and more appearances in the set.

November 7
City Hall, Newcastle-Upon-Tyne

As well as the 'Sheer Heart Attack' material, Queen also incorporated a medley section into the set for this tour, setting a trend for all subsequent tours. On this tour the medley comprised excerpts from 'Killer Queen' and 'Black Queen', together with the largely lyricless 'Leroy Brown'.

Contrary to some collector's lists, both versions of 'In The Lap Of The Gods' were performed live. The first version featured at the start of the medley and the 'revisited' cut ended the show.

November 8
Apollo Theatre, Glasgow

Procession / Now I'm Here / Ogre Battle / Father To Son / White Queen / Flick Of The Wrist / Medley: In The Lap Of The Gods; Killer Queen; The March Of The Black Queen; Bring Back That Leroy Brown / Son & Daughter / Keep Yourself Alive / Seven Seas Of Rhye / Stone Cold Crazy / Liar / In The Lap Of The Gods (Revisited) / Encore Medley: Big Spender; Modern Times Rock'n'Roll / 2nd Encore: Jailhouse Rock / God Save The Queen

Towards the end of this show, Freddie is dragged into the audience, only to be dragged back out again by security men. He later recalls the incident as a rather undignified affair, but the experience teaches him to be more careful in future.

'Sheer Heart Attack' is released in the UK and four days later in America. It reaches Nos. 2 and 12 in the charts respectively. The cost of producing the album reputably falls between £28-30,000, a fraction of the cost of most contemporary albums, but a significant amount in 1974.

Material which never features in the live shows is Freddie's 'Lily Of The Valley', Roger's superbly self sung and much underrated 'Tenement Funster', Brian's 'Dear Friends' and 'She Makes Me' (bafflingly subtitled 'Stormtrooper In Stilettos') and John Deacon's first composition for Queen, 'Misfire'.

Brian: "For some strange reason we seemed to get a rather different feel on 'Sheer Heart Attack' because of the way we were forced to record it (referring to his absence, because of illness), and even allowing for all the problems we had, none of us were really displeased with the final result."

November 9
University, Lancaster

Procession / Now I'm Here / Ogre Battle / Father To Son / White Queen / Flick Of The Wrist / Medley: In The Lap Of The Gods; Killer Queen; The March Of The Black Queen; Bring Back That Leroy Brown / Son & Daughter / Keep Yourself Alive / Seven Seas Of Rhye / Stone Cold Crazy / Liar / In The Lap Of The Gods (Revisited) / Encore Medley: Big Spender; Modern Times Rock'n'Roll / 2nd Encore: Jailhouse Rock / God Save The Queen

November 10
Guildhall, Preston

November 12
Colston Hall, Bristol

November 13
Winter Gardens, Bournemouth
Set: as November 3

November 14
Gaumont, Southampton

November 15
Brangwyn Hall, Swansea

Procession / Now I'm Here / Ogre Battle / Father To Son / White Queen / Flick Of The Wrist / Medley: In The Lap Of The Gods; Killer Queen; The March Of The Black Queen; Bring Back That Leroy Brown / Son & Daughter / Keep Yourself Alive / Seven Seas Of Rhye / Stone Cold Crazy / Liar / In The Lap Of The Gods (Revisited) / Encore Medley: Big Spender; Modern Times Rock'n'Roll / 2nd Encore: Jailhouse Rock / God Save The Queen

November 16
Town Hall, Birmingham

November 18
New Theatre, Oxford

Procession / Now I'm Here / Ogre Battle / Father To Son / White Queen / Flick Of The Wrist / Medley: In The Lap Of The Gods; Killer Queen; The March Of The Black Queen; Bring Back That Leroy Brown / Son & Daughter / Keep Yourself Alive / Seven Seas Of Rhye / Stone Cold Crazy / Liar / In The Lap Of The Gods (Revisited) / Encore Medley: Big Spender; Modern Times Rock'n'Roll / 2nd Encore: Jailhouse Rock / God Save The Queen

November 19/20

Rainbow Theatre, London

Both Nights: *Procession / Now I'm Here / Ogre Battle / Father To Son / White Queen / Flick Of The Wrist / Medley: In The Lap Of The Gods; Killer Queen; The March Of The Black Queen; Bring Back That Leroy Brown / Son & Daughter / Keep Yourself Alive / Seven Seas Of Rhye / Stone Cold Crazy / Liar / In The Lap Of The Gods (Revisited) / Encore Medley: Big Spender; Modern Times Rock'n'Roll / 2nd Encore: Jailhouse Rock / God Save The Queen*

Queen were originally scheduled to play only the one show at this venue, but when it sells out in just two days, promoter Mel Bush adds another show, for the night after. For promotional purposes the second performance is sound recorded and filmed. It was the first time Queen had been professionally filmed live in concert.

The footage is later edited down to thirty minutes and screened at selected British cinemas as an opener for the Led Zeppelin film *The Song Remains The Same*. After a limited run, the film was stored away in the Queen archives, not to see the light of day until almost twenty years later.

In 1991 the original master tapes were discovered, still in pristine condition. The missing sections were then edited back into the cinema cut, and a 53 minute video was issued as part of the 'Box Of Tricks' package, in May the following year. Both versions of the film have featured at Queen fan club conventions. The sound recording was considered for release as Queen's first live album, but when they eventually changed their minds, the project was abandoned. It was a

further five years before Queen got around to issuing 'Live Killers', their first live album.

Both shows saw Queen performing before a capacity crowd of 3,500. In keeping with the band image of the time, their stage costume featured exclusively black and white items. Freddie wore white from head to toe, but changed into all black for the encore. John wore a typically Seventies style velvet jacket and flared trousers, Brian his famous white caped outfit, which was frequently copied thereafter, and Roger, as befits the drummer, was dressed in rather less flamboyant attire.

On the second night Freddie's first words were: "The nasty Queenies are back – what do you think of that? Thank you very much. It really is nice to be back home. It's been so long we've missed you all – we really have. Have you missed us? It's time for 'Ogre Battle'."

EUROPE 1974

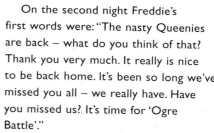

The band's first proper European tour consisted of ten shows in six countries, performed over a two and a half week period. The tour would have been longer, had it not been for the truck transporting their equipment being involved in an accident, and not being able to reach the remaining scheduled venues.

December 4
Frankfurt

December 5
Hamburg

December 6
Cologne

Procession / Now I'm Here / Ogre Battle / Father To Son / White Queen / Flick Of The Wrist / Medley: In The Lap Of The Gods; Killer Queen; The March Of The Black Queen; Bring Back That Leroy Brown / Son & Daughter / Keep Yourself Alive / Seven Seas Of Rhye / Stone Cold Crazy / Liar / In The Lap Of The Gods (Revisited) / Encore Medley: Big Spender; Jailhouse Rock; Stupid Cupid; Be Bop A Lula; Jailhouse Rock (Reprise) / God Save The Queen

December 7
Siegen

Set: as December 6, but with different Rock'n'Roll Medley

December 8
Congress Gebouw, The Hague

Set: as December 6

November 23
Gothenburg

Procession / Now I'm Here / Ogre Battle / Father To Son / White Queen / Flick Of The Wrist / Medley: In The Lap Of The Gods; Killer Queen; The March Of The Black Queen; Bring Back That Leroy Brown / Son & Daughter / Keep Yourself Alive / Seven Seas Of Rhye / Stone Cold Crazy / Liar / In The Lap Of The Gods (Revisited) / Encore Medley: Big Spender; Modern Times Rock'n'Roll / 2nd Encore: Jailhouse Rock / God Save The Queen

November 25
Helsingin Kulttuuritalo, Helsinki

Procession / Now I'm Here / Ogre Battle / Father To Son / White Queen / Flick Of The Wrist / Medley: In The Lap Of The Gods; Killer Queen; The March Of The Black Queen; Bring Back That Leroy Brown / Son & Daughter / Keep Yourself Alive / Seven Seas Of Rhye / Stone Cold Crazy / Liar / In The Lap Of The Gods (Revisited) / Encore: Modern Times Rock'n'Roll / 2nd Encore: Jailhouse Rock / God Save The Queen

December 1
140 Theatre, Brussels

Procession / Now I'm Here / Ogre Battle / Father To Son / White Queen / Flick Of The Wrist / Medley: In The Lap Of The Gods; Killer Queen; The March Of The Black Queen; Bring Back That Leroy Brown / Son & Daughter / Keep Yourself Alive / Seven Seas Of Rhye / Stone Cold Crazy / Liar / In The Lap Of The Gods (Revisited) / Encore Medley: Big Spender; Modern Times Rock'n'Roll / 2nd Encore: Jailhouse Rock / God Save The Queen

December 2
Munich

Set: as previous night

With their equipment truck repaired only two days previously, on the way to this gig the driver attempts to negotiate too small a bridge, and gets stuck.

Another company comes to the rescue and the show goes ahead. A much appreciative Queen employ the services of Edwin Shirley Trucking for every tour thereafter.

December 10
Barcelona

Procession / Now I'm Here / Ogre Battle / Father To Son / White Queen / Flick Of The Wrist / Medley: In The Lap Of The Gods; Killer Queen; The March Of The Black Queen; Bring Back That Leroy Brown / Son & Daughter / Keep Yourself Alive / Seven Seas Of Rhye / Stone Cold Crazy / Liar / In The Lap Of The Gods (Revisited) / Encore: Modern Times Rock'n'Roll / 2nd Encore Medley: Big Spender; Jailhouse Rock; Stupid Cupid; Be Bop A Lula; Jailhouse Rock (Reprise) / God Save The Queen

This was the final show of the tour.

January 17

'Now I'm Here'/'Lily Of The Valley' is released as the second single from 'Sheer Heart Attack'. Though the same song is also issued in Japan (coupled with 'Keep Yourself Alive'), it is, curiously, not issued in America. Unassisted by a promotional video – which would really only commence with 'Bo Rhap' – the single still reaches No.11 in England.

January 18

The band members attended the wedding of John Deacon, to school teacher Veronica Tetzlaff, in London.

USA 1975

January 31

Queen fly to New York to spend seven days rehearsing at the Beacon Theater, before commencing the 38 show, 30 venue American tour. Further shows in late February and April would be cancelled when Freddie develops problems with his throat. Indeed, the proposed final show of the tour, in Portland on April 7, was cancelled. The final two shows of the tour are in Canada, the band's first performances there.

The tour is promoted by Mel Bush, with sound mixing by John Harris. Lighting is organised by James Dann, and the tour manager is Iain Brown.

The support acts are Kansas, the band which had replaced Queen in America the previous May, and Mahogany Rush. Some of the shows on the tour featured Styx as support, instead of Kansas.

February 5
Agora, Columbus, Ohio

Procession / Now I'm Here / Ogre Battle / Father To Son / White Queen / Flick Of The Wrist / Medley: In The Lap Of The Gods; Killer Queen; The March Of The Black Queen; Bring Back That Leroy Brown / Son & Daughter; Guitar Solo / Keep Yourself Alive; Drum Solo / Seven Seas Of Rhye / Stone Cold Crazy / Liar / In The Lap Of The Gods (Revisited) / Encore Medley: Big Spender; Modern Times Rock'n'Roll / 2nd Encore: Jailhouse Rock / God Save The Queen

February 7
Palace Theatre, Dayton, Ohio

February 8
Music Hall, Cleveland, Ohio (Two shows)

Procession / Now I'm Here / Ogre Battle / Father To Son / White Queen / Flick Of The Wrist / Medley: In The Lap Of The Gods; Killer Queen; The March Of The Black Queen; Bring Back That Leroy Brown / Son & Daughter; Guitar Solo / Keep Yourself Alive; Drum Solo / Seven Seas Of Rhye / Stone Cold Crazy / Liar / In The Lap Of The Gods (Revisited) / Encore Medley: Big Spender; Modern Times Rock'n'Roll / 2nd Encore: Jailhouse Rock / God Save The Queen

February 9
Morris Civic Auditorium, South Bend, Indiana

February 10
Ford Auditorium, Detroit, Michigan

February 11
Student Union Auditorium, Toledo, Ohio

February 14
Palace Theater, Waterbury, Connecticut

Procession / Now I'm Here / Ogre Battle / Father To Son / White Queen / Flick Of The Wrist / Medley: In The Lap Of The Gods; Killer Queen; The March Of The Black Queen; Bring Back That Leroy Brown / Son & Daughter; Guitar Solo / Keep Yourself Alive; Drum Solo / Seven Seas Of Rhye / Stone Cold Crazy / Liar / In The Lap Of The Gods (Revisited) / Encore Medley: Big Spender; Be Bop A Lula / 2nd Encore: Modern Times Rock'n'Roll / Jailhouse Rock / God Save The Queen

February 15
Orpheum Theatre, Boston (2 shows)

February 16
Avery Fisher Hall, New York (2 shows)

Procession / Now I'm Here / Ogre Battle / Father To Son / White Queen / Flick Of The Wrist / Medley: In The Lap Of The Gods; Killer Queen; The March Of The Black Queen; Bring Back That Leroy Brown / Son & Daughter; Guitar Solo / Keep Yourself Alive; Drum Solo / Seven Seas Of Rhye / Stone Cold Crazy / Liar / In The Lap Of The Gods (Revisited) / Encore: Modern Times Rock'n'Roll / 2nd Encore: Big Spender / Jailhouse Rock / God Save The Queen

Freddie's first words: "The nasty Queenies are back". He especially liked this expression. When he reaches the front of the stage, he is handed a bouquet of white roses.

Freddie is interviewed after the show by Lisa Robinson for *Circus* magazine. Among other things, she asks whose idea it was to perform "Big Spender": "Oh (he laughs) it was my idea entirely. I like that approach to entertainment. I like that cabaretish sort of thing. I adore Liza Minnelli, I think she's a wow. It does appeal to me, the thought of doing more lavish stage type things, but somehow I would like to combine it with the group, not divorce from it. That's a difficult thing, because you've got to approach the others with it and convince them that it's going to work."

February 17
War Memorial, Trenton, New Jersey

February 19
Lewiston, New York

February 21
Capitol Theater, Passaic, New Jersey

Procession / Now I'm Here / Ogre Battle / Father To Son / White Queen / Flick Of The Wrist / Medley: In The Lap Of The Gods; Killer Queen; The March Of The Black Queen; Bring Back That Leroy Brown / Son & Daughter; Guitar Solo / Keep Yourself Alive; Drum Solo / Seven Seas Of Rhye / Stone Cold Crazy / Liar / In The Lap Of The Gods (Revisited) / Encore Medley: Jailhouse Rock; Big Spender; Be Bop A Lula; Stupid Cupid; Modern Times Rock'n'Roll; Jailhouse Rock (Reprise) / God Save The Queen

February 22
Farm Arena, Harrisburg, Pennsylvania

February 23
Erlinger Theater, Philadelphia, Pennsylvania (2 shows)

Having performed the two shows here with increasing voice problems, Freddie

is taken to see a throat specialist at the Philadelphia University Hospital. The diagnosis is two suspected throat nodes. The specialist recommends that Freddie should refrain from singing and speaking for three months. His initial reaction is "the band will kill me"– they did not get the chance, they had already left for Washington, the venue of the next show.

Not wanting to disappoint the fans, especially at such short notice, Freddie decides he will perform one more show, despite strict advice to rest his voice. His problems do not end there, however. He still has to get to Washington for the next show, and time is running out.

Dave Thomas (of Trident) and Jack Nelson, who have remained behind with Freddie, board a train to Washington, but get no further than Baltimore before they encounter a derailed train blocking their path. As every taxi and hire car has already been booked, an alternative is required, and quickly. By this time it is five o'clock, and Queen are due on stage in three hours.

Eventually another train is found, but it is only a sleeper and has no seats. The three men book it, and spend the duration of the journey on their backs in bunk beds. They eventually arrive at the JFK Center at 7.15 pm. John, Roger and Brian are told that the show will be

Queen's last for at least three months. The band go on stage only slightly later than scheduled, and perform a blistering show, despite Freddie having missed the soundcheck.

Dave Thomas: "They went on stage and did the most amazing gig that I have ever seen them do in my life. It was an amazing show because they seemed to have so much energy, and to our astonishment there was Freddie hitting all the high notes again."

After the show it is suggested that Freddie should seek a second opinion on his throat condition. He sees a specialist in Washington, and is told that nodules are not the cause, but that he has rather severe swelling. He is told to rest his voice, but that three months is excessive, one or two weeks should suffice. To be completely sure, a third consultation in New Orleans, by a specialist who has also advised artists Tom Jones and Barbra Streisand, confirms the swelling diagnosis, and antibiotics are prescribed.

Six concerts are cancelled: Pittsburgh, Kuzton, Buffalo, Toronto, London (Ontario) and Davenport. The tour recommences on March 5.

February 24
Kennedy Center, Washington, Pennsylvania

Set: Same as February 16

March 5
Mary E. Sawyer Auditorium, La Crosse, Wisconsin

In an attempt to save his voice, Freddie keeps his usually considerable between-song banter and vocal improvisations to a minimum for this, and a few subsequent shows. Further dates were cancelled however, when similar problems re-emerged. But rather than cancel a number of consecutive shows, Queen performed some, but just left a greater period of time between each one.

March 6
Madison, Wisconsin

Procession / Now I'm Here / Ogre Battle / Father To Son / White Queen / Flick Of The Wrist / Medley: In The Lap Of The Gods; Killer Queen; The March Of The Black Queen; Bring Back That Leroy Brown / Son & Daughter; Guitar Solo / Keep Yourself Alive; Drum Solo / Seven Seas Of Rhye / Stone Cold Crazy / Liar / In The Lap Of The Gods (Revisited) / Encore Medley: Jailhouse Rock; Big Spender; Modern Times Rock'n'Roll; Jailhouse Rock (Reprise) / God Save The Queen

March 7
Uptown Theater, Milwaukee, Wisconsin

March 8
Aragon Ballroom, Chicago, Illinois

March 9
Keil Auditorium, St Louis, Missouri
'White Queen', 'Killer Queen' and 'Black Queen' are all now featured in the show. They would appear together only during 1975 and 1976.

March 10
Coliseum, Fort Wayne, Indiana

March 12
Municipal Auditorium, Atlanta, Georgia

Procession / Now I'm Here / Ogre Battle / Father To Son / White Queen / Flick Of The Wrist / Medley: In The Lap Of The Gods; Killer Queen; The March Of The Black Queen; Bring Back That Leroy Brown / Son & Daughter; Guitar Solo / Keep Yourself Alive; Drum Solo / Seven Seas Of Rhye / Stone Cold Crazy / Liar / In The Lap Of The Gods (Revisited) / Encore Medley: Big Spender; Modern Times Rock'n'Roll / 2nd Encore: Jailhouse Rock / God Save The Queen

March 13
Civic Auditorium, Charleston, South Carolina

March 15
Marina, Miami, Florida

March 18
St Bernard Civic Auditorium, New Orleans, Louisiana

March 20
Municipal Hall, San Antonio, Texas

Procession / Now I'm Here / Ogre Battle / Father To Son / White Queen / Flick Of The Wrist / Medley: In The Lap Of The Gods; Killer Queen; The March Of The Black Queen; Bring Back That Leroy Brown / Son & Daughter; Guitar Solo / Keep Yourself Alive; Drum Solo / Seven Seas Of Rhye / Stone Cold Crazy / Liar / In The Lap Of The Gods (Revisited) / Encore Medley: Jailhouse Rock; Be Bop A Lula; Big Spender; Modern Times Rock'n'Roll; Jailhouse Rock (Reprise) / God Save The Queen

March 23
McFarlin Auditorium, Dallas, Texas

March 25
Municipal Theater, Tulsa, Oklahoma

March 29
Santa Monica Civic Auditorium, Los Angeles (2 Shows)

Procession / Now I'm Here / Ogre Battle / Father To Son / White Queen / Flick Of The Wrist / Hangman / Medley: In The Lap Of The Gods; Killer Queen; The March Of The Black Queen; Bring Back That Leroy Brown / Son & Daughter; Guitar Solo / Keep Yourself Alive; Drum Solo / Seven Seas Of Rhye / Stone Cold Crazy / Liar / In The Lap Of The Gods (Revisited) / Encore Medley: Big Spender; Modern Times Rock'n'Roll / 2nd Encore: Jailhouse Rock / God Save The Queen

March 30
Winterland, San Francisco, California
Set: as March 29, with longer Rock'n'Roll medley

April 2
Kindmens Fieldhouse, Edmonton, Alberta

Procession / Now I'm Here / Ogre Battle / Father To Son / White Queen / Flick Of The Wrist / Hangman / Medley: In The Lap Of The Gods; Killer Queen; The March Of The Black Queen; Bring Back That Leroy Brown / Son & Daughter; Guitar Solo / Keep Yourself Alive; Drum Solo / Seven Seas Of Rhye / Stone Cold Crazy / Liar / In The Lap Of The Gods (Revisited) / Encore Medley: Jailhouse Rock; Be Bop A Lula / 2nd Encore: Big Spender; Modern Times Rock'n'Roll; Jailhouse Rock (Reprise) / God Save The Queen

This concert was filmed for a subsequent Japanese documentary on the band. Although it was not broadcast as a purely live programme and only a small amount of material was transmitted, numerous bootleg recordings of various types subsequently appeared.

Queen performed this, and the concluding show here, before a capacity audience of 10,000. Sumo wrestlers were employed to keep overzealous fans off the stage. However, when Queen appear, there is a huge surge forward which quickly turns into a potentially dangerous situation. Freddie halts the show momentarily and appeals for calm. The show then continues.

This was Queen's first concert in Canada, they were joined on stage for the encore by the support band Kansas.

April 3
Calgary, Alberta
Set: as April 2, but with different medley (unknown)

April 6
Seattle, Washington
Procession / Now I'm Here / Ogre Battle / Father To Son / White Queen / Flick Of The Wrist / Hangman / Medley: In The Lap Of The Gods; Killer Queen; The March Of The Black Queen; Bring Back That Leroy Brown / Son & Daughter; Guitar Solo / Keep Yourself Alive / Drum Solo / Seven Seas Of Rhye / Stone Cold Crazy / Liar / In The Lap Of The Gods (Revisited) / Encore Medley: Big Spender; Modern Times Rock'n'Roll / 2nd Encore: Jailhouse Rock / God Save The Queen

An additional tour of North America – comprising eighteen concerts – was planned for the summer of 1975, but was ultimately cancelled – despite tickets having been sold for many venues – because of problems with Trident.

In December 1974 Queen had recruited the services of music lawyer Jim Beach to free them from their Trident obligations. Ties with Trident (and the Norman brothers) would eventually be severed in August 1975.

1975 JAPANESE TOUR

April 18
The band arrive in Tokyo to begin their first tour of Japan. All four members are visibly overwhelmed to discover over 3,000 screaming fans have gathered to welcome them. They cover every available vantage point. The phenomenon is christened 'Queen Mania', and would re-occur at every Japanese tour thereafter. Freddie would later cite Japan as his very favourite country, and his shopping expeditions there would become famous.

There is some wonderful footage in the 'Magic Years' videos of a somewhat astonished, bemused and young looking Queen arriving at the airport. Each band member stepping out of the aircraft is clearly shocked at the scene. Banners proclaiming "Japan Welcomes Queen" and "We Love You Brian" were totally unexpected.

The tour opens and concludes at the same venue, the vast Budokan Hall, in Tokyo, which is most commonly employed to stage martial art events and Sumo wrestling competitions. Although the tour entails only eight shows, between them they yield many bootlegs – and very good ones at that.

April 19
Budokan Hall, Tokyo
Procession / Now I'm Here / Ogre Battle / Father To Son / White Queen / Flick Of The Wrist / Hangman / Great King Rat / Medley: In The Lap Of The Gods; Killer Queen; The March Of The Black Queen; Bring Back That Leroy Brown / Son & Daughter / Doing All Right / Stone Cold Crazy / Keep Yourself Alive / Seven Seas Of Rhye / Liar / In The Lap Of The Gods (Revisited) / Encore: Jailhouse Rock / 2nd Encore: See What A Fool I've Been / God Save The Queen

April 22
Aichi Taiikukan, Nagoya
John Deacon commented during this tour that the collective audience noise was so deafening, that it seemed to him as if the whole arena was shaking.

April 23
Nokusai Taikan, Kobe
Procession / Now I'm Here / Ogre Battle / Father To Son / White Queen / Flick Of The Wrist / Hangman / Great King Rat / Medley: In The Lap Of The Gods; Killer Queen; The March Of The Black Queen; Bring Back That Leroy Brown / Son & Daughter / Doing All Right / Stone Cold Crazy / Keep Yourself Alive / Seven Seas Of Rhye / Liar / In The Lap Of The Gods (Revisited) / Encore Medley: Big Spender; Modern Times Rock'n'Roll / 2nd Encore: Jailhouse Rock / See What A Fool I've Been / God Save The Queen

April 25
Kyden Taiikukan, Fukuoka
Set: similar to April 23

Brian: "It's such an amazing novelty, it's so different to everywhere else, because in addition to the immediate feeling you get from the people you're playing to, you have all the real magic of the traditional part of Japanese life which affects you very much while you're there."

It soon became impossible for any member of the band to go anywhere and not be recognised.

Roger Taylor: "I went into a shop to buy a tape recorder and suddenly the shop keeper stared at me. 'Ah so – you Queen' and proceeded to drag a

camera from underneath the counter. He just kept taking pictures all the time, for about ten minutes. I couldn't get another word out of him."

April 28
Taiikukan, Okayama

Procession / Now I'm Here / Ogre Battle / Father To Son / White Queen / Flick Of The Wrist / Hangman / Great King Rat / Medley: In The Lap Of The Gods; Killer Queen; The March Of The Black Queen; Bring Back That Leroy Brown / Son & Daughter / Doing All Right / Stone Cold Crazy / Keep Yourself Alive / Seven Seas Of Rhye / Liar / In The Lap Of The Gods (Revisited) / Encore Medley: Big Spender; Modern Times Rock'n'Roll / 2nd Encore: Jailhouse Rock / See What A Fool I've Been / God Save The Queen

April 29
Yamaha Tsumagoi Hall, Shizuoka

As the main lights dim and a single spotlight picks out Brian for the start of his guitar solo, the other three disappear to the back of the stage, in darkness. Roger bends to sit on a box for the duration of the solo, but unbeknown to him it is overhanging the back of the stage. The box disappears off the edge, and takes Roger with it. Despite somersaulting backwards and landing heavily on his back, he sustains no injuries and continues the show. The audience are unaware of the incident.

April 30
Bunkan Taiikukan, Yokohama

The band come back onto the stage after the encore dressed in traditional Japanese kimonos. The gesture is greatly appreciated by the audience and the band repeated it many times, in Japan, and elsewhere.

May 1
Budokan Hall, Tokyo

Procession / Now I'm Here / Ogre Battle / Father To Son / White Queen / Flick Of The Wrist / Hangman / Great King Rat / Medley: In The Lap Of The Gods; Killer Queen; The March Of The Black Queen; Bring Back That Leroy Brown / Son & Daughter / Doing All Right / Stone Cold Crazy / Keep Yourself Alive / Seven Seas Of Rhye / Liar / In The Lap Of The Gods (Revisited) / Encore Medley: Big Spender; Modern Times Rock'n'Roll / 2nd Encore: Jailhouse Rock / See What A Fool I've Been / God Save The Queen

This show was filmed and later broadcast on Japanese television.

'Shag Out' appears on a handful of bootleg lists (after 'Hangman'). It is actually part of that song.

May 22
Freddie receives an Ivor Novello award for 'Killer Queen'. It was the first such recognition of his songwriting talent.

August
Queen work on new material for their fourth album 'A Night At The Opera'. The sessions eventually conclude in November.

October 31
EMI 2375 is issued as the fifth UK single. Better known as 'Bohemian Rhapsody'/'I'm In Love With My Car', it provides Queen with their first No.1 single. The same pairing is issued on December 2 in America, and peaks at No. 9. The two tracks are a universal pairing.

UK 1975
A Night At The Opera Tour

Following rehearsals at Elstree Studios, at which the promotional video for 'Bohemian Rhapsody' had been filmed, the band kick off their third headlining tour. It begins in familiar Queen territory, with two shows at the Liverpool Empire, and concludes on Christmas Eve with the now famous Hammersmith Odeon show. The support act is Oxford based Mr Big.

The set takes on a very different feel for this tour, now including 'The Prophet's Song' and 'Sweet Lady' from 'A Night At The Opera'. Other material from the album would follow later, specifically 'Death On Two Legs', 'Lazing On A Sunday Afternoon', 'You're My Best

Friend' and ''39'. The album is released during the tour, on November 21.

The tour programme cover reads: "Queen Invite You To A Night At The Opera"

November 14
Empire, Liverpool

Bohemian Rhapsody (Taped Intro) / Ogre Battle / Sweet Lady / White Queen / Flick Of The Wrist / Medley: Bohemian Rhapsody; Killer Queen; The March Of The Black Queen; Bohemian Rhapsody (Reprise); Bring Back That Leroy Brown / Son & Daughter / The Prophet's Song / Stone Cold Crazy / Doing All Right / Keep Yourself Alive / Seven Seas Of Rhye / Liar / In The Lap Of The Gods (Revisited) / Encore: Now I'm Here / 2nd Encore Medley: Jailhouse Rock; Stupid Cupid; Be Bop A Lula; Jailhouse Rock (Reprise) / God Save The Queen

The set now opens with a taped introduction put together by Kenny Everett. In somewhat of a panic, Freddie called him the day before Queen were due to commence the tour because they lacked an appropriate way to begin the shows. Kenny obliged with a typically unorthodox tape, which he got to them just in time for the first show:

"Ladies and Gentlemen... A Night At The Opera/20 second pause/snippet of "Ogre Battle"/opera bit from "Bo Rhap", up to the line: "Beelzebub has the devil put aside for me", and the band enter the stage. This was performed in exactly the same way, as most fans will recall, during the latter Queen tours, when they return to the stage after allowing the light show extravaganza

to replace them, for the opera section. The final verse ("Nothing really matters") is excised. Queen instead segue straight into 'Ogre Battle' which now includes a dramatic false ending. Roger has added a gong to his stage drum kit for the conclusion of 'Bohemian Rhapsody'.

Because "Now I'm Here" no longer opens the show, it is performed instead as the first encore song. Freddie concluded each show by throwing red roses into the audience. Queen's staff had already painstakingly removed the thorns to save Freddie's fingers. He also discarded his tambourine in a similar fashion, having used it first for 'Liar'. This was also the period which saw Freddie painting the finger nails on one hand black. Many fans would subsequently copy the trend.

November 15
Empire, Liverpool

Set: as preceding night, but with 'Modern Times' after 'Keep Yourself Alive'

The 'Prophet's Song' is new to the set. Not surprisingly, it is far too complex to recreate on stage as it was recorded on 'A Night At The Opera', but Queen manage a close enough reading. For the multi-tracked vocal parts, Freddie sings predominantly improvised lines based on the real lyrics, with a delayed echo.

Brian (on 'The Prophet's Song'): "I had a dream about what seemed like revenge on people, and I couldn't

really work out in the dream what it was that people had done wrong. It was something like a flood. Things had gone much too far and as a kind of reparation, the whole thing had to start again.

"In the dream, people were walking on the streets trying to touch each other's hands, desperate to try and make some sign that they were caring about other people.

"I felt that the trouble must be – and this is one of my obsessions anyway – that people don't make enough contact with each other. A feeling that runs through a lot of the songs I write, is that if there is a direction to mankind, it ought to be a coming together, and at the moment, it doesn't seem to be happening very well. I worry about it a lot. I worry about not doing anything about it. Things seem to be getting worse.

"But I wasn't trying to preach in the song at all. I was just trying to put across the questions which are in my mind rather than the answers, which I don't believe I have. The only answer I can see, is to be aware of things like that and to sort of try and put yourself to rights. There is an overseer in the song though, whose cry to the multitudes is to "listen to the warning of the seer."

"In the song is this guy who also appeared in the dream. I don't really know whether he was a prophet or an impostor, but anyway, he's standing up there and saying: 'Look, you've got to mend your ways.' I still don't know whether he's the man who thinks he's sent from God or whether he isn't. The song asks questions rather than gives answers."

November 16
Coventry Theatre, Coventry

Bohemian Rhapsody (Taped Intro) / Ogre Battle / Sweet Lady / White Queen / Flick Of The Wrist / Medley: Bohemian Rhapsody; Killer Queen; The March Of The Black Queen; Bohemian Rhapsody (Reprise); Bring Back That Leroy Brown / Son & Daughter / The Prophet's Song / Stone Cold Crazy / Doing All Right / Keep Yourself Alive / Seven Seas Of Rhye / Liar / In The Lap Of The Gods (Revisited) / Encore: Now I'm Here / 2nd Encore Medley: Big Spender; Jailhouse Rock / God Save The Queen

'Doing All Right' is new to the set on this tour, played almost note for note to the album version, albeit sung by Freddie. It is not played in every show.

In a repeat of the final Budokan show, in May, Freddie emerges for the encore dressed in a kimono. He later discards it and finishes the show in shorts.

November 17/18
Colston Hall, Bristol
Set: as November 16

The *New Musical Express* of November 29, 1975, carried the following headline: THE SUFFERING OF QUEEN FREDDIE (LAST OF THE BIG SPENDERS)... I mean, you try scoring a silk sash in downtown Bristol...

Among other things – most of them unrelated to the concert – interviewer Julie Webb is intrigued by Freddie's Japanese kimono, which now lacks its sash, following the preceding night's show: "Well, you saw it last night. Came on for 'Big Spender' in the kimono (which is apparently worth £2-300) and did the impromptu strip. I took the belt off and thought 'I'll dangle the sash'." He pauses... "I dropped it. Then I thought 'Can I get it back?' Of course I couldn't. Then I spotted this girl obviously after my kimono. I thought: 'No way dearie'. I flung it to safety offstage."

The piece continued: ONE LEAPS in a single terse sentence from trivia to importance. What, one asks, is a mere £200 kimono to the Mercury bankroll when Queen's new LP is being reported widely as The Most Expensive Album Ever Made?

Are you, in truth, Big Spenders, Fred? Freddie doesn't think so, but then he wouldn't know, he says. But seven different studios...

"We wanted to experiment with sound – sometimes we used three studios simultaneously. The actual album took about four months in all

to record. The single took bloody ages – and 'Prophet Song' alone took two-and-a-half to three weeks - but we've had all the freedom we wanted and we've been able to go to greater extremes.

"Fancy doing opera dear, for a start. I believe this album combines the outrageousness of 'Queen II' with the good songs on 'Sheer Heart Attack'. The finest songs *ever* written, dear".

But the cost, Freddie...

"It may have been an expensive album but the bits – *everything* dear – has been done by us. No session men. But the relief of having finished it – I can't tell you..."

November 19
Capitol, Cardiff

Bohemian Rhapsody (Taped Intro) / Ogre Battle / Sweet Lady / White Queen / Flick Of The Wrist / Medley: Bohemian Rhapsody; Killer Queen; The March Of The Black Queen; Bohemian Rhapsody (Reprise); Bring Back That Leroy Brown / Son & Daughter / The Prophet's Song / Stone Cold Crazy / Doing All Right / Keep Yourself Alive / Seven Seas Of Rhye / Liar / In The Lap Of The Gods (Revisited) / Encore: Now I'm Here / 2nd Encore Medley: Big Spender; Be Bop A Lula; Jailhouse Rock / God Save The Queen

November 20

The promotional video for 'Bohemian Rhapsody' is shown on *Top Of The Pops* for the first time. It was directed by Bruce Gowers, who had previously directed on the Rainbow concert footage, in November 1974.

November 21
Odeon, Taunton

The album which Brian May later remarks is Queen's 'Sgt Pepper' is released in the UK. 'A Night At The Opera' is their fourth album, and it provides the band with their first No.1, on December 13. In America Elektra release the album two weeks later.

Only two tracks on the album are not incorporated into the live show. on December 13. In America Elektra release the album two weeks later.

While Brian's charming 'Good Company' is not an entirely surprising absentee, Freddie's vaudeville inspired 'Seaside Rendezvous' most certainly is. Featuring as it does vocal impressions of various brass and woodwind instruments from Roger and Freddie, its visual concert potential is sadly overlooked.

November 23
Winter Gardens, Bournemouth

November 24
Gaumont, Southampton

November 26
Free Trade Hall, Manchester (2 Shows)
First show: Bohemian Rhapsody (Taped Intro) / Ogre Battle / Sweet Lady / White Queen / Flick Of The Wrist / Medley: Bohemian Rhapsody; Killer Queen; The March Of The Black Queen; Bohemian Rhapsody (Reprise); Bring Back That Leroy Brown / Son & Daughter / The Prophet's Song / Stone Cold Crazy / Doing All Right / Keep Yourself Alive / Seven Seas Of Rhye / Liar / In The Lap Of The Gods (Revisited) / Encore: Now I'm Here / 2nd Encore: Jailhouse Rock / God Save The Queen

Second show: Same as first show, but with 'Big Spender' after 'Jailhouse Rock'

Brian encounters problems here while attempting to set up his guitar before the soundcheck. For inexplicable reasons horrible feedback noise is created, but only at certain areas of the stage. After a thorough examination of the stage, the fault is discovered: a hidden electric cable to the generator system. The entire stage earthing is re-wired. The soundcheck goes ahead somewhat delayed, but the show begins on time.

The mood on stage for this show was even more jovial than usual. 'Bo Rhap' had provided Queen with their first number one the previous day.

Freddie, after 'Ogre Battle': "Good evening everybody. You feeling fine? We're just feeling great, so there's gonna be some good fun here tonight."

After 'Sweet Lady': "By the way, I forgot to say, how nice it is to be here

in Manchester. And it's really nice to do two shows. Right now I'd like to drink a toast to all you lovely people here, Cheers. We'll carry on with a number called 'White Queen'."

Brian introduces 'Flick Of The Wrist' next. Freddie opens the song on piano, but it is noticeably shorter than the album version. He cuts it dead after the line: "He's taken an arm, taken a leg, all this time honey". Brian sustains a guitar note, and Freddie concludes: "Baby you've been had".

"I'll tell you what. We'd like right now, to do a special little medley for you, about four songs all rolled up into one, and we're gonna start with a segment from a number called 'Bohemian Rhapsody'." The medley runs through two other tracks, and concludes with the poignant "Any way the wind blows" line, from the song which began it.

Roger then counts the band in for 'Bring Back That Leroy Brown'. Curiously, hardly any words are sung, even though there are many on the 'Sheer Heart Attack' album version. It also features a rather nice little ukulele solo from Brian. Again, it is different to the album cut, and the audience love it.

When numerous fans shout out suggestions as to what song should be performed next, Freddie explains that the request bit comes later, and 'Brighton Rock' begins. The guitar solo has come a long way since the days of 'Son & Daughter' where its origins lie. Even so, it still segues into the song; only later is it played in its own right.

Freddie: "It's now time to do another number from this little album here. Let me see... I think we'll do a number called 'The Prophet's Song'." A breathtaking version of Brian May's 'NATO' track then follows. Using a delayed echo on his voice, Freddie is able to mimic, quite incredibly, the multi-tracked harmonies in the song's mid section. It does, however, end rather strangely, with a speeded up guitar passage, which enables the band to segue into the frenzied mayhem of 'Stone Cold Crazy'.

Freddie then asks for requests. The audience duly respond with 'Seven Seas Of Rhye', 'Liar', 'In The Lap Of The Gods' and the like. "We'll do the lot of 'em" is Freddie's retort: "and this one's called 'Doing All Right'." Once more, he is seated at the piano for the opening section, but is soon on his feet again.

This starts out as a melancholy ballad but then, almost without warning, turns into one of the loudest and heaviest rock numbers in the Queen repertoire. John Deacon and Roger Taylor really go to town here.

Freddie then incites the audience to clap along to the rhythm. When they begin to clap too fast he tells them to slow down. "Stay with us" he advises. 'Keep Yourself Alive' starts and Freddie begins his now customary string of one-liners: "Join in with all the choruses! Are you with us? You in the balcony, sing up!"

"You might recall this one!" exclaims Brian. "It's called the 'Seven Seas Of Rhye'". The concert is nearing its end. And the crowd know it.

"Liar" is up next. It gives each member of the band an opportunity to show off his respective musical/vocal talent. John 'especially' shines. Alternatively, Roger pounds his way around his entire drum kit, setting an identical pace to the album version, and Freddie comments that it's sounding good. It is. After the song the band exit the stage.

Just when the audience think there is no more, Queen return with 'Now I'm Here' and pretty well bring the house down. Brian's guitar parts are faultless: you could almost be listening to a studio recorded demo tape. Before the song fades out, Brian starts the closing song. Freddie misses the first cue, but it is hardly noticed, and 'Jailhouse Rock' kicks off. It includes the odd line or two of 'Bama Lama'.

November 29/30
Hammersmith Odeon, London
First night: Bohemian Rhapsody (Taped Intro) / Ogre Battle / Sweet Lady / White Queen / Flick Of The Wrist / Medley: Bohemian Rhapsody; Killer Queen; The March Of The Black Queen; Bohemian Rhapsody (Reprise); Bring Back That Leroy Brown / Son & Daughter / The Prophet's Song / Stone Cold Crazy / Doing All Right / Keep Yourself Alive / Modern Times Rock'n'Roll / Seven Seas Of Rhye / Liar / In The Lap Of The Gods (Revisited) / Encore: Now I'm Here / 2nd Encore Medley: Jailhouse Rock ; Be Bop A Lula; Jailhouse Rock (Reprise) / God Save The Queen

'Brighton Rock' is also new to the set on this tour. A lengthy guitar work-out for Brian, it enables Freddie, John and Roger to leave the stage for five minutes before returning for the conclusion.

While in London Freddie and Roger are invited to participate in a Capital Radio phone-in. Actually, Freddie ends up appearing on Kenny Everett's programme and Roger on Maggie Norden's. Both answer Queen trivia questions, such as how many drum sticks did Roger get through during the Japanese tour. "Fourteen in ten days," he responds, "I was going wild, chucking them into the audience."

Second night: Bohemian Rhapsody (Intro) / Ogre Battle / Sweet Lady / White Queen / Flick Of The Wrist / Medley: Bohemian Rhapsody / Killer Queen / The March Of The Black Queen / Bring Back That Leroy Brown / Bohemian Rhapsody (Reprise) / Brighton Rock / Son & Daughter / The Prophet's Song / Stone Cold Crazy / Doing All Right / Keep Yourself Alive / Modern Times Rock'n'Roll / Seven Seas Of Rhye / Liar / Now I'm Here / Jailhouse Rock / Be Bop A Lula / Jailhouse Rock (Reprise) / God Save The Queen

December 1/2
Hammersmith Odeon, London

December 7
Civic Hall, Wolverhampton

December 8
Guildhall, Preston
Bohemian Rhapsody (Taped Intro) / Ogre Battle / Sweet Lady / White Queen / Flick Of The Wrist / Medley: Bohemian Rhapsody; Killer Queen; The March Of The Black Queen; Bohemian Rhapsody (Reprise); Bring Back That Leroy Brown / Son & Daughter / The Prophet's Song / Stone Cold Crazy / Doing All Right / Keep Yourself Alive / Modern Times Rock'n'Roll / Seven Seas Of Rhye / Liar / In The Lap Of The Gods (Revisited) / Encore: Now I'm Here / 2nd Encore: Jailhouse Rock / God Save The Queen

December 9/10
Odeon, Birmingham

December 11
City Hall, Newcastle-Upon-Tyne

After this concert the entourage moves on towards Dundee, but after only two miles they encounter a road block. Plain clothes policemen then escort everyone to the local station, on suspicion of being in possession of drugs. The group, crew and tour coach are all searched, before being allowed to continue on their way. Freddie is asked if he has any drugs: "Don't be so impertinent, you stupid little man!" is his retort.

"The strongest drug anyone imbibed was the odd bottle of Southern Comfort or two," Dicken (lead singer of Mr Big) later explained.

December 13
Caird Hall, Dundee

Bohemian Rhapsody (Taped Intro) / Ogre Battle / Sweet Lady / White Queen / Flick Of The Wrist / Medley: Bohemian Rhapsody; Killer Queen; The March Of The Black Queen; Bohemian Rhapsody (Reprise); Bring Back That Leroy Brown / Son & Daughter / The Prophet's Song / Stone Cold Crazy / Doing All Right / Keep Yourself Alive / Modern Times Rock'n'Roll / Seven Seas Of Rhye / Liar / In The Lap Of The Gods (Revisited) / Encore: Now I'm Here / 2nd Encore Medley: Big Spender; Jailhouse Rock; Shake Rattle And Roll; Jailhouse Rock (Reprise) / God Save The Queen

"Shake Rattle And Roll" is included in the set for a short spell. It was always an infrequent addition to the Queen show.

December 14
Capitol, Aberdeen

December 15/16
Glasgow Apollo, Glasgow

Both nights: Bohemian Rhapsody (Taped Intro) / Ogre Battle / Sweet Lady / White Queen / Flick Of The Wrist / Medley: Bohemian Rhapsody; Killer Queen; The March Of The Black Queen; Bohemian Rhapsody (Reprise); Bring Back That Leroy Brown / Son & Daughter / The Prophet's Song / Stone Cold Crazy / Doing All Right / Keep Yourself Alive / Modern Times Rock'n'Roll / Seven Seas Of Rhye / Liar / In The Lap Of The Gods (Revisited) / Encore: Now I'm Here / 2nd Encore Medley: Big Spender; Jailhouse Rock; Be Bop A Lula; Jailhouse Rock (Reprise) / God Save The Queen

'Be Bop A Lula' and the reprised 'Jailhouse Rock' were omitted on the second night.

December 24
Hammersmith Odeon, London

Now I'm Here / Ogre Battle / White Queen / Medley: Bohemian Rhapsody; Killer Queen; The March Of The Black Queen; Bohemian Rhapsody (Reprise); Bring Back That Leroy Brown / Son & Daughter / Keep Yourself Alive / Liar / In The Lap Of The Gods (Revisited) / Encore Medley: Big Spender; Jailhouse Rock; Stupid Cupid; Be Bop A Lula; Shake Rattle And Roll; Jailhouse Rock (Reprise) / Seven Seas Of Rhye / See What A Fool I've Been / God Save The Queen

(Unusual track sequence, but correct)

This show was broadcast live on both Radio One and *The Old Grey Whistle Test*, whose host Bob Harris introduced the band on stage. Due to the television and radio coverage (including numerous brutally edited repeats), it went on to be the most heavily bootlegged in the band's career. Although at one point only three vinyl albums seemed to be in circulation – 'Command Performance', 'Christmas At The Beeb' and the curiously titled 'Halfpence' – since the advent of compact disc, several alternatives have flooded the market: 'Eve Of Christmas', 'London 1975', 'Rhapsody In Red', 'Command Performance', 'X'Mas 1975', 'Live Dates Vol.17', 'Christmas At The Beeb' and 'Unauthorised', to name only a few. Another vinyl offering has now emerged too – 'High Voltage'.

Due to public demand, the radio broadcast was repeated the following year, on December 28.

Freddie looked fantastic in a white silk Dickensian style outfit, with a custom designed mini-jacket, exaggerated flared trousers and white boots. He also wore numerous rings and bangles, and had the finger nails of his left hand painted black. His hair was long, wavy and jet black. John wore white trousers and waistcoat, and a black shirt. Brian too, was clad entirely in white. Wearing Zandra Rhodes designed cape, reminiscent of a white Batman, he looked decidedly God-like.

Following 'White Queen' Freddie speaks: "Now then, we're gonna do a nice tasty little medley for you... just like the one we did the other day, yes, and we're gonna start off with a little segment from a numberrrr called 'Bohemian Rhapsody'."

After just two minutes Freddie is fingering the opening chords of 'Killer Queen' which replace the finger clicking of the album cut. The crowd assist with accompanying handclaps and the band perform the song up to the point where the line "To avoid complications she never kept the same address" is due, then the direction changes again and the band are into 'March Of The Black Queen' which in turn ends with the 'Bo Rhap' reprise: "Ooh yeah - ooh yeah, nothing really matters, anyone can see, nothing really matters, nothing really matters to me." There the medley ends.

"Now then, we're now gonna feature Brian, Brian May on guitar. This number's entitled 'Brighton Rock'. Nearly eleven minutes later and an exhausted Brian (with help from Roger and John) abruptly ends the song.

Roger then opens the next song before Brian's familiar guitar intro identifies 'Keep Yourself Alive'. By now Freddie has changed into a tight fitting frontless black satin jump-suit. Even by today's standards, it is provocative apparel. Freddie: "Now it's time to join in everybody... and you can sing along in all the choruses, give us a helping hand, you can take all your clothes off. What about you in the balcony... are you with us? Everybody at home, let's go." 'Keep Yourself Alive' begins. Roger takes a fifty-second drum solo mid-way through, and Freddie seems just as impressed as the audience.

"And now, a special rendition of a little number called 'Liar'." Roger pounds his way around his drum kit and Freddie quips: "Sock it to 'em Rog."

Brian introduces the next one: "It's been like a party here tonight. Thanks for making it really something for us, it's felt a lot different. Thanks for giving us a good year. We'd like to leave you in the lap of the gods." Following 'The Gods', during which Freddie is partially obscured by an over-active dry ice machine, Brian owns up to a band oversight: "This is where we start I think", he says, realising that a song has been left out of the show. Freddie: "Right, a number we forgot to do in the set... it's called 'Seven Seas Of Rhye'."

For the encore, Freddie returns to the stage in a Japanese kimono, discarding it to reveal tight white shorts and T-shirt. The show ends with hundreds of festively decorated balloons dropping from nets above the hall. Curiously, a number of fully inflated blow-up ladies also descend.

Brian and Freddie's parents met each other for the first time at this show. It turned out they had lived very close to one another for over sixteen years.

Although this show is widely regarded by fans as one of Queen's best, it seems that the band disagree. Brian: "Freddie and I, though me particularly, had dreadful 'flu and could hardly walk, let alone play, so it wasn't one of our greatest performances, but it was still all very exciting. It was the adrenaline that kept us going."

December 27
'A Night At The Opera' reaches No.1 in the British album charts.

USA 1976

January 20

Queen fly to New York for rehearsals ahead of their third American tour, their second as a headlining act. The thirty-three-date tour begins in Connecticut and concludes six weeks later, with five shows in Los Angeles and one in San Diego, on March 13.

January 27

Palace Theater, Waterbury, Connecticut

Bohemian Rhapsody (Taped Intro) / Ogre Battle / Sweet Lady / White Queen / Flick Of The Wrist / Medley: Bohemian Rhapsody; Killer Queen; The March Of The Black Queen; Bohemian Rhapsody (Reprise); Bring Back That Leroy Brown / Brighton Rock / Son & Daughter / The Prophet's Song / Stone Cold Crazy / Doing All Right / Lazing On A Sunday Afternoon / Keep Yourself Alive / Seven Seas Of Rhye / Liar / In The Lap Of The Gods (Revisited) / Encore: Now I'm Here / God Save The Queen

The band introduce a new, somewhat original angle for 'Now I'm Here' on this tour. The audience briefly glimpse a spotlit Freddie on one side of the stage singing 'Now I'm Here', and then apparently see him an instant later, at the opposite side of the stage repeating the line. They are unaware that one of the 'Freddies' is, in fact, the band's personal assistant Pete Brown, dressed in identical costume – "in one of Fred's frocks," as Pete later recalled.

Sadly, Pete Brown died in 1993. He was 38.

January 29

Music Hall, Boston, Massachusetts

Bohemian Rhapsody (Taped Intro) / Ogre Battle / Sweet Lady / White Queen / Flick Of The Wrist / Medley: Bohemian Rhapsody; Killer Queen; The March Of The Black Queen; Bohemian Rhapsody (Reprise); Bring Back That Leroy Brown / Brighton Rock / Son & Daughter / The Prophet's Song / Stone Cold Crazy / Doing All Right / Lazing On A Sunday Afternoon / Keep Yourself Alive / Seven Seas Of Rhye / Liar / In The Lap Of The Gods (Revisited) / Encore Medley: Big Spender; Jailhouse Rock / God Save The Queen

Freddie's quirky 'Lazing On A Sunday Afternoon', recreated as on 'A Night At The Opera', is new to the set on this tour, but it does not remain in the set for long as the band don't consider that it works well enough on stage.

January 30

Music Hall, Boston, Massachusetts

January 31/February 1

Tower Theater, Philadelphia, Pennsylvania

Second night: Bohemian Rhapsody (Taped Intro) / Ogre Battle / Sweet Lady / White Queen / Flick Of The Wrist / Medley: Bohemian Rhapsody; Killer Queen; The March Of The Black Queen; Bohemian Rhapsody (Reprise); Bring Back That Leroy Brown / Brighton Rock / Son & Daughter / The Prophet's Song / Stone Cold Crazy / Doing All Right / Lazing On A Sunday Afternoon / Keep Yourself Alive / Seven Seas Of Rhye / Liar / In The Lap Of The Gods (Revisited) / Encore Medley: Jailhouse Rock; Big Spender; Be Bop A Lula; Jailhouse Rock (Reprise) / God Save The Queen

February 5/6/7/8

Beacon Theater, New York

Second night: Bohemian Rhapsody (Taped Intro) / Ogre Battle / Sweet Lady / White Queen / Flick Of The Wrist / Medley: Bohemian Rhapsody; Killer Queen; The March Of The Black Queen; Bohemian Rhapsody (Reprise); Bring Back That Leroy Brown / Brighton Rock / Son & Daughter / The Prophet's Song / Stone Cold Crazy / Doing All Right / Lazing On A Sunday Afternoon / Keep Yourself Alive / Seven Seas Of Rhye / Liar / In The Lap Of The Gods (Revisited) / Encore: Now I'm Here / God Save The Queen

February 11/12

Masonic Temple, Detroit, Michigan

February 13

Riverfront Coliseum, Cincinnati, Ohio

February 14

Public Hall, Cleveland, Ohio

Back in the UK, *Record Mirror & Disc* magazine publish their annual poll results which feature Queen in several categories:

World's Best Group (1st)
Best Single: *Bohemian Rhapsody* (1st)
World's Best Singer: *Freddie* (6th)
Best British Singer: *Freddie* (5th)
Best British Songwriter: *Freddie* (4th)
Best British Group (1st)

February 23
Auditorium Theater, Chicago, Illinois

February 26
Keil Auditorium, St Louis, Missouri

February 27
**Convention Center, Indianapolis,
Indiana**

February 28
Dane County Coliseum, Wisconsin

February 29
Fort Wayne Coliseum, Indiana State
*Bohemian Rhapsody (Intro) / Ogre Battle / Sweet
Lady / White Queen / Flick Of The Wrist / Hangman /
Medley: Bohemian Rhapsody; Killer Queen; The March
Of The Black Queen; Bohemian Rhapsody (Reprise);
Bring Back That Leroy Brown / Brighton Rock / Son &
Daughter / The Prophet's Song / Stone Cold Crazy / Doing
All Right / Lazing On A Sunday Afternoon / Keep Yourself
Alive / Seven Seas Of Rhye / Liar / In The Lap Of The Gods
(Revisited) / Jailhouse Rock / Big Spender / Be Bop A Lula /
Jailhouse Rock (Reprise) / God Save The Queen*

March 1
**Milwaukee Auditorium, Milwaukee,
Wisconsin**

March 3
**St Pauls Auditorium, Minneapolis,
Minnesota**

March 7
Berkeley Community Hall, Berkeley
*Set: as February 29, but with 'Saturday
Night's Alright For Fighting' in the encore medley,
after 'Big Spender'*

March 9 / 10 / 11 / 12
**Santa Monica Civic Auditorium,
Los Angeles, California**
*Bohemian Rhapsody (Taped Intro) / Ogre Battle /
Sweet Lady / White Queen / Flick Of The Wrist / Medley:
Bohemian Rhapsody; Killer Queen; The March Of The
Black Queen; Bohemian Rhapsody (Reprise); Bring
Back That Leroy Brown / Brighton Rock / Son &
Daughter / The Prophet's Song / Stone Cold Crazy /
Doing All Right / Lazing On A Sunday Afternoon / Keep
Yourself Alive / Seven Seas Of Rhye / Liar / In The Lap
Of The Gods (Revisited) / Jailhouse Rock / God Save
The Queen*

Queen play two shows on March 9.

March 13
**Sports Arena, San Diego,
California**

World's Best Songwriter: *Freddie* (5th)
Best British Musician: *Brian May* (4th)
World's Best Musician: *Brian May* (4th)
Best Album: *A Night At The Opera* (6th)

February 15
Sports Arena, Toledo, Ohio
*Bohemian Rhapsody (Taped Intro) / Ogre Battle /
Sweet Lady / White Queen / Flick Of The Wrist / Medley:
Bohemian Rhapsody; Killer Queen; The March Of The
Black Queen; Bohemian Rhapsody (Reprise); Bring Back
That Leroy Brown / Brighton Rock / Son & Daughter /
The Prophet's Song / Stone Cold Crazy / Doing All Right /
Lazing On A Sunday Afternoon / Keep Yourself Alive /
Seven Seas Of Rhye / Liar / In The Lap Of The Gods
(Revisited) / God Save The Queen*

February 18
Civic Center, Saginaw, Michigan

February 19
**Veterans' Memorial Auditorium,
Columbus, Ohio**

February 20
**Syrian Mosque, Pittsburgh,
Pennsylvania**

February 22
Auditorium Theater, Chicago, Illinois
*Bohemian Rhapsody (Intro) / Ogre Battle /
Sweet Lady / White Queen / Flick Of The Wrist / Medley:
Bohemian Rhapsody; Killer Queen; The March Of The
Black Queen; Bohemian Rhapsody (Reprise); Bring Back
That Leroy Brown / Brighton Rock / Son & Daughter /
The Prophet's Song / Stone Cold Crazy / Doing All Right /
Lazing On A Sunday Afternoon / Keep Yourself Alive /
Seven Seas Of Rhye / Liar / In The Lap Of The Gods
(Revisited) / Big Spender / Jailhouse Rock / God Save
The Queen*

57

JAPAN 1976

Queen arrive in Japan to begin
their second tour there. It entails
eleven shows at seven different venues,
and again kicks off in the capital's
main stadium. It concludes a week
and a half later at the Nichidai Kodo,
also in Tokyo.

March 22
Budokan Hall, Tokyo

*Bohemian Rhapsody (Taped Intro) / Ogre Battle /
Sweet Lady / White Queen / Flick Of The Wrist /
Hangman / Medley: Bohemian Rhapsody; Killer Queen;
The March Of The Black Queen; Bohemian Rhapsody
(Reprise); Bring Back That Leroy Brown / Brighton Rock /
Son & Daughter / The Prophet's Song: incorporating
Death On Two Legs / Stone Cold Crazy / Doing All Right /
Lazing On A Sunday Afternoon / Father To Son / Keep
Yourself Alive / Seven Seas Of Rhye / Liar / In The Lap
Of The Gods (Revisited) / Encore: Now I'm Here / 2nd
Encore Medley: Big Spender; See What A Fool I've Been /
God Save The Queen*

'Death On Two Legs' is incorporated
into 'Prophet's' before it is eventually
performed in its own right.
  Freddie: 'Death On Two Legs'
was the most vicious lyric I ever wrote.
It's so vindictive that Brian felt bad
singing it. I don't like to explain what
I was thinking when I wrote the song."

March 23
Aichi Ken Gymnasium, Nagoya

*Bohemian Rhapsody (Taped Intro) / Ogre Battle /
Sweet Lady / White Queen / Flick Of The Wrist / Medley:
Bohemian Rhapsody; Killer Queen; The March Of The
Black Queen; Bohemian Rhapsody (Reprise); Bring Back
That Leroy Brown / Brighton Rock / Son & Daughter /
The Prophet's Song: incorporating Death On Two Legs /
Stone Cold Crazy / Doing All Right / Lazing On A Sunday
Afternoon / Keep Yourself Alive / Seven Seas Of Rhye /
Liar / In The Lap Of The Gods (Revisited) / Encore:
Now I'm Here / God Save The Queen*

March 24
Kosei Kaikan, Himeji City

*Bohemian Rhapsody (Taped Intro) / Ogre Battle /
Sweet Lady / White Queen / Flick Of The Wrist / Medley:
Bohemian Rhapsody; Killer Queen; The March Of The
Black Queen; Bohemian Rhapsody (Reprise); Bring Back
That Leroy Brown / Brighton Rock / Son & Daughter /
The Prophet's Song: incorporating Death On Two Legs /
Stone Cold Crazy / Doing All Right / Lazing On A Sunday
Afternoon / Keep Yourself Alive / Liar / In The Lap Of The
Gods (Revisited) / Encore: Now I'm Here / God Save
The Queen*

March 26
Kyden Gymnasium, Fukuoka (2 shows)

*Bohemian Rhapsody (Taped Intro) / Ogre Battle /
Sweet Lady / White Queen / Flick Of The Wrist / Medley:
Bohemian Rhapsody; Killer Queen; The March Of The
Black Queen; Bohemian Rhapsody (Reprise); Bring Back
That Leroy Brown / Brighton Rock / Son & Daughter /
The Prophet's Song; Stone Cold Crazy / Doing All Right /
Lazing On A Sunday Afternoon / Keep Yourself Alive / Liar /
In The Lap Of The Gods (Revisited) / Encore: Now I'm
Here / 2nd Encore Medley: Big Spender; Jailhouse Rock;
Shake Rattle And Roll; Stupid Cupid; Be Bop A Lula;
Jailhouse Rock (Reprise) / God Save The Queen*

March 29
Kosei Nenkin Kaikan, Osaka (2 shows)

*Bohemian Rhapsody (Taped Intro) / Ogre Battle /
Sweet Lady / White Queen / Flick Of The Wrist / Medley:
Bohemian Rhapsody; Killer Queen; The March Of The
Black Queen; Bohemian Rhapsody (Reprise); Bring Back
That Leroy Brown / Brighton Rock / Son & Daughter /
The Prophet's Song / Stone Cold Crazy / Doing All Right /
Lazing On A Sunday Afternoon / Keep Yourself Alive / Liar /
In The Lap Of The Gods (Revisited) / Encore: Now I'm
Here / 2nd Encore: Jailhouse Rock / God Save The Queen*

One wonders what the Japanese
audience must have made of the Kenny
Everett introduction to the show.
If the bootleg from this show is anything
to go by, though, they certainly sound
like they appreciated it. They go
berserk at the 'Bo Rhap' opera bit, even
before the band have taken the stage.
Listening to even the best sound quality
recordings of this show is like watching
old newsreel of a Beatles concert, such
is the din emanating from the crowd.
Freddie's opening words of the
show, following 'Ogre Battle', include
"Orichi ma" – Japanese for "Good
evening". After proposing a toast to the
crowd, Freddie introduces a quiet
number, but the delicate opening lines
of 'White Queen' are lost in the
deafening clamour of Japan's youth.
Freddie continues regardless. Brian
also addresses the audience in their
own language and introduces the next
song as something a little heavier,
written by Freddie. 'Flick Of The Wrist'

is received exceptionally well. The crowd join in on the main chorus. Again it finishes somewhat prematurely.

There is a polite silence while Freddie explains the medley sequence, but the crowd roar at the mention of 'Bohemian Rhapsody'. Their enthusiasm is absolutely unprecedented. After Brian is featured on 'Brighton Rock' and a rendering of 'The Prophet's Song', Freddie dedicates 'Stone Cold Crazy' to all the crazy rock'n'roll people present. Next up is 'Doing All Right' from the début album.

"Okay," Freddie continues, "we'd like you all to join in with this next number, it's called 'Lazing On A Sunday Afternoon'." By any standard this is one of Freddie's most self indulgent moments from the 'Opera' album, but also one of the best. Thankfully, the song is performed almost note for note to the studio cut.

'Keep Yourself Alive' follows, along much the same lines as usual, but with different vocal ad-libs from Freddie. An exceptionally enthusiastic drum solo adds something special too. The Japanese fans scream even louder when Roger comes in with his 'Do you think you're better ev'ry day?' line.

After 'Liar' Brian addresses the audience: "To finish off we'd like to do something from 'Sheer Heart Attack'. Thank you for being really nice. This is 'In The Lap Of The Gods'." Freddie's opening piano chords are once again lost in the din, but when he reaches the "Wo wo la la la wo, wo wo la la" part,

the mighty wall of sound shadows every word he sings. Queen leave the stage. A minute later they return for 'Now I'm Here'. Before the last guitar note has totally faded, another begins, and the show concludes with 'Jailhouse Rock'. Though Freddie's voice is starting to show signs of tiredness, he still plays improvised word games with the audience during the mid section. "Thank you – Origato – Sianara – Goodbye". The national anthem begins, Queen bow and leave the stage, waving.

March 31/April 1
Budokan Hall, Tokyo

Second night: Bohemian Rhapsody (Taped Intro) / Ogre Battle / Sweet Lady / White Queen / Flick Of The Wrist / Hangman / Medley: Bohemian Rhapsody; Killer Queen; The March Of The Black Queen; Bohemian Rhapsody (Reprise); Bring Back That Leroy Brown / Brighton Rock / Son & Daughter / The Prophet's Song / Stone Cold Crazy / Doing All Right / Lazing On A Sunday Afternoon / Keep Yourself Alive / Liar / In The Lap Of The Gods (Revisited) / Encore: Now I'm Here / 2nd Encore Medley: Big Spender; Jailhouse Rock; Stupid Cupid; Be Bop A Lula; Jailhouse Rock (Reprise) / 3rd Encore: See What A Fool I've Been / God Save The Queen

April 2
Miyagi Ken Sports Centre, Sendai

Bohemian Rhapsody (Taped Intro) / Ogre Battle / Sweet Lady / White Queen / Flick Of The Wrist / Medley: Bohemian Rhapsody; Killer Queen; The March Of The Black Queen; Bohemian Rhapsody (Reprise); Bring Back That Leroy Brown / Brighton Rock / Son And Daughter / The Prophet's Song / Stone Cold Crazy / Father To Son / Doing All Right / Lazing On A Sunday Afternoon / Keep Yourself Alive / Liar / In The Lap Of The Gods (Revisited) / Encore: Now I'm Here / 2nd Encore Medley: Big Spender; Jailhouse Rock; Shake Rattle And Roll; Stupid Cupid; Jailhouse Rock (Reprise) / God Save The Queen

Similar set as previous night, but with 'Shake Rattle' added, and no 'Hangman'.

April 4
Nichidai Kodo, Tokyo

Bohemian Rhapsody (Taped Intro) / Ogre Battle / Sweet Lady / White Queen / Flick Of The Wrist / Medley: Bohemian Rhapsody; Killer Queen; The March Of The Black Queen; Bohemian Rhapsody (Reprise); Bring Back That Leroy Brown / Brighton Rock / Son & Daughter / The Prophet's Song / Stone Cold Crazy / Father To Son / Doing All Right / Lazing On A Sunday Afternoon / Keep Yourself Alive / Liar / In The Lap Of The Gods (Revisited) / Encore: Now I'm Here / 2nd Encore: Big Spender / God Save The Queen

'Sweet Lady' here featured Roger's voice more prominently than usual. During the middle section of the song, Brian seems to go off into what sounds like an unrehearsed improvised solo, Freddie and Roger ad-libbing accordingly. The overall sound is

incredible, and vastly different from the album cut.

'White Queen' finds Freddie in stunning voice. A lively bass line from John is complemented by haunting guitar solos and subtle piano work, to make this version one of the best I've heard. Queen are in perfect musical harmony for this performance, and Freddie seems especially aware of it. "Listen, listen, listen, listen, please listen to this next medley," Freddie implores. "It comprises four songs, and we're gonna start it with our current single released here, called 'Bohemian Rhapsody'..."

Following Queen's second Japanese tour, Jon Tiven observes in the New York magazine *Back Pages*: "In the Forties, Japanese pilots occasionally dove aeroplanes into passing Allied warships. Today, Japanese teenagers have taken up a more innocent occupation: diving into the four British rockers known as Queen. When Queen landed in Tokyo recently for an extensive tour of the Land of the Rising Sun, the rhapsodic quartet found their plane surrounded by 5,000 frantic fans. But limousines were driven through the throng to the jet's landing steps and the group was rushed down the stairs, flung into the black Cadillacs, and delivered safely to the hotel.

"All in all, Queen's tour of Japan was a triumphant one. The nation's top radio stations had just voted them the world's number-one rock band, and their 12-day, eight concert tour included

three nights at Tokyo's Budokan, the country's largest arena. From there three nights they went to Australia for another eight dates and then to vacation at an unspecified locale. Preparations three nights for a fifth album began immediately afterwards.

"All this followed the group's most successful US tour to date. Arriving on the heels of their 'Night At The Opera' album, the group was greeted with almost universal acclaim. The normally staid Boston *Globe* said the group was so sensational as to make people forget about such other recent sensations as Bruce Springsteen and Patti Smith, and newspapers across the country continually compared them with The Beatles. And luckily, the group made it through the entire thirty-one date twenty-one city schedule without a cancellation – another first. Queen's first American tour had to be cut short because of guitarist Brian's hepatitis, and their second was interrupted when Freddie Mercury developed throat problems. But this time, despite a 'flu attack which threatened to level Brian, their trip continued unabated."

AUSTRALIA 1976

Queen embark on their first proper tour of Australia, an eleven day visit with eight concerts at five different venues. The band had played in Australia on only one previous occasion at the Sunbury Music Festival in Melbourne two years earlier.

The bad experiences of this first visit were not repeated. All eight concerts were sold out, and were attended by extremely appreciative audiences. This time, Queen *were* permitted to perform their encores.

April 11
Entertainments Centre, Perth

Bohemian Rhapsody (Taped Intro) / Ogre Battle / Sweet Lady / White Queen / Flick Of The Wrist / Hangman / Medley: Bohemian Rhapsody; Killer Queen; The March Of The Black Queen; Bohemian Rhapsody (Reprise); Bring Back That Leroy Brown / Brighton Rock / Son & Daughter / The Prophet's Song / Stone Cold Crazy / Doing All Right / Lazing On A Sunday Afternoon / Keep Yourself Alive / Liar / In The Lap Of The Gods (Revisited) / Encore: Now I'm Here / 2nd Encore Medley: Jailhouse Rock; Big Spender; Be Bop A Lula; Jailhouse Rock (Reprise) / God Save The Queen

April 14/15
Apollo Stadium, Adelaide

April 17/18
Horden Pavillion, Sydney

Second night: Bohemian Rhapsody (Taped Intro) / Ogre Battle / Sweet Lady / White Queen / Flick Of The Wrist / Medley: Bohemian Rhapsody; Killer Queen; The March Of The Black Queen; Bohemian Rhapsody (Reprise); Bring Back That Leroy Brown / Brighton Rock / Son & Daughter / The Prophet's Song / Stone Cold Crazy / Father To Son / Doing All Right / Lazing On A Sunday Afternoon / Keep Yourself Alive / Liar / In The Lap Of The Gods (Revisited) / Encore: Now I'm Here / 2nd Encore: Big Spender / God Save The Queen

April 19/20
Festival Hall, Melbourne

April 22
Festival Hall, Brisbane

May 29
Brian May and Chrissy Mullen are married, in Barnes, SW London.

June 18
John Deacon's only composition for 'A Night At The Opera' is released as a single in Europe, America and Japan. 'You're My Best Friend' is paired with Brian May's dream inspired '39', and goes on to give the band Nos. 7 and 16 chart placings, in the UK and America.

Regrettably, no details of Japanese single chart positions are available, hence their conspicuous absence from these pages. As part of the research for an article entitled 'Collecting Japanese 45s' in *Record Collector* magazine in June 1994 (Issue No. 178), the author contacted both EMI/UK and EMI in Japan, but very little information relating to Queen's Japanese catalogue is documented, or if it is, it is not easily accessible.

July
Queen begin work on 'A Day At The Races'. The sessions eventually conclude four months later, in November.

August
In preparation for three British shows, the band book rehearsal time at Shepperton Studios. They work mainly on material from the new album but also on an acoustic version of ''39' from 'A Night At The Opera'.

The set now includes 'Tie Your Mother Down' and 'You Take My Breath Away' from 'A Day At The Races' which is not actually released until December 10. Other material from the album would feature in the set in the US tour the following January: 'White Man', 'Good Old Fashioned Lover Boy', 'Somebody To Love' and 'Millionaire Waltz'. 'Teo Torriatte' would be included too, but only in Japan, beginning in April 1979.

September 1/2
Playhouse Theatre, Edinburgh

First night: Bohemian Rhapsody (Taped Intro) / Ogre Battle / Sweet Lady / White Queen / Flick Of The Wrist / Medley: You're My Best Friend; Bohemian Rhapsody; Killer Queen; The March Of The Black Queen; Bohemian Rhapsody (Reprise); Bring Back That Leroy Brown / Brighton Rock / Son & Daughter / '39 / You Take My Breath Away / The Prophet's Song / Stone Cold Crazy / Doing All Right / Lazing On A Sunday Afternoon / Tie Your Mother Down / Keep Yourself Alive / Liar / In The Lap Of The Gods (Revisited) / Now I'm Here / Big Spender / Jailhouse Rock / God Save The Queen

Queen perform these two shows as part of the Scottish Festival of Popular Music. The venue had just reopened after extensive refurbishment and they appeared alongside Elton John, John Miles, Rainbow and comedian Billy Connelly.

'Tie Your Mother Down' is new to the set, and from this date would be featured in almost every concert Queen ever performed. Brian would later cite it as one of the compositions of which he was most proud, remarking that it always seemed to sound right, even if other material in the set did not.

John Deacon's 'Best Friend' is also featured for the first time, replacing 'Bo Rhap' as the opening song in the medley.

An acoustic segment in the set featured 'Breath Away' and ''39' for the very first time here. Roger emerges from behind the drum kit with a tambourine and accompanies Freddie, John and Brian centre stage. Brian plays an acoustic guitar. Freddie throws his maracas into the audience afterwards, repeating the gesture every night thereafter.

Second night: Bohemian Rhapsody (Taped Intro) / Ogre Battle / Sweet Lady / White Queen / Flick Of The Wrist / Medley: You're My Best Friend; Bohemian Rhapsody; Killer Queen; The March Of The Black Queen; Bohemian Rhapsody (Reprise); Bring Back That Leroy Brown / Brighton Rock / Son & Daughter / '39 / You Take My Breath Away / The Prophet's Song / Stone Cold Crazy / Doing All Right / Lazing On A Sunday Afternoon / Tie Your Mother Down / Keep Yourself Alive / Liar / In The Lap Of The Gods (Revisited) / Encore: Now I'm Here / 2nd Encore: Big Spender / Jailhouse Rock / God Save The Queen

Brian (on 'You're My Best Friend'): "I think his (John) song on the album is

amazing. He went out completely on a limb to do that. It's not the kind of thing we'd done before, but he knew exactly what he wanted."

September 10
Cardiff Castle, Cardiff

Bohemian Rhapsody (Taped Intro) / Ogre Battle / Sweet Lady / White Queen / Flick Of The Wrist / Medley: You're My Best Friend; Bohemian Rhapsody / Killer Queen; The March Of The Black Queen; Bohemian Rhapsody (Reprise); Bring Back That Leroy Brown / Brighton Rock / Son & Daughter / '39 / You Take My Breath Away / The Prophet's Song / Stone Cold Crazy / Doing All Right / Lazing On A Sunday Afternoon / Tie Your Mother Down / Keep Yourself Alive / Liar / In The Lap Of The Gods (Revisited) / Encore: Now I'm Here / Jailhouse Rock / God Save The Queen

Queen headlined a one-day event that also featured Manfred Mann, Andy Fairweather-Low and Frankie Miller's Full House. Bob Harris is the compère.

A much sought after Queen bootleg known as "Queen At The Castle" emerged from this show. Audio cassette recordings circulate today, but vinyl albums were issued originally.

September 18
Hyde Park, London

Bohemian Rhapsody (Taped Intro) / Ogre Battle / Sweet Lady / White Queen / Flick Of The Wrist / Medley: You're My Best Friend; Bohemian Rhapsody; Killer Queen; The March Of The Black Queen; Bohemian Rhapsody (Reprise); Bring Back That Leroy Brown / Brighton Rock / Son & Daughter / '39 / You Take My Breath Away / The Prophet's Song / Stone Cold Crazy / Keep Yourself Alive / Liar / In The Lap Of The Gods (Revisited) / No encore

Repeating an event which The Rolling Stones inaugurated in 1969, Queen perform their first free concert. Between 150,000 and 200,000 people were estimated to have attended. Due to the drought of 1976 and the poor condition of the park as a result

of it, the concert came very close to being cancelled.

The event was conceived by Freddie and Brian, as both a thank you to their British fans for their continued support, and to commemorate the sixth anniversary of the death of Jimi Hendrix. Support acts were Steve Hillage, Kiki Dee and Liverpudlian band Supercharge.

Supercharge singer/saxophonist Albie Donnelly is dressed in a blatantly Mercuryesque white leotard. He struts and prances around the stage like Freddie too, but it is all in good fun, and no one takes offence. One of their songs is a cover of the Bay City Rollers' 'Bye Bye Baby'.

Having enjoyed a No.1 hit in July with 'Don't Go Breaking My Heart', with Elton John, Kiki Dee had invited her co-star to join her on stage at this show. When Elton is unable to attend, Kiki shares the stage with a life size cardboard cut-out of him for her encore.

After the lights dim, the introduction to 'Tie Your Mother Down' from 'A Day At The Races' fills the air. Then, abruptly, it ends and cuts into the Kenny Everett tape, with the opening "Ladies and Gentlemen" line and NATO reference excised. Following the pre-recorded "Has the devil put aside for me" line, Queen bound on to the huge stage. Due to what sounds like a problem at the mixing desk, Freddie's first words of "Bo Rhap" go unheard, but he is soon heard again with: "So you think you can love me and leave me to die".

'Ogre Battle' follows without a break, with Freddie exaggerating the lyrics and emphasising certain lines with body language. The audience love it, and the show is off to a classy start.

"Thank you very much, good evening everybody. Welcome to our picnic by the Serpentine. You all look very beautiful, I must say. We should like to carry on now with a song called... 'Sweet Lady'." 'White Queen' follows, then an ominous sounding 'Flick Of The Wrist'. Brian: "This is a song slightly more in the vicious vein, written by Freddie in one of his more passionate moments, of which he has many."

Freddie: "Now then my darlings – listen. I have been requested by the constabulary, for you not to throw those things around – tin cans or whatever. Make this a peaceful event, okay. Now sit on your arses and listen. This is a medley, and this is a special little one coz we've increased it in length this time round. To start off with, a song called 'You're My Best Friend'." The medley moves through John's NATO ballad and on to 'Bo Rhap', 'Killer' and 'Black Queen' and concludes with Roger striking the gong on the 'Bo Rhap' reprise. 'Black Queen' would never again feature in the set after this show.

After a sprightly rendition of 'Leroy Brown', including Brian's ukulele solo, Freddie announces that was a *slow* version. 'Brighton Rock' follows, and segues into 'Son & Daughter', as usual.

Brian introduces the next song: "From one piece of nonsense to another, I've said it before, this is something which we were gonna do with the London Philharmonic, but they didn't turn up, so we will do the ethnic version... of a song called ''39'." All four members of the band assemble at the front of the stage, Roger with a tambourine, but also operating a bass drum with his foot, and Brian swapping his electric guitar for an acoustic. John assists with minimal bass.

Freddie: "Right now I'm gonna do a very special song. This is a new song from our forthcoming album. It hasn't quite been recorded yet. Anyway, it's a song called 'You Take My Breath Away'." This fine ballad features Freddie alone, accompanying himself at the piano. The audience remain silent throughout, for which Freddie seems relieved. "Something heavy, aye?" he says afterwards, and 'The Prophet's Song' follows with an opening section almost identical to the 'Opera' version and a similar operatic middle section.

'Stone Cold Crazy' proceeds at its usual furious pace and is followed by the contrasting mellowness of the 'Sheer Heart Attack' closing track, which Brian always introduced: "Thank you for making this a great day and a great evening for us. I hope you come again. We're gonna finish in the manner in which we are accustomed. This is 'In The Lap Of The Gods' or something

like that." The rock ballad is performed as usual, and closes with Freddie bidding farewell to his 'darlings', following which Roger bashes the gong a dozen times, and the band exit the stage.

Despite cries of "We want Queen" they do not reappear, because they are not permitted to by the police. Instead, compère Bob Harris walks on: "What a fantastic day today has been. That is the end of the day [laughs nervously]. The band are off and gone, that's the end of the evening, but it's been amazing, thanks to you. Thank you very much indeed, we'll see you soon."

The show was transmitted live on Capital Radio. DJ's Kenny Everett and Nicky Horne provide the commentary. It is also filmed for inclusion in a proposed documentary, put together by Bob Harris.

It was later apparent that Queen's set had overrun by half an hour, and the police warned Freddie that he would be arrested if he attempted to go back on stage, so he grudgingly abandoned the idea. The police, in their infinite wisdom,

pull the power to the stage equipment, not realising that the same power source is also feeding the lighting to the many exit points and surrounding car parks. As a result, thousands of fans are left to find their way out in total darkness.

"As the masses emanated towards Marble Arch and Queensway, people still threw up, fell down and hit each other. But that was the aftermath. The Picnic by the Serpentine was just fine."
(Tim Lott)

A variety of bootlegs emerged from Queen's performance. Some included the radio presenter's commentary, and others offered only edited accounts without it. Predictably, the sound quality of many of the recordings has declined drastically over the years. Most of the tapes currently exchanging hands are sixth or seventh generation copies. The most dominant sound on them is a dreadful background hiss.

One of the organisers of the concert was Virgin boss Richard Branson. During the show preparations, Roger Taylor was introduced to his French personal assistant Dominique Beyrand. They begin dating soon afterwards and eventually marry.

November 12

'Somebody To Love'/'White Man' is released as the first single from 'A Day At The Races'. It is issued almost a month later in America where it peaks at No.13; at home it reaches No.2.

The accompanying promotional video contains snippets of film recorded at the Hyde Park concert.

Incidentally, five of Queen's UK singles peaked at the No.2 position. This was the second such instance. It was kept off the top spot by Chicago's 'If You Leave Me Now'.

December 1

At the last minute Queen pull out of appearing on the *Bill Grundy Today* television programme. EMI are asked to provide a replacement, which they do – in the form of The Sex Pistols. What follows is a watershed in British rock. The Pistols, provoked by the wretched Grundy, shock the nation with their language and, proving the maxim that all publicity is good publicity, become the hottest property in British rock almost overnight. Grundy is sacked.

Whether The Sex Pistols would have gained the same notoriety had Queen appeared on the Grundy show is debatable. However, the catalogue number for 'Somebody To Love' is EMI 2565. The next single in the sequence was 'Anarchy In The UK' by the Pistols (EMI 2566).

December 10

Queen release their second album with a title inspired by a Marx Brothers' film, 'A Day At The Races', which quickly climbs the British album charts to reach No.1 on Christmas Day. The American issue came on

December 18 – it reached No. 5. Although many fans regard the record as an outstanding piece of work in its own right, it inevitably falls victim to comparisons with its predecessor.

The two albums should be regarded as one whole project, as they were by Queen. Brian May would later explain that he would have liked to have seen the two albums released simultaneously, rather than twelve months apart.

Three songs from the album are bypassed for the live show, though all would seem to be ideal candidates:

'Long Away', Brian's subtle, somewhat reflective tale of becoming wealthy and famous too quickly, John's 'You And I' – on which Freddie gave a breathtaking vocal performance – and Roger's greatly underrated 'Drowse'.

Though 'Drowse' was clearly not strong enough to be considered as a single release (it is sung by Roger, and therefore lacks the instantly recognisable Queen sound), it was issued as the B-side to the American and Japanese 'Tie Your Mother Down' singles.

December 13
Queen appear on Capital Radio's *Hullabaloo* programme. It is the station's first interview with all four members. When the interviewer asks Brian exactly what he studied at college, and what the subject entailed reading, the response was...

Brian: "I did a physics degree and about five years of Astronomy..."

Roger interrupts: "This is Roger, and I was reading Superman comics most of the time."

Freddie (laughing audibly): "Obviously."

USA 1977

Queen fly to Boston for ten days of rehearsals before commencing a two month, forty-one show tour of North America. The tour also includes seven shows in Canada. Thin Lizzy are the support act, fronted by Phil Lynott. The tour is rather aptly nicknamed the Queen Lizzy Tour. It is, after all, Queen Elizabeth II's Silver Jubilee year.

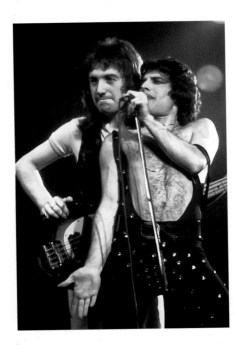

The set now looks very different. While 'Black Queen' has been dropped, 'White Man', 'Somebody To Love' and 'The Millionaire Waltz' (from ADATR) are all new additions. 'Tie Your Mother Down' now opens the show. 'Bo Rhap' is now performed in its entirety. The band do not attempt to re-create the opera section, but leave the stage and let the light show take over.

January 13

Auditorium, Milwaukee, Wisconsin

Intro / Tie Your Mother Down / Ogre Battle / White Queen / Somebody To Love / Medley: Killer Queen; The Millionaire Waltz; You're My Best Friend; Bring Back That Leroy Brown / Sweet Lady / Brighton Rock / Guitar Solo / '39 / You Take My Breath Away / White Man / The Prophet's Song: incorporating Death On Two Legs / Bohemian Rhapsody / Stone Cold Crazy / Keep Yourself Alive / Liar / In The Lap Of The Gods (Revisited) / Encore: Big Spender / Jailhouse Rock / God Save The Queen

Queen's first impressions of Milwaukee are not great. They arrive on the coldest night for over a hundred years. They count their blessings that the venue is not an outdoor gig.

The show opens with the studio recording of 'Tie Your Mother Down' guitar introduction, before the band take the stage and perform the track themselves.

For 'Bohemian Rhapsody' Queen leave the stage during the operatic sequence while the recording plays. Dry ice and a dazzling array of lighting trickery distract the crowd until the band will reappear amid an explosion, at which point Brian begins his blistering guitar solo, and Freddie reclaims his vocal mike on the song's hard rock conclusion.

The support acts for the first few shows are Cheap Trick and Head East. Thin Lizzy take over for most gigs thereafter.

January 14

Dane County Coliseum, Madison, Wisconsin

'Killer Queen' no longer opens the medley, but 'Best Friend' still features in it.

January 15

Columbus Gardens, Columbus, Indiana

'Sweet Lady' has now moved down the set list somewhat. Instead of featuring very early in the set, it now follows the medley tracks.

January 16

Convention Center, Indianapolis, Indiana

January 18

Cobo Hall, Detroit, Michigan

January 20

Civic Center, Saginaw, Michigan

Intro / Tie Your Mother Down / Ogre Battle / White Queen / Somebody To Love / Medley: Killer Queen; The Millionaire Waltz; You're My Best Friend; Bring Back That Leroy Brown / Sweet Lady / Brighton Rock / Guitar Solo / '39 / You Take My Breath Away / White Man / The Prophet's Song: incorporating Death On Two Legs / Bohemian Rhapsody / Stone Cold Crazy / Keep Yourself Alive / Liar / In The Lap Of The Gods (Revisited) / Encore: Big Spender; Jailhouse Rock / 2nd Encore: Now I'm Here / God Save The Queen

January 21

Elliot Hall Of Music, Louisville, Kentucky

January 22

Wings Stadium, Kalamazoo, Michigan

'Killer Queen' is re-created here, like everywhere else, almost exactly the same as the album version, but unlike the studio cut, segues into the next part of the medley before it reaches the final verses. In this case Freddie's 'Millionaire Waltz' follows it. Both songs are typical representations of their respective albums, and explore almost every aspect of the band's musical repertoire at the time, especially the latter example.

January 23

Richfield Coliseum, Cleveland, Ohio

Intro / Tie Your Mother Down / Ogre Battle / White Queen / Somebody To Love / Medley: Killer Queen; The Millionaire Waltz; You're My Best Friend; Bring Back That Leroy Brown / Sweet Lady / Brighton Rock / Guitar Solo / '39 / You Take My Breath Away / White Man / The Prophet's Song: incorporating Death On Two Legs / Bohemian Rhapsody / Stone Cold Crazy / Keep Yourself Alive / Liar / In The Lap Of The Gods (Revisited) / Encore: Big Spender; Jailhouse Rock / God Save The Queen

Queen perform a wonderful version of 'Millionaire Waltz' at this show, with Freddie coping effortlessly with the constant changes in pitch and tempo.

January 25

Central Canadian Exhibition, Ottawa, Ontario

Intro / Tie Your Mother Down / Ogre Battle / White Queen / Somebody To Love / Medley: Killer Queen; The Millionaire Waltz; You're My Best Friend; Bring Back That Leroy Brown / Sweet Lady / Brighton Rock / Guitar Solo / '39 / You Take My Breath Away / White Man / The Prophet's Song: incorporating Death On Two Legs / Bohemian Rhapsody / Stone Cold Crazy / Keep Yourself Alive / Liar / In The Lap Of The Gods (Revisited) / Encore Medley: Jailhouse Rock; Big Spender; Be Bop A Lula; Jailhouse Rock (Reprise) / 2nd Encore: Now I'm Here / God Save The Queen

Like last night's 'Millionaire Waltz', 'Somebody To Love' here catches the band in dazzling form with a sympathetic audience singing along in perfect harmony and with great enthusiasm. It is one of those rare occasions when no-one spoils the mood by shouting out during the quieter passages. All too often songs like 'Love Of My Life', 'Breath Away' and 'Doing All Right' have been spoilt by obnoxious individuals bent on making themselves heard over Brian's quieter guitar passages or distracting Freddie as he reaches for a high note.

January 26

The Forum, Montreal, Quebec

Queen meet up with Roy Thomas Baker and Ian Hunter, of Mott The Hoople, before the show. The two had just finished work on Hunter's new album, and were in attendance to watch Queen's show.

'Prophet's Song' now incorporates segments of 'Death On Two Legs' which is still not yet performed in its own right.

January 28

Chicago Stadium, Chicago, Illinois

Intro / Tie Your Mother Down / Ogre Battle / White Queen / Somebody To Love / Medley: Killer Queen; The Millionaire Waltz; You're My Best Friend; Bring Back That Leroy Brown / Sweet Lady / Brighton Rock / Guitar Solo / '39 / You Take My Breath Away / White Man / The Prophet's Song: incorporating Death On Two Legs / Bohemian Rhapsody / Stone Cold Crazy / Keep Yourself Alive / Liar / In The Lap Of The Gods (Revisited) / Encore Medley: Big Spender; Jailhouse Rock / 2nd Encore: Now I'm Here / God Save The Queen

Ted Joseph writes in the *New York Times*: "It should, by all means and stretches of the imagination, have been the hot show to end the winter freeze-out that finds rock and roll barrenness haunting this windy city in a post-Christmas hangover. But, Thin Lizzy's challenge to Queen's throne turned out to be a rather luke-warm battle.

"Lizzy is obviously looking for a break to stardom in the US after years as headliners in Britain, and this could have been the tour for it to happen. Not this time around. Quite simply, Lizzy's likeable, somewhat spirited music doesn't have much life on stage, due to a number of factors.

"Its stage presence simply isn't that of an up-and-coming '70s band, but rather a ghost-like reminiscence of the rising days of Ten Years After or Black Sabbath. Bassist/lead singer Phil Lynott down on his knees screaming 'baby... baby... baby' seems ridiculously out of place in 1977...

"The superb lighting, pyrotechnics and musical pulse from guitarist Brian May, bassist John Deacon and drummer Roger Taylor have stayed at the same level since they departed the States last year. It's one of the best integrated, most fully developed power trio sounds remaining today, and without a lot of noise to mimic the real music. Deacon and Taylor remain visually unobtrusive, but run together with May like finely lubed cogs; and May's royal leads constantly tug the show to new levels. That's where Lizzy can take a lesson from the royalty: Queen know their own dynamics and their audiences' interdynamics well. Their pacing has become exquisite."

So appalling is the weather that on the way to this show en route from Montreal, the trucks transporting the equipment are blown off the road. Another PA system is hastily arranged and flown in for the Chicago show.

Queen were to play a show the following evening, at the Hara Arena in Dayton, but because of adverse freezing conditions, tanker lorries transporting fuel needed to heat the arena were stranded at harbours with frozen diesel. Despite the band offering to go ahead with the show regardless, the local council refuse permission and the show is cancelled.

January 29
Hara Arena, Dayton, Ohio
(cancelled)

January 30
St. John's Arena, Toledo, Ohio
Intro / Tie Your Mother Down / Ogre Battle / White Queen / Somebody To Love / Medley: Killer Queen; The Millionaire Waltz; You're My Best Friend; Bring Back That Leroy Brown / Sweet Lady / Brighton Rock / Guitar Solo / '39 / You Take My Breath Away / White Man / The Prophet's Song: incorporating Death On Two Legs / Bohemian Rhapsody / Stone Cold Crazy / Keep Yourself Alive / Liar / In The Lap Of The Gods (Revisited) / Encore: Jailhouse Rock / 2nd Encore: Now I'm Here / God Save The Queen

During the customary post-medley champagne toast, Freddie calls the audience a load of tarts. They seem confused at the remark, but cheer anyway. Freddie moves on, and introduces a Brian May number – 'Sweet Lady'.

February 1
Maple Leaf Gardens, Toronto, Ontario

February 3
Civic Center, Springfield, Massachusetts

February 4
College Park, University Of Maryland, Maryland State

Intro / Tie Your Mother Down / Ogre Battle / White Queen / Somebody To Love / Medley: Killer Queen; The Millionaire Waltz; You're My Best Friend; Bring Back That Leroy Brown / Sweet Lady / Brighton Rock / Guitar Solo / '39 / You Take My Breath Away / White Man / The Prophet's Song: incorporating Death On Two Legs / Bohemian Rhapsody / Stone Cold Crazy / Keep Yourself Alive / Liar / In The Lap Of The Gods (Revisited) / Encore: Jailhouse Rock / 2nd Encore: Now I'm Here / God Save The Queen

Following 'Ogre Battle' Freddie addresses the audience for the first time: "Thank you. Good evening everybody. Are you ready for a fun night tonight? Okay then, we're gonna give it to you. It's very nice to be here in Maryland. We'd like to thank you for a very good welcome."

Freddie: "I think we're gonna go straight into something brand new. This was our last released single, it's called 'Somebody To Love'." This song would remain a concert favourite of both the band and their various audiences world-wide. Following the line "I've just got to get out of this prison cell, one day I'm gonna be free," Roger commences a rhythmic, almost anthem-like drum backing which the audience mimic with deafening hand clapping. Then Freddie begins the chorus of "Find - me - somebody - to - love. Find - me - somebody - to - love". Having hit the infamous high note of the song, Freddie makes his way back down the scale for the climax, John and Brian take their cue from Roger, who strikes one drum stick with the other. The audience cannot hear this, but the band can, and come in together for an impressive conclusion. "Thanks a lot for making that a hit here," Brian remarks afterwards.

February 5
Madison Square Garden, New York

After the show Elektra throw a party for the band in a restaurant in New York's Soho. Guests include Peter Frampton and Monty Python star Eric Idle.

February 6
Nassau Coliseum, Nassau, The Bahamas

February 8
War Memorial Auditorium, Syracuse, New York

Freddie: "Has anybody got any requests?" 'Bohemian Rhapsody' and 'Death On Two Legs' are yelled out. "Come on, you must have some more. Yes... yes... we're gonna do 'Liar' later on, and all the rock'n'roll numbers as well... yes. Right then, we'll do one now. This features Mr Brian May on guitar. This is 'Brighton Rock'."

February 9
Boston Garden, Boston, Massachusetts

February 10
Civic Center, Providence, Rhode Island

February 11
Civic Center, Philadelphia, Pennsylvania

Brian's 'Brighton Rock' guitar solo here is absolutely stunning. The acoustics within the venue were obviously ideal. Bootleg recordings from this show are marred only by irritating shouts from the audience, which inevitably come during the quieter moments.

February 19
Sportatorium, Miami, Florida

February 20
Civic Center, Lakeland, Florida

Intro / Tie Your Mother Down / Ogre Battle / White Queen / Somebody To Love / Medley: Killer Queen; The Millionaire Waltz; You're My Best Friend; Bring Back That Leroy Brown / Sweet Lady / Brighton Rock / Guitar Solo / '39 / You Take My Breath Away / White Man / The Prophet's Song: incorporating Death On Two Legs / Bohemian Rhapsody / Stone Cold Crazy / Keep Yourself Alive / Liar / In The Lap Of The Gods (Revisited) / Encore Medley: Jailhouse Rock; Big Spender; Be Bop A Lula; Jailhouse Rock (Reprise) / God Save The Queen

February 21
Fox Theater, Atlanta, Georgia

February 22
Auditorium, Birmingham, Alabama

Freddie offers a stunning version of 'You Take My Breath Away' here which is marred by inappropriate shouts from members of the crowd at all the wrong moments. Most respect his wishes to 'listen carefully'.

Unfortunately the bootleg from this show cuts off just as Freddie approaches the final verse, only to resume on the next side 20 seconds further into the track.

February 24
Kiel Auditorium, St. Louis, Missouri

Freddie is in stunning voice here. Although recordings of this concert are incomplete, and cut through two of the songs half way through, what little does survive is of the very best quality. John's bass playing features prominently too.

February 25
Lloyd Noble Center, Norman, Oklahoma

February 26
Moody Coliseum, Dallas, Texas

"Changing the mood now again ladies and gentlemen. This is for all you heavy people out there okay. This song seems to get better every time we do it. This is 'White Man'." Freddie is not exaggerating... what follows is a first class version of the 'Races' track, on which Roger must surely have exhausted himself. The live version of this song is very different from the studio cut, from the point at which it would normally end with a sudden short crash upon the drums onwards. Thereafter it instead segues into a

rather eerie improvised passage that included various segments of 'The Prophet's Song'. This would later evolve into the equally unpredictable concert version of Freddie's 'Get Down Make Love'.

February 27
Sam Houston, Houston, Texas

March 1
Phoenix Coliseum, Phoenix, Arizona

Tie Your Mother Down / Ogre Battle / White Queen / Somebody To Love / Medley: Killer Queen; The Millionaire Waltz; You're My Best Friend; Bring Back That Leroy Brown / Sweet Lady / Brighton Rock / '39 / You Take My Breath Away / White Man / The Prophet's Song / Bohemian Rhapsody / Stone Cold Crazy / Keep Yourself Alive / Liar / In The Lap Of The Gods (Revisited) / Encore: Now I'm Here / 2nd Encore Medley: Big Spender; Jailhouse Rock / God Save The Queen

March 3/4
Inglewood Forum, Los Angeles, California

First night: Tie Your Mother Down / Ogre Battle / White Queen / Somebody To Love / Medley: Killer Queen; Millionaire Waltz; You're My Best Friend; Bring Back That Leroy Brown / Sweet Lady / Brighton Rock / '39 / You Take My Breath Away / White Man / The Prophet's Song / Bohemian Rhapsody / Stone Cold Crazy / Keep Yourself Alive / Liar / In The Lap Of The Gods (Revisited) / Encore: Jailhouse Rock / 2nd Encore: Saturday Night / Stupid Cupid / God Save The Queen

Here 'Somebody To Love' is amazingly similar to the album version, but has the added bonus of Roger and Brian's harmonies being significantly more audible than usual, something which was not always the case. The audience participation also helps make this a memorable show.

Brian introduces a song: "The next song we were gonna do with an orchestra. Do you think that's a good idea?" "I might play drums," quips Freddie. "You're not supposed to say yes!" Brian adds, and "39' begins.

Queen also perform a wonderful version of 'Jailhouse Rock'. Freddie's vocal ad-libs are many and varied, even if somewhat nonsensical but are all the better for it: "Give it a little swing ah, keep on moving. Yeah, I like it, it's getting to me, can you feel it, ah baby — can I take you home tonight" and so on. Then, almost without a break, the band are off into a cover of Elton John's 'Saturday Night'. Roger's backing vocals are just as loud as Freddie's lead. Brian plays some blistering guitar, while Freddie repeats: "Rock and roll tonight". John takes over where Brian leaves off, and Freddie addresses the masses again: "Thank you for being such a beautiful audience tonight. Thank you very much. We've really had a good time, I just hope you have". A few more made-up lines further on, and Freddie suggests playing 'Stupid Cupid', which the other three respond to immediately. The band then segue back into the 'Jailhouse' reprise, and the medley concludes.

Two different bootleg recordings originate from this show, 'Mania' and 'Duck Soup', and both offer alternative track listings. Neither features the complete show, and there are ruthless edits with nearly every bit of between-song patter excised. 'Duck Soup' takes its name from another Marx Brothers film.

One of the discs on the 'Mercury Is Rising' CD (1993) also features material from this show.

March 16
Jubilee Auditorium, Calgary, Alberta

Following "39', which is every bit as good as the 'Live Killers' version, Freddie announces that just as Queen have done right throughout the tour so far, they would like to continue on a somewhat experimental note. "We are trying out lots of new and different styles," he says. "This is one of them. It's from our latest release, you might even recognise it if you bought 'A Day At The Races'. It's called 'You Take My Breath Away'."

March 17
Jubilee Auditorium, Calgary, Alberta

March 18
Northlands Arena, Edmonton, Alberta

March 25

Elektra issue 'Teo Torriatte'/'Good Old Fashioned Lover Boy' (P-157E) as an exclusively Japanese single. Predictably, it quickly becomes a hugely collectable disc. Like all Queen's Japanese singles, it features a unique full colour picture sleeve, and lyric sheet insert.

April

Sometime during the month John Deacon, whose turn it was to write the quarterly fan club magazine newsletter, recalled details of the recently completed forty-one date America/Canada tour:

"We left for America soon after Christmas on January 4. We flew to Boston, Massachusetts (of Boston Tea Party fame), for ten days' rehearsal before the first show in Milwaukee, Wisconsin. We covered the whole of the US this time and did quite a few shows in Canada too. It was the first time we had played in the very large auditoriums like Los Angeles Forum and Madison Square Garden, New York, so it was very exciting for us to play to 20,000 people in one concert. Our show went over really well in those auditoriums, and the American crowds wouldn't let us go until we had done two or even three encores.

"As you probably know by now, we are doing a UK and European tour

soon, which we're really looking forward to, as we haven't done a concert tour of England since November '75 and we haven't played in Europe for over two years. We hope to include material from our forthcoming album, if we have time to rehearse it well enough before we hit the road.

Brian's introduction to the medley: "Okay then, we have some more goodies for you I think. These are some of the old things we used to do. We've put them all together in a medley which we hope you'll like. We hope you recognise this." 'Killer Queen' follows, with Roger tapping his drumsticks together and Freddie matching each tap with a key on the piano.

May 13
Congresscentrum, Hamburg

Tie Your Mother Down / Ogre Battle / White Queen / Somebody To Love / Medley: Killer Queen; Good Old Fashioned Lover Boy; The Millionaire Waltz; You're My Best Friend; Bring Back That Leroy Brown / Death On Two Legs / Sweet Lady / Brighton Rock / '39 / You Take My Breath Away / White Man / The Prophet's Song / Bohemian Rhapsody / Stone Cold Crazy / Keep Yourself Alive / In The Lap Of The Gods (Revisited) / Encore: Now I'm Here / Liar / 2nd Encore: Jailhouse Rock / God Save The Queen

Slade, who are also in Germany at this time, come to see the show.

May 14
Jahrhunderthalle, Frankfurt

'Good Old Fashioned Lover Boy' is incorporated into the medley, not as the full album version but as a slightly accelerated, short sample.

May 16
Philipshalle, Dusseldorf

When the band pause briefly during 'The Millionaire Waltz', the audience think the song has ended and begin to applaud. In fact, the song is far from over and Freddie continues. The same thing occurred at most shows. Only fans familiar with 'A Day At The Races' remain silent.

May 17
Ahoy Hall, Rotterdam

Tie Your Mother Down / Ogre Battle / White Queen / Somebody To Love / Medley: Killer Queen; Good Old Fashioned Lover Boy; The Millionaire Waltz; You're My Best Friend; Bring Back That Leroy Brown / Death On Two Legs / Sweet Lady / Brighton Rock / '39 / You Take My Breath Away / White Man / The Prophet's Song / Bohemian

Rhapsody / Stone Cold Crazy / Keep Yourself Alive / In The Lap Of The Gods (Revisited) / Encore: Now I'm Here / Liar / 2nd Encore: Jailhouse Rock / God Save The Queen

Despite this show being only the second Queen performance in Holland, all tickets are sold within an hour of going on sale. After the show, a riot ensues at the front of the hall, though no one is seriously hurt.

At an EMI organised reception for the band held aboard a boat, Queen are presented with no less than 38 silver, gold and platinum discs for sales of singles and albums in Holland.

May 19
Sporthalle, Basle

Tie Your Mother Down / Ogre Battle / White Queen / Somebody To Love / Medley: Killer Queen; Good Old Fashioned Lover Boy; The Millionaire Waltz; You're My Best Friend; Bring Back That Leroy Brown / Death On Two Legs / Sweet Lady / Brighton Rock / '39 / You Take My Breath Away / White Man / The Prophet's Song / Bohemian Rhapsody / Stone Cold Crazy / Keep Yourself Alive / In The Lap Of The Gods (Revisited) / Encore: Now I'm Here / Liar / 2nd Encore: Jailhouse Rock / God Save The Queen

This was the last of the European dates. The band flew back home the following day.

SUMMER TOUR 1977
Queen
BACKSTAGE

May 20

Queen issue their first and only extended play single 'Good Old Fashioned Lover Boy'/'Death On Two Legs'/'Tenement Funster'/'White Queen'. Featuring material from the second, third, fourth and fifth albums (contrary to the 'Greatest Hits Vol I' sleeve notes), it ultimately peaks at No.17. It was not issued in Japan or the USA.

Queen insist that the disc be sold at the same price as traditional two track singles.

May 23/24
Hippodrome, Bristol

First night: Tie Your Mother Down / Ogre Battle / White Queen / Somebody To Love / Medley: Killer Queen; Good Old Fashioned Lover Boy; The Millionaire Waltz; You're My Best Friend; Bring Back That Leroy Brown / Death On Two Legs / Sweet Lady / Brighton Rock / '39 / You Take My Breath Away / White Man / The Prophets Song / Bohemian Rhapsody / Stone Cold Crazy / Keep Yourself Alive / In The Lap Of The Gods (Revisited) / Encore: Now I'm Here / Liar / 2nd Encore: I'm A Man / Jailhouse Rock / God Save The Queen

'I'm A Man', the Spencer Davis Group hit, makes an extremely rare appearance here.

Second night: Tie Your Mother Down / Ogre Battle / White Queen / Somebody To Love / Medley: Killer Queen; Good Old Fashioned Lover Boy; The Millionaire Waltz; You're My Best Friend; Bring Back That Leroy Brown / Death On Two Legs / Brighton Rock / '39 / You Take My Breath Away / White Man / The Prophet's Song / Bohemian Rhapsody / Stone Cold Crazy / Sweet Lady / Keep Yourself Alive / In The Lap Of The Gods (Revisited) / Encore: Now I'm Here / Liar / 2nd Encore: Jailhouse Rock / God Save The Queen

'Brighton Rock' on this tour saw Brian's guitar solo extending to the longest it had ever been. Like the show's finale, this would remain a part of the Queen live show right through to the last tour.

May 26/27
Gaumont, Southampton

Freddie (on 'White Man'/'The Prophet's Song'): "Let me tell you about these next two songs. They're two songs rolled into one, both written by Brian. Every night we do this sort of segue thing, and every night it seems to be getting a little better. It depends on the audience really. It starts with a song called 'White Man'."

The band then perform one of the best versions of the pairing to have been captured on tape, albeit unsanctioned tape. The bootleg recording of this show is definitely worth searching for, although it offers only approximately two thirds of the performance.

During 'The Millionaire Waltz' and 'You're My Best Friend' on the second night here, there are slight problems with Freddie's microphone. Although it's nothing serious, it does mar an otherwise faultless performance.

May 29
Bingley Hall, Stafford

No seats were available for this show and the entire audience stands. There is a rush towards the stage when Queen appear, but no one is hurt.

May 30/31
Apollo, Glasgow

First night: Tie Your Mother Down / Ogre Battle / White Queen / Somebody To Love / Medley: Killer Queen; Good Old Fashioned Lover Boy; The Millionaire Waltz; You're My Best Friend; Bring Back That Leroy Brown / Death On Two Legs / Sweet Lady / Brighton Rock / Guitar Solo / '39 / You Take My Breath Away / White Man / The Prophet's Song / Bohemian Rhapsody / Keep Yourself Alive / Stone Cold Crazy / In The Lap Of The Gods (Revisited) / Encore: Now I'm Here / Liar / I'm A Man / 2nd Encore: Jailhouse Rock / God Save The Queen

Freddie's intro: "Good evening everybody. Are you all ready for a rock and roll night? We're gonna give it to you. It's really nice to be back here in Glasgow, and thanks for such a lovely welcome. We have a lot of music to play for you tonight, of various kinds... a lot of the heavy stuff... a lot of the quieter stuff. I think straight away we'd like to do a song entitled 'White Queen'."

The medley section at this show is truly exceptional. Each song segues effortlessly into the next, especially the two 'Races' tracks, which at first glance seem to be a strange coupling to perform back to back. Not so. The two go together well, and bootleg recordings from this concert more than confirm this. The audience clearly know every single word, better than Freddie sometimes, and join in every verse. They do that for the duration of the show, in fact.

Freddie: "Okay, we're gonna do something heavy. This is a song that we only just recently included in the set. It's a song called 'Death On Two Legs'." No four letter expletives are included in the intro at this point. Curiously, that seemed to become a habit only later on, during the 1979 tour.

"I know we do this every time we come here, but every time we come here you give us a little present – a little statuette for getting a full house. But we'd like to drink a toast to you. Queen would like to drink a toast to everybody here tonight... CHEERS GLASGOW!" Freddie then goes on to inform the crowd that Brian is featured next, and 'Brighton Rock' begins.

Queen performed 'I'm A Man' at both shows here. One bootleg recording purporting to come from the first show includes 'Manish Boy' but this was only played on the second night.

Second night: Tie Your Mother Down / Ogre Battle / White Queen / Somebody To Love / Medley: Killer Queen; Good Old Fashioned Lover Boy; The Millionaire Waltz; You're My Best Friend; Bring Back That Leroy Brown / Death On Two Legs / Sweet Lady / Brighton Rock / Guitar Solo / '39 / You Take My Breath Away / White Man / The Prophet's Song / Bohemian Rhapsody / Keep Yourself Alive / Stone Cold Crazy / In The Lap Of The Gods (Revisited) / Encore: Now I'm Here / Liar / I'm A Man / 2nd Encore: Manish Boy / Jailhouse Rock / God Save The Queen

'Manish Boy' and 'I'm A Man' are both played, making the 'Apollo II' bootleg much sought after. I have yet to hear a particularly good quality copy though.

June 2/3
Empire Theatre, Liverpool
First night: Tie Your Mother Down / Ogre Battle / White Queen / Somebody To Love / Medley: Killer Queen; Good Old Fashioned Lover Boy; The Millionaire Waltz; You're My Best Friend; Bring Back That Leroy Brown / Death On Two Legs / Sweet Lady / Brighton Rock / '39 / You Take My Breath Away / White Man / The Prophet's Song / Bohemian Rhapsody / Stone Cold Crazy / Keep Yourself Alive / In The Lap Of The Gods (Revisited) / Encore: Now I'm Here / Liar / I'm A Man / 2nd Encore: Jailhouse Rock / God Save The Queen

Second night: Same as first night but with 'Doing All Right' instead of 'Sweet Lady', and 'Lucille' after 'Now I'm Here'

The band played a small segment of Paul McCartney's 'Mull Of Kintyre' after 'Keep Yourself Alive'.

'Doing All Right' rejoined the set here. It remained only briefly however.

June 6/7

Earls Court, London

First night: Procession / Tie Your Mother Down / Ogre Battle / White Queen / Somebody To Love / Medley: Killer Queen; Good Old Fashioned Lover Boy; Millionaire Waltz; You're My Best Friend; Bring Back That Leroy Brown / Death On Two Legs / Doing All Right / Brighton Rock / '39 / You Take My Breath Away / White Man / The Prophet's Song / Bohemian Rhapsody / Keep Yourself Alive / Stone Cold Crazy / In The Lap Of The Gods (Revisited) / Encore: Now I'm Here / Liar / 2nd Encore Medley: Lucille; Jailhouse Rock; Saturday Night's Alright For Fighting; Stupid Cupid; Be Bop A Lula; Jailhouse Rock (Reprise) / God Save The Queen

Surprised audience members were greeted by bagpipers and a display of frisbee expertise in the foyer as they

enter the auditorium for both concerts. Front row seat tickets for both shows at this venue were reserved for fan club members. The pre-show music is chosen by Freddie, and features passages by Chopin, one of his great favourites.

Both shows at this venue were recorded. Like the Rainbow Theatre shows in November 1974, the band were considering issuing their début live album using material recorded here. No such project ever materialised.

Queen use a brand new £50,000 lighting rig for the first time here. It consists of a huge silver framework covered in black sheets, with copious lights situated at its base. It weighs almost nine and a half tons, is twenty feet high, forty-five feet

deep and fifty-four feet wide, and is referred to as 'The Crown'.

As the house lights slowly dim, the classical music fades and is replaced by the pre-recorded guitar introduction to 'Tie Your Mother Down'. The Crown begins its gradual forty foot ascent to illuminate a smoke-filled stage. As the smoke clears, the taped introduction suddenly ends and the band become visible, bounding on stage. "Before we please you with some heavier rock'n'roll towards the end, I'd like you to listen carefully to a simple little song, with me on piano, it's called 'You Take My Breath Away'. Freddie treats the audience to an extremely moving rendition of a song which many consider to be the finest track on 'A Day At The Races', perhaps the most beautiful version of the song ever performed and, as requested, 17,000 fans listen intently, in absolute silence. They seem almost mesmerised by Freddie's voice.

Although this concert is regularly shown at Queen fan club conventions, it is also unofficially available on video. Like audio cassette bootlegs, however, most of the tapes currently in circulation are third or fourth generation copies, and offer extremely poor sound and picture quality. This concert really does deserve a proper home video release. Along with the Hammersmith Odeon Show from 1975, Hyde Park 1976, and another Hammy Odeon show from late December 1979, which we'll come to later, you really won't find better Queen concert footage than this.

The band were dressed in classic Queen apparel of the period. Freddie wore the famous green, white and orange diamond patterned cat suit, with white ballet slippers, Brian wore the Dickensian style white pleated cape, and John wore a white T-shirt with black waistcoat. Because this is the last show of the tour, and it's in Queen's home town, they perform an unusually long rock'n'roll medley, including a very rare 'Lucille'.

Second night: *Processions / Tie Your Mother Down / Ogre Battle / White Queen / Somebody To Love / Medley: Killer Queen / Good Old Fashioned Lover Boy / Millionaire Waltz / You're My Best Friend / Bring Back That Leroy Brown / Death On Two Legs / Doing All Right / Brighton Rock / '39 / You Take My Breath Away / White Man / The Prophet's Song / Bohemian Rhapsody / Stone Cold Crazy / Sweet Lady / Keep Yourself Alive / In The Lap Of The Gods (Revisited) / Encore: Now I'm Here / Liar / 2nd Encore Medley: Lucille; Jailhouse Rock; Stupid Cupid; Be Bop A Lula; Saturday Night's Alright For Fighting; Jailhouse Rock (Reprise) / God Save The Queen*

This period saw Freddie dressed in some of his most famous costumes. For the first part of the show, he invariably wore a harlequin leotard, an exact replica of that worn by the dancer Nijinsky, before changing into either red striped shorts worn beneath a Japanese kimono, or the infamous, much photographed Lurex outfit.

After the show, numerous celebrities join Queen at a party held in a marquee in London's Holland Park. Among them are Olivia Newton-John, Elton John and Bob Harris.

The band donate the proceeds of this show to the Queen's Silver Jubilee Fund.

June 7
Elektra in America release 'Long Away' as the third single from 'A Day At The Races'. It is paired with John Deacon's 'You And I'. The track is not issued in Europe or Japan, and neither song was performed in the live set.

July
The band spend July, August and September at Basing Street and Wessex Studios working on new material for their next album. They are assisted by Mike Stone, who had engineered all five previous albums, but essentially they produce the album themselves.

'News Of The World' is eventually released in the UK on the same day as Queen record their sixth and final session for the BBC, October 28 1977.

October 6
New London Theatre Centre, London

For the purposes of promoting the new single 'We Are The Champions', five thousand British fan club members are invited to attend the filming of the video. At only four days' notice though,

many receive their invitations too late, and are unable to get to London in time.

As the fans enter the Drury Lane venue, each one is given a copy of the single. The track is played three or four times for the audience to familiarise themselves with it before filming commences. The band perform the song several times, as it is necessary to shoot it from numerous angles. The footage later appears on *Top Of The Pops*.

Following a break after filming, the band return to the stage to play an impromptu performance by way of a thank you. They perform ten of their best known tracks. As radio presenter Bob Harris is present to film additional material for a documentary he was putting together, he introduces Queen to the stage.

The ten tracks performed were:

Tie Your Mother Down / Keep Yourself Alive / Somebody To Love / White Man / The Prophet's Song / Liar / Bohemian Rhapsody / Now I'm Here / Jailhouse Rock / Encore: See What A Fool I've Been

In the Winter 1977 fan club magazine, a handwritten letter from Bob Harris is printed. He refers not only to the 'We Are The Champions' video filming, but also to the documentary that he and Queen are involved in putting together: "All this brings me on to the film that the band and I are currently making together. It's a one hour documentary, tracing their history (through films from The Rainbow, Hyde Park, Earls Court concerts and stacks of promotional material very few people have ever seen). In fact, I'm off to America next week to finish off the remainder of the concert footage, (from the gigs in Texas, as well as filming the major interview with all the band).

Then we have to edit it all, fit it all together and get it ready for the television by mid-way through January. (I say that knowing that these things always take much longer than everybody expects) but keep a look out for it on *Whistle Test* towards the end of this series."

October 7

'We Are The Champions'/'We Will Rock You' is released in the UK. It provides the band with their sixth Top Ten chart placing. The same pairing was issued universally. The American release was delayed until October 25, to coincide with the beginning of the tour.

October 28

Maida Vale Studio, London

Spread Your Wings / It's Late / My Melancholy Blues / We Will Rock You

Returning to Maida Vale for the second time, Queen record their final session for the BBC. On this occasion, four tracks from 'News Of The World', which was released the same day, are reworked. The session is produced by Jeff Griffin and engineered by Mike Robinson, and is eventually broadcast two weeks later, on November 14.

Most of the tapes in circulation from this session (which are all unofficial bootlegs since it has yet to be officially issued) feature extremely irritating audience cheering, whistling and clapping, all of which have been blatantly added later (not by Queen), in an attempt to simulate the concert environment, an exercise which fails miserably, and ruins an otherwise faultless performance. The noise level of the audience remains unrealistically consistent throughout, and does not even quieten when a song concludes. While Brian May's 'It's Late' and 'We Will Rock You' are not entirely destroyed by the din, the sentiment of 'Spread Your Wings' and 'My Melancholy Blues' are altogether lost. Such sacrilege has only ever been paralleled (in Queen's case) by the 1974 American 'Liar' single edit.

It would appear that the audience noise was added later for release on various bootleg formats, and passed off as an enigmatic rare live recording. While the original John Peel radio transmission featured the four tracks in their proper form, most of the subsequent bootlegs have included the unwelcome addition. 'No News Is Good News' (SLA 0009) perhaps being the best known. The 1991 CD 'Tribute' (MF 284) is one of the few discs to offer a proper representation, albeit

as a third or fourth generation copy of a copy.

Another odd fact about session No.6 is the inclusion of a curious narrative passage, which precedes 'We Will Rock You'. Immediately following an explosion, an effect which would later be used to commence the live shows of 1978/79/80, and just prior to the familiar opening chords of 'We Will Rock You' (fast version), a female voice cuts in briefly with the tale of a Buddha and Brahmanism. When the band assembled in the control room to play back material just recorded, they were surprised to discover on the tape additional material which was not theirs. The tape contained a Radio 4 programme, which had also been recorded in that studio, a few days earlier, though it had not yet been broadcast. So bemused were the band that they incorporated a small segment of this into their own work!

'It's Late' contains a unique improvised section which is absent from the album version. There are many similarities with 'Get Down Make Love' (from the same album) which is largely due to a custom made tape delay machine which the band took with them into the studio. Because no commercially available device existed to supply the desired length of delay, the band designed their own.

This session take of 'It's Late' offers the only recorded version in that form. Even the many live versions did not see the song performed in this experimental manner.

The sixth album 'News Of The World' is released in the UK. Although Queen produced 'A Day At The Races' without assistance, this seemed to suffer from a somewhat shorter recording schedule.

While the band took three months and five months respectively,

to record 'Opera' and 'Races', barely ten weeks was allocated to 'News Of The World'. An American tour was planned to commence in mid November 1977, so Queen were obliged to record the album in nearly half the time they would normally take.

While the album did yield a great deal of well produced material – 'Rock You', 'Champions', 'Fight From The Inside', 'Get Down Make Love', 'It's Late' and 'Melancholy Blues', other tracks lacked the usual polish.

Brian May's exquisite 'All Dead All Dead' would unquestionably have benefited from additional production time. Only when Hollywood Records released their re-mastered compact disc of the album in 1991 was its full charm and subtlety properly evident. For the first time Freddie's vocals are clearly audible alongside Brian's lead vocal. The ballad emerges as the duet it was intended to be. John Deacon's 'Spread Your Wings' and in particular 'Who Needs You' sound too much like demo versions for comfort.

'News Of The World' was the only Queen album to chart higher in America than it did in England. It peaked at No.4 at home, but one place higher across the Atlantic. Three of it's tracks do not feature in the live show – 'Who Needs You', 'All Dead All Dead', and 'Fight From The Inside' – which was scandalously ignored as a single release. It seems that 'Sleeping On The Sidewalk' was played only once, on November 11, but was dropped because it did not work as well as expected.

USA 1977
US Tour (2nd Leg)

On November 4, the band flew to America. Three days later they moved on to the Metro Coliseum in New Haven to make final adjustments to the show. Queen now tour with over sixty tons of equipment, including a specially modified Crown lighting rig, which was first seen at the London Earls Court gigs. It is necessary for the lighting rig to be as easy as possible to move into and out of each new venue, so a Boston based sail making company are given the task of redesigning it.

The actual stage consists of three catwalks and a further two raised platforms, which are constructed above the PA system, giving the band access to all areas of the stage, and the ability to see the entire audience, including those seated behind the stage.

No support act will be employed for the tour, which allows Queen to play a two and a quarter hour set which includes new material from 'News Of The World': 'We Will Rock You' (fast and slow versions), 'Get Down Make Love', 'Sheer Heart Attack', 'Spread Your Wings' and 'My Melancholy Blues'. 'It's Late' would be incorporated into the show later in the tour. 'Sweet Lady', 'Ogre Battle', 'White Queen' and 'Liar' are all dropped from the set list.

November 11
Cumberland County Civic Center, Portland, Maine

We Will Rock You (Slow) / We Will Rock You (Fast version) / Brighton Rock / Somebody To Love / Medley: Death On Two Legs; Killer Queen; Good Old Fashioned Lover Boy; I'm In Love With My Car / Get Down Make Love; The Millionaire Waltz; You're My Best Friend / Spread Your Wings / It's Late / Sleeping On The Sidewalk / Now I'm Here / Love Of My Life / '39 / My Melancholy Blues / White Man / Improvisation / The Prophet's Song / Liar / Keep Yourself Alive / Bohemian Rhapsody / Tie Your Mother Down / Encore: We Will Rock You / We Are The Champions / 2nd Encore: Sheer Heart Attack / Jailhouse Rock / God Save The Queen

The stage is an extremely impressive sight, and features the immense custom built lighting rig suspended over it. As the show commences the crown rises slowly, amid an eerie cloud of smoke, which is bellowing across stage from hidden dry ice machines.

The show now opens with the slow album/single version of 'We Will Rock You'. Instead of the football terrace stamp-stamp-clap opening beat, as seen in the accompanying video, Roger Taylor provides a pounding drum accompaniment, although he and John are not yet visible to the audience. When Brian has concluded the track with a guitar solo, Roger and John are revealed when a curtain in front of the drum kit suddenly parts, and an explosion creates clouds of smoke. A much accelerated 'We Will Rock You' then ensues. An example of the fast, live version is contained on the first 'Greatest Flix' video compilation.

For the first time on stage, Roger sings his 'Opera' song, 'I'm In Love With My Car'. Another first is the addition of Freddie's beautiful 'Love Of My Life', also from 'Opera'. This is performed in a very different form from that of the album version. John and Roger leave the stage to Freddie and Brian, who perform it acoustically, often seated on stools in the centre of the stage. When Freddie stops singing half way through the song, to let the already word perfect audience continue without him, they willingly do so. It sets a precedent which Freddie continues from that show on. This does not remain exclusive to English speaking audiences. In subsequent years, the band are pleasantly surprised to discover European, Japanese and South American audiences singing along in perfect English too.

'Tie Your Mother Down' is no longer the opening track of the show. It was never omitted from the Queen live set. Brian would later comment that the song was the easiest track for getting on and off stage too. The second encore sees Freddie return adorned in the famous lurex suit to conclude the show with 'Sheer Heart Attack' and 'Jailhouse Rock'.

The show now concludes with the 'Rock You'/'Champions' finale and would remain that way for virtually every concert thereafter. On the odd occasion, the pairing would be separated by another track, as with 'Friends Will Be Friends' in 1986.

November 12
Boston Garden, Boston, Massachusetts

Because John sports a severely short cropped hair cut during this tour, photographs originating from this period are easy to date.

November 13
Civic Center, Springfield, Massachusetts

Although the length of 'Get Down Make Love' tended to differ from one night to the next, depending largely on the overall atmosphere at a given theatre, it usually featured a certain amount of improvised material. Because the stage lights were often kept low, to set the mood, and the band members could not always see each other, a whistle was blown as the cue for everyone to come in together for the dramatic conclusion. A good example of this is contained on the 'Live Killers' cut.

Brian: "It's just an exercise in using guitar harmonizer effects together with noises from Freddie... a sort of erotic interlude."

November 15
Civic Center, Providence, Rhode Island

We Will Rock You (Slow/Fast) / Brighton Rock / Somebody To Love / Medley: Death On Two Legs; Killer Queen; Good Old Fashioned Lover Boy; I'm In Love With My Car; Get Down Make Love; The Millionaire Waltz; You're My Best Friend / Spread Your Wings / Liar / Love Of My Life / '39 / My Melancholy Blues / White Man / Improvisation / The Prophet's Song / Keep Yourself Alive / Stone Cold Crazy / Bohemian Rhapsody / Tie Your Mother Down / Encore: We Will Rock You / We Are The Champions / 2nd Encore: Sheer Heart Attack / Jailhouse Rock / God Save The Queen

November 16
Memorial Coliseum, New Haven, Connecticut

November 18/19
Cobo Hall, Detroit, Michigan

November 21
Maple Leaf Garden, Toronto, Ontario

The next day the band fly to Philadelphia – in their own aeroplane. Previously they had resisted hiring their own air transport as they considered commercial flights to be a safer option.

November 23/24
The Spectrum, Philadelphia, Pennsylvania

First night: We Will Rock You (Slow/Fast) / Brighton Rock / Somebody To Love / Medley: Death On Two Legs; Killer Queen; Good Old Fashioned Lover Boy; I'm In Love With My Car; Get Down Make Love / The Millionaire Waltz; You're My Best Friend / Spread Your Wings / Liar / Love Of My Life / '39 / My Melancholy Blues / White Man / Improvisation / The Prophet's Song / Keep Yourself Alive / Stone Cold Crazy / Bohemian Rhapsody / Tie Your Mother Down / Encore: We Will Rock You / We Are The Champions / 2nd Encore: Sheer Heart Attack / Jailhouse Rock / God Save The Queen

Following the two shows at this venue, the band flew to Norfolk, Virginia, home

of Frank Kelly Freas, the artist whom Queen had commissioned to rework an original painting for the 'News Of The World' album sleeve.

The band met him at the Chrysler Museum of Art, where he was exhibiting his work, including the original robot painting. The event was covered by local press and TV.

November 25
Scope Arena, Norfolk, Virginia

November 27
Richfield Coliseum, Cleveland, Ohio

Before the show Queen are visited backstage by ELO drummer Bev Bevan, who is in town on a promotional tour.

November 29
Capitol Center, Washington DC

While at this venue, the band stay at the famous Watergate Hotel which Freddie finds most agreeable.

December 1/2
Madison Square Garden, New York

When Freddie appears for the first encore, he is dressed in a jacket and hat sporting the New York Yankees logo. The baseball team had just won the World Series, and had adopted 'We Are The Champions' as their theme tune. Freddie appreciated the gesture.

Second night: We Will Rock You (Slow/Fast) / Brighton Rock / Somebody To Love / It's Late / Medley: Death On Two Legs; Killer Queen; Good Old Fashioned Lover Boy; I'm In Love With My Car; Get Down Make Love; The Millionaire Waltz; You're My Best Friend / Spread Your Wings / Liar / Love Of My Life / '39 / My Melancholy Blues / White Man / Vocal Improvisation / The Prophet's Song / Now I'm Here / Stone Cold Crazy / Bohemian Rhapsody / Tie Your Mother Down / Encore: We Will Rock You / We Are The Champions / 2nd Encore: Sheer Heart Attack / Jailhouse Rock / God Save The Queen

While in New York, the band take time out to see various shows. Freddie attends Liza Minnelli's *The Act*, and together all four members see Daryl Hall and John Oates in concert. Three of the Hall and Oates band had previously worked with Elton John, and were therefore old friends of Queen.

Only hours before Queen are scheduled to leave New York, Freddie goes shopping and purchases a Japanese style grand piano, which he has shipped home. He would subsequently write many songs on it.

December 4
University Arena, Dayton, Ohio

December 5
Chicago Stadium, Chicago, Illinois

We Will Rock You (Slow/Fast) / Brighton Rock / Somebody To Love / Medley: Death On Two Legs; Killer Queen; Good Old Fashioned Lover Boy; I'm In Love With My Car; Get Down Make Love; The Millionaire Waltz; You're My Best Friend / Spread Your Wings / Liar / Love Of My Life / '39 / My Melancholy Blues / White Man / Vocal Improvisation / The Prophet's Song / Now I'm Here / Stone Cold Crazy / Bohemian Rhapsody / Tie Your Mother Down / Encore: We Will Rock You / We Are The Champions / 2nd Encore: Sheer Heart Attack / Jailhouse Rock / God Save The Queen

December 8
The Omni, Atlanta, Georgia

Bob Harris arrives with a film crew to cover two shows for a proposed documentary. They begin with the Fort Worth gig on December 10, and conclude with the wonderful show the following night in Houston, Texas, a show which frequently features at the annual fan club conventions, and is represented on the 'Rare Live' video collection.

Though the film crew fly home, Bob remains and travels with the band to the next venue, in Las Vegas, where additional interview material is recorded.

December 10
Tarrant County Convention Center, Fort Worth, Texas

December 11
The Summit, Houston, Texas

We Will Rock You (Slow/Fast) / Brighton Rock / Somebody To Love / Medley: Death On Two Legs; Killer Queen; Good Old Fashioned Lover Boy; I'm In Love With My Car; Get Down Make Love; The Millionaire Waltz; You're My Best Friend / Spread Your Wings / Liar / Love Of My Life / '39 / My Melancholy Blues / White Man / Vocal Improvisation / The Prophet's Song / Now I'm Here / Stone Cold Crazy / Bohemian Rhapsody / Tie Your Mother Down / Encore: We Will Rock You / We Are The Champions / 2nd Encore: Sheer Heart Attack / Jailhouse Rock / God Save The Queen

This is without doubt one of the very best Queen performances to have been captured on film, and one which finds the band in truly dazzling form. Part of the show was filmed. Pieces of it have subsequently materialised on video, most notably on the August 1989 'Rare Live' compilation. Unlike the Rainbow show of 1974, however, this show has yet to be given a proper home video release, long overdue though it is.

Parts have been available as a bootleg video for many years. Although it really should not be, like most videos of its kind, it is relatively easy to come by at record fairs up and down the country. It's probably fair to suggest that Queen's bootleg video catalogue is fast becoming as popular as those of the audio and compact discs. (The band really do need to address the situation quickly, and officially issue early concert footage before the situation escalates to the same proportion as CD bootlegs, of which there are now over 80.)

'My Melancholy Blues' sees Freddie once again seated at the piano: "Okay, we'd like to try something very different right now. This is from the new album 'News Of The World'. Have you got it yet? The album, that is. You might just about recognise this... this is 'My Melancholy Blues'". Having sung the opening line, he then counts in Roger by clicking his fingers. Roger and John (who is seated on a stool) provide only a subtle accompaniment. Brian does not feature in the song at all. This is a much underrated song, and this version is as good as you are ever likely to hear.

This version later appeared as a bonus track on the 12" and CD single formats of 'The Miracle' single in November, 1989. The 7" disc featured a live take of 'Stone Cold Crazy' recorded in 1974 at The Rainbow Theatre. It was also the second track on the 12" and CD single.

While Queen are in Houston, Roger Taylor takes the opportunity to attend a Rod Stewart show in Los Angeles, as he too is in the middle of an American tour.

December 15
Aladdin Center, Las Vegas, Nevada

December 16
Sports Arena, San Diego, California

Bootleg recordings from this show are worth locating for the wonderful version of John Deacon's 'Spread Your Wings'. This song remained in the set – on and off – until late 1979.

December 17
County Coliseum, Oakland, California

With only four shows of the tour left, John Deacon somehow manages to put his hand through a plate glass window. The injury requires nineteen stitches to his arm and hand, but the tour continues with John playing with a bandaged right arm.

December 20/21
Long Beach Arena, Long Beach, California

While here, the band were the subject of a fifteen minute NBC six o'clock news slot, which included a rare insight into the stage being set up, and interviews with them.

Second night: We Will Rock You (Slow/Fast) / Brighton Rock / Somebody To Love / Medley: Death On Two Legs; Killer Queen; Good Old Fashioned Lover Boy; I'm In Love With My Car; Get Down Make Love / The Millionaire Waltz; You're My Best Friend / Spread Your Wings / Liar / Love Of My Life / '39 / My Melancholy Blues / White Man / Vocal Improvisation / The Prophet's Song / Now I'm Here / Stone Cold Crazy / Bohemian Rhapsody / Tie Your Mother Down / Encore: We Will Rock You / We Are The Champions / 2nd Encore: Sheer Heart Attack / Jailhouse Rock / God Save The Queen

December 22
Inglewood Forum, Los Angeles, California

For the final encore, the band's six and a half foot bodyguard takes to the stage, dressed as Father Christmas carrying on his back a huge sack from which Freddie emerges. An assortment of people then join the band on stage, also attired in unusual costumes. Included in the somewhat strange line-up is the director of EMI, dressed as a ginger bread man, John Reid (Queen's Manager) dressed as an elf, and other unknown individuals assuming the roles of reindeers, clowns and walking Christmas trees.

Freddie and Brian perform a specially rehearsed acoustic rendition of 'White Christmas', during which 5,000 balloons are released into the audience, and mock snow and glitter is shot across the stage, to add to the festive atmosphere.

Following a party after the show, John Harris (sound engineer) is taken seriously ill and rushed to hospital.

He would spend almost an entire year in hospital, before making a full recovery.

Queen fly back to the UK on Christmas Eve. On the same day, the first half of a two part two hour documentary on the band was broadcast on Radio One. It concluded on Boxing Day.

February 10

'Spread Your Wings' is released as the eleventh UK single. The choice of B-side is Roger Taylor's manic 'Sheer Heart Attack', a track which was originally written for the album of the same name, but when it could not be completed in time, it was included later on 'News Of The World'. 'Wings' was not issued in America. Brian May's epic 'It's Late' was considered a better alternative, though it had the same flip side as the UK issue. The same pairing was also released in Japan, where it included the added bonus of an exclusive shortened edit of the main track. The American disc contained the full six and a half minute album cut.

EUROPE 1978

In April the band embark on a four week European tour of twenty shows in nine countries at thirteen different venues. The final three shows are consecutive nights at the Wembley Empire Pool, in London.

Fitting the huge crown lighting rig into some of the theatres would prove to be unexpectedly troublesome. Enabling the rig to be raised properly required a minimum height above the stage, and the theatres at Copenhagen and Hamburg proved to be too small to accommodate the full rig, so just the base lights were used.

April 12
Ice Stadium, Stockholm

We Will Rock You (Slow/Fast) / Brighton Rock / Somebody To Love / Medley: Death On Two Legs; Killer Queen; Good Old Fashioned Lover Boy; I'm In Love With My Car; Get Down Make Love; The Millionaire Waltz; You're My Best Friend / Spread Your Wings / It's Late / Now I'm Here / Love Of My Life / '39 / My Melancholy Blues / White Man / Instrumental Improvisation / The Prophet's Song / Stone Cold Crazy / Bohemian Rhapsody / Keep Yourself Alive / Tie Your Mother Down / Encore: We Will Rock You / We Are The Champions / 2nd Encore: Sheer Heart Attack / Jailhouse Rock / God Save The Queen

April 13
Falkoner Theatre, Copenhagen

We Will Rock You (Slow/Fast) / Brighton Rock / Somebody To Love / Medley: Death On Two Legs; Killer Queen; Good Old Fashioned Lover Boy; I'm In Love With My Car; Get Down Make Love; The Millionaire Waltz; You're My Best Friend / Spread Your Wings / It's Late / Now I'm Here / Love Of My Life / '39 / My

Melancholy Blues / Medley: White Man; The Prophet's Song: incorporating You Take My Breath Away; Guitar Solo; The Prophet's Song (Reprise) / Stone Cold Crazy / Bohemian Rhapsody / Keep Yourself Alive / Tie Your Mother Down / Encore: We Will Rock You / We Are The Champions / 2nd Encore: Sheer Heart Attack / Jailhouse Rock / God Save The Queen

"Good evening everybody, we're gonna have a good rock'n'roll night tonight, okay! We'll do a song called 'Brighton Rock'," exclaims Freddie, as he greets the audience for the first time. This rendition of the song is very similar to the album version. It lacked the lengthy guitar solo from Brian as did every version of the song performed on this tour.

Freddie introduces the newly updated medley: "It's really nice to see you guys here. We have a lot of music for you tonight, that's why we don't have a support (act). I just wish there were a few more of you. Right now we'd like to do a sort of a medley, this is about six or seven songs all rolled in together. This is a song called 'Death On Two Legs'." On this occasion 'Lover Boy' is the third track in the medley, but in later shows 'Bicycle Race' would replace it. Indeed that would be the medley that ultimately appeared on the 'Live Killers' album in 1979.

During 'I'm In Love With My Car' Freddie assists Roger with rather more backing vocal than usual. The two sing the main chorus together, one of the very few occasions on which this occurred.

At a dinner party after the show, arranged by EMI, the band were presented with silver discs for sales of 'A Night At The Opera' which had topped one hundred thousand.

April 14
Ernst Merck Halle, Hamburg

'It's Late' wasn't performed that often, but when it was, Roger's vocals were well to the fore, and Brian allowed himself a degree of guitar improvisation. This song is the ultimate Queen live track, the perfect song for the concert environment. Freddie would invariably introduce the next song, 'Spread Your Wings', by informing the audience that John Deacon wrote it, as he had the previous track, 'You're My Best Friend'.

April 16/17
Forêt Nationale, Brussels

Problems with the lighting rig at the beginning of the set threatened to jeopardise the show. The immense weight of the crown requires it to be lifted hydraulically, in a sequence controlled by four switches, but the sequence fails and only one side rises, causing the other to be dragged downward. There is much confusion both on and off stage, before it is decided that the show should restart, which it does. It proceeded without further interruption.

As part of the promotion for the gigs in Brussels, a large mock up of the 'News Of The World' album sleeve robot was driven around the city before each show. It had originally been constructed on the back of a car by local Queen fans, specifically for the Mardi Gras carnival in Antwerp, but was borrowed by the concert promoters, who'd spotted it at the carnival and transferred it to the back of a trailer. By the end of the second day, however, little was left of the robot – courtesy of Belgium's over-zealous Queen fans.

After the second show the band hold a press conference, during which they are presented with further awards: gold discs for 'A Night At The Opera', 'A Day At The Races' and 'News Of The World' (250,000 sales).

April 19/20
Ahoy Hall, Rotterdam

First night: We Will Rock You (Slow/Fast) / Brighton Rock / Somebody To Love / Medley: Death On Two Legs; Killer Queen; Good Old Fashioned Lover Boy; I'm In Love With My Car; Get Down Make Love; The Millionaire Waltz; You're My Best Friend / Spread Your Wings / It's Late / Now I'm Here / Love Of My Life / '39 / My Melancholy Blues / Medley: White Man; The Prophet's Song; Guitar Solo; The Prophet's Song (Reprise) / Stone Cold Crazy / Bohemian Rhapsody / Keep Yourself Alive / Tie Your Mother Down / Encore: We Will Rock You / We Are The Champions / 2nd Encore: Sheer Heart Attack / Jailhouse Rock / God Save The Queen

As a welcome for the band, EMI arrange for a small aeroplane to circle the band's hotel, with a trailing banner which reads "EMI Welcome Queen". The gesture is appreciated by Queen, but local fans descend upon the hotel in their hundreds.

While in Holland, the 'News Of The World' and 'A Night At The Opera' albums earn Queen single and double platinum awards respectively.

Second night: *We Will Rock You (Slow/Fast) / Brighton Rock / Somebody To Love / Medley: Death On Two Legs; Killer Queen; Good Old Fashioned Lover Boy; I'm In Love With My Car; Get Down Make Love; The Millionaire Waltz; You're My Best Friend / Spread Your Wings / Liar / It's Late / Now I'm Here / Love Of My Life / '39 / My Melancholy Blues / Medley: White Man; The Prophet's Song; Instrumental Improvisation; The Prophet's Song (Reprise) / Stone Cold Crazy / Bohemian Rhapsody / Keep Yourself Alive / Tie Your Mother Down / Encore: We Will Rock You / We Are The Champions / 2nd Encore: Sheer Heart Attack / Jailhouse Rock / Stupid Cupid / Be Bop A Lula / Jailhouse Rock (Reprise) / God Save The Queen*

April 21
Forêt Nationale, Brussels

This show (the third at this venue) was added because demand for tickets for the first two shows was so great. Queen were the first band to sell out three nights at the Forêt Nationale, the largest concert hall in Belgium.

April 23/24
Pavillion De Paris, Paris

We Will Rock You (Slow/Fast) / Brighton Rock / Somebody To Love / Medley: Death On Two Legs; Killer Queen; Good Old Fashioned Lover Boy; I'm In Love With My Car; Get Down Make Love; The Millionaire Waltz; You're My Best Friend / Spread Your Wings / It's Late / Now I'm Here / Love Of My Life / '39 / My Melancholy Blues / Medley: White Man; Instrumental Inferno; The Prophet's Song / Stone Cold Crazy / Bohemian Rhapsody / Keep Yourself Alive / Tie Your Mother Down / Encore: We Will Rock You / We Are The Champions / 2nd Encore: Sheer Heart Attack / Jailhouse Rock / God Save The Queen

Having drunk a toast to the audience, Freddie tells them that it has taken Queen six years to get to Paris; indeed, this was the band's very first performance anywhere in France.

'Death On Two Legs' opens with an unusual keyboard special effects sequence which accompanies Freddie's piano and the two guitars until Roger comes in with drums. This had not always been the case. 'Killer Queen' and 'I'm In Love With My Car' sound exactly like the versions on the 'Live Killers' album. The latter is an incredible

rendition, featuring Roger singing lead vocals and drumming simultaneously.

Freddie forgets a few of the words to 'Lover Boy' and improvises with the odd "bub bub bubba" line instead, something which he did frequently throughout Queen's concerts. Freddie had a knack of going off on vocal improvisations during a song, which added to the impact of the overall performance. In later years, 'Another One Bites The Dust' greatly benefited from Freddie's ad-libs.

The second, slower, version of 'We Will Rock You' is played here, as 'Bohemian Rhapsody' might be in the UK and 'Teo Torriatte', in Japan. This was because the song had spent twelve weeks at No.1 in France the previous year, only to be replaced by 'We Are The Champions'. France being a notoriously difficult market for rock'n'roll artists to penetrate, this was no small feat.

Due to problems at previous concerts at the Pavillion, local police had enforced a limit on the number of people allowed into the hall. For Queen's shows however, a number of tickets above that limit had already been sold. The restriction was lifted only for the second show – as no trouble occurred during the first.

The band agree to 'We Are The Champions' appearing on a French compilation album called 'La Cadeau De La Vie', in aid of cancer research.

After the second show, *Record Mirror* carries a report by Tim Lott,

ostensibly reporting from Paris at the *start* of Queen's European tour. Aside from the two Paris Pavillion shows not being the start of the tour (eight other shows preceded them), Tim Lott's summary gave readers a vivid insight into a show from a period which many fans consider to be the band's most exciting. There was nevertheless the customary note of journalistic sarcasm hanging over his report:

"At 8.21 Freddie makes his entrance – a predictable but dramatic spectacle as he taunts and postures to the thud of 'We Will Rock You'. His dress sense is as gauche as always, a harlequin leotard with neckline sweeping to his waist, and a small leather belt round his hips. The lights go up to reveal Queen units B, C and D.

"Brian May in benign intensity stands on a protruding plinth on the opposite side of the stage to Freddie. John Deacon looks monumentally uninterested, as always. There go Freddie's cheeks again right between his back teeth. Bonjour madames et messieurs, comment ça va? A cliché is a cliché even in Gallic.

"'Brighton Rock' provokes untrammelled jumping up and down from the audience. Freddie stalks through still more physical graffiti, wielding his mike stand as if he were practising guitar in front of the mirror with a tennis racquet."

"With the sort of predictability that made Max Bygraves famous, Freddie

86

takes up his champagne glass and toasts the crowd with an arrogance that only just passes for sophistication. This is the customary cue for 'Somebody To Love' standard version.

"OK. OK. This is what we call a medley," announces the pouting caveman. Automatically the medley is 'Death On Two Legs', 'Killer Queen' and 'Old Fashioned Lover Boy'. Then 'Get Down Make Love', a rather cloddish funk number, and the spotlights sweep the audience – another well worked device.

"OK. OK," says Fred again, in a rather uninspired fashion, 'My Best Friend', an exercise in the twee side of the group, is followed by the somnolent 'Spread Your Wings' which is greeted less than rapturously.

"In between numbers Fred attempts a spot of 'Parley' but the most lucid statement he can come up with is 'Voulez-vous couchez avec moi ce soir'. He still has a nasty habit of treating audiences like naughty schoolchildren. "Listen, he scolds, as a preamble to 'It's Late', a song so lacking in interest that I start noticing irrelevant details in an absent minded way.

"For instance, Fred has very small nipples. I can see them quite clearly. I am glad that he is not inhibited by their obvious lack of development. And that gormless robot face peers out from the drum kit blankly. Machines, machines.

"It does occur to me that Fred's voice is to be marvelled at for its purity and range. If only he could think of something exciting and new to do with it. A bit more pidgin French from Brian that I can't begin to fathom. The audience start shouting something like 'parsley'. Are they referring to Roger Taylor's slight resemblance to Parsley the Lion? Or is it some Gallic primal chant?

"The problem is soon forgotten as Queen do their Seekers' impression. 'Listen, listen,' chides Fred again. 'This is another one from 'News Of The World'. A mixture of polite cheers and, I suspect, quiet groans greet the news, it's 'My Melancholy Blues' the third newcomer to the set and it sounds like Johnny Ray doing a Dickie Valentine number. Quite funny in a way.

"'White Man' is extremely powerful, demonstrating that they can

still get tough when they need to, but it is too much of a price to pay for what follows. Up until this point Queen have been unenterprising but sensible.

"Now. In a spate of laboured self indulgence Freddie and Brian spend 20 minutes farting about playing 'Little Sir Echo' with their technical gadgets in a modified 'Prophet's Song'. The rest of the band whip backstage for a game of Monopoly.

"'Stone Cold Crazy' is hardly a redeemer, but 'Bohemian Rhapsody' the song that made Queen famous in Britain at least, retains all its grace and atmosphere.

"Freddie isn't changing his cozzie as much as he did last year when he undressed and dressed with the zeal of an obsessive stripper. But he starts to in 'Keep Yourself Alive' and, oh God... no, it's all right. The drum solo stops short and Freddie tosses his tambourine into the audience in relief.

"That suspect ditty about incestuous bondage 'Tie Your Mother Down' ends the set. Crash, bang, hooray et l'encore. By doing 'We Will Rock You' a second time, they re-affirm their lack of pioneering spirit, as does Freddie's 'My Way' and 'We Are The Champions', a song so ponderous it might have been more appropriately titled 'We Were The Champions.'

"Unnecessarily, they end with 'Jailhouse Rock' and Fred throws carnations into the audience. One lands on my head. Queen vanish. I squeeze out of the auditorium and take the Metro to the Pigalle. Sitting in the café, a shabby old man stands in front of me and frightens passers by with a plastic rat. At first a crowd stand and watch him, but as he does it again, and again, the crowd thin out and eventually disappear.

"If only Fred could have watched that man with me, I could have shown him what a terrible mistake he was making."

April 26
Westfallenhalle, Dortmund

April 28
Deutschlandhalle, Berlin

We Will Rock You (Slow/Fast) / Brighton Rock / Somebody To Love / Medley: Death On Two Legs; Killer Queen; Good Old Fashioned Lover Boy; I'm In Love With My Car; Get Down Make Love; The Millionaire Waltz; You're My Best Friend / Spread Your Wings / It's Late / Now I'm Here / Love Of My Life / '39 / My Melancholy Blues / Medley: White Man; The Prophet's Song; Instrumental Inferno; The Prophet's Song (Reprise) / Stone Cold Crazy / Bohemian Rhapsody / Keep Yourself Alive / Tie Your Mother Down / We Will Rock You / We Are The Champions / Encore: Big Spender / Sheer Heart Attack / 2nd Encore: Jailhouse Rock / God Save The Queen

This was Queen's first-ever show in Berlin.

April 30
Hallenstadion, Zurich

We Will Rock You (Slow/Fast) / Brighton Rock / Somebody To Love / Medley: Death On Two Legs; Killer Queen; Good Old Fashioned Lover Boy; I'm In Love With My Car; Get Down Make Love; The Millionaire Waltz; You're My Best Friend / Spread Your Wings / It's Late / Now I'm Here / Love Of My Life / '39 / My Melancholy Blues / Medley: White Man; Instrumental Inferno; The Prophet's Song / Stone Cold Crazy / Bohemian Rhapsody / Keep Yourself Alive / Tie Your Mother Down / Encore: We Will Rock You / We Are The Champions / 2nd Encore: Sheer Heart Attack / 3rd Encore: Jailhouse Rock / God Save The Queen

Queen performed a stunning version of the encore track 'Sheer Heart Attack' here. Although it is as fast and furious as ever, every word is clearly audible.

May 2

Stadthalle, Vienna

We Will Rock You (Slow/Fast) / Brighton Rock /
Somebody To Love / Medley: Death On Two Legs ; Killer
Queen; Good Old Fashioned Lover Boy; I'm In Love
With My Car; Get Down Make Love; The Millionaire
Waltz; You're My Best Friend / Spread Your Wings /
It's Late / Now I'm Here / Love Of My Life / '39 /
My Melancholy Blues / Medley: White Man;
The Prophet's Song; Instrumental Inferno; The Prophet's
Song (Reprise) / Stone Cold Crazy / Bohemian Rhapsody /
Keep Yourself Alive / Tie Your Mother Down / Encore:
We Will Rock You / We Are The Champions / 2nd Encore:
Sheer Heart Attack / 3rd Encore: Jailhouse Rock /
God Save The Queen

This was Queen's début show in
Vienna. It was attended by the winners
of a competition organised by the *Daily
Mirror* newspaper in Britain. The winners
were flown out specially for the show,
and later met the band in person.

May 3

Olympiahalle, Munich

Before the show commences,
the catwalk at the front of the stage
collapses under the pressure of the
audience. No one is seriously hurt, and
following a slight delay the show does
go ahead as planned.

The last twenty minutes of this
show was filmed for a German television programme called *Szene 78*.

May 6/7

Bingley Hall, Stafford

We Will Rock You (Slow/Fast) / Brighton Rock /
Somebody To Love / Medley: Death On Two Legs;
Killer Queen; Good Old Fashioned Lover Boy; I'm In
Love With My Car; Get Down Make Love; The Millionaire
Waltz; You're My Best Friend / Spread Your Wings /
It's Late / Now I'm Here / Love Of My Life / '39 / My
Melancholy Blues / Medley: White Man; The Prophet's
Song; Instrumental Inferno; The Prophet's Song
(Reprise) / Stone Cold Crazy / Bohemian Rhapsody /
Keep Yourself Alive / Tie Your Mother Down / We Will Rock
You / We Are The Champions / Encore: Sheer
Heart Attack / 2nd Encore: Jailhouse Rock / God Save
The Queen

During 'Love Of My Life' Freddie
decides to stop singing and let the
crowd take over. They do so with great
vigour, and the band are extremely
touched. From this show on, the
audience taking over the vocals of
numerous verses of the song, becomes

something of a tradition, and a high
point of the show.

Under the headline LATE - BUT
GREAT! the following report of the
second show by Maurice Rotheroe
appears in the *Birmingham Evening Mail*
of May 8, 1978.

"THEIR Highnesses deigned to
give audience to their adoring subjects
thirty-five minutes late.

"But what's that to the
converted thousands, many of whom
have been queuing since the previous
day?

"Their arrival, accompanied by
majestic music of the spheres and a fair
representation of a spaceship take-off,
transforms what should be a pop
concert into more of a rock mass.

"The barn-like hall takes on the
atmosphere of a cathedral.

"The regal quartet have style and
swagger – and the skill to accompany it,
as they pulsate their way through
their rhythmic hymnal. The show is

ostentatious, exciting, and the only
lull as they skip from heavy, to light and
fantastic, is during indulgent guitar and
vocal solos which are electronic
exercises rather than music.

"Quicksilver Freddie Mercury, in
black plastic trousers and red braces
makes 'Bohemian Rhapsody' into
something of a revelation."

May 11/12/13

Empire Pool, London

First night: We Will Rock You (Slow/Fast) /
Brighton Rock / Somebody To Love / Medley: Death On
Two Legs; Killer Queen; Good Old Fashioned Lover Boy;
I'm In Love With My Car; Get Down Make Love; The
Millionaire Waltz; You're My Best Friend / Spread Your
Wings / It's Late / Now I'm Here / Love Of My Life /
'39 / My Melancholy Blues / Medley: White Man; The
Prophet's Song; Instrumental Inferno; The Prophet's Song
(Reprise) / Stone Cold Crazy / Bohemian Rhapsody /
Keep Yourself Alive / Tie Your Mother Down / Encore:
We Will Rock You / We Are The Champions / 2nd Encore:
Sheer Heart Attack / 3rd Encore: Jailhouse Rock /
God Save The Queen

Final night: We Will Rock You (Slow/Fast) / Brighton Rock / Somebody To Love / White Queen / Medley: Death On Two Legs; Killer Queen; Good Old Fashioned Lover Boy; I'm In Love With My Car; Get Down Make Love; Millionaire Waltz; You're My Best Friend / Spread Your Wings / It's Late / Now I'm Here / Love Of My Life / '39 / My Melancholy Blues / Medley: White Man; The Prophet's Song; Instrumental Inferno; The Prophet's Song (Reprise) / Stone Cold Crazy / Bohemian Rhapsody / Keep Yourself Alive / Tie Your Mother Down / Encore: Sheer Heart Attack / 2nd Encore: We Will Rock You / We Are The Champions / God Save The Queen

For this, the last show of the European leg of the tour, Queen change the encore, to conclude with 'We Will Rock You'/'We Are The Champions'.

July

Queen work on material for their seventh album 'Jazz'. The sessions are recorded at Mountain Studios, in Switzerland, and Superbear Studios in Southern France. The recording is finished by October.

October 13

'Fat Bottomed Girls'/'Bicycle Race', the first single from 'Jazz', is released in the UK – their second double A-sided issue. Though promotional videos for both tracks are filmed, the 'Bicycle Race' footage is deemed unsuitable for television broadcast in its original form. The infamous footage of sixty-five female models cycling naked around Wimbledon Stadium (as depicted in the poster which accompanied the UK

album – but not the US version) was obscured with special effects for its few television screenings. The uncensored cut is on the 'Magic Years' video documentary. Regardless of the censorship, the disc peaked at No.11 in the UK, and No.24 in America.

October 24

Four days prior to the beginning of American tour dates, 'Bicycle Race'/'Fat Bottomed Girls' is issued in the US, as a double A-sided disc.

USA 1978
North American Tour

In late October Queen flew to Dallas to prepare for a thirty-five show, seven week tour of North America. Five concerts in Canada were also included. The tour concludes with three consecutive shows at the Inglewood Forum, in Los Angeles.

A new hydraulic operated lighting rig is unveiled on this tour. It weighs five tons and utilises six hundred lights which radiate so much heat that the rig earns the nickname 'The Pizza Oven'.

The tour programme cover features similar graphics to those used for the 'Jazz' album, and includes some wonderful on and off stage photographs of the band.

The brand new set now features material from the 'Jazz' album – due for a British release on November 10, and four days later in America – 'Let Me Entertain You', 'Bicycle Race', 'If You Can't Beat Them', 'Dreamers Ball' and 'Fat Bottomed Girls'. 'Don't Stop Me Now' and 'Mustapha' will also feature in

the set, but not yet. 'Lover Boy', 'Stone Cold Crazy', 'Prophet's Song', 'My Melancholy Blues' and 'White Man' are all dropped from the set. The medley is now that featured on 'Live Killers'.

At Madison Square Garden in November, the band are joined on stage by topless female cyclists clad only in tiny G-strings. Since the nude ladies cycling around Wimbledon Stadium poster had not been included in the album package in America (only an application to order it), Queen decided to compensate by giving the audience the real thing instead. The local press had a field day next day.

October 28
Convention Center, Dallas, Texas

We Will Rock You / Let Me Entertain You / Somebody To Love / If You Can't Beat Them / Medley: Death On Two Legs; Killer Queen; Bicycle Race; I'm In Love With My Car; Get Down Make Love; You're My Best Friend / Now I'm Here / Spread Your Wings / Dreamers Ball / Love Of My Life / '39 / It's Late / Brighton Rock / Fat Bottomed Girls / Keep Yourself Alive / Bohemian Rhapsody / Tie Your Mother Down / Encore: Sheer Heart Attack / 2nd Encore: We Will Rock You / We Are The Champions / God Save The Queen

Like its predecessor, the new rig moves above the stage throughout the show, and ultimately comes to rest facing out towards the audience – a spectacular sight, which very few photographs captured properly.

John Deacon now sports a severely cropped hair cut.

This show's live 'Bo Rhap' was quite outstanding, with Freddie and audience singing together with uncanny synchronicity.

October 29
Mid South Coliseum, Memphis, Tennesse

We Will Rock You / Let Me Entertain You / Somebody To Love / If You Can't Beat Them / Medley: Death On Two Legs; Killer Queen; Bicycle Race; I'm In Love With My Car; Get Down Make Love; You're My Best Friend / Now I'm Here / Spread Your Wings / Dreamers Ball / Love Of My Life / '39 / It's Late / Brighton Rock / Fat Bottomed Girls / Keep Yourself Alive / Bohemian Rhapsody / Tie Your Mother Down / Encore: Sheer Heart Attack / Jailhouse Rock / 2nd Encore: We Will Rock You / We Are The Champions / God Save The Queen

Although 'Jailhouse Rock' was dropped from the set during this tour, the band perform it here as a tribute to Elvis Presley. Elvis had died in 1977, and this was the first opportunity Queen had to offer an appropriate tribute to him in his home town.

October 31

Civic Auditorium, New Orleans
Following the show, a huge party takes place for the world premier of the 'Jazz' album. It is the very first event jointly organised by EMI and Elektra, and includes an elaborate assortment of entertainment: fire-eaters, African dancers, unicyclists, strippers, drag artists and local jazz bands. The event is such a success that the album is never actually played.

November 3
Sportorium, Miami

November 4
Civic Center, Lakeland, Florida

The day after the show in Lakeland, the band fly to Florida in a private jet. They spend the day in Disney World, before flying on to Washington.

November 6
Capitol Center, Washington DC

November 7
New Haven Coliseum, Connecticut

November 9/10

Cobo Arena, Detroit

'Jazz', Queen's seventh album, is released in the UK. It reaches No. 2 in the charts. In America it peaks at No. 6. It is the first Queen LP to have been recorded in a studio outside the UK.

As with every album, a proportion of the material is not used in the live show, despite most of it seeming easily adaptable to the stage. The most glaring omission has to be Brian May's track 'Dead On Time', which, with its frantic pace, exceptional lyrics and 'Courtesy of God' thunderclap (taped by Brian during a power failure at a recording session), really would have made a wonderful addition to the set.

Likewise, the band evidently deemed John Deacon's 'In Only Seven Days' as unsuitable, as they did Brian's emotive 'Leaving Home Ain't Easy', Freddie's 'Jealousy' and Roger's 'More Of That Jazz'. Only part of 'Fun It', it would seem, was performed live, and then on only one occasion, in Paris.

The running order of 'Jazz' is somewhat erratic, or at the very least disorganised. 'Jealousy', for example, is entirely misplaced between 'Fat Bottomed Girls' and 'Bicycle Race' which should have appeared back to back. Though 'Let Me Entertain You' is an obvious choice for the opening track, it actually concludes Side 1, and 'Dead On Time' does not segue well into John Deacon's cleverly written 'In Only Seven Days'. Fortunately, the advent of programmable CD players has enabled fans to experiment with alternative track sequences.

November 11

Wings Stadium, Kalamazoo, Michigan

The very first Queen Fan Club Convention is held on this date at the Empire Ballroom in London's Leicester Square. A general invitation is issued in the Autumn fan club magazine, and hundreds of eager fans from all around the UK assemble outside the Leicester Square venue.

Alan Freeman hosts the event, which unlike subsequent conventions, is a half day affair, held on a Saturday afternoon. It kicks off with Freeman explaining the programme for the afternoon, and continues with him playing various tracks from the albums, commencing with 'Keep Yourself Alive'. The music is accompanied by a slide show of pictures of the band.

The promotional videos for 'Bohemian Rhapsody', 'You're My Best Friend', 'Somebody To Love', 'Tie Your Mother Down', 'We Will Rock You', 'We Are The Champions' and 'Spread Your Wings' were also shown.

The afternoon concludes with a complete play-through of the brand new album 'Jazz', before a telegram sent from America by the band, is read out.

November 13

Boston Gardens, Boston, Massachusetts

November 14

Civic Center, Providence, Rhode Island

November 16/17

Madison Square Garden, New York

First night: We Will Rock You / Let Me Entertain You / Somebody To Love / If You Can't Beat Them / Medley: Death On Two Legs; Killer Queen; Bicycle Race; I'm In Love With My Car; Get Down Make Love; You're My Best Friend / Now I'm Here / Spread Your Wings / Dreamers Ball / Love Of My Life / '39 / It's Late / Brighton Rock / Fat Bottomed Girls / Keep Yourself Alive / Bohemian Rhapsody / Tie Your Mother Down / Encore: Sheer Heart Attack / 2nd Encore: We Will Rock You / We Are The Champions / God Save The Queen

The band perform a blistering set here. 'Somebody To Love', 'Dreamers Ball', ''39', 'It's Late' and 'Tie Your Mother Down' in particular, are exceptional. Freddie has much to say, and takes full advantage of an enthusiastic and compliant audience.

Second night: We Will Rock You / Let Me Entertain You / Somebody To Love / If You Can't Beat Them / Medley: Death On Two Legs; Killer Queen; Bicycle Race; I'm In Love With My Car; Get Down Make Love; You're My Best Friend / Now I'm Here / Spread Your Wings / Dreamers Ball / Love Of My Life / '39 / It's Late / Brighton Rock / Fat Bottomed Girls / Keep Yourself Alive / Bohemian Rhapsody / Tie Your Mother Down / Encore: Sheer Heart Attack / 2nd Encore: We Will Rock You / We Are The Champions / God Save The Queen

During 'Bicycle Race' the band are joined on stage by a number of girls on bicycles, wearing only G-strings. Since the poster of the sixty-five nude ladies cycling around Wimbledon Stadium had not been included in the American album package, Queen decided to offer the audience the real thing instead.

In an article headlined Regal Queen At The Garden in the *Brooklyn College Kingsmen* dated December 8, 1978, Richard Torregrossa writes:

...''They also treated their listeners to songs off the new album, 'Jazz'.

'Bad Bottom Girl' (mis-spelled) was performed as five girls, adequately described by the song's title, rode across the stage in outfits quite risqué, as the male populace seated in the upper promenades frantically reached for the binoculars...

..."Mercury bowed and gestured to the audience as he emphasised the lyrics in 'We Are The Champions': You've brought me fame and fortune and everything that goes with it - I Thank You All...

..."As the final notes from Brian May's self-made guitar echoed throughout the Garden after the band's third and final encore, fearless Freddie sauntered to the front of the stage, bowed graciously and said brashly: "I thank you for your time and I thank you for your money!"

November 19
Nassau Coliseum, Uniondale, Long Island, New York

November 20
Spectrum, Philadelphia, Pennsylvania

November 22
Nashville Auditorium, Nashville, Tennessee

November 23
Checkerdome, St Louis, Missouri

November 25
Richfield Coliseum, Cleveland, Ohio

November 26
Riverfront Coliseum, Cincinnati, Ohio

November 28
War Memorial Auditorium, Buffalo, New York

Brian composes a letter for the Winter fan club magazine. In it he recalls:

"We're almost exactly half-way through our two and a half month tour of America and it is going spectacularly well. Every city has given us a great welcome. Many of the radio stations are transmitting 'mini-Queen concerts' on the nights of the shows.

"We were very happy to be presented with a special plaque from Madison Square Garden, for being one of the very few groups to sell over 100,000 tickets in New York City. Our album 'Jazz' entered the US charts at 30 – our previous highest being 65 – so everything looks great. As you probably know, our touring schedule takes us to Europe in January and to Japan after that..."

November 30
Central Canadian Exhibition Center, Ottawa, Ontario

December 1
The Forum, Montreal, Quebec
We Will Rock You / Let Me Entertain You / Somebody To Love / If You Can't Beat Them / Medley: Death On Two Legs; Killer Queen; Bicycle Race; I'm In Love With My Car; Get Down Make Love; You're My Best Friend / Now I'm Here / Spread Your Wings / Dreamers Ball / Love Of My Life / '39 / It's Late / Brighton Rock / Fat Bottomed Girls / Keep Yourself Alive / Bohemian Rhapsody / Tie Your Mother Down / Encore: Sheer Heart Attack / 2nd Encore: We Will Rock You / We Are The Champions / God Save The Queen

Another show which mirrors almost exactly the 'Live Killers' album set. The six medley songs ('Death' – 'Best Friend') appear here in the same order as they do on the album. Only three songs do not appear on the album – 'Somebody To Love', 'It's Late' and 'Fat Bottomed Girls'. All are regrettable omissions.

December 3/4
Maple Leaf Garden, Toronto, Ontario
First night: We Will Rock You / Let Me Entertain You / Somebody To Love / If You Can't Beat Them / Medley: Death On Two Legs; Killer Queen; Bicycle Race; I'm In Love With My Car; Get Down Make Love; You're My Best Friend / Now I'm Here / Spread Your Wings / Dreamers Ball / Love Of My Life / '39 / It's Late / Brighton Rock / Fat Bottomed Girls / Keep Yourself Alive / Bohemian Rhapsody / Tie Your Mother Down / Encore: Sheer Heart Attack / 2nd Encore: We Will Rock You / We Are The Champions / God Save The Queen

December 6
Dane County Coliseum, Madison, Wisconsin

December 7
Chicago Stadium, Chicago
We Will Rock You / Let Me Entertain You / Somebody To Love / If You Can't Beat Them / Medley: Death On Two Legs; Killer Queen; Bicycle Race; I'm In Love With My Car; Get Down Make Love; You're My Best Friend / Now I'm Here / Spread Your Wings / Dreamers Ball / Love Of My Life / '39 / It's Late / Brighton Rock / Fat Bottomed Girls / Keep Yourself Alive / Bohemian Rhapsody / Tie Your Mother Down / Encore: Sheer Heart Attack / 2nd Encore: We Will Rock You / We Are The Champions / God Save The Queen

December 8
Kemper Arena, Kansas City, Missouri

December 12
Seattle Coliseum, Seattle

December 13
Portland Coliseum, Portland, Oregon

December 14
PNE Coliseum, Vancouver, British Columbia

December 16
Oakland Coliseum, Oakland, California
We Will Rock You / Let Me Entertain You / Somebody To Love / If You Can't Beat Them / Medley: Death On Two Legs; Killer Queen; Bicycle Race; I'm In Love With My Car; Get Down Make Love; You're My Best Friend / Now I'm Here / Spread Your Wings / Dreamers Ball / Love Of My Life / '39 / It's Late / Brighton Rock / Fat Bottomed Girls / Keep Yourself Alive / Bohemian Rhapsody / Tie Your Mother Down / Encore: Sheer Heart Attack / 2nd Encore: We Will Rock You / We Are The Champions / God Save The Queen

December 18/19/20
Inglewood Forum, Los Angeles

The third night was the last show of the tour, and indeed the year. The band played 'Jailhouse Rock' and 'Big Spender'.

December 23
When the band arrive back in London, they announce their intention to perform a concert on the Centre Court at Wimbledon. Their application is predictably rejected by the Club's management.

The band spend Christmas at home, which in Roger's case is a beautiful newly acquired house set in 20 acres of ground on the outskirts of Guildford, Surrey. The house had apparently once belonged to Dr Crippen's lawyer.

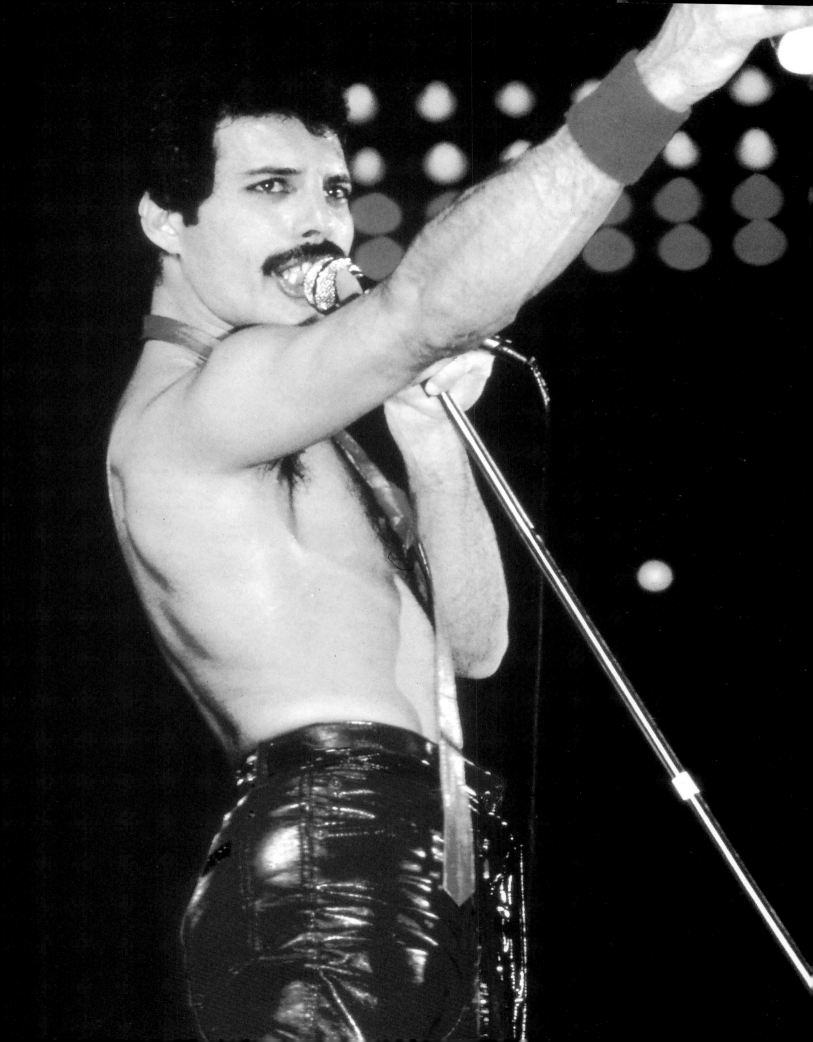

EUROPE 1979
European Tour

After spending Christmas at home, the band travel to Germany to start their biggest European tour yet. The tour comprises twenty-eight shows, in seven countries, over a six week period, and includes Queen's first shows in Yugoslavia.

January 17
Ernst Merckhalle, Hamburg

We Will Rock You / Let Me Entertain You / Somebody To Love / If You Can't Beat Them / Medley: Death On Two Legs; Killer Queen; Bicycle Race; I'm In Love With My Car; Get Down Make Love; You're My Best Friend / Now I'm Here / Don't Stop Me Now / Spread Your Wings / Dreamers Ball / Love Of My Life / '39 / It's Late / Brighton Rock / Guitar Solo / Keep Yourself Alive / Bohemian Rhapsody / Tie Your Mother Down / Encore: Sheer Heart Attack / 2nd Encore: We Will Rock You / We Are The Champions / God Save The Queen

Both 'Bicycle Race' and 'Fat Bottomed Girls' make chart appearances while the band are in Germany.

January 18
Ostee Hall, Kiel

January 20
Stadthalle, Bremen

We Will Rock You / Let Me Entertain You / Somebody To Love / If You Can't Beat Them / Medley: Death On Two Legs; Killer Queen; Bicycle Race; I'm In Love With My Car; Get Down Make Love; You're My Best Friend / Now I'm Here / Don't Stop Me Now / Spread Your Wings / Dreamers Ball / Love Of My Life / '39 / It's Late / Brighton Rock / Guitar Solo / Keep Yourself Alive / Bohemian Rhapsody / Tie Your Mother Down / Encore: Sheer Heart Attack / 2nd Encore: We Will Rock You / We Are The Champions / God Save The Queen

'Don't Stop Me Now' is now featured in the set. It is a slightly accelerated account to that which is contained on the 'Jazz' album, and is also one of the most exciting tracks to have appeared in any Queen set, due largely to an immensely powerful drumming accompaniment and backing vocal from Roger. The live renderings of the song seemed to be injected with a vibrancy and edge not present on the studio cut. This is amply demonstrated on the 'Live Killers' album. Indeed, Side Three of that album ('Don't Stop Me Now', 'Spread Your Wings', 'Brighton Rock'),

offers arguably the finest 23 minutes of Queen live material available.

January 21
Westfallenhalle, Dortmund

January 23
Messesportspalace, Hanover

January 24
Deutschlandhalle, Berlin

We Will Rock You / Let Me Entertain You / Somebody To Love / Medley: Death On Two Legs; Killer Queen; Bicycle Race; I'm In Love With My Car; Get Down Make Love; You're My Best Friend / Now I'm Here / Don't Stop Me Now / Spread Your Wings / Dreamers Ball / Love Of My Life / '39 / It's Late / Brighton Rock / Guitar Solo / Fat Bottomed Girls / Keep Yourself Alive / Bohemian Rhapsody / Tie Your Mother Down / Encore: Sheer Heart Attack / 2nd Encore: We Will Rock You / We Are The Champions / God Save The Queen

January 26
Forêt Nationale, Brussels

We Will Rock You / Let Me Entertain You / Somebody To Love / Medley: Death On Two Legs; Killer Queen; Bicycle Race; I'm In Love With My Car; Get Down Make Love; You're My Best Friend / Now I'm Here / Don't Stop Me Now / Spread Your Wings / Dreamers Ball / Love Of My Life / '39 / It's Late / Brighton Rock / Guitar Solo / Fat Bottomed Girls / Keep Yourself Alive / Bohemian Rhapsody / Tie Your Mother Down / Encore: Sheer Heart Attack / 2nd Encore: We Will Rock You / We Are The Champions / God Save The Queen

EMI release the band's thirteenth single, 'Don't Stop Me Now' coupled with John Deacon's 'In Only Seven Days', which goes on to attain a No.9 chart position. The American issue featured instead Roger Taylor's 'More Of That Jazz' as its flipside, as did the Japanese version, but

it only reached a disappointing No.86 in the *Billboard* chart.

January 27
Forêt Nationale, Brussels

January 29/30
Ahoy Hall, Rotterdam

First night: We Will Rock You / Let Me Entertain You / Somebody To Love / If You Can't Beat Them / Medley: Death On Two Legs; Killer Queen; Bicycle Race; I'm In Love With My Car; Get Down Make Love; You're My Best Friend / Now I'm Here / Don't Stop Me Now / Spread Your Wings / Dreamers Ball / Love Of My Life / '39 / It's Late / Brighton Rock / Guitar Solo / Keep Yourself Alive / Bohemian Rhapsody / Tie Your Mother Down / Encore: Sheer Heart Attack / 2nd Encore: We Will Rock You / We Are The Champions / God Save The Queen

Second night: The band performed 'Fat Bottomed Girls' in place of 'Beat Them'

February 1
Sportshalle, Cologne

We Will Rock You / Let Me Entertain You / Somebody To Love / If You Can't Beat Them / Medley: Death On Two Legs; Killer Queen; Bicycle Race; I'm In Love With My Car; Get Down Make Love / You're My Best Friend / Now I'm Here / Band Intro / Don't Stop Me Now / Spread Your Wings / Dreamers Ball / Love Of My Life / '39 / Brighton Rock / Guitar Solo / Keep Yourself Alive / Bohemian Rhapsody / Tie Your Mother Down / Encore: Sheer Heart Attack / 2nd Encore: We Will Rock You / We Are The Champions / God Save The Queen

Freddie's introduction to 'Death On Two Legs' here sheds interesting light on to what was frustratingly bleeped out of the 'Live Killers' album version: "This next song comes from 'A Night At The Opera'. It was conceived and written during the time we were having a lot of trouble with our managers... you understand what I mean! He was a real motherfucker of a gentleman, I don't know what you would call him over here... Schweinhund or whatever, but we also call him 'Death On Two Legs'."

When 'Death On Two Legs' appeared on the 'Opera' album credits with a "Dedicated To..." subtitle, EMI are believed to have paid an aggrieved Norman Sheffield a substantial sum of money not to delay its intended pre-Christmas release date with court proceedings. Sheffield had assumed it was an unsubtle dig at him, even though Queen had never actually intimated as much. No chances were taken with 'Live Killers' and the offending words were removed and replaced by three bleeps.

As you might imagine, Queen's split from Trident in 1975 was acrimonious to say the least. Freddie would later liken the experience to a lavatorial visit: "As far as Queen are concerned, our old management is deceased. They cease to exist in any capacity with us whatsoever. We feel so relieved. One leaves them behind like one leaves excreta."

After 'Love Of My Life', for which Roger and John were both absent, Brian reintroduced the band as follows: "I would like to welcome back to the stage, the rest of the band. On drums

and percussion... Mr Roger Meddows-Taylor. And on bass... Mr John Deacon. And on wondrous vocals... Mr Freddie Mercury." On 'Live Killers', he says: "I'd like to welcome back to the stage the rest of the Queen group. On drums and tiger skin trousers... Mr Roger Taylor. And on dazzling tie and bass guitar... Mr John Deacon. And on maracas and sometimes vocals... Mr Freddie Mercury."

February 2
Festhalle, Frankfurt

We Will Rock You / Let Me Entertain You / Somebody To Love / Medley: Death On Two Legs; Killer Queen; Bicycle Race; I'm In Love With My Car; Get Down Make Love; You're My Best Friend / Now I'm Here / Don't Stop Me Now / Spread Your Wings / Dreamers Ball / Love Of My Life / '39 / It's Late / Brighton Rock / Keep Yourself Alive / Bohemian Rhapsody / Tie Your Mother Down / Encore: Sheer Heart Attack / 2nd Encore: We Will Rock You / We Are The Champions / God Save The Queen

"'39' and 'Now I'm Here' from this show were used for the 'Live Killers' album. It has not been possible to establish which specific show each track on 'Live Killers' was recorded at. No-one, it seems, kept a record or documented such information and even Brian May cannot recall which songs were recorded at what venue.

February 4
Hallenstadium, Zurich

We Will Rock You / Let Me Entertain You / Somebody To Love / Medley: Death On Two Legs; Killer Queen; Bicycle Race; I'm In Love With My Car; Get Down Make Love; You're My Best Friend / Now I'm Here / Don't Stop Me Now / Spread Your Wings / Dreamers Ball / Love Of My Life / '39 / It's Late / Brighton Rock / Keep Yourself Alive / Bohemian Rhapsody / Tie Your Mother Down / Encore: Sheer Heart Attack / 2nd Encore: We Will Rock You / We Are The Champions / God Save The Queen

February 6
Dom Sportova, Zagreb

February 7
Tivoli Halle, Ljubljana

February 10/11
Basketball Halle, Munich

Bootleg recordings from this show present the set listing in entirely the wrong sequence, indicating that whoever was responsible for compiling the bootleg was unfamiliar with Queen's typical shows. Every one of Queen's tours is represented by at least two examples of this, and some of the track sequences are absurd.

February 13
Sporthalle Boeblingen, Stuttgart

February 15
Saalandhalle, Saarbrucken

February 17
Palais De Sport, Lyon

February 19/20/21
Palacio De Deportef, Barcelona

On the 20th, the band perform a dazzling 'Get Down Make Love' with vocal improvisation from Freddie that is even more elaborate than usual.

February 23
Pabellon Del Real Madrid

February 25
Les Arenas, Poitiers

February 27/28/March 1
Pavillion De Paris, Paris

All three shows at this venue were filmed for possible use in a documentary

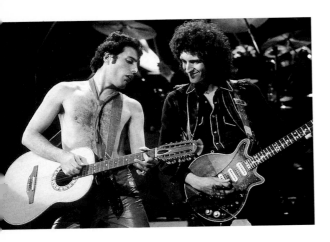

which ultimately never materialised. One of the shows, however, does feature at the annual Queen fan club conventions, but its general quality is clearly not worthy of a proper home video release. Unlike the familiar live video issues, the shows were filmed from one or two vantage points only, without the usual elaborate camera set-ups.

First night: *We Will Rock You / Let Me Entertain You / Somebody To Love / Fat Bottomed Girls / Medley: Death On Two Legs; Killer Queen; Bicycle Race; I'm In Love With My Car; Get Down Make Love; You're My Best Friend / Now I'm Here / Don't Stop Me Now / Spread Your Wings; Dreamers Ball / Love Of My Life / '39 / It's Late / Brighton Rock / Keep Yourself Alive / Fun It (Part Of) / Bohemian Rhapsody / Tie Your Mother Down / Encore: Sheer Heart Attack / 2nd Encore: We Will Rock You / We Are The Champions / God Save The Queen*

Second night: *We Will Rock You / Let Me Entertain You / Somebody To Love / If You Can't Beat Them / Medley: Death On Two Legs; Killer Queen; Bicycle Race; I'm In Love With My Car; Get Down Make Love; You're My Best Friend / Now I'm Here / Don't Stop Me Now / Spread Your Wings / Dreamers Ball / Love Of My Life / '39 / It's Late / Brighton Rock / Keep Yourself Alive / Bohemian Rhapsody / Tie Your Mother Down / Encore: Sheer Heart Attack / 2nd Encore: We Will Rock You / We Are The Champions / God Save The Queen*

Third night: *'Fat Bottomed Girls' was performed after 'Somebody', 'Beat Them' followed 'Don't Stop Me Now' and 'Mustapha (Intro)' preceded 'Bo Rhap', which was used for the 'Live Killers' album*

When Freddie notices that the same faces are again present in the front two rows of the audience, he acknowledges them by remarking aloud that the Royal Family are here again. The name sticks, and Freddie makes numerous further references to them at subsequent concerts.

The family consists mostly of British fans who travelled all around Europe with the band since the tour began. They also make a point of delivering a bouquet of flowers backstage to the band at every show too.

Each member of the family attending this concert did so with one additional item – a bicycle bell. At the appropriate point in the set they united in a chorus of bell-ringing, much to the surprise of the band and the French audience who promptly copied the idea the following night. By March 1, hundreds of bells were ringing, and they can even be heard on the 'Live Killers' album. Indeed, a bell can be seen on top of the piano of the album's back cover photograph, which was also taken in Paris.

On one occasion in France, members of the Royal Family approached a roadie before the show and handed him a bicycle bell to pass on to Freddie for use in the show. The confused roadie accepted the bell and disappeared with it. Sure enough, during the concert, Freddie walked over to the grinning faces in the front row – by now familiar to him – produced the bell and rang it. On another occasion, when the family discovered that John Deacon was rather fond of dry roasted peanuts, they handed out packets of them to fans entering the theatre prior to the show. When 'You're My Best Friend' – a John Deacon song – begins, the band were showered in nuts from all directions. Although their immediate reaction is one of shock, the band laugh when they realise the significance.

JAPAN 1979
Japan Tour

Queen embark upon what would prove to be their biggest ever tour of Japan – though by American and European standards, it is relatively small. Three weeks of performances open with two shows at the Budokan Hall in Tokyo, and move through a further seven cities. The tour ends with two shows in Sapporo.

'Teo Torriatte' is performed during this tour. Queen only ever included it in the set for Japanese shows.

April 13/14
Budokan Hall, Tokyo

First night: *We Will Rock You / Let Me Entertain You / Somebody To Love / Fat Bottomed Girls / Medley: Death On Two Legs; Killer Queen; Bicycle Race; I'm In Love With My Car; Get Down Make Love; You're My Best Friend / Now I'm Here / Teo Torriatte / Don't Stop Me Now / Dreamers Ball / Love Of My Life / '39 / It's Late / Brighton Rock / Keep Yourself Alive / Bohemian Rhapsody / Tie Your Mother Down / Encore: Sheer Heart Attack / 2nd Encore: We Will Rock You / We Are The Champions / God Save The Queen*

This concert was filmed and later broadcast on Japanese television.

April 19/20
Festival Hall, Osaka

First night: *We Will Rock You / Let Me Entertain You / Somebody To Love / Medley: Death On Two Legs; Killer Queen; Bicycle Race; I'm In Love With My Car; Get Down Make Love; You're My Best Friend / Now I'm Here / Teo Torriatte / Don't Stop Me Now / Spread Your Wings / Dreamers Ball / Love Of My Life / '39 / It's Late / Brighton Rock / Keep Yourself Alive / Bohemian Rhapsody / Tie Your Mother Down / Encore: Sheer Heart Attack / 2nd Encore: We Will Rock You / We Are The Champions / God Save The Queen*

April 21
Practica Ethics Commemoration Hall, Kanazawa

April 23/24/25
Budokan Hall, Tokyo

Second night: *We Will Rock You / Let Me Entertain You / Somebody To Love / Fat Bottomed Girls / Medley: Death On Two Legs; Killer Queen; Bicycle Race; I'm In Love With My Car; Get Down Make Love; You're My Best Friend / Now I'm Here / Teo Torriatte / Don't Stop Me Now / Dreamers Ball / Love Of My Life / '39 / It's Late / Brighton Rock / Keep Yourself Alive / Bohemian Rhapsody / Tie Your Mother Down / Encore: Sheer Heart Attack / Jailhouse Rock / 2nd Encore: We Will Rock You / We Are The Champions / God Save The Queen*

April 27
Central International Display, Kobe

'Jealousy'/'Fun It' (E46039) is released as an exclusively American single. Both tracks are taken from the 'Jazz' album, though because neither one ever featured in the live set, the disc fails to chart.

April 28
International Display, Nagoya

April 30/May 1
Kyuden Athletic Association, Fukuoka

May 2
Prefectural Athletic Association, Yamaguchi

May 5/6
Makomani Ice Arena, Sapporo

First night: We Will Rock You / Let Me Entertain You / Somebody To Love / Fat Bottomed Girls / Medley: Death On Two Legs; Killer Queen; Bicycle Race; I'm In Love With My Car; Get Down Make Love; You're My Best Friend / Now I'm Here / Teo Torriatte / Don't Stop Me Now / Dreamers Ball / Love Of My Life / '39 / It's Late / Brighton Rock / Keep Yourself Alive / Bohemian Rhapsody / Tie Your Mother Down / Encore: Sheer Heart Attack / 2nd Encore: We Will Rock You / We Are The Champions / God Save The Queen

June 22
Queen release their first live album, the long awaited and much overdue 'Live Killers'. A double album, it comprises twenty-two tracks recorded at various locations on the European tour, between January and March, 1979. It is issued four days later in America. In Japan it is made available in two forms: a double album available in red and green coloured vinyl, and an edited single album.

Despite four sides of material, there were some unavoidable omissions from the album, notably: 'Somebody To Love', 'If You Can't Beat Them', 'Fat Bottomed Girls', and 'It's Late'. EMI might have been better advised issuing a triple set.

One reason for Queen agreeing to issue a live album, which they would have much preferred not to have done, was to try and kerb the growth of bootlegs. In reality, it had come far too late. Fans were crying out for concert recordings as far back as 1974.

Brian: "Live albums are inescapable really. Everyone tells you you have to do them, and when you do, you find that they're very often not of mass appeal, and in the absence of a fluke condition, you sell your live album to the converted – the people who already know your stuff, and come to the concerts."

Many of the tracks from 'Live Killers' were used as B-sides on singles. Two, 'We Will Rock You' and 'Love Of My Life', were A-sides.

June 29
The first and only UK Queen single to feature two tracks recorded in concert is issued. 'Love Of My Life'/'Now I'm Here' are both lifted from the 'Killers' album, released just one week earlier. Packaged in a dull plain black sleeve, and given little promotion, the single stalls at No.63.

The same pairing is issued in Japan, though its unique full colour picture cover and lyric sheet makes it far more attractive than the UK equivalent.

'Love Of My Life' was not released in America. Instead Elektra went with an entirely different coupling from 'Live Killers': the two opening tracks, 'We Will Rock You' and 'Let Me Entertain You' (E46532), released August 24, 1979. While Japanese collectors received the same pairing (P486E) in a different sleeve, UK fans were denied it. They were given the opportunity to purchase the two tracks later, when they were issued as B-sides to the 'Crazy Little Thing Called Love' and 'Save Me' singles.

July
Queen purchase Mountain Studios in Montreux, Switzerland. The band first used the studios in 1978 to record parts of the 'Jazz' album, and later mixed 'Live Killers' there. David Richards is the resident sound engineer, and becomes good friends with Queen. He would later go on to co-engineer 'Hot Space' and 'A Kind Of Magic' (with Mack), co-engineer 'The Miracle' (with numerous others), and co-produce/ engineer the band's final album 'Innuendo'.

Roger Taylor also recorded his first solo album, 'Fun In Space', and some of his second, 'Strange Frontier', at Mountain Studios, and Queen would record the 'Flash Gordon' sessions and the David Bowie collaboration there also. Other artists who have recorded at Mountain Studios include David Bowie, Bryan Ferry, Chaka Khan, Chris Rea, Rick Wakeman and Status Quo.

August 18
Ludwigsparkstadion, Saarbrucken

We Will Rock You / Let Me Entertain You / If You Can't Beat Them / Medley: Mustapha; Death On Two Legs; Killer Queen; I'm In Love With My Car; Get Down Make Love; You're My Best Friend / Now I'm Here / Somebody To Love / Don't Stop Me Now / Spread Your Wings / Love Of My Life / '39 / It's Late / Keep Yourself Alive / Brighton Rock / Fat Bottomed Girls / Bohemian Rhapsody / Tie Your Mother Down / Encore: Sheer Heart Attack / Jailhouse Rock / 2nd Encore: We Will Rock You / We Are The Champions / God Save The Queen

Queen are the headlining act at this one day outdoor festival. Other artists on the bill are: Rory Gallagher, Red Baron, Molly Hatchet, Lake, Alvin Lee and Ten Years After, Voyager, and The Commodores, 30,000 people attend the show. Although the capacity crowd is not the largest to have attended a Queen show, the band are very aware that for a German venue, the turnout is hugely significant and a great compliment.

Due to a failed attempt at dying his hair earlier in the day, Roger is forced to play this show with bright green hair. He later recalls the experience as one of the most embarrassing of his life, not least because Freddie seizes every opportunity to ridicule him during the set. He manages to restore it to the intended colour immediately after the show.

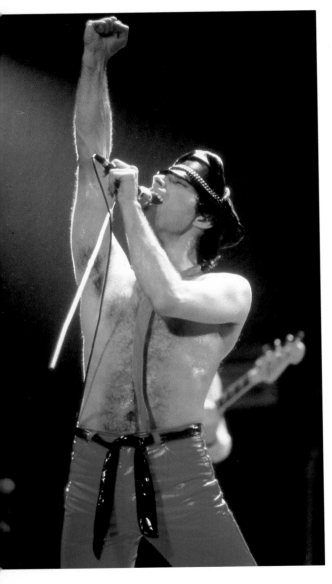

Photographs from this gig are few and far between. Perhaps Roger tracked them all down and disposed of them. Rumour has it that Roger demolished his drum kit after this show. He considered that a whole series of technical problems had spoilt his

performance, and so channelled his frustration into destroying the kit.

October 5

'Crazy Little Thing Called Love' is released in the UK as the first single from 'The Game' album. The 'Live Killers' opening track 'We Will Rock You' is chosen as the B-side. Unlike subsequent changes in musical direction, this one is extremely well received by most fans. Some, however, view the rockabilly song as Queen selling out, and joining the conformity bandwagon. The motorbike and leather image of the accompanying video is considered decidedly 'unQueen'.

At home the track peaks (yet again) at No. 2 but in America it gives Queen their long awaited first No. 1. The B-side, however, is different to the UK... the 'Live Killers' cut of John Deacon's 'Spread Your Wings' is chosen instead, as it is for Japanese release.

'Crazy Little Thing Called Love' also reached No. 1 in Canada, Mexico, Holland, Australia and New Zealand.

October 7
London Coliseum, London

Freddie takes part in a charity gala ballet. The event is organised to benefit the City of Westminster Society for Mentally Handicapped Children. Many of the world's most respected ballet companies offer their services, including Margot Fonteyn, Peter Schaufuss, Wayne Sleep and Anthony Dowell.

Having rehearsed his routine several times at the London Dance Centre earlier in the week, assisted by Derek Dene and Wayne Eagling (both principal dancers with the Royal Ballet), Freddie provided the finale to the show when he danced and sang 'Bohemian Rhapsody' and 'Crazy Little Thing Called Love' with an orchestral accompaniment.

When Freddie invites the audience to sing along to 'Crazy', he forgets that the song was only released two days earlier. Only the few Queen fans in attendance (and Roger Taylor), are able to comply. The event is a huge success, and one which Freddie enjoys immensely, and is very proud of.

Roger: "I was more nervous than he was. I mean, I wouldn't do it. That's

just not my scene. I'd like to see anyone else have the courage to do that – and carry it off as well as he did. He had a lot of balls to go on that stage. He loves all that stuff."

UK 1979
The Crazy Tour

The band begin a twenty date, four week tour which is made up of mostly small venues, in direct contrast to the huge stadiums which had for so long been the location of Queen's live shows. Although the band enjoy performing at large venues, and to the huge audiences that such places entail, they are also aware of the personal contact that is sacrificed in doing so. They now decide to revert to the type of venue more typical of their early concerts.

Tour organiser Gerry Stickells is given the task of locating any suitably appropriate sites. Among those he comes up with are: Tiffany's in Purley, The Lewisham Odeon and The Mayfair in Tottenham. The tour is christened the 'Crazy Tour'. The lighting rig for the shows on this tour was a modified version of the so called Pizza Oven.

The tour gets under way at the Royal Dublin Society Hall, and concludes at the Alexandra Palace, on December 22. The show on Boxing Day at the Hammersmith Odeon, is performed as a charity event.

November 22
Royal Dublin Society Hall, Dublin

Let Me Entertain You / Somebody To Love / If You Can't Beat Them / Medley: Mustapha; Death On Two Legs; Killer Queen; I'm In Love With My Car; Get Down Make Love; You're My Best Friend / Save Me / Now I'm Here / Don't Stop Me Now / Love Of My Life / '39 / Fat Bottomed Girls / Brighton Rock / Keep Yourself Alive / Bohemian Rhapsody / Tie Your Mother Down / Encore: Danny Boy / Crazy Little Thing Called Love / 2nd Encore: Sheer Heart Attack / We Will Rock You / We Are The Champions

Although the accelerated version of 'We Will Rock You' no longer opens the show, the slower version still features late in the set.

'Save Me' is performed for the very first time. Freddie introduces it as a song written by Brian, which will be released as the band's new single. Brian plays piano, but is handed his guitar in time for the solo.

'Save Me' is released in the UK eight weeks later, as the second single from 'The Game'.

'Mustapha' from the 'Jazz' album is used during this tour to commence the medley. 'Fat Bottomed Girls', 'Bicycle Race' and 'Dreamers Ball' are all dropped.

This was Queen's first show in Ireland. They perform a specially rehearsed version of 'Danny Boy'. It is the one and only time they do so. They do not close the show with 'God Save The Queen'.

November 24
National Exhibition Centre, Birmingham

Let Me Entertain You / Somebody To Love / If You Can't Beat Them / Medley: Mustapha; Death On Two Legs; Killer Queen; I'm In Love With My Car; Get Down Make Love; You're My Best Friend / Save Me / Now I'm Here / Don't Stop Me Now / Love Of My Life / '39 / Brighton Rock / Keep Yourself Alive / Bohemian Rhapsody / Tie Your Mother Down / Crazy Little Thing Called Love / Encore: Sheer Heart Attack / 2nd Encore: We Will Rock You / We Are The Champions / God Save The Queen

During 'Don't Stop Me Now' member's of the 'Royal Family' do a Conga at the back of the hall. The venue's security staff also partake.

With 14,000 attending, this was the largest venue on the tour.

Under the headline Cold And Dirty in the *Birmingham Evening Mail* on November 26, 1979, Stafford Hildred writes:

"QUEEN got a right royal reception from 14,000 loyal subjects in the giant Hall at the NEC.

"It's a pity the setting was so unsuitable. Cold, dirty and acoustically appalling, at £4 a ticket the fans deserved more, much more.

"Still the stars of the show were in impressive form. The range and versatility that have elevated Queen to super-group status was all there.

"But the outfit were forced to pump out such volume to fill the hall that the distortion of the sound ruined the effect, unless you joined the Twickenham-style maul in front of the stage.

"After battling to be with the seething mass of real enthusiasts, the performance sounded much better. I didn't think the intricate recordings that Queen delight in would be possible to recreate live.

"And they weren't quite, but they came so close you couldn't complain. NEC organisers have tried to improve the concert sound quality, but they certainly haven't got it right yet."

November 26/27
Apollo Theatre, Manchester

First night: Let Me Entertain You / Somebody To Love / Medley: Mustapha; Death On Two Legs; Killer Queen; I'm In Love With My Car; Get Down Make Love; You're My Best Friend / Save Me / Now I'm Here / Don't Stop Me Now / Love Of My Life / '39 / Brighton Rock / Keep Yourself Alive / Bohemian Rhapsody / Tie Your Mother Down / Encore: Sheer Heart Attack / 2nd Encore: We Will Rock You / We Are The Champions / God Save The Queen

Second night: Begins with 'Rock You (Fast)', and 'Liar' followed 'Brighton Rock'

Having already been at the preceding night's show, members of the Royal Family are again in attendance at this gig. They record the show, and from the cassette transcribe the lyrics to the not yet available 'Save Me'. The following night they hand out copies to fans as they enter the theatre. When Freddie introduces the song as the band's next single, he is unprepared for fans joining in with him and accompanying the song almost word perfect. It is only when Freddie spots fans reading and singing from their prompt sheets, that the explanation is apparent. He appreciates the gesture.

Prior to the show on the second night, the Royal Family send a card to the band. Because 'Liar' had been absent from the previous night's show, the card reads; "If you want to get to Glasgow alive, you'd better play 'Liar' tonight". They do.

Mick Middles, of *Sounds*, attended this show, and apparently realised a fondness for Queen he had not anticipated. Beneath the headline MORE THAN OK, Fred, he wrote:

"THE ULTIMATE rock show. Glittering and glorious. A music form that has long since reached its peak. I hate good/bad old rock music, but I can even enjoy cricket when it's played properly. The music of Queen pours from the sky and unless you are equipped with suitable weatherwear, you are going to get wet. I was drenched.

"I have never felt the slightest desire to listen to a Queen album since the heady days of 'Night At The Opera'. A string of awful (albeit cleverly awful) singles have succeeded only in transforming my lack of desire into a snobbish lack of respect. Do you catch my drift? You are anticipating another hatchet job, right? You are wrong. Y'see, I really hated Queen until... 8.45 Monday evening, when the rock band Queen ceremoniously exploded into life on the Manchester Apollo stage.

"Queen's Freddie Mercury bobbed charismatically into the centre of the crowd's attention, a confusing mass of flashing lights and pounding opening chords turned the initial tenseness into a staggering spectacle. Queen played with courage and, to my utter surprise, total conviction. I never imagined for one moment that they could be THIS good. The show (for it was a show rather than a gig) continued to impress me with its professional ferocity. Dozens of familiar and totally meaningless songs seemed to change into enjoyable tunes packed with satirical humour. A humour that was never apparent to me before...

"I left the Apollo in a state of absolute amazement. The realisation that I'd actually enjoyed every second of a credibility-blowing Queen gig was beginning to burn away at my confused mind. There is no hope for me now."

November 30/December 1
Apollo Theatre, Glasgow

We Will Rock You / Let Me Entertain You / Somebody To Love / If You Can't Beat Them / Medley: Mustapha; Death On Two Legs; Killer Queen; I'm In Love With My Car; Get Down Make Love; You're My Best Friend / Save Me / Now I'm Here / Don't Stop Me Now / Spread Your Wings / Love Of My Life / '39 / Fat Bottomed Girls / Keep Yourself Alive / Brighton Rock / Crazy Little Thing Called Love / Bohemian Rhapsody / Tie Your Mother Down / Encore: Sheer Heart Attack / 2nd Encore: We Will Rock You / We Are The Champions / God Save The Queen

On the second night 'Liar' was performed after 'Brighton Rock'.

'Crazy Little Thing Called Love' featured Brian swapping his beloved red-special home made guitar for a Fender Stratocaster, while Freddie assisted on a twelve-string acoustic guitar, the strings of which he would frequently break. Fred Mandel meanwhile, who provided 'rip-roaring' piano on 'Works' album tracks (among other things), also joined the band on stage to help out on piano.

Although the track featured constantly throughout the remaining Crazy tour shows, and in all subsequent tours, amazingly it was not included on the 'Live Magic' album of December 1986. It is one of a handful of tracks which was sacrificed because of the lack of space.

On the second night, having sung only the opening lines of 'I'm In Love With My Car', Roger experiences a mental block and forgets the rest. He continues with an occasional word or two, until Freddie eventually helps out with some improvised vocals. The bootleg copy of this show is worth getting hold of, if only to hear this rare moment.

December 3/4
City Hall, Newcastle-Upon-Tyne

First night: We Will Rock You / Let Me Entertain You / Somebody To Love / If You Can't Beat Them / Medley: Mustapha; Death On Two Legs; Killer Queen; I'm In Love With My Car; Get Down Make Love; You're My Best Friend / Save Me / Now I'm Here / Don't Stop Me Now / Spread Your Wings / Love Of My Life / '39 / Fat Bottomed Girls / Keep Yourself Alive / Crazy Little Thing Called Love / Bohemian Rhapsody / Tie Your Mother Down / Encore: Sheer Heart Attack / 2nd Encore: We Will Rock You / We Are The Champions / God Save The Queen

Second night: Jailhouse Rock / We Will Rock You / Let Me Entertain You / Somebody To Love / If You Can't Beat Them / Medley: Mustapha; Death On Two Legs; Killer Queen; I'm In Love With My Car; Get Down Make Love; You're My Best Friend / Save Me / Now I'm Here / Don't Stop Me Now / Spread Your Wings / Love Of My Life / '39 / Keep Yourself Alive / Guitar Solo / Liar / Crazy Little Thing Called Love / Bohemian Rhapsody / Tie Your Mother Down / Encore: Sheer Heart Attack / 2nd Encore: We Will Rock You / We Are The Champions / God Save The Queen

The title of the bootleg from this show – 'Mack Attack' – would seem to have been inspired by Rheinhardt Mack, who was responsible for co-producing (with Queen) and engineering 'The Game' album, even though only two tracks from it, 'Save Me' and 'Crazy Little Thing...', actually feature in the set at this time. Mack would subsequently co-produce the 'Flash Gordon' soundtrack, and co-produce/engineer 'Hot Space', 'The Works' and 'A Kind Of Magic' albums.

December 6/7
Empire Theatre, Liverpool

December 9
Hippodrome, Bristol

December 10/11
Brighton Centre, Brighton

Harvey Goldsmith Entertainments Presents

QUEEN

CRAZY TOUR OF LONDON
at The Lyceum Ballroom
The Strand WC2
on Thursday 13th December 1979
show starts 8.00 p.m.

Tickets £4.75 each   N° 4416

December 13
Lyceum Ballroom, London

December 14
Rainbow Theatre, London

December 17
Tiffany's, Purley

December 19
Tottenham Mayfair, London

The band performed this show with no lighting rig. The venue is too small to accommodate it.

Freddie is very talkative during the show, and discusses the presents he is buying for Christmas.

December 20
Lewisham Odeon, London

December 22
Alexandra Palace, London

Most of the 'Save Me' promotional video footage was recorded at this show. The finished film, which includes animated sections conceived by Brian May, later featured on popular British

CONCERTS FOR THE PEOPLE OF
KAMPUCHEA

THE CLASH
ELVIS COSTELLO & THE ATTRACTIONS
IAN DURY & THE BLOCKHEADS
PAUL McCARTNEY & WINGS
PRETENDERS QUEEN ROCKESTRA
ROCKPILE THE SPECIALS
THE WHO

television programmes of the time including *Swap Shop* and *Tiswas*.

December 26
Hammersmith Odeon, London

Jailhouse Rock / We Will Rock You / Let Me Entertain You / Somebody To Love / If You Can't Beat Them / Medley: Mustapha; Death On Two Legs; Killer Queen; I'm In Love With My Car; Get Down Make Love; You're My Best Friend / Save Me / Now I'm Here / Don't Stop Me Now / Spread Your Wings / Love Of My Life / '39 / Fat Bottomed Girls / Keep Yourself Alive / Silent Night (Part Of) / Crazy Little Thing Called Love: Crazy Reprise / Bohemian Rhapsody / Tie Your Mother Down / Encore: Sheer Heart Attack / 2nd Encore: We Will Rock You / We Are The Champions / God Save The Queen

Queen were approached by Paul McCartney to perform this show as part of the Concerts For Kampuchea. Apart from his own band Wings, he, and promoter Harvey Goldsmith had secured performances from several other artists.

Four separate shows are planned but Queen would be the only group to appear on the first night. Unlike most other artists, they played a full set. All four shows were conceived, organised and promoted by Harvey Goldsmith, on behalf of the High Commission For Refugees and UNICEF, for the sole purpose of raising funds to purchase food and aid for the people of Kampuchea (now Cambodia).

The concerts were filmed and later edited for a television broadcast. It was eventually screened in the UK in March 1980. Peter Ustinov introduced Queen's material ('Now I'm Here' and 'Crazy Little Thing Called Love') and this was later utilised in the 'Magic Years' video, but in an entirely different context.

It was also given an American television airing at some point, and some of the remaining Queen material has since been screened at fan club conventions. It provides conclusive evidence that the entire programme is another example of concert footage worthy of a proper release. It really is exceptional.

Bootleg recordings of this show feature 'Silent Night' as the first track. It in fact preceded 'Crazy', as part of Brian's guitar solo. The solo also incorporated parts of 'Three Blind Mice'.

January 25

Brian May's 'Save Me' is issued in the UK as the second single from 'The Game'. It is backed with 'Let Me Entertain You' from the double live set, and reaches No.11 in the charts. Though 'Save Me' is also released in Japan, backed with the live cut of 'Spread Your Wings', it remains unissued in America.

May 30

'Play The Game' is issued in the UK as the third single from 'The Game', even though the actual album was still not yet available – a most unusual situation. Roger Taylor's non-album track 'A Human Body' is the B-side. In America the same pairing (released a week later to coincide with American and Canadian dates) peaks at No.42, while at home it fared better in reaching No.14.

USA 1980
The Game Tour

Queen fly to Los Angeles on June 19 for seven days of rehearsals ahead of the impending American tour. It entails forty-six shows over a three month period, the biggest tour Queen would ever undertake. Every one of the forty-six shows was performed before a capacity audience. The itinerary included four consecutive nights at the Los Angeles Forum and four at Madison Square Garden in New York.

The new lighting rig is called 'The Fly Swatters', and is made up of a number of moving arms (operated by a hidden roadie) covered in banks of lights, which rise up and down during the show. The crew refer to the individual pieces as G2 Razors. When the numerous sections work together in unison, they are an awesome sight. The rig would also be utilised on the 1980 Winter European tour (including the UK dates), the five Japanese Budokan shows (in February 1981) and for the two Canadian (Forum) shows in November 1981. The rig can be seen on the 'We Will Rock You' video.

As well as opening with 'Jailhouse Rock', the set now includes new material from 'The Game' – 'Play The Game', 'Need Your Loving Tonight' and 'Dragon Attack'. 'Save Me' and 'Crazy' had already been incorporated

into the set the previous November. 'Rock It' would feature in the set later. 'Fat Bottomed Girls' is back in the set again, on quite a regular basis.

June 30
PNE Coliseum, Vancouver, British Columbia

Jailhouse Rock / We Will Rock You / Let Me Entertain You / Need Your Loving Tonight / Play The Game / Medley: Mustapha; Death On Two Legs; Killer Queen; I'm In Love With My Car; Get Down Make Love / Somebody To Love / Save Me / Now I'm Here / Dragon Attack / Fat Bottomed Girls / Love Of My Life / Keep Yourself Alive / Brighton Rock / Guitar Solo / Crazy Little Thing Called Love / Bohemian Rhapsody / Tie Your Mother Down / Encore: Another One Bites The Dust / Sheer Heart Attack / 2nd Encore: We Will Rock You / We Are The Champions / God Save The Queen

June 30

'The Game' is released worldwide and reaches No.1 all over Europe. It is also Queen's first chart topping album in North America. Although the original album title is 'Play The Game', it is shortened when Roger objects to its implications of conformity.

Though seven tracks from the album are included in the live set (at various times), three are not. Roger Taylor's provocatively titled 'Coming Soon' is perhaps an inevitable omission, but Brian May's 'Sail Away Sweet Sister' would have been ideal for the acoustic part of the show. Ironically, this ballad later materialised at a Guns n' Roses live show, during one of their tours in 1990/91, for which Brian made a guest appearance. Freddie's tongue in cheek 'Don't Try Suicide' was the other concert absentee. 'You're My Best Friend' is dropped from the set on this tour.

July 1
Seattle Coliseum, Seattle

July 2
Portland Coliseum, Portland, Oregon

July 5
Sports Arena, San Diego

During 'Crazy Little Thing Called Love' Freddie breaks a guitar string. He makes a joke of it by explaining to the audience that in twenty years he only ever managed to master two chords. This was not an isolated incident, he can also be seen at the 1979 Kampuchia benefit concert, playing with a broken string.

July 6
Compton Terrace, Phoenix

July 8/9/11/12
The Forum, Los Angeles

Third night: Jailhouse Rock / We Will Rock You / Let Me Entertain You / Need Your Loving Tonight / Play The Game / Medley: Mustapha; Death On Two Legs; Killer Queen; I'm In Love With My Car; Get Down Make Love / Somebody To Love / Save Me / Now I'm Here / Dragon Attack / Fat Bottomed Girls / Love Of My Life / Keep Yourself Alive / Brighton Rock / Guitar Solo / Crazy Little Thing Called Love / Bohemian Rhapsody / Tie Your Mother Down / Encore: Another One Bites The Dust / Sheer Heart Attack / 2nd Encore: We Will Rock You / We Are The Champions / God Save The Queen

Final night: We Will Rock You / Let Me Entertain You / Need Your Loving Tonight / Play The Game / Medley: Mustapha; Death On Two Legs; Killer Queen; I'm In Love With My Car; Get Down Make Love / Somebody To Love / Save Me / Now I'm Here / Dragon Attack / Fat Bottomed Girls / Love Of My Life / Keep Yourself Alive / Brighton Rock / Guitar Solo / Crazy Little Thing Called Love / Bohemian Rhapsody / Tie Your Mother Down / Encore: Another One Bites The Dust / Sheer Heart Attack / 2nd Encore: Jailhouse Rock / We Will Rock You / We Are The Champions / God Save The Queen

July 13/14
Oakland Coliseum, Oakland, California

Second night: We Will Rock You / Let Me Entertain You / Need Your Loving Tonight / Play The Game / Medley: Mustapha; Death On Two Legs; Killer Queen; I'm In Love With My Car; Get Down Make Love / Somebody To Love / Save Me / Now I'm Here / Dragon Attack / Fat Bottomed Girls / Love Of My Life / Keep Yourself Alive / Brighton Rock / Guitar Solo / Crazy Little Thing Called Love / Bohemian Rhapsody / Tie Your Mother Down / Encore: Another One Bites The Dust / Sheer Heart Attack / 2nd Encore: Jailhouse Rock / We Will Rock You / We Are The Champions / God Save The Queen

August 5
Mid South Coliseum, Memphis, Tennessee

August 6
Riverside Centroplex, Baton Rouge, Louisiana

August 8
City Myriad, Oklahoma, Oklahoma City

August 9
Reunion, Dallas, Texas

August 10
Summit, Houston, Texas

August 12
The Omni, Atlanta, Georgia

'Another One Bites The Dust' is released in the US, as 'The Game's' third single. It is coupled with Freddie's 'Don't Try Suicide', and provides Queen with their second American number one. At home Brian May's 'Dragon Attack' was chosen to back the track. It was issued ten days later, and reached No.7. The Japanese issue, which featured the same pairing as the US, was held back until September 25.

August 13
Charlotte Coliseum, Charlotte, North Carolina

August 14
Greensboro Coliseum, Greensboro, North Carolina

August 16
Civic Center, Charleston, South Carolina

August 17
Riverton Coliseum, Cincinnati, Ohio

August 20
Civic Center, Hartford, Connecticut

August 22
Spectrum, Philadelphia, Pennsylvania

The UK's fourth and last single from 'The Game' is released. Backed with 'Dragon Attack', John Deacon's 'Another One Bites The Dust' reaches No.7 in England, but is a spectacular success in America, where it storms into the charts at No.1, and remains there for over a month. The disc sells over 3 million copies. It is Elektra's first single to do so. Both the American and Japanese issues featured 'Don't Try Suicide' as the B-side.

August 23
Civic Center, Baltimore, Maryland

August 24
Civic Center, Pittsburgh, Pennsylvania

August 26
Civic Center, Providence, Rhode Island

Jailhouse Rock / We Will Rock You / Let Me Entertain You / Play The Game / Medley: Mustapha; Death On Two Legs; Killer Queen; I'm In Love With My Car; Get Down Make Love / Somebody To Love / Save Me / Now I'm Here / Dragon Attack / Fat Bottomed Girls / Love Of My Life / Keep Yourself Alive / Brighton Rock / Guitar Solo: Drum Solo / Crazy Little Thing Called Love / Bohemian Rhapsody / Tie Your Mother Down / Encore: Another One Bites The Dust / Sheer Heart Attack / 2nd Encore: We Will Rock You / We Are The Champions / God Save The Queen

August 27
Spectrum, Portland, Maine

August 29
The Forum, Montreal, Quebec

August 30
CNE Grandstand, Toronto

Jailhouse Rock / We Will Rock You / Let Me Entertain You / Play The Game / Medley: Mustapha; Death On Two Legs; Killer Queen; I'm In Love With My Car; Get Down Make Love / Somebody To Love / Save Me / Now I'm

Here / Dragon Attack / Fat Bottomed Girls / Love Of My Life / Keep Yourself Alive / Brighton Rock / Guitar Solo / Crazy Little Thing Called Love / Bohemian Rhapsody / Tie Your Mother Down / Encore: Another One Bites The Dust / Sheer Heart Attack / 2nd Encore: We Will Rock You / We Are The Champions / God Save The Queen

After this show the band fly home for a six day break before resuming the tour again in Milwaukee.

September 10
Mecca, Milwaukee, Wisconsin

Jailhouse Rock / We Will Rock You / Let Me Entertain You / Play The Game / Medley: Mustapha; Death On Two Legs; Killer Queen; I'm In Love With My Car; Get Down Make Love / Somebody To Love / Save Me / Now I'm Here / Dragon Attack / Fat Bottomed Girls / Love Of My Life / Keep Yourself Alive / Brighton Rock / Guitar Solo / Crazy Little Thing Called Love / Bohemian Rhapsody / Tie Your Mother Down / Encore: Another One Bites The Dust / Sheer Heart Attack / 2nd Encore: We Will Rock You / We Are The Champions / God Save The Queen

September 11
Market Square Arena, Indianapolis, Indiana

September 13
Civic Center, Omaha, Nebraska

September 14
St Paul Civic Center, Minneapolis, Minnesota

September 16
Kemper Arena, Kansas City, Missouri

September 17
Checkerdome, St Louis, Missouri

September 19
Horizon, Chicago, Illinois

Jailhouse Rock / We Will Rock You / Let Me Entertain You / Play The Game / Medley: Mustapha; Death On Two Legs; Killer Queen; I'm In Love With My Car; Get Down Make Love / Somebody To Love / Save Me / Now I'm Here / Dragon Attack / Fat Bottomed Girls / Love Of My Life / Keep Yourself Alive / Brighton Rock / Guitar Solo / Crazy Little Thing Called Love / Bohemian Rhapsody / Tie Your Mother Down / Encore: Another One Bites The Dust / Sheer Heart Attack / 2nd Encore: We Will Rock You / We Are The Champions / God Save The Queen

Freddie's opening lines here: "Do you realise that this is the first time we've come here when there's no snow on the ground... fucking good job too... I'll tell ya!"

Later on: "Do you think I should keep this moustache?" – (mixed reaction) – "Did you say no? Fuck off! Actually a lot of people really hated it in San Francisco... they told me to shave it off... and I told them to fuck off, I really did. We're gonna detour for a dirty song right now. We're gonna dedicate this next song to anybody here with a huge pair of tits - BIG PAIR OF TITS - and a BIG arse. Do you know what I'm talking about? 'Fat Bottomed Girls'."

The acoustics at this venue were evidently not as good as they might have been. This irritated Brian in particular, as he encountered problems during augmented guitar solos: "There seems to be just a little bit of echo in this place. We used to play in a place called The Stadium... isn't that right? They told us this place was better, is that right too? I really don't know. In this age of computer acoustic design, how they can design a place this bad, I do not understand... it's very strange. There's only one reason for coming to this place, and that's one of the best rock and roll audiences in the country – you really are. I'd better stop talking." Someone shouts: "Yeah... play that guitar!" Brian complies: "This is a song we used to do some time ago, and we've just revived it. It's called 'Love Of My Life'."

September 20
Joe Louis Arena, Detroit

September 21
Cleveland Coliseum, Cleveland, Ohio

September 23
Veterans' Memorial Coliseum, New Haven, Connecticut

September 24
War Memorial, Syracuse, New York
Set: Same as September 19

September 26
Boston Gardens, Boston, Massachusetts

September 28/29/30/ October 1
Madison Square Garden, New York

Following a holiday the band work upon the *Flash Gordon* soundtrack album. The sessions conclude in November.

September 28,29,30 1980
Madison Square Garden

November 20

Queen leave London and head for Zurich, for two days' rehearsal, before the European Tour begins.

EUROPEAN TOUR 1980

November 23
Hallenstadion, Zurich

Jailhouse Rock / We Will Rock You / Let Me Entertain You / Play The Game / Medley: Mustapha; Death On Two Legs; Killer Queen; I'm In Love With My Car; Get Down Make Love / Need Your Loving Tonight / Save Me / Now I'm Here; Dragon Attack; Now I'm Here (Reprise) / Fat Bottomed Girls / Love Of My Life / Keep Yourself Alive / Instrumental Inferno / Battle Theme / The Hero / Brighton Rock / Guitar Solo / Crazy Little Thing Called Love / Bohemian Rhapsody / Tie Your Mother Down / Encore: Another One Bites The Dust / Sheer Heart Attack / 2nd Encore: We Will Rock You / We Are The Champions / God Save The Queen

The Support band are fellow Brits Straight Eight.

'Flash's Theme', 'Battle Theme' and 'The Hero' from the *Flash Gordon* soundtrack album, are all performed during this tour.

For the first encore Freddie is carried on stage on the shoulders of the Darth Vader character from the *Star Wars* film, in reality band bodyguard Wally Verson. During the 1979 UK tour Freddie had been carried on stage by Superman.

November 24

The only single to be issued from the *Flash Gordon* soundtrack album is released in the UK. Backed with 'Football Fight', the film's main theme

'Flash' reaches No.10. The same pairing is issued universally, but in most cases, not until January 1981.

November 25
Le Bourget La Retonde

Jailhouse Rock / We Will Rock You / Let Me Entertain You / Play The Game / Medley: Mustapha; Death On Two Legs; Killer Queen; I'm In Love With My Car; Get Down Make Love / Need Your Loving Tonight / Save Me / Now I'm Here; Dragon Attack; Now I'm Here (Reprise) / Fat Bottomed Girls / Love Of My Life / Keep Yourself Alive / Instrumental Inferno / Battle Theme / The Hero / Brighton Rock / Guitar Solo / Crazy Little Thing Called Love / Bohemian Rhapsody / Tie Your Mother Down / Encore: Another One Bites The Dust / Sheer Heart Attack / 2nd Encore: We Will Rock You / We Are The Champions / God Save The Queen

November 26
Sportshalle, Cologne

Set: same as previous night

November 27
Groenoordhalle, Leiden

Set: same as November 25

November 29
Grundhalle, Essen

Jailhouse Rock / We Will Rock You / Let Me Entertain You / Play The Game / Medley: Mustapha; Death On Two Legs; Killer Queen; I'm In Love With My Car; Get Down Make Love / Need Your Loving Tonight / Save Me / Now I'm Here; Dragon Attack; Now I'm Here (Reprise) / Fat Bottomed Girls / Love Of My Life / Keep Yourself Alive / Instrumental Inferno / Battle Theme / The Hero / Brighton Rock / Guitar Solo / Crazy Little Thing Called Love / Bohemian Rhapsody / Tie Your Mother Down / Encore: Another One Bites The Dust / Sheer Heart Attack / 2nd Encore: We Will Rock You / We Are The Champions / God Save The Queen

November 30
Deutschlandhalle, Berlin

Set: same as previous night

The band have a synthesizer on stage for the first time on this tour, so that the 'Flash Gordon' medley can be performed.

December 1
Stadthalle, Bremen

December 5/6
NEC, Birmingham

Jailhouse Rock / We Will Rock You / Let Me Entertain You / Play The Game / Medley: Mustapha; Death On Two Legs; Killer Queen; I'm In Love With My Car; Get Down Make Love / Need Your Loving Tonight / Save Me / Now I'm Here; Dragon Attack; Now I'm Here (Reprise) / Fat Bottomed Girls / Love Of My Life / Keep Yourself Alive / Battle Theme / The Hero / Brighton Rock / Guitar Solo / Crazy Little Thing Called Love / Bohemian Rhapsody / Tie Your Mother Down / Encore: Another One Bites The Dust / Sheer Heart Attack / 2nd Encore: We Will Rock You / We Are The Champions / God Save The Queen

Queen were the first band to play at this (all seat) venue.

A press review the following morning by *Melody Maker's* Patrick Humphries summarised the show rather well, although he was evidently unfamiliar with many Queen traditions such as the band leaving the stage during the 'Bo Rhap' operatic section, and leaving a taped recording and lighting rig extravaganza to fill the space, and a reference to an acoustic 'Save Me', in fact relates to 'Love Of My Life'.

"If you want to be absolutely accurate, Queen are not the first band to play Birmingham's National Exhibition Centre. That honour fell to Straight Eight, who have been the opening act for Queen on their current European tour. They delivered a crisp, fast-paced set, but which tended to get lost in the vast auditorium.

"But the capacity 10,500 people had not come to see Straight Eight, they were there to pay yearly homage to the visiting monarch. The Arena is a perfect venue for a rock show, everything under one roof, from trains to fish and chips. Acoustically, from where I was sitting, Queen sounded fine.

"...The cheers escalate to a crescendo as the band hit the stage and crash straight into 'Jailhouse Rock'. A tacit acknowledgement from Mercury greets the hysteria which followed the first number, and it's off into 'We Will Rock You'. Well no quibbles about the beginning, straight, no-nonsense down the line rock'n'roll. That was the real eye-opener of the evening as far as I was concerned. Wrenched away from the antiseptic cotton wool of the recording studio, Queen tore through their set with a force that could have registered on the Richter Scale.

"The deliberate crowd-pleasers fulfilled their function – 'Rock You', 'We Are The Champions', 'Mustapha' (ample proof of Mercury's extraordinary voice), 'Love Of My Life' and 'Play The Game'. But it was the ranch-filled rockers that got more upraised arms than a Nuremberg Rally. 'Killer Queen', 'Fat Bottomed Girls' (great opening) and 'Crazy Little Thing Called Love': a neat amalgam of Fats Domino's 'I'm Ready' and The Everly Brother's 'Bye Bye Love'.

"As front man, ringmaster and manipulator, Mercury is incomparable. Exhorting, cajoling the audience, worshipped because of his inaccessibility, a perfect post-Ziggy Stardust idol, remote and idolised. If that's how you like your heroes, then fine.

"As a guitarist, Brian May is superb, running the gamut of guitar virtuosity, utilising all manner of technical effects, but never disguising his innate ability. 'Save Me' was simply Brian May and Mercury and acoustic guitar, the audience doing most of the singing, demonstrating the empathy

between band and crowd. 'Bohemian Rhapsody' worked well, apart from the fact the band weren't on stage during the middle of it.

"The hugely successful 'Another One Bites The Dust' (I wonder if John Deacon had been listening to Chic's 'Good Times'?) and 'Sheer Heart Attack' wrapped it up. Queen quit the stage, while the crowd sang 'You'll Never Walk Alone', then the band returned to rock us all again. Mercury was carried on by Darth Vadar ('Darth On Two Legs'?).

"'God Save The Queen'. End. The lights go up, the crowd go home, their fantasies fulfilled. I enjoyed it considerably more than I thought I would. As an event, a Queen gig is certainly impressive, and however objectively you may view Queen and their music, it is difficult not to be impressed by the spectacle.

"Impressed, but not necessarily involved. It is a strange feeling to be alone at the heart of a crowd. Queen

fans are familiar with, and expect, every cadence and note, variation is permitted within reason, but it is familiarity that breeds content. The kid next to me had come down from Leeds for the gig. 'And it were bloody worth it,' according to him. That is who Queen are playing for."

Second night: same as first night but with 'Flash' between 'Battle Theme' and 'The Hero'

December 8/9/10
Wembley Arena, London
First night: Jailhouse Rock / We Will Rock You / Let Me Entertain You / Play The Game / Medley: Mustapha; Death On Two Legs; Killer Queen; I'm In Love With My Car; Get Down Make Love / Need Your Loving Tonight / Save Me / Now I'm Here; Dragon Attack; Now I'm Here (Reprise) / Fat Bottomed Girls / Love Of My Life / Keep Yourself Alive / Flash / The Hero / Brighton Rock / Guitar Solo / Crazy Little Thing Called Love / Bohemian Rhapsody / Tie Your Mother Down / Encore: Another One Bites The Dust / Sheer Heart Attack / 2nd Encore: We Will Rock You / We Are The Champions / God Save The Queen

Following the opening number, Freddie greets the London audience with the words: "It's fucking cold in this auditorium, especially for those at the back. Don't worry, we'll soon set your arses on fire!" He then launches into a blistering recitation of 'We Will Rock You'.

On December 8, the *Flash Gordon* soundtrack album is released in the UK. Because it consists of snippets of dialogue from the movie, with predominantly instrumental accompaniment, only three tracks ('Flash's Theme', 'Battle Theme' and 'The Hero') are appropriate for the live show. All are Brian May compositions.

The American release was held back until January 27, 1981. It reaches No. 23 in the *Billboard* charts. In the UK it peaked at No. 10.

Second night: We Will Rock You / Let Me Entertain You / Play The Game / Medley: Mustapha; Death On Two Legs; Killer Queen; I'm In Love With My Car; Get Down Make Love / Save Me / Now I'm Here; Dragon Attack; Now I'm Here (Reprise) / Fat Bottomed Girls / Love Of My Life / Imagine / Keep Yourself Alive / Instrumental Inferno / Battle Theme / Flash /The Hero / Brighton Rock / Guitar Solo / Crazy Little Thing Called Love / Bohemian Rhapsody /Tie Your Mother Down / Encore: Another One Bites The Dust / Sheer Heart Attack / 2nd Encore: We Will Rock You /We Are The Champions / God Save The Queen

Queen play 'Imagine' as a tribute to John Lennon, who had been shot dead by deranged Beatle fan Mark Chapman in New York the previous day. Like everyone touched by Lennon's spirit, the band were devastated by the news and wanted to pay tribute to Lennon in their show. Limited rehearsal time did not permit quite as good a rendition of the ballad as the band would have liked, but the technical quality was secondary to the gesture.

Roger (in 1981): "John Lennon was my ultimate hero. He was the best living songwriter, and one of the best rock'n'roll voices I've ever heard. And when you think of what he did in his life, he stood up for what he thought was right. I just couldn't believe it, I still haven't quite come to terms with the fact that he's not here any more."

Final night: *Jailhouse Rock / We Will Rock You / Let Me Entertain You / Play The Game / Medley: Mustapha; Death On Two Legs; Killer Queen; I'm In Love With My Car; Get Down Make Love / Save Me / Now I'm Here; Dragon Attack; Now I'm Here (Reprise) / Fat Bottomed Girls / Love Of My Life / Keep Yourself Alive / Flash / The Hero / Brighton Rock / Guitar Solo / Crazy Little Thing Called Love / Bohemian Rhapsody / Tie Your Mother Down / Encore: Another One Bites The Dust / Sheer Heart Attack / 2nd Encore: We Will Rock You / We Are The Champions / God Save The Queen*

December 12/13
Forêt Nationale, Brussels

Second night: *Jailhouse Rock / We Will Rock You / Let Me Entertain You / Play The Game / Medley: Mustapha; Death On Two Legs; Killer Queen; I'm In Love With My Car; Get Down Make Love / Save Me / Now I'm Here; Dragon Attack; Now I'm Here (Reprise) / Fat Bottomed Girls / Love Of My Life / Keep Yourself Alive / Instrumental Inferno / Battle Theme / Flash / The Hero / Brighton Rock / Guitar Solo / Crazy Little Thing Called Love / Bohemian Rhapsody / Tie Your Mother Down / Encore: Another One Bites The Dust / Sheer Heart Attack / 2nd Encore: We Will Rock You / We Are The Champions / God Save The Queen*

December 14
Festhalle, Frankfurt

Same set as previous night, but with 'Imagine' making its second and last ever appearance in the set, following 'Love Of My Life'.

December 16
Hall Rheus, Strasbourg

December 18
Olympiahalle, Munich

Jailhouse Rock / We Will Rock You / Let Me Entertain You / Play The Game / Medley: Mustapha; Death On Two Legs; Killer Queen; I'm In Love With My Car; Get Down Make Love / Save Me / Now I'm Here; Dragon Attack; Now I'm Here (Reprise) / Fat Bottomed Girls / Love Of My Life / Keep Yourself Alive / Instrumental Inferno / Battle Theme / Flash / The Hero / Brighton Rock / Guitar Solo / Crazy Little Thing Called Love / Bohemian Rhapsody / Tie Your Mother Down / Encore: Another One Bites The Dust / Sheer Heart Attack / 2nd Encore: We Will Rock You / We Are The Champions / God Save The Queen

December 19
The band fly back to the UK, to spend Christmas at home. By the end of 1980, Queen had sold 45 million albums and 25 million singles worldwide.

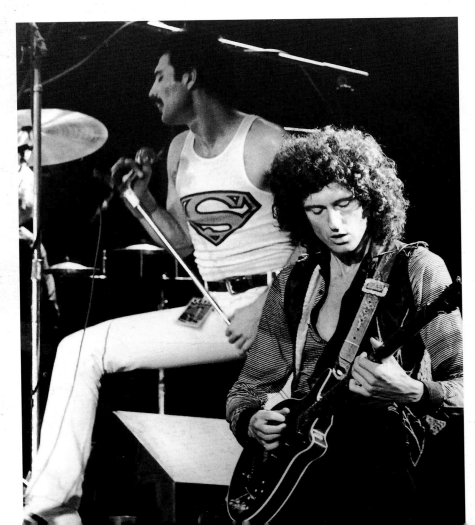

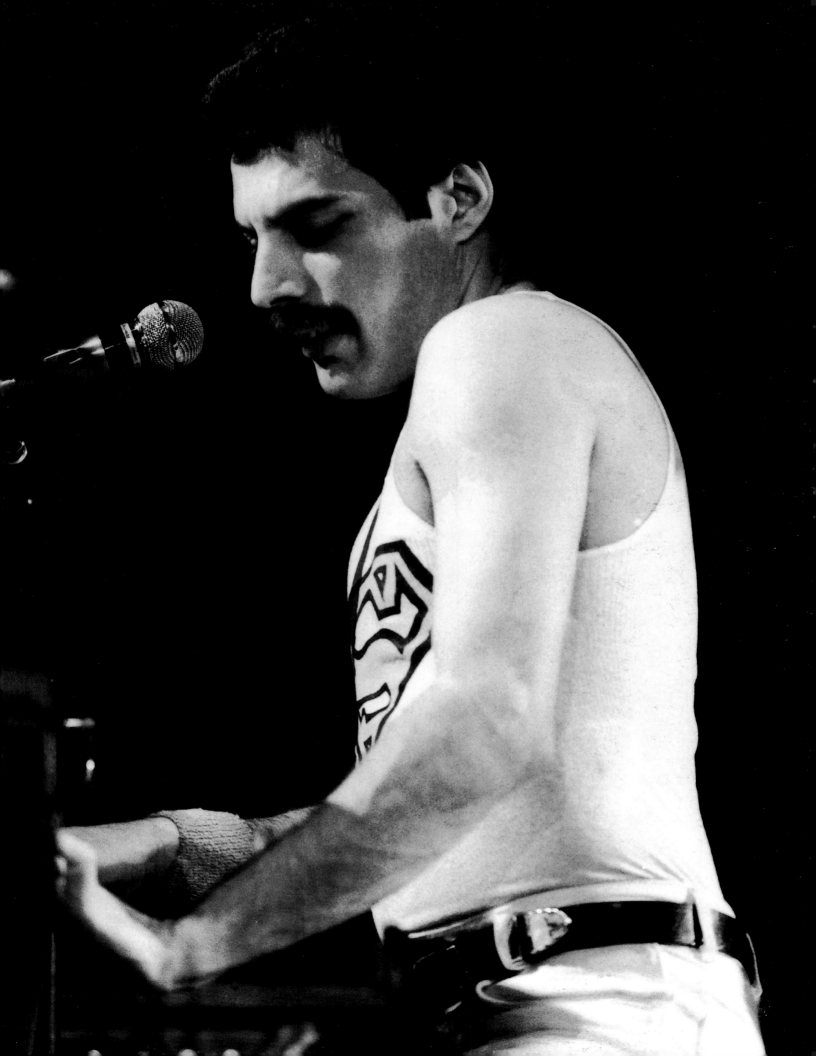

JAPAN 1981
Japan Tour

On February 8, the band leave London and head for Japan for brief rehearsals before playing five consecutive shows at the vast Budokan Hall in Tokyo. On the same flight as the band is the Nottingham Forest Football team, who are travelling to Japan to play in the World Championships. On a rare day off between shows, Roger, Brian and John attend one of the matches. The English club loses 1-0.

February 10

The Japanese première of the *Flash Gordon* film takes place in Tokyo, to which Queen are invited as honoured

guests. The band are interviewed on stage by top Japanese DJ Yuki Okazaki before the film is screened.

February 12/13/16/17/18
Budokan Hall, Tokyo

First night: Jailhouse Rock / We Will Rock You / Let Me Entertain You / Play The Game / Medley: Mustapha; Death On Two Legs; Killer Queen; I'm In Love With My Car; Get Down Make Love / Save Me / Now I'm Here; Dragon Attack; Now I'm Here (Reprise) / Fat Bottomed Girls / Love Of My Life / Keep Yourself Alive / Instrumental Inferno / Vultan's Theme / Battle Theme / Flash / The Hero / Brighton Rock / Guitar Solo / Crazy Little Thing Called Love / Bohemian Rhapsody / Tie Your Mother Down / Encore: Another One Bites The Dust / Sheer Heart Attack / 2nd Encore: We Will Rock You / We Are The Champions / God Save The Queen

Queen perform all five shows here before capacity audiences of 12,000.

Curiously, 'Teo Torriatte' is not performed every night at any of the shows.

Second night: same as previous night, but with 'Need Your Loving Tonight' after the medley and before 'Save Me'.

Queen performed only extracts of 'Flash Gordon' material, never complete versions. 'The Hero' was the longest excerpt, appearing here as part of the 'Flash' medley. In 1982 it would open the show.

Third night: Jailhouse Rock / We Will Rock You / Let Me Entertain You / Play The Game / Medley: Mustapha; Death On Two Legs; Killer Queen; I'm In Love With My Car; Get Down Make Love / Rock It / Save Me / Now I'm Here; Dragon Attack; Now I'm Here (Reprise) / Fat Bottomed Girls / Love Of My Life / Keep Yourself Alive / Instrumental Inferno / Vultan's Theme / Battle Theme / Flash / The Hero / Brighton Rock / Guitar Solo / Crazy Little Thing Called Love / Bohemian Rhapsody / Tie Your Mother Down / Encore: Another One Bites The Dust / Sheer Heart Attack / 2nd Encore: We Will Rock You / We Are The Champions / God Save The Queen

Gary Numan attends all three shows here. He was also in Japan for a brief tour.

While Queen are in Japan for these shows, *Music Life* magazine release a commemorative book entitled 'Queen The Miracle' which contains 104 pages of beautifully illustrated full colour pictures and text. Apart from concert photographs, others relate to press conferences, rehearsals, public appearances and picture shoots.

Japanese single and album discographies are also detailed, though many of the sleeve illustrations are absent. The photographic reproduction is far superior to anything available elsewhere, and copies today are very collectable among Queen fans.

Final night: same as previous night, but with 'Teo Torriatte' after 'Save Me'

Following the shows, Freddie decides to stay on in Japan to conclude last minute shopping. Having left himself the minimum amount of time to reach the airport, when he does eventually arrive for his flight to New York, he boards the wrong aircraft, albeit to the right destination. For reasons best known to himself, Freddie detested DC 10s, and was prepared to wait an additional twelve hours for an alternative plane.

SOUTH AMERICA 1981
Gluttons For Punishment Tour

In mid February, Queen flew to Rio De Janeiro for final preparations for their first (and only) tour of South America. From there they moved on to Buenos Aires, where they are greeted at the airport by their own music playing over the public address system. The band are also permitted to bypass lengthy arrival procedures, at the express orders of Argentina's President.

Their press conference is broadcast live on national TV, and such is the interest in Queen's movements throughout the tour that local radio and TV companies (Radio Cidade and TV Bandeirantes) run frequent Queen news bulletins which interrupt or replace scheduled programmes.

Following the first press conference, the band encounter a phenomenon which will occur many times throughout the tour. John Deacon: "We just about made it to our cars in time, rattled and bruised. We had only gone a few hundred yards when the driver stopped for petrol. Within seconds the car was surrounded by girls battering on the windows and roof. The driver had no idea what was going on. They'd never had to deal with anything like that before."

The equipment required to stage these shows consists of seventy-two specially built speakers, sixteen tons of scaffolding, one hundred rolls (three tons) of artificial turf (to protect the sacred football pitches), three hundred and fifty aircraft landing lights (which

make up the lighting rig). Every inch of aircraft space was filled. The collective weight of the gear was a staggering seventy-five tons. Each concert costs around £25,000 to stage. The tour entourage consisted of thirty-four people.

Because equipment hire opportunities do not exist in South America, twenty tons of sound equipment was shipped in from Japan. Not only was the flight from Tokyo to Buenos Aires hideously expensive, it was also, at thirty-six hours, the longest direct flight anywhere. A further forty tons of equipment was flown in from Miami, which included additional artificial turf to cover football fields on which the band will perform, plus

sixteen tons of stage scaffolding from Los Angeles, and five tons of lighting gear.

When the band's production manager, Chris Lamb, arrived in Buenos Aires, after an exhausting eighteen hour flight from Los Angeles, he was promptly arrested for being in possession of obscene material. The offending items were the tour stage passes, which featured an illustration of a Japanese girl facing Carmen Miranda. Both ladies wore only suggestive grins and native head attire, and one was shown holding a peeled banana in a none-too-subtle manner. Although Lamb took an unscheduled detour to the local police station, he was soon released.

Meanwhile, the equipment, which had thus far survived its mammoth journey from Japan without incident, encountered problems of its own. When one of the forty foot transporter containers falls off the truck into the street, it remains there for two days until a crane large enough to lift it can be located.

Despite every Customs document being labelled with strict warnings that they be retained at every step along the tour, tour manager Gerry Stickells was somewhat alarmed at observing every one being ripped to shreds and binned by the first Customs official they encounter. Stickells later recalled that "No explanation was forthcoming".

Because setting up the stage often entailed working in extreme temperatures – frequently over one hundred degrees – many of the crew took to wearing shorts and caps, as did the local hired labour. This seemingly harmless choice of attire later proved to be surprisingly troublesome, when one of the crew ventured into town on an errand, and was arrested. Unbeknown to the Queen staff, there was a strict law which forbade men to wear shorts in public. Following a brief spell in jail, the unfortunate individual was released.

Roger: "In some ways I was surprised that we didn't get more criticism for playing South America. I didn't think we were being used as tools by political régimes, although obviously we have to co-operate with them. We were playing for the people. We didn't go there with the wool pulled over our eyes. We know fully what the situation is like in some of those countries. But for a time we made thousands of people happy. Surely that must count for something. We weren't playing for the government, we were playing to lots of ordinary Argentinean people. In fact, we were asked to meet the President, President Viola, and I refused. I didn't want to meet him because that would have been playing into their hands."

February 28
Velez Sarfield, Buenos Aires

We Will Rock You / Let Me Entertain You / Play The Game / Somebody To Love / Medley: Mustapha; Death On Two Legs; Killer Queen; I'm In Love With My Car; Get Down Make Love / Need Your Loving Tonight / Rock It / Save Me / Now I'm Here; Dragon Attack; Now I'm Here (Reprise) / Fat Bottomed Girls / Love Of My Life / Keep Yourself Alive / Instrumental Inferno / Flash / The Hero / Brighton Rock / Guitar Solo / Crazy Little Thing Called Love / Bohemian Rhapsody / Tie Your Mother Down / Encore: Another One Bites The Dust / Sheer Heart Attack / 2nd Encore: We Will Rock You / We Are The Champions / God Save The Queen

Prior to the tour the band had been apprehensive that fans unfamiliar with their show might be confused by their habits. How might they react, for instance, to the band walking off stage during 'Bo Rhap', or to Freddie inviting them to sing along with him? They need not have worried. The audience would exceed everyone's expectations of them, and considerably more besides. When it came time for Freddie and Brian to perform 'Love Of My Life', they joined in from the very first word and could easily have continued right through without any prompting from Freddie: "I stood there blinking away like mad and swallowing hard, with the same feeling that the last night of the proms gives me."

Queen perform before a capacity 54,000 people at this venue, and go on to play sell-out shows at every venue thereafter.

'Jailhouse Rock' no longer commences most of the shows, and 'Mustapha' begins the medley only occasionally.

Meanwhile back in the UK, Nina Myskow's coverage of the tour in The Sun newspaper is read over toast and marmalade on March 20, 1981, beneath the headline: DON'T CRY FOR QUEEN ARGENTINA.

"Supergroup numero uno: That is the new title that Queen have been crowned in South America. Amid scenes of Beatle-type adulation and frenzy, the four-man British rock band have sparked another revolution in the turbulent history of Argentina. A rock revolution. In the first of a series of huge outdoor concerts, they conquered new territory with a dazzling display of rock at its best."

March 1
Velez Sarfield, Buenos Aires

We Will Rock You / Let Me Entertain You / Play The Game / Somebody To Love / Medley: Death On Two Legs; Killer Queen; I'm In Love With My Car; Get Down Make Love / Need Your Loving Tonight / Save Me / Now I'm Here; Dragon Attack; Now I'm Here (Reprise) / Fat Bottomed Girls / Love Of My Life / Keep Yourself Alive / Instrumental Inferno / Flash / The Hero / Brighton Rock / Guitar Solo / Crazy Little Thing Called Love / Bohemian Rhapsody / Tie Your Mother Down / Encore: Another One Bites The Dust / Sheer Heart Attack / 2nd Encore: We Will Rock You / We Are The Champions / God Save The Queen

This show is broadcast live on national television, and is watched by an incredible 35 million people in Argentina and Brazil. Bootleg (edited) audio and video copies of the show are quickly circulated. Many find their way to Europe and North America, and fast become very sought-after collectors' items. The show has never received an official home video release. The specially adapted set entails a running order not played elsewhere, and fans are anxious to familiarise themselves with it.

In Rolling Stone magazine James Henke writes: "When I return to Velez Sarfield that evening for the show, the stadium is swarming with kids – and cops. These are crusty, corpulent tough guys – not the boot-camp boys I saw at the airport. And it doesn't take long to find out that they mean business. When one American writer snaps a photo of the twenty-odd billy-club-wielding policemen who are cordoning off the backstage area, he's pinned against a government owned Falcon and threatened at knife point with the loss of a finger until he yields his film. "No problem." Sure.

"'Un supergrupo numero uno,' the MC announces as the lights dim, and with a burst of smoke, Queen appears on stage and begins hammering out its anthem, 'We Will Rock You.' Mercury – dressed in a white, sleeveless Superman T-shirt, red vinyl pants and a black vinyl jacket – frequently stops singing and dares the audience to carry the weight. And carry the weight they do: the fans seem to know all the lyrics throughout the 110-minute show – which, if for no other reason, is impressive for the number of hits the group is able to offer, such as 'Keep Yourself Alive', 'Killer Queen', 'Bohemian Rhapsody', 'Fat Bottomed Girls' and 'Bicycle Race'.

"Though the band-audience interaction is remarkable, the crowd responds with such unquestioning devotion I get the feeling that if Freddie Mercury told them to shave their heads, they'd do it...

..."For the encore, the band reprises 'We Will Rock You', then bounds into 'We Are The Champions'. Mercury, by this time wearing only a pair of black leather short shorts and a matching policeman's leather hat, struts around the stage like some hybrid of Robert Plant and Peter Allen, climactically kicking over a speaker cabinet and bashing it with his microphone stand. Pretty ridiculous in this day and age, but the kids love it."

March 4
Estadio Municipal, Mar Del Plata

We Will Rock You / Let Me Entertain You / Play The Game / Somebody To Love / Medley: Death On Two Legs; Killer Queen; I'm In Love With My Car; Get Down Make Love / Need Your Loving Tonight / Save Me / Now I'm Here; Dragon Attack; Now I'm Here (Reprise) / Fat Bottomed Girls / Love Of My Life / Keep Yourself Alive / Instrumental Inferno / Flash / The Hero / Brighton Rock / Guitar Solo / Crazy Little Thing Called Love / Bohemian Rhapsody / Tie Your Mother Down / Encore: Another One Bites The Dust / Sheer Heart Attack / 2nd Encore: We Will Rock You / We Are The Champions / God Save The Queen

This and the following night's show, are performed in front of record breaking audiences.

March 6
Alletico Rosario Central, Rosario

March 8
Velez Sarfield, Buenos Aires

We Will Rock You / Let Me Entertain You / Play The Game / Somebody To Love / Medley: Death On Two Legs; Killer Queen; I'm In Love With My Car; Get Down Make Love / Need Your Loving Tonight / Rock It / Save Me / Now I'm Here; Dragon Attack; Now I'm Here (Reprise) / Fat Bottomed Girls / Love Of My Life / Keep Yourself Alive / Instrumental Inferno / Flash / The Hero / Brighton Rock / Guitar Solo / Crazy Little Thing Called Love / Bohemian Rhapsody / Tie Your Mother Down / Encore: Another One Bites The Dust / Sheer Heart Attack / 2nd Encore: We Will Rock You / We Are The Champions / God Save The Queen

This concert was also broadcast on national television. Again, a proportion of it can be seen on 'Rare Live': 'Another One Bites The Dust' and a lengthy improvised passage. Queen performed 'Rock It' which featured in their set only

rarely and featured Roger's vocals. They also played a special rehearsed 'Inferno' improvisation.

Such was the hysteria surrounding the shows that the band encountered problems leaving the stadium and had to be given a police escort led by four motorcycles.

While in Buenos Aires, the band were invited to the home of General Viola (President Designate of Argentina), and introduced to footballer Diego Maradona.

Before playing the final two shows of the tour, the band take a short break. John and Roger head for London, Freddie flew to New Orleans and Brian remained in Rio. Additional shows in Venezuela and Mexico, which followed in September, had not at this time been finalised. Concerts in New Zealand and Australia were also mooted but ultimately dismissed.

March 20/21
Morumbi Stadium, Sao Paulo

First night: We Will Rock You / Let Me Entertain You / Play The Game / Somebody To Love / Medley: Mustapha; Death On Two Legs; Killer Queen; I'm In Love With My Car; Get Down Make Love / Need Your Loving Tonight / Save Me / Now I'm Here; Dragon Attack; Now I'm Here (Reprise) / Fat Bottomed Girls / Love Of My Life / Keep Yourself Alive / Instrumental Inferno / Flash / The Hero / Brighton Rock / Guitar Solo / Crazy Little Thing Called Love / Bohemian Rhapsody / Tie Your Mother Down / Encore: Another One Bites The Dust / Sheer Heart Attack / 2nd Encore: We Will Rock You / We Are The Champions / God Save The Queen

Queen break yet more records at this venue, attracting the biggest paying audience in history. There are 131,000 people at the opening, with a further 120,000 the second night.

This stadium is the second biggest in the world. The band had intended to play the biggest — Maracana Stadium in Rio — but had been refused permission. This would have held 206,000 people.

Second night: same as previous night, but with 'Rock It' instead of 'Need Your Loving Tonight'.

Because the first night at the venue had sold out so quickly, this show was added. It also sold out.

UK rock writer Ray Coleman reported: "Flanked by the menacing security gorillas as they make their way down the players' tunnel to face the

wall of noise emanating from the 130,000 fans before whom they will play, they appear small and fragile. But once on stage, emerging from the billowing clouds of their smoke machine and

illuminated by the dazzling colours of their kaleidoscopic lighting equipment, the seductive power of rock music takes its own control, and the armed guards who surrounded Queen watch in bewilderment, as the youth of Sao Paulo open their hearts and lungs to the first rock concerts they have ever seen, in a touching non-violent dialogue of music and friendship."

Immediately after the tour, the valuable equipment is hastily loaded on to a specially chartered New York bound 747 cargo plane before any local Custom and Excise red tape can delay it, or before it can be confiscated, as had apparently happened to Earth Wind & Fire. Gerry Stickells had observed that some of the spotlights supplied by local concert organisers carried their name. He would not be taking any risks with Queen's equipment.

By now it seemed that all the problems encountered throughout the tour were finally behind them but this was not the case. The jumbo developed compass problems during flight, and was forced to land in Puerto Rico. The four crew members left behind to supervise the equipment complete the appropriate paperwork and book into a hotel for the night. When they return the next morning they discover that the airport ground crew have broken the steering gear, and the flight is delayed yet further. Eventually the crew and stage gear do reach their American destination. The equipment remains in storage there, until it is needed for the second leg of the tour, in September.

In his letter to the fan club members (Autumn 1981 issue), John Deacon reflects briefly on the forthcoming shows: "...When you read this we should have finished our recording session in Montreux, Switzerland and be on our way to Caracas, Venezuela. We hope to be playing Rio in Brazil before moving on to Mexico. It's always very exciting to play in a country for the first time, and 1981 has really been our year for discovering new audiences we didn't even know existed.

September

The band spend the early part of September working on new material for what will later emerge as the 'Hot Space' album. Work is interrupted for the second visit to South America, two Canadian shows and a Christmas break, but resumes again in the New Near. The sessions are at an end by March 1982.

SOUTH AMERICA 1981
Gluttons For Punishment Tour (2nd Leg)

On September 15, Queen travel to New Orleans for rehearsals before resuming the South American tour. They then fly to Caracas on the 21st.

As with the American tour in 1980, the lighting rig used throughout all the South American dates, is 'Fly Swatters'.

September 25/26/27
Poliedro De Caracas, Caracas

First night: We Will Rock You / Let Me Entertain You / Play The Game / Somebody To Love / Medley: Killer Queen; I'm In Love With My Car; Get Down Make Love / Save Me / Now I'm Here; Dragon Attack; Now I'm Here (Reprise) / Fat Bottomed Girls / Love Of My Life / Keep Yourself Alive / Instrumental Inferno / Flash / The Hero / Brighton Rock / Guitar Solo / Crazy Little Thing Called Love / Bohemian Rhapsody / Tie Your Mother Down / Encore: Another One Bites The Dust / Sheer Heart Attack / 2nd Encore: We Will Rock You / We Are The Champions / God Save The Queen

Despite a six month gap between shows, there are no significant changes to the set list. 'Death On Two Legs' no longer features, with 'Killer Queen' taking its place as the medley opening number.

An additional two shows proposed for this venue, scheduled originally for September 29 and 30, were cancelled, as was a second show at Monterey on October 10. Two shows at a venue in Guadalajara, Mexico on October 15 and 16 were moved to Puebla on the 16th and 17th instead.

On September 30 the band flew back to New Orleans for a week's final rehearsals. They then travel on to Mexico on October 8.

Two other shows in Venezuela (scheduled for September 29 and 30) were cancelled when former President Romulo Ethancourt died, and the country's population went into a period of mourning. Ethancourt's gradually deteriorating health had already jeopardised the three main shows, but he'd held on long enough for them to go ahead.

When an advance party of crew members attempted to cross the border into Mexico, they were told that it was impossible to issue all eighteen with visas. Only six per day could be issued, and only three of those could be granted to one party.

Threatened with spending six unplanned days awaiting passage into Mexico, and faced with a second refusal the following day, the crew needed a plan – and quick. With inflexible schedules to be met and time running out fast, there was only one alternative... bribery. The crew are soon given the required visas, and all eighteen are permitted to cross the border together. Gerry Stickells later puts it down to "British ingenuity triumphing yet again."

October 9
Estadion Universitano, Monterey

We Will Rock You / Let Me Entertain You / Play The Game / Somebody To Love / Medley: Killer Queen; I'm In Love With My Car; Get Down Make Love / Save Me / Now I'm Here; Dragon Attack; Now I'm Here (Reprise) / Fat Bottomed Girls / Love Of My Life / Keep Yourself Alive / Instrumental Inferno / Flash / The Hero / Brighton Rock / Guitar Solo / Crazy Little Thing Called Love / Bohemian Rhapsody / Tie Your Mother Down / Encore: Another One Bites The Dust / Sheer Heart Attack / 2nd Encore: We Will Rock You / We Are The Champions / God Save The Queen

The night before this show, Gerry Stickells is contacted at his hotel by an anxious journalist calling to confirm the time of an interview with the band the next day. She had apparently been promised exclusive time with them, and had rather naïvely paid the local promoter 10,000 pesos for the privilege. Queen knew nothing of the arrangement! This was not an isolated incident.

October 11
Queen return to the US for three days' break, before flying back for the two Puebla, Mexico shows.

A Concert Documentary

October 16/17
Estadion Cuahtermoc, Puebla

First night: Jailhouse Rock / We Will Rock You / Let Me Entertain You / Play The Game / Somebody To Love / Medley: Killer Queen; I'm In Love With My Car; Get Down Make Love / Save Me / Now I'm Here; Dragon Attack; Now I'm Here (Reprise) / Love Of My Life / Keep Yourself Alive / Instrumental Inferno / Flash / The Hero / Brighton Rock / Guitar Solo / Crazy Little Thing Called Love / Bohemian Rhapsody / Tie Your Mother Down / Encore: Another One Bites The Dust / Sheer Heart Attack / 2nd Encore: We Will Rock You / We Are The Champions / God Save The Queen

'Jailhouse Rock' begins the show here for the very last time. Thereafter it was always performed as an encore song, or as part of the rock'n'roll medley.

Anyone attending this show with the intention of making a fast buck (or peso) by bootlegging it will no doubt have been aggrieved to find security staff awaiting them as they passed through the turnstile. Each person was thoroughly searched, and any batteries found were confiscated. Once inside the stadium there was a stall which sold batteries - newly confiscated second hand batteries – at highly inflated prices.

Second night: same as previous night, but without 'Jailhouse Rock'

In early 1983, Jim Beach and Gerry Stickells flew back to South America for discussions concerning the possibility of further gigs. Although venues and dates were proposed for the end of year, they were eventually shelved, when the enormous costs involved proved too great.

The six proposed concerts were to take place at the Belo Horizonte, Porte Allegro, Sao Paulo Morumbi, Coritiba and Rio Maracana Stadia, the last of which is the largest stadium in the world (capacity crowd 206,000).

Queen did return to Brazil in January 1985 to perform at the two day Rock In Rio Festival. This would be Queen's last visit to South America.

October 26

A full seven months ahead of the 'Hot Space' album release, on which it would appear, 'Under Pressure' is released in the UK. Coupled with the enigmatic non-album cut "Soul Brother", the David Bowie joint venture gives Queen their second No.1. Surprisingly, the same pairing reaches only No.29 in America. 'Under Pressure' was the only single released in the UK in 1981.

November 2

'Greatest Hits' is issued in the UK, having been put back two weeks from an October 12 release date. Originally planned for release in December 1980 (as EMC 3350), it was shelved to make way for the *Flash Gordon* soundtrack project, issued as EMC 3351. Because of the band's various single successes in different territories, numerous variations are issued. 'Love Of My Life' is included on the South American disc, as it had spent many weeks at number one there. 'Seven Seas Of Rhye' is omitted to make way for it. Likewise, the Japanese counterpart includes Brian May's 'Teo Torriatte' instead of 'Seven Seas'.

Other variations include 'Keep Yourself Alive' on the American, Australian, Canadian and New Zealand editions (despite its failure to chart there), 'Sweet Lady' on the Bulgarian and Russian issues, and 'Tie Your Mother Down' on the Canadian, Australian and New Zealand versions. All variations have since become extremely collectable.

In conjunction with the album, two sister products are also issued: 'Greatest Flix', an eighteen track video compilation, and a *Greatest Pix* book. This triple marketing concept was later re-employed for the 'Greatest Hits II' issues, in October 1991.

November 22

The band travel to Canada for rehearsals and last minute preparations for two concerts which are to be filmed. The shows are organised purely because the band want to put together a full length film to properly document their live show.

The footage from both shows is edited together to give the impression of just one. On September 10, 1984, a twenty-one track aptly titled 'We Will Rock You' video is released. It was the first commercially available film of Queen in concert.

'Under Pressure' was included in the set for the first time, and 'Need Your Loving Tonight' was omitted.

November 24/25
Forum, Montreal, Quebec

Both nights: We Will Rock You / Let Me Entertain You / Play The Game / Somebody To Love / Medley: Killer Queen; I'm In Love With My Car; Get Down Make Love / Save Me / Now I'm Here; Dragon Attack; Now I'm Here (Reprise) / Love Of My Life / Under Pressure / Keep Yourself Alive / Brighton Rock / Guitar Solo; Drum Solo / Crazy Little Thing Called Love / Bohemian Rhapsody / Tie Your Mother Down / Encore: Another One Bites The Dust / Sheer Heart Attack / 2nd Encore: We Will Rock You / We Are The Champions / God Save The Queen

All the above material appears on the 'We Will Rock You' video. There were no omissions.

Although this video was a welcome addition to Queen collections, many fans would have preferred something representative of 1979 instead. Every piece of footage from that period seems to feature the band

in dazzling form. The music of that era is arguably Queen's best, as are their costumes and lighting set-up. Video footage of something from the 'Live Killers' period, is very long overdue.

Freddie's opening words: "Hello Montreal... long time no see. You wanna get crazy? Okay let's go!"

November 26

Queen fly home for the Christmas period.

December 6

The band go to Munich to continue sessions for the 'Hot Space' album with the studio's resident producer Rheinhardt Mack.

Meanwhile, in the Christmas issue of the fan club magazine, the results of the first proper Fan's Favourite Queen Album and Track poll is published. The poll includes all material released up to, and including, 'Flash Gordon'. one hundred and twenty-three different tracks are listed, the top song receives 7,696 votes and the worst ('The Ring' from the 'Flash' album) receives only one vote.

The Top 20 tracks are: Bohemian Rhapsody / Somebody To Love / Killer Queen / March Of The Black Queen / We Are The Champions / Liar / The Prophet's Song / Brighton Rock (Live Killers version) / Brighton Rock / Another One Bites The Dust / Don't Stop Me Now / Save Me / Love Of My Life / Crazy Little Thing Called Love / It's Late / '39 / Keep Yourself Alive / Spread Your Wings / Tie Your Mother Down / White Queen

The Top 10 albums are: A Night At The Opera / Queen II / The Game / Live Killers / Sheer Heart Attack / A Day At The Races / Jazz / News Of The World / Queen / Flash Gordon

EUROPE 1982
The Hot Space Tour

Following several days' rehearsals, the band fly to Gothenburg on April 8 for the opening show of the European tour which comprises thirty performances in nine cities, at twenty-two different venues. It would have included one more show had things gone according to plan.

Although applications to play gigs at both Manchester United and Arsenal football grounds (Old Trafford and Highbury) were made, both are turned down. Magistrates refuse to issue licences because of objections from local residents, despite the all-clear being given by the local Council and the Police. Apart from that, there were no chemical toilet facilities available to hire, all had already been booked for Pope John Paul II's personal appearances around the country. The proposed Manchester show is replaced by one in Leeds (May 29), and the Arsenal show by one at Milton Keynes (June 5).

Plans for a further show at the Albert Hall were abandoned because of fears that the famous ceiling might cave in under the weight of the lighting rig.

The support act for the tour is British band Bow Wow Wow. Regrettably, they would not stay for the full duration of the tour because fans pelted them with bottles. Queen are appalled at the fans' behaviour. Brian

May later recalled that he had never imagined such a situation ever arising at a Queen show. He was particularly disappointed that the group quit the tour before they had an opportunity to play any of the twelve planned shows in Germany where they had enjoyed some success with single sales. Bow Wow Wow's final dates were at Leiden, Holland (April 24/25).

Brian: "We liked them very much. There was this certain section in the audience that didn't like them, who found them very modern. Our audience, it's a sad comment, is perhaps a little narrow minded in that way. It's only a small percentage. Most people gave them a very good hearing, but there were a few people who went so far as to throw things at them, which to be honest I was pretty disgusted at. Unfortunately Bow Wow Wow decided to throw them back, as a matter of policy. On a couple of nights in particular it just snowballed into a big fight, which became very silly."

Annabella of Bow Wow Wow: "The fans were extremely hostile. We decided to come home before one of us got badly hurt. There was no point in carrying on really."

Matthew Ashman of Bow Wow Wow: "All those tossers wanted to do was kiss Queen's arse... well bollocks to them."

Another British band called Airrace are drafted in as the replacement support act, for the remaining dates.

The set now included new material from the 'Hot Space' album: 'Action This Day', 'Staying Power', 'Body Language' and 'Back Chat'. 'Under Pressure' had already been incorporated into the set for the two filmed Canadian shows. Other material from the album would feature in the set in subsequent concerts, but was for now absent: 'Put Out The Fire', 'Calling All Girls' and 'Life Is Real'. 'We Will Rock You' (Fast version), 'Let Me Entertain You' and 'Sheer Heart Attack' are all now dropped from the set, but 'Liar' and 'Mustapha' make more frequent appearances once more.

Other material is just shuffled about, but still remains. Queen employed that concept on many occasions throughout their touring career, as evident from the set lists herein. To inject a fresh feel

into a set which may perhaps comprise songs which have been performed for some time, the band would instead re-organise the running order: 'Jailhouse Rock', 'Bohemian Rhapsody', 'Death On Two Legs', 'Brighton Rock', 'Liar', 'Flash', 'Keep Yourself Alive', 'Sweet Lady', 'Fat Bottomed Girls', 'We Will Rock You (Slow)', and especially 'Now I'm Here' and 'Tie Your Mother Down' are all good examples of this.

April 9
Scandinavium, Gothenburg

April 10
Isstadion, Stockholm

Flash / The Hero / Tie Your Mother Down / Action This Day / Play The Game / Somebody To Love / Staying Power / Get Down Make Love / Body Language / Under Pressure / Fat Bottomed Girls / Love Of My Life / Save Me / Guitar Solo / Liar / Crazy Little Thing Called Love / Bohemian Rhapsody / Now I'm Here; Dragon Attack / Now I'm Here (Reprise) / Encore: Another One Bites The Dust / Bohemian Rhapsody / Sheer Heart Attack / 2nd Encore: We Will Rock You / We Are The Champions / God Save The Queen

'Action This Day' features Roger's backing vocals every bit as prominently as on the album. Although by no means the strongest track on 'Hot Space', it took on a new life in concert.

April 12
Drammenshallen, Oslo

April 16/17
Hallenstadion, Zurich

First night: Flash / The Hero / Tie Your Mother Down / Action This Day / Play The Game / Somebody To Love / Get Down Make Love / Body Language / Back Chat (Rhythm Version) / Liar / Love Of My Life / Save Me / Mustapha / Fat Bottomed Girls / Crazy Little Thing Called Love / Bohemian Rhapsody / Now I'm Here; Dragon Attack; Now I'm Here (Reprise) / Encore: Another One Bites The Dust / Bohemian Rhapsody / Sheer Heart Attack / 2nd Encore: We Will Rock You / We Are The Champions / God Save The Queen

This set listing is correct – as unlikely as it seems.

'Back Chat' is not performed quite unlike the album version, while on 'Staying Power', making an early appearance in the set, Freddie replaces Arif Mardin's horn arrangement with vocal ad-libs. 'Liar' makes a welcome return.

April 19/20
Palais De Sport, Paris

First night: *Flash* / *The Hero* / *Tie Your Mother Down* / *Action This Day* / *Play The Game* / *Staying Power* / *Somebody To Love* / *Get Down Make Love* / *Body Language* / *Back Chat (Rhythm Version)* / *Under Pressure* / *Love Of My Life* / *Save Me* / *Back Chat* / *Fat Bottomed Girls* / *Crazy Little Thing Called Love* / *Bohemian Rhapsody* / *Now I'm Here; Dragon Attack; Now I'm Here (Reprise)* / *Encore: Another One Bites The Dust* / *Sheer Heart Attack* / 2nd *Encore: We Will Rock You* / *We Are The Champions* / *God Save The Queen*

On April 19, the band's twentieth UK single is released. 'Body Language' is the second track lifted from the 'Hot Space' album. The single fails to make the top twenty, and peaks at No.25. The choice of B-side is universal: Freddie's tribute to John Lennon entitled 'Life Is Real'.

Released on the same day in America too, the pairing fares rather better than at home, peaking at No.11. The accompanying promo video is considered too provocative for television broadcast, and was also ignored on the 'Greatest Pix' video collections.

April 22/23
Forêt Nationale, Brussels

Second night: *Flash* / *The Hero* / *We Will Rock You* / *Action This Day* / *Play The Game* / *Staying Power* / *Somebody To Love* / *Get Down Make Love* / *Instrumental Inferno* / *Under Pressure* / *Liar* / *Love Of My Life* / *Save Me* / *Fat Bottomed Girls* / *Crazy Little Thing Called Love* / *Bohemian Rhapsody* / *Tie Your Mother Down* / *Now I'm Here; Dragon Attack; Now I'm Here (Reprise)* / *Encore: Another One Bites The Dust* / *Sheer Heart Attack* / 2nd *Encore: We Will Rock You* / *We Are The Champions* / *God Save The Queen*

April 24/25
Groenoordhalle, Leiden

Second night: *Flash* / *The Hero* / *Tie Your Mother Down* / *Action This Day* / *Play The Game* / *Somebody To Love* / *Get Down Make Love* / *Instrumental Inferno* / *Under Pressure* / *Love Of My Life* / *Save Me* / *Fat Bottomed Girls* / *Crazy Little Thing Called Love* / *Bohemian Rhapsody* / *Now I'm Here; Dragon Attack; Now I'm Here (Reprise)* / *Back Chat* / *Staying Power* / *Liar* / *Encore: Another One Bites The Dust* / *Sheer Heart Attack* / 2nd *Encore: We Will Rock You* / *We Are The Champions* / *God Save The Queen*

April 28/29
Festhalle, Frankfurt

First night: *Flash* / *The Hero* / *Tie Your Mother Down* / *Action This Day* / *Play The Game* / *Staying Power* /

Somebody To Love / *Now I'm Here; Dragon Attack; Now I'm Here (Reprise)* / *Love Of My Life* / *Save Me* / *Get Down Make Love* / *Guitar Solo* / *Under Pressure* / *Fat Bottomed Girls* / *Crazy Little Thing Called Love* / *Back Chat (Piano Improvisation)* / *Bohemian Rhapsody* / *Encore: Another One Bites The Dust* / *Sheer Heart Attack* / 2nd *Encore: We Will Rock You* / *We Are The Champions* / *God Save The Queen*

One of the two shows at this venue (it's unclear which one) was filmed and later broadcast on German television.

May 1
Westfallenhalle, Dortmund

Flash / *The Hero* / *Tie Your Mother Down* / *Action This Day* / *Play The Game* / *Staying Power* / *Somebody To Love* / *Now I'm Here; Dragon Attack; Now I'm Here (Reprise)* / *Love Of My Life* / *Save Me* / *Get Down Make Love* / *Instrumental Inferno; Guitar Solo (Prolonged)* / *Under Pressure* / *Fat Bottomed Girls* / *Crazy Little Thing Called Love* / *Bohemian Rhapsody* / *Encore: Another One Bites The Dust* / *Sheer Heart Attack* / 2nd *Encore: We Will Rock You* / *We Are The Champions* / *God Save The Queen*

May 3
Palais De Sport, Paris

Flash / *The Hero* / *Tie Your Mother Down* / *Action This Day* / *Play The Game* / *Staying Power* / *Somebody To Love* / *Now I'm Here; Dragon Attack; Now I'm Here (Reprise)* / *Love Of My Life* / *Save Me* / *Get Down Make Love* / *Instrumental Inferno* / *Under Pressure* / *Fat Bottomed Girls* / *Crazy Little Thing Called Love* / *Bohemian Rhapsody* / *Encore: Another One Bites The Dust* / *Sheer Heart Attack* / 2nd *Encore: We Will Rock You* / *We Are The Champions* / *God Save The Queen*

May 5
Eilenriedehalle, Hanover

May 6/7
Sporthalle, Cologne

May 9
Carl Diem Halle, Wurzburg

Flash / *The Hero* / *We Will Rock You* / *Action This Day* / *Play The Game* / *Back Chat* / *Somebody To Love* / *Now I'm Here; Dragon Attack; Now I'm Here (Reprise)* / *Love Of My Life* / *Save Me* / *Get Down Make Love* / *Instrumental Inferno* / *Under Pressure* / *Fat Bottomed Girls* / *Crazy Little Thing Called Love* / *Bohemian Rhapsody* / *Tie Your Mother Down* / *Encore: Another One Bites The Dust* / *Sheer Heart Attack* / 2nd *Encore: We Will Rock You* / *We Are The Champions* / *God Save The Queen*

May 10
Sporthalle, Stuttgart

May 12/13
Stadthalle, Vienna

First night: *Flash* / *The Hero* / *We Will Rock You* / *Action This Day* / *Play The Game* / *Back Chat* / *Somebody To Love* / *Now I'm Here; Dragon Attack; Now I'm Here (Reprise)* / *Love Of My Life* / *Save Me* / *Get Down Make Love* / *Instrumental Inferno* / *Under Pressure* / *Fat Bottomed Girls* / *Crazy Little Thing Called Love* / *Bohemian Rhapsody* / *Tie Your Mother Down* / *Encore: Another One Bites The Dust* / *Sheer Heart Attack* / 2nd *Encore: We Will Rock You* / *We Are The Champions* / *God Save The Queen*

This show was apparently filmed (in its entirety), for a possible local television broadcast. Whether the transmission ever went ahead however, is unclear.

Second night: *Flash* / *The Hero* / *We Will Rock You* / *Action This Day* / *Play The Game* / *Staying Power* / *Somebody To Love* / *Now I'm Here; Dragon Attack; Now I'm Here (Reprise)* / *Love Of My Life* / *Save Me* / *Body Language* / *Get Down Make Love* / *Instrumental Inferno* / *Under Pressure* / *Fat Bottomed Girls* / *Crazy Little Thing Called Love* / *Bohemian Rhapsody* / *Tie Your Mother Down* / *Encore: Another One Bites The Dust (Incorporating Back Chat)* / *Sheer Heart Attack* / 2nd *Encore: We Will Rock You* / *We Are The Champions* / *God Save The Queen*

This show was filmed for the band's archives. A superb segment of 'Dust' is contained on 'Rare Live', and sees Freddie parading around the stage in a hooded towelling robe.

May 15
Waldbuehne, Berlin

Flash / The Hero / We Will Rock You / Action This Day / Play The Game / Staying Power / Somebody To Love / Now I'm Here; Dragon Attack; Now I'm Here (Reprise) / Love Of My Life / Save Me / Get Down Make Love / Instrumental Inferno / Under Pressure / Body Language / Back Chat / Fat Bottomed Girls / Crazy Little Thing Called Love / Bohemian Rhapsody / Tie Your Mother Down / Encore: Another One Bites The Dust / Sheer Heart Attack / 2nd Encore: We Will Rock You / We Are The Champions / God Save The Queen

May 16
Ernst-Mercke Halle, Hamburg

May 18
Eissporthalle, Kassel

Flash / The Hero / Sheer Heart Attack / Action This Day / Play The Game / Staying Power / Somebody To Love / Now I'm Here; Dragon Attack; Now I'm Here (Reprise) / Love Of My Life / Save Me / Guitar Solo / Get Down Make Love / Instrumental Inferno / Under Pressure / Fat Bottomed Girls / Crazy Little Thing Called Love / Bohemian Rhapsody / Tie Your Mother Down / Encore: Another One Bites The Dust / 2nd Encore: We Will Rock You / We Are The Champions / God Save The Queen

May 21
Olympiahalle, Munich

Flash / The Hero / Sheer Heart Attack / Action This Day / Play The Game / Staying Power / Somebody To Love / Now I'm Here; Dragon Attack; Now I'm Here (Reprise) / Love Of My Life / Save Me / Get Down Make Love / Instrumental Inferno / Under Pressure / Fat Bottomed Girls / Crazy Little Thing Called Love / Bohemian Rhapsody / Tie Your Mother Down / Encore: Another One Bites The Dust / 2nd Encore: We Will Rock You / We Are The Champions / God Save The Queen

Queen's eleventh studio album 'Hot Space' is released in the UK. It peaks at No.4, and No.22 in America, where it is issued on May 25.

Three tracks are not included in the live set. The Deacon/Mercury co-composition 'Cool Cat' is not an unsurprising omission, but 'Las Parablas De Amor' and 'Dancer' (both Brian May songs) certainly are. Neither is performed even once.

UK 1982
The Hot Space Tour

May 29
Elland Road Football Stadium, Leeds

Flash / The Hero / We Will Rock You / Action This Day / Play The Game / Staying Power / Somebody To Love / Now I'm Here; Dragon Attack; Now I'm Here (Reprise) / Love Of My Life / Save Me / Get Down Make Love / Instrumental Inferno / Under Pressure / Fat Bottomed Girls / Crazy Little Thing Called Love / Bohemian Rhapsody / Tie Your Mother Down / Encore: Another One Bites The Dust / Sheer Heart Attack / 2nd Encore: We Will Rock You / We Are The Champions / God Save The Queen

This show went ahead despite local residents' objections. Signed petitions were submitted to the City Council, but given that the site is commonly used as a venue for football matches, the objections were regarded lightly. A house opposite the ground is commandeered on the night of the concert to monitor Queen's noise level but they did not exceed any noise limitations.

Despite encountering problems with maintaining the tuning of his guitar (as was always a problem with open air venues), Brian May later cites this show as one of Queen's best ever live performances. It is made more enjoyable for him because he has family living in Leeds. A capacity 38,000 people witness the show.

Brian is interviewed before the show at the Dragonara Hotel where the band are staying. The interviewer is irritated because Freddie will not speak with him:

Q: "What's up with fruitcake Fred?"

Brian: "He's been torn apart and bitten so many times before, that he doesn't want to say anything. It's very difficult being a frontman in a band, because the things you say often get twisted. In my position I can stand away and be objective, Freddie comes in for abuse. He's part of the team and he doesn't like it when he's singled out. Would you?"

Although "Les Parablas De Amor" never featured in this show - nor any other for that matter - the band did perform it at rehearsals on the evening before this show. It is most likely that they felt it had not worked well enough to include in any concert.

Support Acts: The Teardrop Explodes, Heart, Joan Jett & The Blackhearts.

June 1/2
Ingliston Showground, Edinburgh

First night: Flash / The Hero / We Will Rock You / Action This Day / Play The Game / Staying Power / Somebody To Love / Now I'm Here; Dragon Attack; Now I'm Here (Reprise) / Love Of My Life / Save Me / Back Chat / Get Down Make Love / Instrumental Inferno (Incorporating I Go Crazy) / Under Pressure / Fat Bottomed Girls / Crazy Little Thing Called Love / Bohemian Rhapsody / Tie Your Mother Down / Encore: Another One Bites The Dust / 2nd Encore: We Will Rock You / We Are The Champions / God Save The Queen

The support act for the two shows here is The Teardrop Explodes.

Despite the fact that 'Las Palabras De Amor' was issued in the UK as the third single from 'Hot Space' on this day, it still failed to feature in the live set. It was backed with 'Cool Cat', and peaked at a disappointing No.17 – not helped by the absence of an accompanying promo video. The same track was issued in Japan only as a B-side to 'Back Chat' (P-1708), and was not released at all in America.

June 5

Milton Keynes Bowl, Buckinghamshire

Highlighted tracks featured in the television broadcast.

Flash / **The Hero** / **We Will Rock You** / *Action This Day* / **Play The Game** / *Staying Power* / **Somebody To Love** / *Now I'm Here*; **Dragon Attack**; *Now I'm Here (Reprise)* / **Love Of My Life** / *Save Me* / *Back Chat* / *Get Down Make Love* / **Guitar Solo** / **Drum Solo** / *Under Pressure* / *Fat Bottomed Girls* / *Crazy Little Thing Called Love* / **Bohemian Rhapsody** / *Tie Your Mother Down* / *Encore: Another One Bites The Dust* / *2nd Encore:* **We Will Rock You** / **We Are The Champions** / *God Save The Queen*

The show does not actually begin with 'Flash' proper, a pre-recorded backing track is played instead. The band perform 'The Hero' as their first number.

Freddie's first words come after 'Rock You': "Hello ev'rybody, okay. You know it's not very often that we do shows in the daylight – I fucking wish we had before – I can see you all now! And there's some beauties here tonight I can tell you. On with the show...This is 'Action'."

Queen perform a superb version of 'Play The Game' here, intro'd by a wonderful piano ad-lib from Freddie. He also improvises during the song too: "This is your bloody life," he sings. "Don't play hard to get. It's a free world, all you have to do is play the game".

"Hey hey hey, heyooooh, heyooooh." Freddie is off again down the 'everything I sing, you sing' road... first he showers the front rows with his drink, then addresses them: "Now most of you know that we've got some new sounds out, in the last week, and for what it's worth, we're gonna do a few songs in the funk / black category... whatever you call it. That doesn't mean we've lost our rock and roll feel, okay!... I mean it's only a bloody record. People get so excited about these things. We just want to try out a few sounds. This is 'Staying Power'." The amazing horn arrangement on the album is replaced on stage by Freddie's vocal interpretation.

An unusual vocal/piano improvisation precedes the next song. When Freddie hits a particularly difficult high note he grins, and turns to the audience: "Are

you ready? Huh, are you ready brothers and sisters?...". An enthusiastic "Yeah" comes back, and Queen commence 'Somebody To Love'. This is Queen – and Freddie in particular – at their very best.

"I feel positively knackered, I tell ya" says Fred after 'Now I'm Here', then he's off again: "Okay everybody, let's play games uh?... I'm gonna make you sing like Aretha Franklin." This time it ends with him telling the masses that they can join the band. During an ad-libbed segment Brian is heard to encounter tuning problems with his guitar so, momentarily, Roger provides a blistering solo. Then 'Dragon Attack' begins.

When Brian and Freddie are left on stage alone, seated on stools at the front centre of stage, Brian says: "This is the guitarist's chance to say a few words. Thank you for coming first of all. Thank you for making this long trip to Milton Keynes. I think it was worth it, what do you think?... I'm gonna dedicate this next one – this is a little unusual. I'd like to dedicate this particular song to all those people who are not like us, who sit here and have a good time listening to music – no matter where they come from – people who have given up their lives for what they believe." 'Love Of My Life' follows.

With no introduction at all, the band slide into another ballad, and everyone takes a turn on 'Save Me'. John's 'Back Chat' follows, again without formal introduction. 'Get Down Make Love' follows that, complete with lengthy mid-song interlude which is predictably edited out of the television broadcast. Brian then gives a punishing guitar solo which he looks relieved to finish, before Roger comes in with a short unexpected drum solo introduction to 'Under Pressure'.

Freddie's intro to 'Crazy Little Thing': "Ten years ago I only knew about three chords on the guitar, and now in 1982, I know three chords on the guitar. Before this wonderful intro that I'm gonna give you, right now I'd like to introduce to you Mr Morgan Fisher on piano – in that wonderful PINK! He's either AC or he's DC – I don't know. This is for anyone that's crazy out there."

The show nears the end with 'Bo Rhap' and 'Mother Down' – Queen would not be permitted to leave the

stage without performing them. 'Dust' follows. They then move into another frantic paced 'Sheer Heart Attack', which often seemed out of place in the set during this tour, before finishing with 'Rock You' and 'Champs'.

This show was filmed by Tyne Tees Television (in its entirety), and later broadcast on British TV's *The Tube* programme in January the following year on Channel 4, edited down to sixty minutes. Gavin Taylor, *The Tube's* resident director, directs the filming, which so impresses Queen that they later invite him to direct the Wembley Stadium (July 12, 1986) show, which is later released on video. The footage receives its American TV première on August 20, 1983, on the MTV network.

The broadcast also features brief snippets of pre-show interviews with Roger and Brian, as well as with a fan who says that he is attending his twenty-third Queen concert, and up to that point, has travelled 8,000 miles in all to see them. In addition to that, a policeman comments that if the crowd remain in the mood they have been in all morning, he will enjoy as good a day as them.

"Why have you travelled all this way to see Queen?" asks a local journalist. The replies are varied: "Sheer technical brilliance, good songs and a good show"/"I've been waiting four years to see them"/"They're one step ahead of everybody - well, three steps ahead of everybody"/"Coz we luv 'em, we luv 'em all".

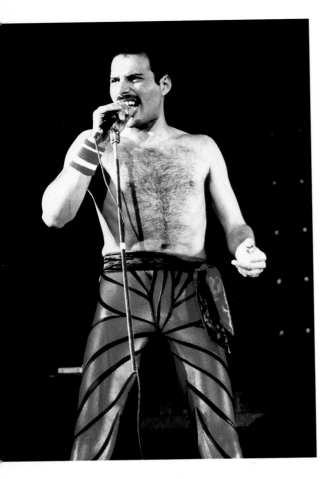

Stage manager Rick O'Brien talking about the lights: "Those cost $9,000 apiece, they are custom built for this show. They've (the manufacturers) taken a standard follow-spot and rebuilt the optics to our specifications, and then built that custom housing for it. It's being used in a very unique application. All the operator has to do is point it at whatever it is he's following, all the other spotlight controls and colour changing is done by remote – for all the spotlights – so it's an amazing piece of work.

"Once the band is on stage, most of my worries are over – the show really runs itself. We've got a very professional crew, and the band is very professional. It's getting them on stage that is the hard part – getting everything working, and perfect for them. What you want to do is create a sixty by forty foot universe that never changes for the band. So they just come up, and play – whether it be in Argentina, or in Europe, or in the States, on stage is the same wherever they go. The band shouldn't have anything else to worry about except playing for their fans."

The band arrive at the venue in a helicopter. Immediately prior to the start of the show, they are seen hanging around backstage, waiting to play. It is a rare insight, and shows a somewhat anxious looking Roger and John. Freddie meanwhile, clad in white jeans and striking matching leather jacket, looks fantastic, anything but nervous.

Support acts are the same as Elland Road on June 29, with one extra band: The Anti Nowhere League. The Teardrop Explodes finish their set early, when the audience become restless and begin to throw things at the stage, an all too common occurrence on this tour.

After the show Queen hold a 'shorts or suspenders' party at the Embassy club, in London.

July 19

'Calling All Girls'/'Put Out The Fire' is issued as an exclusively American single. It precedes Canadian and North American dates by only two days and eventually reaches No.60 in the *Billboard* charts.

USA 1982
Rock'n'America Tour '82

Queen fly to Montreal on July 18 to embark upon what would prove to be their final tour of North America. It entails forty shows at twenty-nine different venues, performed over a seven week period. Four of the shows are in Canada. It concludes with two concerts in California, at the Inglewood Forum, on September 14 and 15.

The support act is Billy Squier who had become a good friend of the band over the years. Freddie, Brian and Roger had all made appearances on his albums, either by playing their respective instruments or by providing backing vocals.

The show now includes material from 'Hot Space' which was previously absent: 'Calling All Girls', 'Body Language', 'Life Is Real' and 'Put Out The Fire'. The set was not otherwise much different from that played in Europe, but shuffled around somewhat. Roger Taylor's 'Rock It (Prime Jive)' was promoted to the second track performed. It replaced 'The Hero' which was dropped from the set despite being an apparently perfect choice for American audiences.

July 21
Forum, Montreal, Quebec

Flash / Rock It / We Will Rock You / Action This Day / Play The Game / Staying Power / Now I'm Here; Dragon Attack; Now I'm Here (Reprise) / Save Me / Calling All Girls / Back Chat / Get Down Make Love / Instrumental Inferno / Under Pressure / Fat Bottomed Girls / Crazy Little Thing Called Love / Bohemian Rhapsody / Tie Your Mother Down / Body Language / Encore: Another One Bites The Dust / 2nd Encore: We Will Rock You / We Are The Champions / God Save The Queen

July 23
Boston Gardens, Boston, Massachusetts

July 23 is declared official Queen Day in Boston. As such, the band are presented with a certificate to recognise the fact and given the freedom of the City, by the Mayor.

July 24
Spectrum, Philadelphia, Pennsylvania

July 25
Capitol Center, Washington DC

July 27/28
Madison Square Garden, New York

First night: Flash / Rock It / We Will Rock You / Action This Day / Play The Game / Staying Power / Now I'm Here; Dragon Attack; Now I'm Here (Reprise) / Save Me / Calling All Girls / Back Chat / Get Down Make Love / Instrumental Inferno / Under Pressure / Fat Bottomed Girls / Crazy Little Thing Called Love / Bohemian Rhapsody / Tie Your Mother Down / Body Language / Encore: Another One Bites The Dust / 2nd Encore: We Will Rock You / We Are The Champions / God Save The Queen

Queen make an in-store appearance at Crazy Eddies, the largest in a chain of New York record and audio shops.

Second night: Flash / Rock It / We Will Rock You / Action This Day / Play The Game / Somebody To Love / Now I'm Here; Dragon Attack / Save Me / Calling All Girls / Get Down Make Love / Instrumental Inferno / Body Language / Under Pressure / Fat Bottomed Girls / Crazy Little Thing Called Love / Bohemian Rhapsody / Tie Your Mother Down / Encore: Another One Bites The Dust / 2nd Encore: We Will Rock You / We Are The Champions / God Save The Queen

Female mud wrestlers are hired backstage – for the entertainment of the crew. They are present at both Madison Square Garden shows.

July 31

Richfield Coliseum, Cleveland, Ohio

August 2

Maple Leaf Gardens, Toronto, Ontario

Flash / Rock It / We Will Rock You / Action This Day / Play The Game / Staying Power / Now I'm Here; Dragon Attack / Save Me / Calling All Girls / Get Down Make Love / Instrumental Inferno / Body Language / Under Pressure / Fat Bottomed Girls / Crazy Little Thing Called Love / Bohemian Rhapsody / Tie Your Mother Down / Encore: Another One Bites The Dust / 2nd Encore: We Will Rock You / We Are The Champions / God Save The Queen

August 3

Maple Leaf Gardens, Toronto, Ontario

August 5

Market Square Arena, Indianapolis, Indiana

August 6

Joe Louis Arena, Detroit, Michigan

Flash / Rock It / We Will Rock You / Action This Day / Play The Game / Staying Power / Now I'm Here; Dragon Attack; Now I'm Here (Reprise) / Save Me / Calling All Girls / Back Chat / Get Down Make Love / Instrumental Inferno / Body Language / Under Pressure / Fat Bottomed Girls / Crazy Little Thing Called Love / Bohemian Rhapsody / Tie Your Mother Down / Encore: Another One Bites The Dust / 2nd Encore: We Will Rock You / We Are The Champions / God Save The Queen

August 7

Riverfront Coliseum, Cincinnati, Ohio

August 9

Brendon Burn Coliseum, Meadowlands, New Jersey

Flash / Rock It / We Will Rock You / Action This Day / Play The Game / Somebody To Love / Now I'm Here; Dragon Attack; Now I'm Here (Reprise) / Save Me / Calling All Girls / Get Down Make Love / Instrumental Inferno (Prolonged) / Body Language / Under Pressure / Life Is Real / Fat Bottomed Girls / Crazy Little Thing Called Love / Bohemian Rhapsody / Tie Your Mother Down / Encore: Another One Bites The Dust / 2nd Encore: We Will Rock You / We Are The Champions / God Save The Queen

This show sees rare live versions of 'Calling All Girls' and 'Life Is Real'. Neither was performed during the preceding European shows.

After the show the band throw a party at the famous Danceteria Club. It is co-organised by the American record company Elektra, and is attended by a host of famous celebrities including Irene Cara, Andy Warhol, Ian Hunter, Johnny Rotten and Vitas Gueralitis.

While no single was released in America on this day, in Britain the final track taken from 'Hot Space' was issued. 'Back Chat'/'Staying Power' fails to make much impression on the British public, struggling to reach No.40. Allowing for the generally uninspiring reception given to the second, third and fourth dance orientated 'Hot Space' singles, EMI may well have been better advised to have released the heavier Brian May songs 'Put Out The Fire' and 'Dancer'.

August 10

New Haven Coliseum, Connecticut

August 13/14

Poplar Creek, Chicago, Illinois

Second night: Flash / Rock It / We Will Rock You / Action This Day / Play The Game / Calling All Girls / Now I'm Here; Dragon Attack; Now I'm Here (Reprise) / Save Me / Get Down Make Love / Life Is Real / Body Language / Under Pressure / Fat Bottomed Girls / Crazy Little Thing Called Love / Bohemian Rhapsody / Tie Your Mother Down / Encore: Another One Bites The Dust / 2nd Encore: We Will Rock You / We Are The Champions / God Save The Queen

August 15

Civic Center Arena, St Paul, Minnesota

August 19

Civic Center, Biloxi, Mississippi

Flash / Rock It / We Will Rock You / Action This Day / Play The Game / Calling All Girls / Now I'm Here; Dragon Attack; Now I'm Here (Reprise) / Save Me / Get Down Make Love / Life Is Real / Body Language / Under Pressure / Fat Bottomed Girls / Crazy Little Thing Called Love / Bohemian Rhapsody / Tie Your Mother Down / Encore: Another One Bites The Dust / 2nd Encore: We Will Rock You / We Are The Champions / God Save The Queen

August 20

Summit, Houston, Texas

August 21

Reunion, Dallas, Texas

August 24

The Omni, Atlanta, Georgia

August 25

Mid South Coliseum, Memphis, Tennessee

August 27

City Myriad, Oklahoma

Flash / Rock It / We Will Rock You / Action This Day / Somebody To Love / Calling All Girls / Now I'm Here / Put Out The Fire / Dragon Attack / Love Of My Life / Save Me / Get Down Make Love / Instrumental Inferno / Guitar Solo / Body Language / Back Chat / Under Pressure / Fat Bottomed Girls / Crazy Little Thing Called Love / Saturday Night's Alright For Fighting / Bohemian Rhapsody / Tie Your Mother Down / Jailhouse Rock / Encore: Another One Bites The Dust / 2nd Encore: We Will Rock You / We Are The Champions / God Save The Queen

August 28

Kemper Arena, Kansas City, Missouri

August 30

McNichols Arena, Denver, Colorado

September 2

Portland Coliseum, Portland, Oregon

Flash / Rock It / We Will Rock You / Action This Day / Play The Game / Calling All Girls / Now I'm Here; Put Out The Fire; Dragon Attack ; Now I'm Here (Reprise) / Save Me / Get Down Make Love / Instrumental Inferno / Body Language / Under Pressure / Fat Bottomed Girls / Crazy Little Thing Called Love / Bohemian Rhapsody / Tie Your Mother Down / Encore: Another One Bites The Dust / 2nd Encore: We Will Rock You / We Are The Champions / God Save The Queen

September 3

Seattle Coliseum, Seattle, Washington

September 4

PNE Coliseum, Vancouver, British Columbia

September 7

Oakland Coliseum, Oakland, California

Flash / Rock It / We Will Rock You / Action This Day / Play The Game / Calling All Girls / Now I'm Here; Put Out The Fire; Dragon Attack; Now I'm Here (Reprise) / Save Me / Get Down Make Love / Instrumental Inferno / Body Language / Under Pressure / Fat Bottomed Girls / Crazy Little Thing Called Love / Bohemian Rhapsody / Tie Your Mother Down / Encore: Another One Bites The Dust / 2nd Encore: We Will Rock You / We Are The Champions / God Save The Queen

During a promotional interview for 'Hot Space', Brian is asked by DJ Richard Skinner to explain why 'Put Out The Fire' appears directly before the John Lennon tribute song ('Life Is Real') in the album's running sequence. The song suggests that guns alone do not kill people, people do. Skinner remarks that perhaps the gesture is rather too blatant.

Brian: "I think it is a good idea to put out the fire in many respects. In some songs you can subtle-out yourself. We've put little things like that in previous albums, and they've been overlooked." In a separate interview he added: "It's seldom that people actually pick them up, except the few real close fans who listen very carefully. It was deliberate."

September 10
ASU Arena, Temple, Texas

September 11/12
Irving Meadows, Irving, Texas

September 14/15
The Inglewood Forum, Los Angeles, California

Second night: Flash / Rock It / We Will Rock You / Action This Day / Somebody To Love / Calling All Girls / Now I'm Here ; Put Out The Fire ; Dragon Attack / Love Of My Life / Save Me / Get Down Make Love / Instrumental Inferno / Guitar Solo / Body Language / Back Chat / Under Pressure / Fat Bottomed Girls / Crazy Little Thing Called Love / Saturday Night's Alright For Fighting / Bohemian Rhapsody / Tie Your Mother Down / Encore: Another One Bites The Dust / Jailhouse Rock / 2nd Encore: We Will Rock You / We Are The Champions / God Save The Queen

Queen were joined on stage by Billy Squier for the 'Jailhouse Rock' encore on the second night. Squier had been the support act throughout the American dates. In attendance at this show are friends of the band Michael Jackson, Rod Stewart and Donna Summer.

September 25
Queen appear on the American television programme *Saturday Night Live*, in the first of a new series, performing 'Crazy Little Thing Called Love' and 'Under Pressure'. They are also followed around for several days by another television crew, who are filming and recording material for an *Entertainment Tonight* programme.

JAPAN 1982
Japan (Hot Space) Tour

Queen fly to Japan once again to begin their fifth tour there, a two week visit entailing only six shows, in five cities.

Unusually, the vast Budokan Hall venue, in the capital city, is not one of them.

The sixth show is filmed, and later issued as an exclusively Japanese video. It very soon becomes an extremely difficult-to-locate collectors' item, and a very expensive one too.

The set features 'The Hero' back in its rightful place as the opening track. Other than the inclusion once again of 'Teo Torriatte', there are no significant changes to the set.

October 19/20
Kyuden Auditorium, Fukuoka

October 24
Hankyu Nishinomiyakyujo, Osaka

Flash / The Hero / We Will Rock You / Action This Day / Somebody To Love / Calling All Girls / Now I'm Here; Put Out The Fire; Dragon Attack; Now I'm Here (Reprise) / Love Of My Life / Improvisation / Save Me / Get Down Make Love / Instrumental Inferno / Body Language / Under Pressure / Fat Bottomed Girls / Crazy Little Thing Called Love / Saturday Night's Alright For Fighting / Bohemian Rhapsody / Tie Your Mother Down / Encore: Another One Bites The Dust / Jailhouse Rock / 2nd Encore: Teo Torriatte / We Will Rock You / We Are The Champions / God Save The Queen

This concert was filmed for the band's own archive. Some of it features on the 1989 'Rare Live' video. 'Crazy Little Thing' is without doubt one of the best renditions ever captured on tape, and especially on film. The band are assisted on stage by Morgan Fisher on piano, and it is largely due to him that the song is so good.

While in Osaka, Queen hold a press conference to satisfy the huge demand for their time. So many radio stations, TV programmes and newspapers had requested time with them that it was decided everyone should attend one big conference.

October 26
Kokusai Tenjijo, Nagoya

October 29
Hokkaidoritso Sangyo Kyoshinakaijo, Sapporo

Flash / The Hero / We Will Rock You / Action This Day / Somebody To Love / Calling All Girls / Now I'm Here; Put Out The Fire; Dragon Attack; Now I'm Here (Reprise) / Love Of My Life / Improvisation / Save Me / Get Down Make Love / Instrumental Inferno / Body Language / Under Pressure / Fat Bottomed Girls / Crazy Little Thing Called Love / Saturday Night's Alright For Fighting /

Bohemian Rhapsody / Tie Your Mother Down / Encore: Another One Bites The Dust / Jailhouse Rock / 2nd Encore: Teo Torriatte / We Are The Champions / God Save The Queen

Queen perform 'Take Me Home' during this set, but it is not known where in the set it featured.

November 3
Seibu Lions Stadium, Tokyo

Highlighted tracks featured in the Japanese video.

*Flash / The Hero / Rock It / We Will Rock You / Action This Day / Somebody To Love / **Now I'm Here**; Improvisation; **Put Out The Fire**; Dragon Attack; **Now I'm Here (Reprise)** / **Love Of My Life** / **Save Me** / Get Down Make Love / **Guitar Solo** (AKA Instrumental Inferno) / Body Language / Back Chat / **Under Pressure** / Fat Bottomed Girls / **Crazy Little Thing Called Love** / **Bohemian Rhapsody** / **Tie Your Mother Down** / Encore: **Teo Torriatte** / 2nd Encore: **We Will Rock You** / **We Are The Champions** / God Save The Queen*

The entire set was filmed and later issued on video, exclusive to the Japanese market as the very first commercially available footage of Queen in concert. The rest of the world would have to wait until September 1984 for their first offering, the November 24/25, 1981, Montreal Forum, Canada show, issued as 'We Will Rock You'.

The Japanese video release offered just an edited account of the show but it features the only officially available concert footage of 'Teo Torriatte' and 'Put Out The Fire'.

November 4
While Brian and John travel straight home to the UK after the shows, Freddie stays on for further shopping sprees in his beloved Japan, and Roger flies to Hong Kong for a short holiday before moving on to Bangkok and Thailand.

November 13
Roger screens the final sixty-minute edited 'We Will Rock You' live video at his home during a fireworks party. John and Brian are also in attendance.

There would be no Queen concerts in 1983.

January 23
Roger Taylor's 'Radio Ga Ga' is released in the UK as the first single from the forthcoming 'Works' album. It is backed with Brian's 'I Go Crazy', a track which was left off the album and from the live shows, and it reaches No.2. The same pairing is released in America on February 7. It peaks at No.16.

The UK disc carries QUEEN 1 as its catalogue number. It is the first of the personalised numbers which will eventually conclude with QUEEN 20 with the 'Bo Rhap'/'These Are The Days Of Our Lives' single issued in December 1991 as a tribute to Freddie.

February 3
Queen fly to Italy to headline in the annual San Remo Song Festival. The event is broadcast live throughout Europe, and is watched by 30 million people. Other artists appearing include Paul Young, Bonnie Tyler and Culture Club. It was Queen's first performance in Italy. They perform 'Radio Ga Ga' in front of a studio audience of 2000.

When Freddie sees Culture Club's performance, he is much impressed, and later remarks that Boy George possesses a great talent, and is very brave, a reference to his camp image. He observes similarities during Queen's early years between George and himself.

February 27
Queen release their eleventh studio album 'The Works' in the UK, and a day later in America. The numerous subsequent singles from it yield a wide range of non-album material, not least

'I Go Crazy' in which Freddie protests he "ain't gonna go and see The Rolling Stones no more" and adds "I ain't gonna go and see Queeeeeen". The track is an astonishing omission from the album (despite there being ample room to accommodate it) and was released only as B-side to 'Radio Ga Ga'. Not only is it left off the album, it is also overlooked for a single release and is absent in the live show too. Given its concert related theme, it would certainly have been well received.

'The Works' is unprecedented in that it is the only Queen album to feature material which was all issued as either a main single, or a B-side. 1984 proved to be a very expensive period for collectors.

'Radio Ga Ga', 'It's A Hard Life', 'I Want To Break Free' and 'Hammer To Fall' were all issued as main singles, 'Tear It Up', 'Man On The Prowl', 'Machines (Or Back To Humans)', 'Keep Passing The Open Windows' and 'Is This The World We Created' all appeared as flipsides. In addition to that, extended cuts of 'Ga Ga', 'Hard Life', 'Prowl', 'Break Free' and 'Windows', instrumental cuts of 'Ga Ga' and 'Machines', and edited and 'Headbanger' versions of 'Hammer To Fall' also emerged.

Regardless of the prolific vinyl output, several songs from 'Works' did not appear in the live show. As well as 'I Go Crazy', Freddie's 'Keep Passing The Open Windows' and 'Man On The Prowl', and the Taylor/May co-composition 'Machines' were also overlooked.

Although all shows on the Works Tour commenced with the 'Machines' backing track, the full vocal version was never actually performed. The song centres around a hypothetical argument exploring the pros and cons of computers over human beings. An

ingenious lyric and driving guitar/drum backing gives the song immense concert potential – conjuring up visions of an on stage argument scenario, between Freddie and Brian perhaps.

When Hollywood Records reissued the Queen back catalogue on compact disc in 1991, they included 'I Go Crazy', and 'Radio Ga Ga'/'Break Free (Extended Versions)' as bonus tracks. They could certainly have appeared on the original album as a thirty-seven minute running time would have permitted the space. Four of the album's six extended mixes were to crop up later on the September 1992 'Box Of Tricks' boxed set, as well as the superb instrumental cut of 'Machines' which had previously been available only on the American 'Break Free' single (as B-side).

Aimed blatantly at 1984's Christmas market, EMI issued a three track seven and twelve inch disc in November 1984, which entailed Queen's second only A-side song not to appear on an album ('Flash' was the first). 'Thank God It's Christmas' (another May/Taylor collaboration) was backed with the album cuts of 'Man On The Prowl' and 'Keep Passing The Open Windows' on seven inch format, and extended cuts of both tracks for the twelve inch. Despite the two track flipside, the festive disc still narrowly missed the Top 20 (it peaked at 21).

March/April
On March 24 John and Roger left London for Tokyo where they undertook a gruelling two week tour promoting 'The Works' album. They cram an average of six radio and television interviews into each day, which include appearances on Tokyo Rock TV and a *Music Life* magazine special. The two then move on to Seoul, for more interviews, and then fly on to Sydney on April 1. On April 5 they moved onwards once again, to Melbourne, for yet more appointments, before concluding the tour in Los Angeles, on April 8.

Between them, John and Roger gave a total of 112 interviews in only 16 days. They then take a short holiday in Spain – where the word 'Works' was avoided at all costs.

April 2

'I Want To Break Free' is released as the second single from 'The Works'. Coupled with the May/Taylor co-composition 'Machines (Or Back To Humans)', it provides Queen with a No.3 hit in the UK.

Although Elektra issued an exclusive instrumental version of the B-side in America, it could only reach No.45 in the charts. The single has subsequently become hugely collectable because of the otherwise unavailable instrumental track, though with the May 1992 Hollywood Records 'Box Of Tricks' release, it is now available on compact disc. In the UK, no less than six different picture sleeves were issued, four 7" sleeves and two 12".

May 12

Queen appear at the four day Golden Rose Pop Festival which commences on May 10 and runs through to the 13th. They are the headlining act on the 12th. None of the performances are live, however, and miming to the songs presents Freddie with occasional problems: he forgets the odd lyric, or comes in too late. They perform 'Radio Ga Ga', 'Tear It Up', 'I Want To Break Free' and 'It's A Hard Life'. Also featured on the same day as Queen are Adam Ant, Status Quo and Madness.

The event was recorded by both Swiss TV and the BBC, and was eventually broadcast to over forty countries around the world – which was the main reason for Queen's attendance. Despite having a dislike of miming material, they viewed the huge potential audience as too good an opportunity to pass up.

Cliff Richard, Shakin' Stevens, Duran Duran, Rod Stewart and Elton John also appear at the event.

May 22

Freddie attends an Elton John concert in Munich. He does not join him on stage, however, as his foot and leg are in plaster, following a severe knee ligament injury he sustained.

June 28

Queen attend the Music Therapy Awards dinner, and are presented with a Silver Clef award for outstanding contribution to music.

July 16

The penultimate single from 'The Works' is released in the UK. Backed with the acoustic May/Mercury ballad 'Is This The World We Created', 'It's A Hard Life' eventually reaches No.6. Issued ten days earlier in America, the same pairing of songs struggles to reach No.72. A somewhat unorthodox promotional video, which even members of the band were not entirely comfortable with, did little to inspire sales.

The other three members of the band ridicule Freddie when they see his now legendary costume. Predominently red and featuring giant eyes, Roger was overheard to comment that Freddie looked like a gigantic prawn.

EUROPE 1984
Queen Works!
(The Works Tour)

Queen begin what is commonly referred to as The Works Tour which entails twenty-three shows at fourteen different sites in seven cities. The nine British shows begin on August 28 with two shows in Dublin and three consecutive gigs at the National Exhibition Centre in Birmingham. Four shows at London's Wembley Arena follow that.

The stage backdrop is based on scenes from the Fritz Lang silent movie *Metropolis*, made in 1930. Two giant cogwheels rotate slowly in front of immense skyscrapers, partly obscured by clouds of steam. Strobe lights illuminate the entire backdrop during 'Radio Ga Ga'.

The set has now undergone a major face lift to incorporate much of the material from 'The Works' album, released six months earlier: 'Tear It Up', 'It's A Hard Life', 'Is This The World We Created', 'Hammer To Fall', 'Radio Ga Ga', 'I Want To Break Free' and a predominantly improvised keyboard version of 'Machines'. The 'Machines' backing track also starts the show.

As might be expected, most of the 'Hot Space' and 'Game' tracks, as well as other material, is dropped to accommodate the newer maaterial. A handful of songs which could never be considered for omission still remain, but are juggled around somewhat: 'Love Of My Life', 'Bo Rhap', 'Tie Your Mother Down', 'Under Pressure', 'Brighton Rock' and 'Somebody To Love'. Some others are brought out of retirement to appear again: 'Seven Seas Of Rhye', 'Stone Cold Crazy' and parts of 'Liar' and 'Great King Rat'.

By the time the tour began, the album and related singles had already sold impressive numbers, as the accompanying tour programme summarised: "The album has gone either gold or platinum in over a dozen countries. The album's first single, 'Radio Ga Ga' was a massive world-wide hit, reaching No.1 in an incredible nineteen countries. The follow up, 'I Want To Break Free' followed the tried and trusted Queen path, going gold more frequently than Sebastian Coe! And the Queen machine rolls on: a new single 'It's A Hard Life' looks set to follow its predecessors into the charts." 'Hard Life' actually reached No.6.

August 24
Forest Nationale, Brussels

Machines (Intro) / Tear It Up / Tie Your Mother Down / Under Pressure / Medley: Somebody To Love; Killer Queen; Seven Seas Of Rhye; Keep Yourself Alive; Liar / It's A Hard Life / Staying Power / Dragon Attack / Now I'm Here / Is This The World We Created / Love Of My Life / Stone Cold Crazy / Great King Rat / Machines (Keyboard Improv) / Guitar Solo / Brighton Rock / Another One Bites The Dust / Crazy Little Thing Called Love / Bohemian Rhapsody / Hammer To Fall / Radio Ga Ga / Encore: I Want To Break Free / Sheer Heart Attack / 2nd Encore: We Will Rock You / We Are The Champions / God Save The Queen

This show was filmed so that the 'Hammer To Fall' promotional video could be made. Members of the audience were also invited back the following day for additional filming. The concert environment was recreated and then filmed again. David Mallett was the director.

A photograph taken of the event, which depicts the extraordinary lighting display, was used to illustrate the front cover of early 'Hammer To Fall' single sleeves. Due to objections, apparently from Brian May, the sleeves were withdrawn and replaced with a plain red jacket. A number of the live sleeves did circulate, however, and have since become hugely collectable. The same photograph was later used to promote the 'Greatest Hits II' video and album releases.

As if by magic, during 'Radio Ga Ga' everyone in the audience unites to recreate the synchronised handclapping which features in the video. An incredible sea of arms are seen to clap twice above the respective heads, and then thrust into the night sky with clenched fists. It was almost as if the audience had arrived hours beforehand and rehearsed it. This would occur at every subsequent live performance.

August 28/29
Royal Dublin Society Showgrounds, Dublin

First night: Machines (Intro) / Tear It Up / Tie Your Mother Down / Under Pressure / Medley: Somebody To Love; Killer Queen; Seven Seas Of Rhye; Keep Yourself Alive; Liar / It's A Hard Life / Staying Power / Dragon Attack / Now I'm Here / Is This The World We Created / Love Of My Life / Stone Cold Crazy / Great King Rat / Machines (Keyboard Improv) / Guitar Solo / Brighton Rock / Another One Bites The Dust / Hammer To Fall / Crazy Little Thing Called Love / Bohemian Rhapsody / Radio Ga Ga / Encore: I Want To Break Free / Sheer Heart Attack / 2nd Encore: We Will Rock You / We Are The Champions / A Day At The Races (Outro)

Because it was considered inappropriate to close the two shows here with 'God Save The Queen', the band instead concluded the first one with the musical passage from 'A Day At The Races'. When the music was absent from the second performance, members of the audience improvised by singing the national anthem themselves.

For 'Hammer To Fall' on this tour, Brian is joined on stage by Spike Edney who provides additional guitar.

August 31/September 1/2
NEC, Birmingham

First night: Machines (Intro) / Tear It Up / Tie Your Mother Down / Under Pressure / Medley: Somebody To Love; Killer Queen; Seven Seas Of Rhye; Keep Yourself Alive; Liar / Improvisation / It's A Hard Life / Staying Power / Dragon Attack / Now I'm Here / Is This The World We Created / Love Of My Life / Stone Cold Crazy / Great King Rat / Machines (Keyboard Improvisation) / Guitar Solo / Brighton Rock / Hammer To Fall / Another One Bites The Dust / Crazy Little Thing Called Love / Bohemian Rhapsody / Radio Ga Ga / Encore: I Want To Break Free / Sheer Heart Attack / 2nd Encore: We Will Rock You / We Are The Champions / God Save The Queen

All three shows at this venue are sold out. Eleven thousand people each night fill the NEC to its capacity.

Roger Trapp reviews this concert in the *Birmingham Evening Mail* of September 1 under the headline: "NEC SHOW'S A REAL DAZZLER".

"Chart topping rock group Queen began their three-night stand in Birmingham last night with one of the most spectacular shows the NEC Arena has ever seen. Back in Britain for the first time in two years, the four-man group, who have scored numerous hits in the last decade, performed with enormous energy and enthusiasm for nearly two hours.

"...While lead singer Freddie Mercury – clad for much of the show in just skin-tight red Spiderman trousers – strutted and pranced about the stage, the multi-coloured lights on the huge rig rose and fell and gigantic wheels spun against a mechanical landscape back-drop.

"Queen – who have a reputation for producing excessive concerts – had promised their fans something

special this time. None of them can have been disappointed. The only low point was when guitarist Brian May took a sustained – and by the end rather tedious – solo spot. Otherwise he, Mercury, drummer Roger Taylor and bass player John Deacon – with help from an extra musician and the special effects – held the audience's rapt attention.

"All the favourites - from 'Seven Seas Of Rhye', through 'Killer Queen' and 'Under Pressure' to the recent No.1 'Radio Ga Ga' were there and performed with a staggering panache. So thrilled at their reception were the group that Mercury vowed they would keep playing concerts as long as their records sold."

Second night: Machines (Intro) / Tear It Up / Tie Your Mother Down / Under Pressure / Medley: Somebody To Love; Killer Queen; Seven Seas Of Rhye; Keep Yourself Alive; Liar / Improvisation / It's A Hard Life / Staying Power / Dragon Attack / Now I'm Here / Is This The World We Created / Love Of My Life / Stone Cold Crazy / Great King Rat / Machines (Keyboard Improvisation) / Guitar Solo / Brighton Rock / Hammer To Fall / Another One Bites The Dust / Crazy Little Thing Called Love / Saturday Night's Alright For Fighting / Bohemian Rhapsody / Radio Ga Ga / Encore: I Want To Break Free / Sheer Heart Attack / 2nd Encore: We Will Rock You / We Are The Champions / God Save The Queen

The support act is General Public, a group consisting of two former members of The Beat – Dave Wakeling and Ranking Roger. They also supported at the four London shows.

The shows were attended by a variety of celebrities, which included Andy Taylor (Duran Duran), Tony Hadley (Spandau Ballet) and Jimmy Lea and Dave Hill from Slade.

Highlighted tracks featured in the video
Final night: Machines (Intro) / **Tear It Up** / Tie Your Mother Down / Under Pressure / Medley: Somebody To Love; Killer Queen; Seven Seas Of Rhye; Keep Yourself Alive; **Liar** / Improvisation / **It's A Hard Life** / **Staying Power** / **Dragon Attack** / Now I'm Here / **Is This The World We Created** / **Love Of My Life** / **Stone Cold Crazy** / Great King Rat / Machines (Keyboard Improvisation) / Guitar Solo / Brighton Rock / **Hammer To Fall** / **Another One Bites The Dust** / **Crazy Little Thing Called Love** / Saturday Night's Alright For Fighting / Bohemian Rhapsody / **Radio Ga Ga** /

Encore: I Want To Break Free / Sheer Heart Attack / 2nd Encore: We Will Rock You / We Are The Champions / God Save The Queen

Freddie's opening words: "Hello how you doing? Listen, I must say it's nice to be back on the road again after two years of absence. It seems kind of different, but as long as you guys are here it'll be alright.

"A lot of people are saying that this is gonna be our last tour. That is completely untrue, okay. If we wanted to break up we'd let you know, but as long as you buggers buy the records we're gonna be here. Just to prove it, this is 'Staying Power'."

When the audience begin singing the opening lines of 'Love Of My Life' without Freddie, he stops Brian from continuing and suggests that they start again from the top. Just then, an audience member gives two hoots on a hand held horn. "Don't mess about," Freddie snaps, then he jokingly chastises the culprit: "How dare you sing without my command". Before he is permitted to resume though, he must first face a barrage of "We love you Freddie" repeated about twenty times. "That's what I like – a really intelligent bunch," he adds, laughing. "Look shall we sing this bugger or not?". The song eventually goes ahead – faultlessly.

Most audio bootlegs of this show include the pre-show soundcheck tracks (as highlighted in the set list). They were not played in the concert sequence, and most were not full length versions. The sound quality is typically poor.

September 4/5/7/8
Wembley Arena, London
First night: Machines (Intro) / Tear It Up / Tie Your Mother Down / Under Pressure / Medley: Somebody To Love; Killer Queen; Seven Seas Of Rhye; Keep Yourself Alive; Liar / Improvisation / It's A Hard Life / Staying Power / Dragon Attack / Now I'm Here / Is This The World We Created / Love Of My Life / Stone Cold Crazy / Great King Rat / Machines (Keyboard Improvisation) / Guitar Solo / Brighton Rock / Hammer To Fall / Another One Bites The Dust / Not Fade Away / Crazy Little Thing Called Love / Bohemian Rhapsody / Radio Ga Ga / Encore: I Want To Break Free / Sheer Heart Attack / 2nd Encore: We Will Rock You / We Are The Champions / God Save The Queen

When the band return for their first encore here, Freddie is dressed in the

wig he wore for the infamous 'I Want To Break Free' video, and has an enormous pair of false breasts beneath his pink sleeveless jumper. He takes great delight in exposing them to the already uproarious onlookers.

'Not Fade Away' is not performed in its entirety, Freddie merely sings a few opening verses as a segue into 'Crazy Little Thing'.

Second night: Machines (Intro) / Tear It Up / Tie Your Mother Down / Under Pressure / Medley: Somebody To Love; Killer Queen; Seven Seas Of Rhye; Keep Yourself Alive; Liar / Improvisation / It's A Hard Life / Staying Power / Dragon Attack / Now I'm Here / Is This The World We Created / Love Of My Life / Stone Cold Crazy / Great King Rat / Machines (Keyboard Improvisation) / Guitar Solo / Brighton Rock / Hammer To Fall / Another One Bites The Dust / Crazy Little Thing Called Love / Bohemian Rhapsody / Radio Ga Ga / Encore: I Want To Break Free / Sheer Heart Attack / 2nd Encore: We Will Rock You / We Are The Champions / God Save The Queen

Following 'Dragon Attack' the audience sing 'Happy Birthday' to Freddie who is thirty-eight. He acknowledges them with a smile, bows, and then proceeds to shower the front rows with the contents of a plastic beaker. Then he opens a card handed to him from the audience: "I can't read *this*" he declares. After a couple of minutes of improvised vocal ad-libbing, the band then break into 'Now I'm Here'.

During the 'Break Free' encore, Freddie lifts up his pink T-shirt to expose the now customary breasts, strutting around the stage showing them to anyone who wants to look, and finally thrusting them into John Deacon's face. Both laugh as cameras flash everywhere.

Freddie takes the opportunity during the show to respond to yet more tedious tabloid misrepresentation: "You've all been reading a lot of things in the press today. Let me just say that the stories about us splitting up are all unfucking true, alright." The audience seem relieved, and roar in appreciation. "We love you!" he adds, and the show continues.

Rick Parfitt (Status Quo) joins Queen on stage to assist with additional guitar backing and vocals on 'Shake Rattle And Roll'. Freddie's thirty-eighth birthday ensures that spirits are high throughout.

After the show the band and friends make their way to the Xenon nightclub in Piccadilly. Celebrations last well into the next morning, and Freddie is presented with two huge cakes – one a superbly decorated Rolls Royce with FM 1 as its licence number.

Third night: Machines (Intro) / Tear It Up / Tie Your Mother Down / Under Pressure / Medley: Somebody To Love; Killer Queen; Seven Seas Of Rhye; Keep Yourself Alive; Liar / Improvisation / It's A Hard Life / Staying Power / Dragon Attack / Now I'm Here / Is This The World We Created / Love Of My Life / Stone Cold Crazy / Great King Rat / Machines (Keyboard Improvisation) / Guitar Solo / Brighton Rock / Another One Bites The Dust / Hammer To Fall / Crazy Little Thing Called Love / Saturday Night's Alright For Fighting / Bohemian Rhapsody / Radio Ga Ga / Encore: I Want To Break Free / Sheer Heart Attack / 2nd Encore: We Will Rock You / We Are The Champions / God Save The Queen

TEN YEARS AFTER

Roll up ! Roll up ! Step this way !

"For a mere £9 you too can visit Mercury's Amazing Time Machine and be whisked back to a time when you could play and enjoy heavy metal and not be ashamed of it.

..."The band are ten minutes late and plenty of eyes are being cast down at watches. Suddenly the lights dimmed and the Arena erupts. The impressive backdrop of pulleys and cogs ('The Works' – geddit?) springs into life, flashpots ignite and with a bang they're onstage at last...

..."It was obvious that Freddie's overworked vocal chords were suffering, but with an impressive light show and the band on such form, there weren't any complaints. "You sing it!" he invites the crowd before 'Somebody To Love', and they dutifully obliged. His control over the crowd throughout was almost frightening to behold. One word was the signal for a roar of almost atomic proportions."

Final night: Machines (Intro) / Tear It Up / Tie Your Mother Down / Under Pressure / Medley: Somebody To Love; Killer Queen; Seven Seas Of Rhye; Keep Yourself Alive; Liar / It's A Hard Life / Staying Power / Dragon Attack / Now I'm Here / Is This The World We Created / Love Of My Life / Stone Cold Crazy / Great King Rat / Machines (Keyboard Improvisation) / Guitar Solo / Brighton Rock / Another One Bites The Dust / Hammer To Fall / Crazy Little Thing Called Love / Saturday Night's Alright For Fighting / Bohemian Rhapsody / Radio Ga Ga / Encore: I Want To Break Free / Sheer Heart Attack / 2nd Encore: We Will Rock You / We Are The Champions / God Save The Queen

Following the acoustic guitar introduction to 'Love Of My Life', Freddie misses Brian's cue to begin singing and general confusion between the two follows. Freddie ponders a while and then exclaims: "Well we fucked that up between us," and both give a good humoured grin, and restart the song. The front rows of the audience erupt into laughter.

As with the shows in Birmingham, all four nights at this venue were sold out, each attended by capacity audiences of 8,000 per night. Similarly, they were attended by numerous celebrities, including John Taylor of Duran Duran, racing driver Jackie Stewart, various members of Def Leppard, and actor John Hurt and his new wife. The Hurts had been guests at Freddie's birthday party, and were married the next morning.

Due largely to the seven NEC and Wembley Arena shows, in the week ending September 21, 1984, no less than nine Queen albums appeared in the UK Top 200 album chart.

They were:
The Works (No.9)
Greatest Hits (No.22)
A Night At The Opera (No.85)
A Day At The Races (No.123)
Sheer Heart Attack (No.134)
The Game (No.138)
Queen II (No.148)
Live Killers (No.160)
News Of The World (No.161)

September 10

'Hammer To Fall (Edit)'/'Tear It Up' (both written by Brian May) is issued in the UK. Though two other tracks, 'Man On The Prowl' and 'Keep Passing The Open Windows', later accompany the non-album 'Thank God It's Christmas' single, this is the last track to be released as a main single from 'The Works'. It peaks in the charts at No.13, due largely to the promotional film, shot in Brussels two weeks earlier.

The two tracks were a universal coupling although, surprisingly, Japan was overlooked. In America the disc was released a month later.

Also released on this day is the first officially available Queen live video aside from 'Live In Japan' which was issued in Japan only. 'We Will Rock You' is a long awaited twenty-one track visual documentation of the two Montreal shows of November 1981. It enters the UK video charts, in true Queen style, at No.1.

The video was directed by Saul Swimmer, who was also responsible for co-producing The Beatles *Let It Be* film. Although it was originally scheduled for a Christmas 1982 release, it was apparently delayed because of problems with the eight track Dolby sound system.

The footage is also shown at selected British cinemas throughout September and October, and continues showing until early March 1985 as attendance figures are rather better than anticipated, especially considering that none of the programmes begin before 11 p.m. The promotional videos for 'Ga Ga', 'Hard Life', 'Break Free' and 'Hammer To Fall' accompany the film as the support programme.

September 12
Westfallenhalle, Dortmund

September 14/15
Sportspalace, Milan

First night: Machines (Intro) / Tear It Up / Tie Your Mother Down / Under Pressure / Medley: Somebody To Love; Killer Queen; Seven Seas Of Rhye; Keep Yourself Alive; Liar / It's A Hard Life / Staying Power / Dragon Attack / Now I'm Here / Is This The World We Created / Love Of My Life / Stone Cold Crazy / Great King Rat / Machines (Keyboard Improvisation) / Guitar Solo / Brighton Rock / Another One Bites The Dust / Hammer To Fall / Crazy Little Thing Called Love / Bohemian Rhapsody / Radio Ga Ga / Encore: I Want To Break Free / Sheer Heart Attack / 2nd Encore: We Will Rock You / We Are The Champions / God Save The Queen

Second night: Machines (Intro) / Tear It Up / Tie Your Mother Down / Under Pressure / Somebody To Love / Medley: Killer Queen; Seven Seas Of Rhye; Keep Yourself Alive; Liar / It's A Hard Life / Staying Power / Dragon Attack / Now I'm Here / Is This The World We Created / Love Of My Life / Stone Cold Crazy / Great King Rat / Machines (Keyboard Improvisation) / Guitar Solo / Brighton Rock / Another One Bites The Dust / Hammer To Fall / Crazy Little Thing Called Love / Bohemian Rhapsody / Radio Ga Ga / Encore: I Want To Break Free / Jailhouse Rock / 2nd Encore: We Will Rock You / We Are The Champions / God Save The Queen

These were the first of only two shows played in Italy on 'The Works' tour.

September 16
Olympic Hall, Munich

September 18
Omnisports, Paris

Machines (Intro) / Tear It Up / Tie Your Mother Down / Under Pressure / Medley: Somebody To Love; Killer Queen; Seven Seas Of Rhye; Keep Yourself Alive; Liar / Improvisation / It's A Hard Life / Dragon Attack / Now I'm Here / Is This The World We Created / Love Of My Life / Stone Cold Crazy / Great King Rat / Machines (Keyboard Improvisation) / Guitar Solo / Brighton Rock / Another One Bites The Dust / Hammer To Fall / Crazy Little Thing Called Love / Bohemian Rhapsody / Radio Ga Ga / Encore: I Want To Break Free / Jailhouse Rock / 2nd Encore: We Will Rock You / We Are The Champions / God Save The Queen

September 20
Groenoordhalle, Leiden

Machines (Intro) / Tear It Up / Tie Your Mother Down / Under Pressure / Medley: Somebody To Love; Killer Queen; Seven Seas Of Rhye; Keep Yourself Alive; Liar / It's A Hard Life / Dragon Attack / Now I'm Here / Is This The World We Created / '39 / Love Of My Life / Stone Cold Crazy / Great King Rat / Machines (Keyboard Improvisation) / Guitar Solo / Brighton Rock / Another One Bites The Dust / Hammer To Fall / Crazy Little Thing Called Love / Bohemian Rhapsody / Radio Ga Ga / Encore: I Want To Break Free / Jailhouse Rock / 2nd Encore: We Will Rock You / We Are The Champions / God Save The Queen

The band performed an impromptu recital of "39" here. They sing only a small segment of it, in response to the audience's prompting. The audience sing the opening verses, and Queen oblige by joining in with additional verses.

September 21
Forêt Nationale, Brussels

Machines (Intro) / Tear It Up / Tie Your Mother Down / Under Pressure / Somebody To Love / Medley: Killer Queen; Seven Seas Of Rhye; Keep Yourself Alive; Liar / Improvisation / It's A Hard Life / Dragon Attack / Now I'm Here / Is This The World We Created / Love Of My Life / Stone Cold Crazy / Great King Rat / Machines (Keyboard Improvisation) / Brighton Rock / Guitar Solo / Another One Bites The Dust / Hammer To Fall / Crazy Little Thing Called Love / Mustapha (Intro) / Bohemian Rhapsody / Radio Ga Ga / Encore: I Want To Break Free / Jailhouse Rock / 2nd Encore: We Will Rock You / We Are The Champions / God Save The Queen

September 22
Europhalle, Hanover

During 'Hammer To Fall', Freddie slips on stage and further damages his already injured knee. He is helped to the piano and performs three more songs. Two songs are left out of the set, and the show concludes prematurely with Freddie still seated at the piano. The 'show must go on' philosophy was never more true.

When the lights go down, Freddie is carried straight to a waiting car and driven to hospital. He performs the remaining five European shows with his leg heavily bandaged.

September 24
Deutschlandhalle, Berlin

September 26
Festhalle, Frankfurt

Machines (Intro) / Tear It Up / Tie Your Mother Down / Under Pressure / Medley: Somebody To Love; Killer Queen; Seven Seas Of Rhye; Keep Yourself Alive; Liar / Improvisation / It's A Hard Life / Dragon Attack / Now I'm Here / Is This The World We Created / Love Of My Life / Stone Cold Crazy / Great King Rat / Machines (Keyboard Improvisation) / Brighton Rock / Guitar Solo / Another One Bites The Dust / Hammer To Fall / Crazy Little Thing Called Love / Bohemian Rhapsody / Radio Ga Ga / Encore: I Want To Break Free / Jailhouse Rock / 2nd Encore: We Will Rock You / We Are The Champions / God Save The Queen

September 27

Schleyerhalle, Stuttgart

Machines (Intro) / Tear It Up / Tie Your Mother Down / Under Pressure / Medley: Somebody To Love; Killer Queen; Seven Seas Of Rhye; Keep Yourself Alive; Liar / It's A Hard Life / Dragon Attack / Now I'm Here / Is This The World We Created / Love Of My Life / Stone Cold Crazy / Great King Rat / Machines (Keyboard Improvisation) / Brighton Rock / Guitar Solo / Another One Bites The Dust / Hammer To Fall / Crazy Little Thing Called Love / Saturday Night's Alright For Fighting / Bohemian Rhapsody / Radio Ga Ga / Encore: I Want To Break Free / Jailhouse Rock / 2nd Encore: We Will Rock You / We Are The Champions / God Save The Queen

September 29/30

Stadthalle, Vienna

First night: *Machines (Intro) / Tear It Up / Tie Your Mother Down / Under Pressure / Medley: Somebody To Love; Killer Queen; Seven Seas Of Rhye; Keep Yourself Alive; Liar / Improvisation / It's A Hard Life / Dragon Attack / Now I'm Here / Is This The World We Created / Love Of My Life / Stone Cold Crazy / Great King Rat / Machines (Keyboard Improvisation) / Brighton Rock / Guitar Solo / Another One Bites The Dust / Hammer To Fall / Crazy Little Thing Called Love / Saturday Night's Alright For Fighting / Bohemian Rhapsody / Radio Ga Ga / Encore: I Want To Break Free / Jailhouse Rock / 2nd Encore: We Will Rock You / We Are The Champions / God Save The Queen*

Final night: *Machines (Intro) / Tear It Up / Tie Your Mother Down / Under Pressure / Medley: Somebody To Love; Killer Queen; Seven Seas Of Rhye; Keep Yourself Alive; Liar / Improvisation / It's A Hard Life / Dragon Attack / Now I'm Here / Is This The World We Created / Love Of My Life / Stone Cold Crazy / Great King Rat / Machines (Keyboard Improvisation) / Brighton Rock / Guitar Solo / Another One Bites The Dust / Hammer To Fall / Crazy Little Thing Called Love / Bohemian Rhapsody / Radio Ga Ga / Encore: I Want To Break Free / Jailhouse Rock / 2nd Encore: We Will Rock You / We Are The Champions / God Save The Queen*

SOUTH AFRICA 1984
The Works Tour

Having concluded the European tour, Queen fly home for a few days before their controversial South African shows which had provoked such a media storm since being announced earlier that May.

The band were greatly apprehensive about the shows, having never before played there. Twelve shows are scheduled in all, but only seven were played because Freddie again encountered problems with his throat. The unplayed shows were scheduled for October 6, 7, 9 and 12.

October 5/10/13/14/18/19/20
Super Bowl, Sun City, Bophuthatswana (now known as Northern Transvaal)

Machines (Intro) / Tear It Up / Tie Your Mother Down / Under Pressure / Medley: Somebody To Love; Killer Queen; Seven Seas Of Rhye; Keep Yourself Alive; Liar / Improvisation / It's A Hard Life / Dragon Attack / Now I'm Here / Is This The World We Created / Love Of My Life / Stone Cold Crazy / Great King Rat / Machines (Keyboard Improvisation) / Guitar Solo / Brighton Rock / Another One Bites The Dust / Hammer To Fall / Crazy Little Thing Called Love / Bohemian Rhapsody / Radio Ga Ga / Encore: I Want To Break Free / Jailhouse Rock / 2nd Encore: We Will Rock You / We Are The Champions / God Save The Queen

The sets differed hardly at all throughout the seven shows. This was the most common set performed.

When Freddie walked back on stage for the 'Break Free' encore, clad in the false breasts and wig props (as unveiled at Wembley Arena), he was greeted with contempt. John Deacon's song had become widely recognised by South Africans as a gesture against apartheid and dictatorship generally, and was not something to be taken lightly or in any way mocked or ridiculed. Freddie's comic attire seemed to undermine its importance. When the audience responded by hurling cans and stones at him, Freddie wisely discarded the offending items, and the show continued without further incident.

An article about Live Aid published in *The Sun*, in April 1986, refers to a remark made by Radio One presenter John Peel regarding Queen's controversial South African shows. Peel had referred to the band as "Sun City Boys Queen" and Roger in particular took exception to this: "I was totally disgusted by that remark. Peel is an ageing hypocrite trying to jump on some moral bandwagon. Now millions of people might think that we are racists, which is far from the case, because of some glib remark."

The article goes on to redress the balance, and points out that the band had repeatedly said that they played Sun City specifically because there was a mixed audience, and that white and black fans were not segregated. "Our songs are very popular in South Africa," added Roger. "'I Want To Break Free' is an unofficial anthem among the African National Congress Movement. And 'Another One Bites The Dust' is one of the biggest-selling songs in South African black history. It was ridiculous of Peel to say what he did."

In a separate article in *Smash Hits* in March 1986, Brian May added: "The criticisms are absolutely and definitely not justified. We're totally against apartheid and all it stands for, but I feel that by going there we did a lot of bridge building. We actually met musicians of both colours. They all welcomed us with open arms. The only criticism we got was from outside South Africa."

As a direct result of the Sun City visit, EMI decide to issue an edited version of the 'Live Killers' album in South Africa. It had previously been issued as a double album (in June 1979). A single disc is compiled and released, and very quickly becomes an elusive collectors' item. All proceeds from the album are donated to the Kutlwamong School for deaf and blind children. Likewise, EMI donate their royalties too, and the money raised goes towards purchasing a new wing for the school.

This edited album was also issued in numerous other countries. Details of all of them are contained in the Live Discography section in this book.

November 26

EMI release Queen's 28th UK single. 'Thank God It's Christmas', backed with the only two remaining unissued tracks from 'The Works', is timed to exploit the Christmas market. The three track disc fails to make the Top 20, however, missing it by only one place.

BRAZIL 1985
Rock In Rio

January 12/19
Rock In Rio Festival, Rio De Janeiro

Highlighted tracks appear on the video.

Both nights: Machines (Intro) / Tear It Up / **Tie Your Mother Down** / *Under Pressure* / Medley: *Somebody To Love; Killer Queen;* **Seven Seas Of Rhye; Keep Yourself Alive; Liar** / *Rock In Rio Blues* / **It's A Hard Life** / *Dragon Attack* / **Now I'm Here** / **Is This The World We Created** / **Love Of My Life** / *Improvisation (incorporating Let Me Out)* / **Brighton Rock** / *Guitar Solo* / *Another One Bites The Dust* / **Hammer To Fall** / *Crazy Little Thing Called Love* / **Bohemian Rhapsody** / **Radio Ga Ga** / Encore: **I Want To Break Free** / 2nd Encore: **We Will Rock You** / **We Are The Champions** / **God Save The Queen**

Queen are the headline act for the huge Rock In Rio Festival. Though the festival runs for ten days, Queen perform on only two nights, the 12th and the 19th. The warm-up bands for Queen are Iron Maiden and Def Leppard for the first show, and The Go Go's and B52's for the second.

An estimated audience of between 250,000 and 300,000 attend each show, edited highlights of which are later shown on Globo television throughout South America, watched by nearly 200 million people. Queen take to the stage at 2.00 a.m. for both their appearances.

'Rock In Rio Blues' is similar to the piano improvisation played at previous European dates, but was reworked to incorporate lyrics written exclusively for the South American audience. Brian's introduction to 'Love Of My Life': "You want to sing with us? Alright. Well, this is especially for you. I have to tell you that this song is very special to the people of South America, and we thank you very much for making it special throughout the world. This is called 'Love Of My Life'." Freddie starts the ballad off, but the audience are anxious to show off their newly acquired English vocabulary, and almost drown him out before he allows them to continue without him. Freddie is visibly moved, as is everyone on the stage. He blows them a kiss, and Brian remarks "You sing very nicely."

When Freddie stops singing to let Brian begin his acoustic solo, a barrage of "BRIAN... BRIAN... BRIAN" fills the vast stadium. It was Brian's turn to swallow hard. Later, he incorporated parts of the track 'Let Me Out' from his 1983 'Star Fleet' solo project into his guitar solo.

When Freddie appears with wig and false boobs for 'I Want To Break Free' there is a similar response to that encountered in South Africa. This time, half expecting the reaction, he laughs and then discards the offending items. He later remarks: "I may have been stoned like the Queen of Sheba but I'm not giving up my boobs for anyone."

Following 'Rock You', Freddie emerges holding a large Union Jack flag above his head. He walks to the front of the stage and turns 180 degrees to reveal the Argentinean equivalent on the reverse side. A quarter of a million people cheer and applaud the gesture. Freddie then throws it into the audience. A fireworks display begins as 'God Save The Queen' plays out. Meanwhile the band are hurrying to their cars for their traditional speedy exit.

Quite apart from Globo Television's coverage of the festival, the second Queen show is filmed with the intention of issuing it on home video, if all goes well - which it does. A sixteen track video (as highlighted above) is eventually released on May 13, 1985.

While Queen are in Brazil, EMI throw yet another huge party in their honour. It is held around the swimming pool which Freddie's suite overlooks, at the Copacabana Palace Hotel in Rio. Every artist playing at the festival is invited, and many attend. Meanwhile, down on the beach near to the hotel, local Queen fans enjoy a party of their own, and place five hundred lighted candles in the sand, spelling out the band's name. Brian hears about it and he and his daughter leave the 'official' party for a while and join the fans. The gesture is much appreciated.

NEW ZEALAND 1985

On April 5 Queen flew to New Zealand for their very first show there. Despite what they consider to have been a blatant anti-apartheid gesture in performing in South Africa, they find themselves in considerable trouble with the Musicians' Union, and they are met at the airport by anti-apartheid demonstrators. They encounter similar problems when they arrive at their hotel.

Again, the set is that already performed in Europe, South Africa and Brazil. Nothing is dropped or added. The sequence of songs played towards the latter part of the show did vary slightly sometimes, but not significantly.

April 13
Mount Smart Stadium, Auckland

Machines (Intro) / Tear It Up / Tie Your Mother Down / Under Pressure / Medley: Somebody To Love; Killer Queen; Seven Seas Of Rhye; Keep Yourself Alive; Liar / Improvisation / It's A Hard Life / Dragon Attack / Now I'm Here / Is This The World We Created / Love Of My Life / Improvisation / Brighton Rock / Another One Bites The

Dust / Hammer To Fall / Crazy Little Thing Called Love / Bohemian Rhapsody / Radio Ga Ga / Encore: I Want To Break Free / Jailhouse Rock / 2nd Encore: We Will Rock You / We Are The Champions / God Save The Queen

When the band discover that Tony Hadley of Spandau Ballet has flown in from Australia specially to see their show, they invite him to join them on stage for the 'Jailhouse Rock' encore.

Parts of this show were filmed, and later broadcast throughout New Zealand. It yielded a number of bootlegs.

AUSTRALIA 1985

Queen commence a short, two week, two venue mini tour of Australia, their first since 1976, performing four consecutive shows in Melbourne and Sydney. The band flew into Melbourne hoping that their show would be accepted rather better than it had been almost a decade previously. It was.

The band had hoped to perform concerts in the Far East following the eight shows here. For a multitude of reasons, no such shows ever materialised.

April 16/17/18/20
Sports & Entertainment Centre, Melbourne

First night: Machines (Intro) / Tear It Up / Tie Your Mother Down / Under Pressure / Medley: Somebody To Love; Killer Queen; Seven Seas Of Rhye; Keep Yourself Alive; Liar / Improvisation / It's A Hard Life / Dragon Attack / Now I'm Here / Is This The World We Created / Love Of My Life / Improvisation / Brighton Rock / Another One Bites The Dust / Hammer To Fall / Crazy Little Thing Called Love / Bohemian Rhapsody / Radio Ga Ga / Encore: I Want To Break Free / Jailhouse Rock / 2nd Encore: We Will Rock You / We Are The Champions / God Save The Queen

Because the band have no show on April 18th, they go instead to watch Phil Collins in concert. He duly returns the compliment by attending the Queen show on April 20.

Third night: Machines (Intro) / Tear It Up / Tie Your Mother Down / Under Pressure / Medley: Somebody To Love; Killer Queen; Seven Seas Of Rhye; Keep Yourself Alive; Liar / Improvisation / It's A Hard Life / Dragon Attack (Guitar Version) / Now I'm Here / Is This The World We Created / Love Of My Life / Improvisation / Brighton

Rock / Guitar Solo / Another One Bites The Dust / Hammer To Fall / Crazy Little Thing Called Love / Bohemian Rhapsody / Radio Ga Ga / Encore: I Want To Break Free / Jailhouse Rock / 2nd Encore: We Will Rock You / We Are The Champions / God Save The Queen

Final night: Machines (Intro) / Tear It Up / Tie Your Mother Down / Under Pressure / Medley: Somebody To Love; Killer Queen; Seven Seas Of Rhye; Keep Yourself Alive; Liar / Improvisation / It's A Hard Life / Dragon Attack / Now I'm Here / Is This The World We Created / Love Of My Life / Improvisation / Brighton Rock / Guitar Solo / Another One Bites The Dust / Hammer To Fall / Crazy Little Thing Called Love / Bohemian Rhapsody / Radio Ga Ga / Encore: I Want To Break Free / Jailhouse Rock / 2nd Encore: We Will Rock You / We Are The Champions / God Save The Queen

This show was marred not only by the lighting rig, which gives up the ghost mid-way through the show, but also re-occurring sound problems. As luck would have it, this was the concert that Phil Collins attended. He later talked about the various difficulties on the 'Magic Years' video, recalling the performance as enjoyable despite the problems.

April 25/26/28/29
Entertainments Centre, Sydney

First and second nights: *Machines (Intro) / Tear It Up / Tie Your Mother Down / Under Pressure / Medley: Somebody To Love; Killer Queen; Seven Seas Of Rhye; Keep Yourself Alive; Liar / Improvisation / It's A Hard Life / Dragon Attack / Now I'm Here / Is This The World We Created / Love Of My Life / Improvisation / Brighton Rock / Guitar Solo / Another One Bites The Dust / Hammer To Fall / Crazy Little Thing Called Love / Bohemian Rhapsody / Radio Ga Ga / Encore: I Want To Break Free / Jailhouse Rock / 2nd Encore: We Will Rock You / We Are The Champions / God Save The Queen*

While in Sydney, Brian and John attend the Opera House as guests of John Reid, Elton John's manager and Queen's ex-manager.

Third night: *Machines (Intro) / Tear It Up / Tie Your Mother Down / Under Pressure / Medley: Somebody To Love; Killer Queen; Seven Seas Of Rhye; Keep Yourself Alive; Liar / Improvisation / It's A Hard Life / Dragon Attack / Now I'm Here / Is This The World We Created / Love Of My Life / Improvisation / Brighton Rock / Guitar Solo / Another One Bites The Dust / Hammer To Fall / Crazy Little Thing Called Love / Bohemian Rhapsody / Radio Ga Ga / Encore: I Want To Break Free / Jailhouse Rock / 2nd Encore: We Will Rock You / We Are The Champions / God Save The Queen*

On April 30 Queen return home to London for a few days off, and to prepare for what would be their final visit to Japan.

JAPAN 1985

Queen continue to play an identical set to that already performed in five other continents. The only surprise is the omission of 'Teo Torriatte', which is arguably the Japanese fans' favourite ballad, for obvious reasons.

May 7/9
Budokan Hall, Tokyo

First night: *Machines (Intro) / Tear It Up / Tie Your Mother Down / Under Pressure / Medley: Somebody To Love; Killer Queen; Seven Seas Of Rhye; Keep Yourself Alive; Liar / Fooling Around (Instrumental Jam) / It's A Hard Life / Dragon Attack / Now I'm Here / Is This The World We Created / Love Of My Life / Improvisation / Brighton Rock / Guitar Solo / Another One Bites The Dust / Hammer To Fall / Crazy Little Thing Called Love / Bohemian Rhapsody / Radio Ga Ga / Encore: I Want To Break Free / Jailhouse Rock / 2nd Encore: We Will Rock You / We Are The Champions / God Save The Queen*

An identical show to that played in Melbourne the preceding month, but with the addition of the 'Fooling Around' jam. This experimental song was later included in the 1986 'Magic' tour set.

Second night: *Machines (Intro) / Tear It Up / Tie Your Mother Down / Under Pressure / Medley: Somebody To Love; Killer Queen; Seven Seas Of Rhye; Keep Yourself Alive; Liar / Fooling Around (Instrumental Jam) / It's A Hard Life / Dragon Attack / Now I'm Here / Is This The World We Created / Love Of My Life / Improvisation / Brighton Rock / Guitar Solo / Another One Bites The Dust / Hammer To Fall / Crazy Little Thing Called Love / Bohemian Rhapsody / Radio Ga Ga / Encore: I Want To Break Free / Jailhouse Rock / 2nd Encore: We Will Rock You / We Are The Champions / God Save The Queen*

May 10/11
Yogishi Swimming Pool Auditorium, Tokyo

Second night: *Machines (Intro) / Tear It Up / Tie Your Mother Down / Under Pressure / Medley: Somebody To Love; Killer Queen; Seven Seas Of Rhye; Keep Yourself Alive; Liar / Fooling Around (Instrumental Jam) / It's A Hard Life / Dragon Attack / Now I'm Here / Is This The World We Created / Love Of My Life / Improvisation / Brighton Rock / Guitar Solo / Another One Bites The Dust / Hammer To Fall / Crazy Little Thing Called Love / Bohemian Rhapsody / Radio Ga Ga / Encore: I Want To Break Free / Jailhouse Rock / 2nd Encore: We Will Rock You / We Are The Champions / God Save The Queen*

This show is another of Queen's most widely bootlegged shows.

May 13
Aichi Auditorium, Nagoya

Machines (Intro) / Tear It Up / Tie Your Mother Down / Under Pressure / Medley: Somebody To Love; Killer Queen; Seven Seas Of Rhye; Keep Yourself Alive; Liar / Improvisation / It's A Hard Life / Dragon Attack / Now I'm Here (incorporating Johnny B. Goode) / Is This The World We Created / Love Of My Life / Improvisation / Brighton Rock / Guitar Solo / Another One Bites The Dust / Hammer To Fall / Crazy Little Thing Called Love / Saturday Night's Alright For Fighting / Bohemian Rhapsody / Radio Ga Ga / Encore: I Want To Break Free / Jailhouse Rock / 2nd Encore: We Will Rock You / We Are The Champions / God Save The Queen

Picture Music International release 'Live In Rio'. The sixteen track video offers an edited account of Queen's second concert at the Rock In Rio Festival, recorded on January 19. As 'We Will Rock You' had done, it enters the British video charts at No.1.

May 15
Jo Hall, Osaka

Machines (Intro) / Tear It Up / Tie Your Mother Down / Under Pressure / Medley: Somebody To Love; Killer Queen; Seven Seas Of Rhye; Keep Yourself Alive; Liar / Improvisation / It's A Hard Life / Dragon Attack / Now I'm Here / Is This The World We Created / Love Of My Life / Improvisation / Brighton Rock / Guitar Solo / Another One Bites The Dust / Mustapha / Hammer To Fall / Crazy Little Thing Called Love / Saturday Night's Alright For Fighting / Bohemian Rhapsody / Radio Ga Ga / Encore: I Want To Break Free / Jailhouse Rock (incorporating Whole Lotta Shakin Going On) / 2nd Encore: We Will Rock You / We Are The Champions / God Save The Queen

May 17

Queen fly home.

June 21

Brian attends a Trade Fair in New Orleans to promote and demonstrate a newly produced copy of his guitar by Guild. During his stay he visits a local club, and ends up on stage in a jam session with John Entwistle and Eddie Van Halen.

July 13

Live Aid, Wembley Stadium, London

Bohemian Rhapsody / Radio Ga Ga / Hammer To Fall / Crazy Little Thing Called Love / We Will Rock You / We Are The Champions

London line up: (in order of appearance) Status Quo, The Style Council, The Boomtown Rats, Adam Ant, Ultravox, Spandau Ballet, Elvis Costello, Nik Kershaw, Sade, Sting, Phil Collins, Reo Speedwagon, Howard Jones, Bryan Ferry, Paul Young, Alison Moyet, U2, Dire Straits (with Sting), Queen, David Bowie, The Who, Elton John, Kiki Dee, Wham, Brian May & Freddie Mercury, Paul McCartney, Finale.

Queen's performance at Live Aid is a triumph of colossal proportions which both revitalises the band and gains them thousands of new fans. It was clear that they had given much thought to the rehearsals for their 20-minute set which took place at the Shaw Theatre.

There was no question that Queen, U2 and perhaps David Bowie stole the show in London.

Live Aid featured sixty-three different acts, performing in London and Philadelphia at no cost. All 72,000 tickets for the show sold out within four hours of going on sale, each at a cost of £25 – no small sum in 1985.

The concert was conceived by Bob Geldof, as was the Band Aid single which preceded it in late 1984. Geldof was so appalled by the images he saw on Michael Buerke's harrowing television famine news reports from Ethiopia that he immediately set about contacting every established name in the music industry to secure their services for the event. He eventually secured Queen's performance by tracking Jim Beach down in New Zealand, having first made contact in Japan and then Australia.

The entire show was broadcast live by BBC TV and Radio One, and was beamed via satellite to over 160 countries, reaching a combined audience of one and a half billion people (a third of the Earth's population) on 80 per cent of the televisions on the planet. It was the perfect setting for Freddie Mercury.

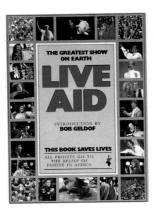

The event proves to be an unparalleled technical and logistical nightmare, but is ultimately a fantastic and unprecedented success, raising over £50 million for the starving people of Ethiopia and neighbouring African countries.

Queen are introduced on stage by comedians Mel Smith and Griff Rhys Jones, both of whom are dressed in police uniforms... "Her Majesty... Queen". Queen bound onto stage. The time is precisely 6.44 pm. Because of the time difference, Queen are the first act to be seen in Philadelphia, where the parallel concert is taking place. This was no accident.

Freddie seats himself at the piano, and 'Bo Rhap' begins immediately. Before the operatic part begins, Freddie is handed his microphone and struts around the stage with it singing 'Radio

Ga Ga'. Despite a throat infection and doctor's advice not to perform, he looks and sounds at his best. During the main verses of the song, the vast Wembley audience once again unite in a wave of overhead clapping. It is executed, as ever, with military type precision.

Freddie walks to centre stage and indulges the crowd with some of his vocal improvisation. They respond gladly. Then he initiates 'Hammer To Fall', Queen's Live Aid *pièce de résistance*. When Freddie is pursued around the

stage by a cameraman, he stops and spins around him, his face only inches from the lens. When the impromptu play acting is over, Freddie walks away with his thumb pointing backwards over his shoulder – as if to gesture that the cameraman is mad. This is truly wonderful stuff, but it is still not officially available on home video, although the concert was obviously videoed by many thousands of people. Following 'Hammer', Freddie grabs a guitar and addresses the masses again:

Queen Live '85

140

future. An article which appeared in *The Sun* in April 1986, focused on just that. Entitled "How Live Aid Saved Our Queen", Martin Dunn's feature included numerous quotes from Roger on the general mood and feeling within the band prior to receiving the telephone call from Bob Geldof: "Whenever we have a band meeting, it's like World War III. We had been living in each others' pockets for months and I had frequently argued with May over everything. Our act had become jaded and stale. We were all determined to get away from Queen for a long while.

"We were playing at the huge San Remo festival in Italy and were due on stage in five minutes. I was really screaming at everyone, especially Brian. I hated some of the things he'd chosen to play in the concert, and he hated the stage settings we'd dreamed up. The atmosphere was so highly charged anything could have happened.

"This next song is only dedicated to beautiful people here tonight – that means all of you. Thank you for coming along, and making this such a great occasion". 'Crazy' begins. Freddie remains static for the most part, standing at the microphone. When Brian takes his guitar solo, a horrible feedback squeal accompanies the first half. The band finish their 20 minute 'global jukebox' show with 'Rock You' segueing into 'Champions' and Freddie is once again back at the piano. For the final verse he gets up on his feet again inciting the audience to sing along with him. They do. Even reluctant anti-Queenists are persuaded to sing. Queen finish. They have not only guaranteed yet more record sales, and reminded the world that they are still one of the planet's biggest rock music forces, but they have confirmed in their own minds that Queen is too important an entity to terminate.

Freddie and Brian later return to the stage (at 9.48 pm), just prior to the finale. Introduced by actor John Hurt, they perform the acoustic 'Works' track 'Is This The World We Created', a song they composed together which features lyrics as appropriate to the occasion as any song performed that day. Unfortunately, their performance is marred by recurring feedback.

Roger Taylor: "The whole thing was magnificent. Geldof did it out of the purest motives. I cannot believe arseholes like Jonathan King can denigrate something that's done real good, when he's done no good to mankind except litter the planet with dreadful records. How dare he? How worthless parasitic specks like him can have a go at something that's so good I don't know!"

Prior to the Live Aid show, there had been speculation about Queen's

"Then someone realised that Freddie wasn't ready. They burst into his changing room and found him still sitting in his underpants and vest, eating a bowl of cornflakes. We just all collapsed in hysterics. And that's Freddie's secret, he will always do the most unexpected thing and bring us back together.

"Live Aid proved a fantastic tonic for us. Now we can't wait to hit the stage again."

November 4

Queen's only single of the year is released. Preceding the 'A Kind Of Magic' album by almost exactly six months, 'One Vision' provides an unexpectedly positive conclusion to the year by reaching No.7 in the UK charts. Backed with the non-album mish mash track 'Blurred Vision', the disc is another universal pairing. Once again though, the American sales figures do nothing to inspire confidence, when the disc peaks at a miserable No.61.

December 2

'The Complete Works' boxed set is released only in the UK. It comprises all the albums up to 'The Works' (excluding 'Greatest Hits'), and an extra seven track rarities album called 'Complete Vision'. Every disc was repackaged in a plain white embossed sleeve, and contained digitally remastered material for the first time.

The tracks on the bonus album were: 'See What A Fool I've Been' / 'A Human Body' / 'Soul Brother' / 'I Go Crazy' / 'Thank God It's Christmas' / 'One Vision' / 'Blurred Vision'. All were unavailable at that time, other than as single A- and B-sides.

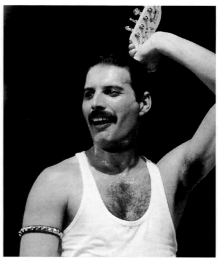

March 17
Roger Taylor's 'A Kind Of Magic' single is released from the soon to follow album of the same name. Backed with the non-album instrumental track 'A Dozen Red Roses For My Darling' (also written by Roger), it goes on to be a No. 3 hit in the UK. The American release (on June 4) is instead coupled with the frantic Brian May gem 'Gimme The Prize'. It reaches No. 42. EMI in Japan also issued the Roger Taylor pairing. The single is aided greatly by a superb, partially animated promotional video, something which had not been done since 'Save Me', in 1980.

April 7
'Princes Of The Universe'/'A Dozen Red Roses For My Darling' is released in America. Apart from Japan, where it is coupled with 'Who Wants To Live

Forever', it is completely overlooked for release elsewhere, despite being one of the 'Magic' album's standout tracks, and having the support of one of Queen's finest promotional videos, in which Christopher Lambert made a cameo appearance. The track was never employed in the live set; one of the most notable concert absentees of the band's entire career.

May 15
The promotional video for 'Friends Will Be Friends' is filmed at a studio in Wembley which Queen are using for rehearsals. Some eight hundred and fifty Queen fans are drafted in to assist, though not all are fan club members, as is usually the case. Following the filming, the band perform an impromptu short live set by way of a thank you.

May
Queen return to the annual Golden Rose rock festival in Montreux, as they had done in 1984. This time they mime to three tracks from the 'Magic' album ('One Vision', 'Friends Will Be Friends', and the title track), and to 'Hammer To Fall' from 'The Works'.

June 2
'A Kind Of Magic' Queen's twelfth studio album is released in the UK. Though the material is written for Russel Mulcahy's *Highlander* film, it is not regarded as a soundtrack album as 'Flash Gordon' had been six years earlier.

Of the nine tracks, five never appear in the live set. John Deacon must have been most frustrated as two of the five victims were his songs. 'Pain Is So Close To Pleasure' (co-written with Freddie) is the most heavily dance oriented song on the album, and probably accounts for its exclusion, but why 'One Year Of Love' could not be incorporated is a mystery. The remaining

tracks are among the most extraordinary omissions of Queen's entire concert history. Written by Brian, Roger and Freddie respectively, 'Gimme The Prize', 'Don't Lose Your Head' and 'Princes Of The Universe' all contain classic Queen trademarks, and would have converted brilliantly to the stage environment. None were played even once.

EUROPE 1986
The Magic Tour

Following an unusually long period of rehearsal in London during May, Queen travel to Stockholm for the first Magic Tour shows. Roger Taylor tells journalists that the tour will feature the most elaborate lighting set-up ever seen in a Queen show. It is the most expensive stage production ever undertaken too. "We are going to play on the biggest stage ever built at Wembley, with the greatest light show ever seen. I think we are probably the best live band in the world at the moment, and we are going to prove it. No one who comes to see us will be disappointed." His comments would prove not to be exaggerated.

The Magic Tour incorporates the UK and nine European countries only. It is never taken to America, Japan or Canada, as were most other tours. It consists of twenty-six performances at twenty separate locations, played over an eight week period. It includes Queen's first and only show in Budapest, Hungary (which is filmed, and later issued on video), and also their only concert at the beautiful Knebworth Park site, in Hertfordshire. The 15th century mansion house would be a fitting location for what would sadly prove to be Queen's very last concert.

The stage is sixty-four feet long and has two wings each side which add another forty feet each and covers 6,000 sq ft in total. For the Wembley and Knebworth Park shows, two sixty feet x fifteen feet Starvision screens are used, which alone weigh twenty tons. They are supported by a custom made two piece bridge like structure, made by an engineering company normally involved in motorway and bridge construction. Six trucks are required to transport it. Such is the weight of the completed structure that it is counterbalanced behind the stage, by a vast water tank. Nine trucks in all, are required to transport the stage equipment.

The lighting rig weighs in at nine and a half tons and by itself occupies four of the forty feet trucks. The PA system consists of one hundred and eighty Claire Brothers S4 speaker cabinets, one hundred and fifty Carver amplifiers, sixty-four input channels (on two Audio mixing desks), and four racks of electronics, which put out a combined total of 245,000 watts of power.

During the tour the trucks which transport the equipment, cover just over 165,000 miles, the equivalent of nearly seven times around the Earth.

The set has now changed drastically. Although the previous album ('The Works') is still well represented by 'Tear It Up', 'Break Free', 'Is This The World', 'Hammer To Fall' and 'Ga Ga', the new one is represented rather less than might have been expected. While 'One Vision', 'Who Wants To Live Forever', 'Friends Will Be Friends' and 'A Kind Of Magic' all now feature, five others do not.

'One Vision' opens the show,

'Machines' disappears completely, as do 'Killer Queen', 'Somebody To Love', 'Dragon Attack', 'Liar', 'Great King Rat', 'Jailhouse Rock' and 'Keep Yourself Alive', but an exciting new rock'n'roll medley now includes '(You're So Square) Baby I Don't Care', 'Tutti Frutti', 'Hello

Mary Lou', and occasional renderings of 'Gimme Some Lovin'' and 'Saturday Night's Alright For Fighting', as well as snippets of 'Stupid Cupid' and 'Shake Rattle & Roll'.

June 7
Rasunda Fotbollstadion, Stockholm

One Vision / Tie Your Mother Down / Medley: In The Lap Of The Gods (Revisited); Seven Seas Of Rhye; Tear It Up / A Kind Of Magic / Under Pressure / Another One Bites The Dust / Who Wants To Live Forever / I Want To Break Free / Improvisation / Now I'm Here / Love Of My Life / Is This The World We Created / Medley: (You're So Square) Baby I Don't Care; Hello Mary Lou; Tutti Frutti / Bohemian Rhapsody / Hammer To Fall / Crazy Little Thing Called Love / Radio Ga Ga / Encore: We Will Rock You / Friends Will Be Friends / We Are The Champions / God Save The Queen

The band encounter anti-apartheid protesters outside the stadium. They were responding to comments Brian had made for a Swedish magazine article. Typically, he had been quoted out of context.

During this show, a sound engineer conducts a noise check on the audience, which results in the startling news that the joint audience vocal output is only one decibel less than that put out by Queen's vast bank of loudspeakers.

The support act was Gary Moore.

June 9

'Friends Will Be Friends' coupled with 'Seven Seas Of Rhye' from 1974, is released in the UK. Assisted by a promotional video which featured fan club members interacting with Queen, it achieves a No.14 chart placing. In America and Japan 'Pain Is So Close To Pleasure' and 'Princes Of The Universe' respectively, were issued instead (B5633 / EMI 17663).

June 11/12

Groenoordhalle, Leiden

First night: One Vision / Tie Your Mother Down / Medley: In The Lap Of The Gods (Revisited); Seven Seas Of Rhye; Tear It Up / A Kind Of Magic / Under Pressure / Another One Bites The Dust / Who Wants To Live Forever / I Want To Break Free / Improvisation / Now I'm Here / Love Of My Life / Is This The World We Created / Medley: (You're So Square) Baby I Don't Care; Hello Mary Lou; Tutti Frutti / Bohemian Rhapsody / Hammer

To Fall / Crazy Little Thing Called Love / Radio Ga Ga / Encore: We Will Rock You / Friends Will Be Friends / We Are The Champions / God Save The Queen

Second night: One Vision / Tie Your Mother Down / Medley: In The Lap Of The Gods (Revisited); Seven Seas Of Rhye; Tear It Up / A Kind Of Magic / Under Pressure / Another One Bites The Dust / Who Wants To Live Forever / I Want To Break Free / Improvisation / Gimme Some Lovin' / Now I'm Here / Love Of My Life / Is This The World We Created / Medley: (You're So Square) Baby I Don't Care; Hello Mary Lou; Tutti Frutti / Big Spender / Bohemian Rhapsody / Hammer To Fall / Crazy Little Thing Called Love / Radio Ga Ga / Encore: We Will Rock You / Friends Will Be Friends / We Are The Champions / God Save The Queen

The band play 'Gimme Some Lovin' at this show. Again, this song very rarely featured in the set.

June 14

Hippodrome De Vincennes

One Vision / Tie Your Mother Down / Medley: In The Lap Of The Gods (Revisited); Seven Seas Of Rhye; Tear It Up / A Kind Of Magic / Under Pressure / Another One Bites The Dust / Who Wants To Live Forever / I Want To Break Free / Improvisation / Now I'm Here / Love Of My Life / Is This The World We Created / Medley: (You're So Square) Baby I Don't Care; Hello Mary Lou; Tutti Frutti / Bohemian Rhapsody / Hammer To Fall / Crazy Little Thing Called Love / Radio Ga Ga / Encore: We Will Rock You / Friends Will Be Friends / We Are The Champions / God Save The Queen

June 17

Forêt Nationale, Brussels

One Vision / Tie Your Mother Down / Medley: In The Lap Of The Gods (Revisited); Seven Seas Of Rhye; Tear It Up / A Kind Of Magic / Under Pressure / Another One Bites The Dust / Who Wants To Live Forever / I Want To Break Free / Improvisation / Now I'm Here / Love Of My Life / Is This The World We Created / Medley: (You're So Square) Baby I Don't Care; Hello Mary Lou; Tutti Frutti / Bohemian Rhapsody / Hammer To Fall / Crazy Little Thing Called Love / Radio Ga Ga / Encore: We Will Rock You / Friends Will Be Friends / We Are The Champions / God Save The Queen

June 19

Groenoordhalle, Leiden

One Vision / Tie Your Mother Down / Medley: In The Lap Of The Gods (Revisited); Seven Seas Of Rhye; Tear It Up / A Kind Of Magic / Under Pressure / Another One Bites The Dust / Who Wants To Live Forever / I Want To Break Free / Improvisation / Now I'm Here / Love Of My Life / Is This The World We Created / Medley: (You're So Square) Baby I Don't Care; Hello Mary Lou; Tutti Frutti / Bohemian Rhapsody / Hammer To Fall / Crazy Little Thing Called Love / Radio Ga Ga / Encore: We Will Rock You / Friends Will Be Friends / We Are The Champions / God Save The Queen

June 21

Maimarktgelande, Mannheim

One Vision / Tie Your Mother Down / Medley: In The Lap Of The Gods (Revisited); Seven Seas Of Rhye; Tear It Up / A Kind Of Magic / Under Pressure / Another One Bites The Dust / Who Wants To Live Forever / I Want To Break Free / Improvisation (incorporating Gimme Some Lovin') / Improvisation / Now I'm Here / Love Of My Life / Is This The World We Created / Medley: (You're So Square) Baby I Don't Care; Hello Mary Lou; Tutti Frutti / Bohemian Rhapsody / Hammer To Fall / Crazy Little Thing Called Love / Radio Ga Ga / Encore: We Will Rock You / Friends Will Be Friends / We Are The Champions / God Save The Queen

During the soundcheck Freddie decides to make his initial entrance on stage via a metal bucket which will be lowered down by a crane. The equipment is drafted in, but soon returned when Freddie discovers that being crammed into a metal bucket and hoisted up high is somewhat undignified, not to mention terrifying. The idea is abandoned.

Fish (from Marillion) joins the band on stage for "Tutti Frutti".

This concert was broadcast live on German radio, British national anthem and all, and also later featured on a US radio series *Off The Record*,

titled *Done Under Pressure*. The show has since become widely bootlegged, and is available in countless different forms, on various formats.

June 26
Waldbuehne, Berlin

One Vision / Tie Your Mother Down / Medley: In The Lap Of The Gods (Revisited); Seven Seas Of Rhye; Tear It Up / A Kind Of Magic / Under Pressure / Another One Bites The Dust / Who Wants To Live Forever / I Want To Break Free / Immigrant Song / Improvisation / Now I'm Here / Love Of My Life / Is This The World We Created / Medley: (You're So Square) Baby I Don't Care; Hello Mary Lou; Tutti Frutti / Bohemian Rhapsody / Hammer To Fall / Crazy Little Thing Called Love / Radio Ga Ga / Encore: We Will Rock You / Friends Will Be Friends / We Are The Champions / God Save The Queen

Queen perform an extremely rare rendition of Led Zeppelin's 'Immigrant Song' at this show. Bootleg copies, of which there are at least two different ones, are worth purchasing just for this, even if both do offer relatively poor sound reproduction.

June 28/29
Olympiahalle, Munich

First night: One Vision / Tie Your Mother Down / Medley: In The Lap Of The Gods (Revisited); Seven Seas Of Rhye; Tear It Up / A Kind Of Magic / Under Pressure / Another One Bites The Dust / Who Wants To Live Forever / I Want To Break Free / Improvisation / Now I'm Here / Love Of My Life / Is This The World We Created / Medley: (You're So Square) Baby I Don't Care; Hello Mary Lou; Tutti Frutti / Bohemian Rhapsody / Hammer To Fall / Crazy Little Thing Called Love / Radio Ga Ga / Encore: We Will Rock You / Friends Will Be Friends / We Are The Champions / God Save The Queen

July 1/2
Hallenstadion, Zurich

First night: set same as June 28, but with 'Mustapha (Intro)' after 'Tutti Fruitti'.

Second night: set same as June 28, but with no 'In The Lap Of The Gods (Revisited)' or 'Who Wants To Live Forever'.

July 5
Slane Castle, Dublin

One Vision / Tie Your Mother Down / Medley: In The Lap Of The Gods (Revisited); Seven Seas Of Rhye; Tear It Up / A Kind Of Magic / Under Pressure / Another One Bites The Dust / Who Wants To Live Forever / I Want To Break Free / Improvisation / Gimme Some Loving / Guitar Solo / Now I'm Here / Love Of My Life / Is This The World We Created / Medley: (You're So Square) Baby I Don't Care; Hello Mary Lou; Tutti Frutti / Bohemian Rhapsody / Hammer To Fall / Crazy Little Thing Called Love / Radio Ga Ga / Encore: We Will Rock You / Friends Will Be Friends / We Are The Champions / God Save The Queen

The 95,000 crowd begin to descend on the ground here, at 9 am, as soon as the gates opened, and nine hours before Queen were due on stage.

As 'Seven Seas Of Rhye' nears its end, Freddie is forced stop the show when an inebriated member of the audience staggers over a cable and rips it out. The cable is one of many which is linking the stage mixing desk to a 24-track mobile recording studio the band are using to record the show.

The support acts here were The Bangles, Fountainhead and Chris Rea.

The show finishes early, due to the lack of lights on site and the possible hazard to those making their way out of the grounds.

July 9
St James Park, Newcastle-Upon-Tyne

One Vision / Tie Your Mother Down / Medley: In The Lap Of The Gods (Revisited); Seven Seas Of Rhye; Tear It Up / A Kind Of Magic / Under Pressure / Another One Bites The Dust / Who Wants To Live Forever / I Want To Break Free / Improvisation / Now I'm Here / Love Of My Life / Is This The World We Created / Medley: (You're So Square) Baby I Don't Care; Hello Mary Lou; Tutti Frutti / Bohemian Rhapsody / Hammer To Fall / Crazy Little Thing Called Love / Radio Ga Ga / Encore: We Will Rock You / Friends Will Be Friends / We Are The Champions / God Save The Queen

The show is the largest ever staged in Newcastle. The queue for tickets was longer than that seen in 1974, when

Newcastle United reached the FA Cup Final. All 38,000 tickets were sold within an hour. The proceeds are donated to the Save The Children Fund. Many local children who have benefited from projects run by the charity attend the show, and meet the band afterwards. Brian dedicates 'Is This The World We Created' to the fund during the show.

Jim Beach would later recall that Queen were so overwhelmed by Newcastle's enthusiasm to see them that they wanted to offer some token of appreciation. Princes Anne's dedication to Save The Children provided the perfect opportunity.

July 11/12
Wembley Stadium, London

First night: *One Vision / Tie Your Mother Down /* Medley: *In The Lap Of The Gods (Revisited); Seven Seas Of Rhye; Tear It Up / A Kind Of Magic / Under Pressure / Another One Bites The Dust / Who Wants To Live Forever / I Want To Break Free / Improvisation / Now I'm Here / Love Of My Life / Is This The World We Created /* Medley: *(You're So Square) Baby I Don't Care; Hello Mary Lou; Tutti Frutti / Bohemian Rhapsody / Hammer To Fall / Crazy Little Thing Called Love / Radio Ga Ga /* Encore: *We Will Rock You / Friends Will Be Friends / We Are The Champions / God Save The Queen*

When major problems are encountered attempting to fit the stage into position, the crew are baffled and somewhat panic stricken. On investigation it is discovered that the architectural plans for Wembley Stadium are precisely four feet out, making it impossible to fit the already designed stage construction into place. Working from the plans, the crew had designed a stage to fit into one complete end of the stadium. When it proved to be over a yard too long, everyone pulls together to rebuild one which does fit in time for the show. An apparently minor oversight very nearly resulted in Queen's first home town gig since Live Aid being cancelled.

Support acts were Status Quo, The Alarm and INXS. Attendance each night was 72,000

As Queen begin 'A Kind Of Magic', four huge inflatable caricature dummies

of the band are released into the air. While two of them are quickly dragged into the audience, the others escape. Though the author cannot recall exactly what happened to John, he vividly remembers watching Freddie's grinning face floating higher and higher into the London night sky, and becoming harder and harder to spot. A somewhat startled lady several miles away apparently found the half deflated guest in her garden the next morning.

'Is This The World' as recorded here is later used for the 'Live Magic' album, as was 'Hammer To Fall' from the following evening's performance.

Second night: *One Vision / Tie Your Mother Down /* Medley: *In The Lap Of The Gods (Revisited); Seven Seas Of Rhye / A Kind Of Magic / Under Pressure / Another One Bites The Dust / Who Wants To Live Forever / I Want To Break Free / Improvisation / Now I'm Here / Love Of My Life / Is This The World We Created /* Medley: *(You're So Square) Baby I Don't Care; Hello Mary Lou; Tutti Frutti / Gimme Some Loving / Bohemian Rhapsody / Hammer To Fall / Crazy Little Thing Called Love / Big Spender / Radio Ga Ga /* Encore: *We Will Rock You / Friends Will Be Friends / We Are The Champions / God Save The Queen*

This show is filmed by Tyne Tees Television, and later broadcast as their first ever radio/television simulcast, transmitted to all 48 stations in the Independent Radio Network. The stereo radio sound is beamed via satellite to the stations and requires a quarter second delay to ensure it synchronises exactly with the television pictures. Satellites are used only because no land lines exist to carry the signals.

As at the June 1982 Milton Keynes Bowl show, Gavin Taylor was employed to direct the programme. He ultimately uses fifteen different cameras, which are not only situated in every conceivable place on and around the stage, but are mounted on cranes outside the stadium and operated by remote control. As an extra touch, he sites a hidden 35mm stills camera on the stage. Still shots from this are incorporated into the programme during final editing.

When the show is finally broadcast, on October 25 (on Channel 4), it is a wonderfully produced and entertaining programme – even for non-Queen enthusiasts – and is watched by 3.5 million people. The programme is titled 'Real Magic' and it was also broadcast in America as part of Westwood One's *Superstar Concert* series. To confuse matters further, some unofficial recordings of the TV/radio broadcasts circulate under the guise of 'Don't Lose Your Seat'. Due to public demand Channel 4 eventually repeat the programme, on January 2, 1987.

The following morning's *Sun* carried this report by Mydrim Jones: "Freddie Mercury, the outrageous leader of Queen, reigned supreme at Wembley Stadium as he brought the house down amid plumes of smoke and brilliantly coloured lights. He whipped up the fans to fever pitch for the second night running and put himself among the all-time rock'n'roll greats.

"Only The Rolling Stones and Bruce Springsteen have ever had two consecutive sell-out concerts at Wembley. Before last night's show Freddie had feared his voice would fail. But once on stage – it was covered in 6,000 sq. ft. of expensive carpet – he pranced around in his king's crown and cloak, singing encore after encore.

"Five electrical generators pumped 500,000 watts along miles of cable to operate the sound and lighting systems. And the fans loved every marvellous minute of it. Among them were *Minder* star Dennis Waterman, his girlfriend Rula Lenska and *EastEnders* actress Anita 'Angie' Dobson. And sitting in the middle of the swaying, waving fans was the old king himself – Mick Jagger. He quietly watched the performance with his daughter Jade. And clearly he saw a new ruler in the magic kingdom of rock."

July 16

Maine Road, Manchester

One Vision / Tie Your Mother Down / Medley: In The Lap Of The Gods (Revisited); Seven Seas Of Rhye; Tear It Up / A Kind Of Magic / Under Pressure / Another One Bites The Dust / Who Wants To Live Forever / I Want To Break Free / Piano Solo / Guitar Solo / Now I'm Here / Love Of My Life / Is This The World We Created / Medley: (You're So Square) Baby I Don't Care; Hello Mary Lou;

Tutti Frutti / Bohemian Rhapsody / Hammer To Fall / Crazy Little Thing Called Love / Radio Ga Ga / Encore: We Will Rock You / Friends Will Be Friends / We Are The Champions / God Save The Queen

July 19

Muengersdorfer Stadion, Cologne

One Vision / Tie Your Mother Down / Medley: In The Lap Of The Gods (Revisited); Seven Seas Of Rhye; Tear It Up / A Kind Of Magic / Under Pressure / Another One Bites The Dust / Who Wants To Live Forever / I Want To Break Free / Improvisation / Now I'm Here / Love Of My Life / Is This The World We Created / Medley: (You're So Square) Baby I Don't Care; Hello Mary Lou; Tutti Frutti / Saturday Night's Alright For Fighting / Bohemian Rhapsody / Hammer To Fall / Crazy Little Thing Called Love / Radio Ga Ga / Encore: We Will Rock You / Friends Will Be Friends / We Are The Champions / God Save The Queen

July 21/22

Stadthalle, Vienna

First night: *One Vision / Tie Your Mother Down / Medley: In The Lap Of The Gods (Revisited); Seven Seas Of Rhye; Tear It Up / A Kind Of Magic / Under Pressure / Another One Bites The Dust / Who Wants To Live Forever / I Want To Break Free / Improvisation / Now I'm Here / Love Of My Life / Is This The World We Created / Medley: (You're So Square) Baby I Don't Care; Hello Mary Lou; Tutti Frutti / Bohemian Rhapsody / Hammer To Fall / Crazy Little Thing Called Love / Radio Ga Ga / Encore: We Will Rock You / Friends Will Be Friends / We Are The Champions / God Save The Queen*

Second night: *One Vision / Tie Your Mother Down / Medley: In The Lap Of The Gods (Revisited); Seven Seas Of Rhye; Tear It Up / A Kind Of Magic / Under Pressure /*

Another One Bites The Dust / Who Wants To Live Forever / I Want To Break Free / Improvisation / Now I'm Here / Love Of My Life / Is This The World We Created / Medley: (You're So Square) Baby I Don't Care; Hello Mary Lou; Tutti Frutti / Bohemian Rhapsody / Hammer To Fall / Crazy Little Thing Called Love / Radio Ga Ga / Encore: We Will Rock You / Friends Will Be Friends / We Are The Champions / God Save The Queen

July 27

Nepstadion, Budapest

Highlighted tracks are those featured on the 'Live In Budapest' video.

One Vision / **Tie Your Mother Down** / Medley: **In The Lap Of The Gods**; **Seven Seas Of Rhye**; Tear It Up / **A Kind Of Magic** / **Tavaszi Szel Vizet Araszt** / **Under Pressure** / Another One Bites The Dust / **Who Wants To Live Forever** / **I Want To Break Free** / Guitar Solo / **Now I'm Here** / **Love Of My Life** / **Tavaszi Szel Vizet Araszt** / **Is This The World We Created** / Medley: You're So Square; Hello Mary Lou; **Tutti Frutti** / **Bohemian Rhapsody** / **Hammer To Fall** / **Crazy Little Thing Called Love** / **Radio Ga Ga** / Encore: **We Will Rock You** / **Friends Will Be Friends** / **We Are The Champions** / **God Save The Queen**

This performance – Queen's first and last in Hungary – was filmed by the Hungarian Film State company Mafilm Dialog, as was the soundcheck. The filming necessitates using nearly every available 35mm television camera in the country, seventeen in all.

An edited eighty-five-minute account was eventually broadcast in December throughout the Communist Bloc, including China, Poland, Czechoslovakia, East Germany, Yugoslavia and Mongolia, as well as to fifty-nine Hungarian cinemas for general release on New Year's Day 1987. The director was Janos Zsombolyai. Other footage of the band – on and off stage in addition to that available on the video – was used to complement television news reports.

The sixty-strong crew members had arrived some days prior to the band. Having driven across Europe in fifteen trucks, with the huge custom designed one hundred and eight-foot long stage, they then spent two full days piecing it all together. Two sixty-foot towers were constructed, which were then fitted with searchlights to dazzle the audience from both sides of the stadium during the show. Eight miles of cables are required to connect everything.

Unlike audiences in every other nation in which Queen had played, the Hungarians were unfamiliar with the many customary Queen concert traditions. This was, after all, the first ever such event in that territory; indeed, it was the first such undertaking anywhere behind the Iron Curtain. For this reason, local newspapers published guides to rock concert etiquette and protocol in the days leading up to the show.

The band themselves were equally apprehensive and, ultimately, the fans would exceed all expectations, and play

their part in the proceedings as efficiently as any of the audiences before them. It was like Sao Paulo, Brazil, all over again, with 80,000 pairs of hands

united in a 'Radio Ga Ga' promo video revisited.

Freddie's introduction was unorthodox. Instead of the usual "Good evening everybody," he sang his opening words: "Hello everybody… it's really nice to be here today… it's really nice to be here tonight."

For the opening of 'Who Wants To Live Forever', Brian sat at an electronic keyboard, as he would throughout all the shows on the Magic tour, leaving it for the first guitar solo. 'Now I'm Here' contained an especially nice, although brief, vocal improvisation from Freddie.

Unusually, there was no proper introduction to 'Love Of My Life'. Instead Brian merely commented: "This is a night that we're never gonna forget". Brian, sat on a stool, played the opening segment of the ballad, and Freddie, who was not seated, offered a lovely version of the song. Next, he walked over to Brian, and with a big grin upon his face, comments: "Now comes the difficult bit… tonight, for the very first time… this is a very special song from Queen… to you". Reading from the scribbled lyrics on his hand, he then sang a modest rendering of an old Hungarian folk song. The audience are impressed by the gesture and join in with him. For a second verse, Freddie instead hums the melody, and prompts the crowd to sing. 'Tavaszi Szel Vizet Araszt' roughly translates as 'Spring wind shields the rain'. Remaining in acoustic vane, Freddie then performed 'Is This The World' to a sea of illuminated matches and cigarette lighters.

Roger and John then returned to stage, Roger with a tambourine, for a short good humoured ad-libbed jam, before segueing into 'Tutti Frutti'. For the song's conclusion, Roger sneaks back to the drum kit and Brian exchanges guitars again. Spike Edney assists with piano backing.

'Bo Rhap' brings the house down. Even the Hungarians know this track, and sing along like any other audience, but they seem confused when Queen leave the stage for the mid-section. The extraordinary light show keeps them occupied until the band return, having changed their clothes. Queen ally Spike Edney again helps out on 'Hammer To Fall', but this time with guitar.

For 'Crazy Little Thing', Freddie walks around the stage with his guitar. At one point he sits on the edge of the piano stool with Edney, before setting off again.

Queen then leave the stage again, but return to revive 'Ga Ga' which was curiously absent from the 'Live In Budapest' video credits although it does appear.

The set concludes in a similar fashion to other shows of the tour: 'Rock You' merges into 'Friends' which in turn segues into 'Champions': "Good night. Thank you very much you beautiful people. We love you. God bless you".

The support was provided by a local group called Z'Zi Labor, who perform a curious rendition of The Rolling Stones' 'Honky Tonk Woman' (backed by a choir of women dressed in peasant costumes) in their set, and Dutch band Craaft.

In the book *Queen – A Magic Tour*, Peter Hillmore wrote: "Darkness fell, the noise of the crowd rose, the stage lights flashed even more brightly and the smoke billowed even more violently – and out of the mist, Queen came on stage. Freddie Mercury began to flash like the lights and chase the smoke around the stage. Roger Taylor crouched behind his drums pounding out the rhythm, seemingly intent on smashing them to oblivion; John Deacon's face was tight with concentration as he played his bass, and Brian May fought a musical duel with Freddie Mercury. 'One Vision' was an apt title for the opening number."

In February 1987, the performance was issued as the band's fourth live video 'Live In Budapest' (MVN 99 1146 2). It enters the UK video chart straight at No.1.

Unlike its predecessors, the video also includes footage of the band offstage. Freddie is seen on stage inside an empty arena, rehearsing material which later features in the show, and John is seen talking with a young English girl he encounters walking around the city.

'A Kind Of Magic' and 'Under Pressure' from this show, were used for the 'Live Magic' album.

July 30
Amphitheatre, Fréjus

One Vision / Tie Your Mother Down / Medley: In The Lap Of The Gods (Revisited); Seven Seas Of Rhye; Tear It Up / A Kind Of Magic / Under Pressure / Another One Bites The Dust / Who Wants To Live Forever / I Want To Break Free / Improvisation / Now I'm Here / Love Of My Life / Is This The World We Created / Medley: You're So Square; Hello Mary Lou; Tutti Frutti / Bohemian Rhapsody / Hammer To Fall / Crazy Little Thing Called Love / Radio Ga Ga / Encore: We Will Rock You / Friends Will Be Friends / We Are The Champions / God Save The Queen

August 1
Monumental Plaza De Toros, Barcelona

August 3
Rayo Vallecano, Madrid

August 5
Estadio Municipal, Marbella

This was to have been the last show of the tour, but due to the huge interest in the tour and because virtually every show had sold out so quickly, a further British date was added. Promoter Harvey Goldsmith had foreseen the possibility of an extra show, and had provisionally booked the venue anyway.

August 9
Knebworth Park, Stevenage, Hertfordshire

The highlighted tracks later appear on the band's penultimate live album 'Live Magic', issued in December 1986. Segments of 'We Are The Champions' also appear on the 1989 'Rare Live' video.

*One Vision / **Tie Your Mother Down** / Medley: In The Lap Of The Gods (Revisited); **Seven Seas Of Rhye**; Tear It Up / A Kind Of Magic / Under Pressure / **Another One Bites The Dust** / Who Wants To Live Forever / **I Want To Break Free** / Improvisation / Now I'm Here / Love Of My Life / Is This The World We Created / Medley: You're So Square; Hello Mary Lou; Tutti Frutti / **Bohemian Rhapsody** / Hammer To Fall / Crazy*
*Little Thing Called Love / **Radio Ga Ga** / Encore: **We Will Rock You / Friends Will Be Friends / We Are The Champions** / God Save The Queen*

Support acts for this day-long show are Belouis Some, Status Quo and Big Country. As in London, the concert is shown on a huge (six hundred sq ft) screen, above the stage, for those who are too far from the front to see everything. One hundred and eighty speakers throw out 500,000 watts of power, the equivalent of approximately 10,000 home hi-fi systems.

No-one knew it at the time but this was to be Queen's last ever public performance, and it seems appropriate now that it took place in the heart of the English countryside on a beautiful summer's day and not on some distant foreign stage. Before an audience variously estimated at between 160,000 and 200,000, Queen certainly went out in style.

They also arrived in style too, descending from cloudless skies in a custom decorated helicopter, provoking a massive cheer from the audience during Big Country's set as they flew overhead. A stunning photograph depicting the scene was later used for the inside illustration of the tour's commemorative live album ('Live Magic'). The helicopter is pictured as it approaches the two hundred acre 15th century grounds of the house.

A souvenir puzzle (of the same scene) was also issued.

Following a dazzling opening to Queen's set and 'Tie Your Mother Down' on which it seemed *everyone* had joined in, Freddie addressed the audience: "Hello... This is what you wanted, this is what you're gonna get. Is everybody okay, and having a nice day?... Yeah, not too bad huh! Now you gotta put up with us!" During 'In The Lap Of The Gods' there's a deafening chorus' of "Wo wo la la wo" from the audience which drowns out Freddie. Someone in the crowd begins to sing, heartily, an extra verse, before he realises his mistake and feigns a somewhat embarrassed cough, and shuts up. Moments later the opening piano chords of 'Seven Seas' ring out, and Freddie is joined again by the masses for a rendition of Queen's first ever hit.

Brian plays an intriguing segue into the next song. A riff from 'Liar' misleads the fans into expecting Freddie singing "I have sinned dear Father" but it doesn't come. A brief riff from 'Dragon Attack' follows just to confuse matters further, and then he's into 'Tear It Up', and the fans at last know where they are. The track starts with the main chorus instead of the proper album cut opening, but even those unfamiliar with the song can join in with the "Oh yeah" bits - and they do.

A few unusual sounds baffle the audience once again. Then Freddie enlightens them: "It's a kinda magic - it's a kinda magic." After a typically *big* finish to Roger's 'Magic', Freddie speaks again: "This is an ENORRRRRMOUS place, even by our standards – I tell you. It looks beautiful from up here, it's frightening." After a pause, Freddie is off down the crowd participation road again: "Da da da da da da da do" – the audience repeat it. Freddie continues, they again repeat, and similar lines follow, higher and lower. He makes it as difficult for the crowd to repeat as he can, but eventually submits: "You fuckers are good, I tell you! I'll get you after a couple of songs though, you wait!"

Roger begins 'Under Pressure' with a simple cymbal introduction, and John's instantly recognisable bass line lets everyone know exactly what song is next. There were rumours that David

Bowie might turn up to join Queen, especially as this was the last show on the tour. He didn't.

"This next song calls for a boogie. It means I throw my c**t around the stage even more than I've done." That's the cue for 'Another One Bites The Dust'. When the first verse comes up Freddie invites the crowd to sing it. They do, and Freddie says "Thank you", in time to the beat. Thereafter they sing everything with him. This version of 'Dust' is probably the best ever recorded, and can be found on the 'Live Magic' album with the introductory expletives excised. The audience are in brilliant voice, but Freddie is in even better form. The 'Live At Wembley' cut also features an improvised vocal section. "I told you I was gonna get you," Freddie says as the song reaches the halfway point. Again he invites the masses to repeat all that he sings.

They cope admirably.

"I think most of you know that is the last stop on our tour... you know that don't you? It's such a beautiful way to end it, I mean look at them (points to the mass of heads, as far back as the eye can see) the lot of you. I might also add that this has been the best European tour for us, thanks to every single one of you. And earlier on there were rumours of us splitting up, but I mean – fuck 'em – I mean really, look at this. How can you split up when you have an audience like this... I mean really. We're not that stupid. So. Now we're gonna do a song called 'Who Wants To Live Forever'." An especially poignant version follows.

'I Want To Break Free' starts without an introduction from Freddie. The audience sing the opening line before Freddie comes in. The band perform a semi-improvised operatic

153

In Rio Blues' from 1985. This segues into an unusual guitar solo from Brian that forms the opening of 'Now I'm Here', and Freddie reappears on stage. Roger and John join in together and Knebworth rocks to a stunning version of one of Queen's oldest and best loved anthems.

As was always the case, Roger and John leave the stage at this point, leaving Brian and Freddie to perform alone. The two sit on stools at the front centre of stage, with just one spotlight on them. While checking the tuning of the guitar he has just been handed, Brian says: "I would just like to say that you're a joy to play to. You are great. This is it." A moving acoustic version of 'Love Of My Life' begins, and Freddie is joined by a 100,000 voice choir.

They remain seated. Brian speaks again: "As some of you may know, the proceeds of this concert are going to the Save The Children people. So we would like to dedicate this to you and to all the people who work for Save The Children the whole year round. 'Is This The World We Created' follows.

"Okay, it's time to fool around a little, come on... everybody." The band then begin their Fifties style rock'n'roll medley. Elvis Presley's '(You're So Square) Baby I Don't Care' sees Roger at the forefront of the stage with the other three, returning to his drums when 'Tutti Frutti' calls for an extra punch. "This next one is a Ricky Nelson song. See if you know it," says Freddie. They obviously do, and many sing along with him. Freddie gets carried away with an extra line of "Awopbopalubop awopbamboom," as Roger crashes in over him with a ferocious thrashing drum roll intro.

Freddie walks around the stage briefly, sipping a drink, and then seats himself at the piano again. The very first notes he plays provoke the audience into roars of encouragement. 'Bo Rhap' begins. Afterwards, cries of "FREDDIE - FREDDIE - FREDDIE" begin somewhere in the front rows, and soon spread to every corner of the park. His reaction is simply... "And it's... 'Hammertafall'."

With a frenzied 'Hammer To Fall' behind them, the band settle down

to a less physically demanding attempt at 'Crazy'. Freddie is handed a guitar but he seems indifferent to it. "This guitar only plays three chords for me... who gives a shit!" he says. "This is a... sort of a crazy kind of song." He seems far more at home later in the song, when he abandons the guitar and settles down at the piano.

As ever, 'Radio Ga Ga' features the traditional synchronised hanclapping from the audience, made even more impressive by the sheer volume of numbers that participate. A massive sea of hands above heads accompanies the main verse, exactly as in the promo video. After this song, Queen leave the stage, and the lights dim.

When 'We Will Rock You' begins, the crowd know that the show is rapidly nearing its conclusion. What they do not know, however, is that Queen are performing it for the very last time. 'Rock You' is followed not by 'Champions' but by 'Friends Will Be Friends'. 'Champions' follows that, after which Freddie addresses his fans: "Thank you lovely people, you've been a wonderful audience - God bless you. Good night, thank you."

After the show departing fans created one of the biggest traffic jams in British recorded history. The situation was made worse because the local authorities had chosen to close parts of the main A1 near Stevenage.

During the show a woman in the audience goes into labour, and actually gives birth within the grounds, in a St. John's ambulance. However, a Status Quo fan in the audience is stabbed, and bleeds to death before medical personnel can reach him. Queen are extremely upset by the news, which mars an otherwise spectacular climax to their concert career.

Since the tour had begun, on June 7, the band played to a fraction over one million people. The millionth fan - whoever it was, was present at the show here.

December 1, '86

EMI release the band's second live album 'Live Magic' in the UK. It was not issued in America. Consisting of material recorded between July and August during the Magic tour, the fifteen track album goes on to peak at No.3 in the charts. It is produced by Queen and Trip Khalaf, Queen's concert sound engineer of ten years.

Because the band are reluctant to issue another double album, some of the tracks are heavily edited, to their detriment. The compact disc, however, did offer the full versions of 'A Kind Of Magic', 'Another One Bites The Dust' and 'Hammer To Fall'. Considering the huge volume of live Queen recordings known to exist, this comes as a big disappointment to fans.

September 15

The last single from 'A Kind Of Magic' is released in the UK. Once again nothing new is offered as the B-side, even though numerous extended mixes exist. Brian May's 'Who Wants To Live Forever' is instead backed with 'Killer Queen'. It reaches No. 24. On the 12" vinyl disc, however, a beautiful piano version of 'Forever' is contained as a bonus track, in addition to both single and album cuts of the main track.

Brian May, speaking in 1991: "When we gave up touring I suddenly realised 'Oh, you've never really stopped to enjoy this, and now it's ending'. That was the beginning of a major crisis for me. My dad died at the same time, and my marriage broke up. For a while I didn't exist as a person. I'd look at myself in the mirror and think 'Oh he's alright, he's a rock star'. Inside there was almost nothing there. I can't describe how bad it was. I know who I am again now, but no amount of fame or money can insulate you from that sort of pain. I'm okay, I'm productive again. I took a major part on the new album ('Innuendo'). In fact, the other three have all had a lot to deal with in the last

year, and I was the one saying 'OK, I'll hold the fort'."

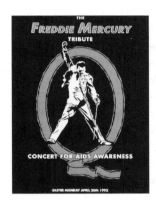

April 20, '92
Wembley Stadium, London
The Freddie Mercury Tribute Concert -
For Aids Awareness
Part 1: Various Artists:
Metallica: Enter Sandman / Sad But True / Nothing Else Matters. Extreme: Medley: Mustapha / Bohemian Rhapsody / Keep Yourself Alive / I Want To Break Free / Bicycle Race / Another One Bites The Dust / We Will Rock You / Radio Ga Ga / Stone Cold Crazy / Radio Ga Ga / Love Of My Life / More Than Words. Def Leppard: Animal / Let's Get Rocked / Now I'm Here (with Brian). Bob Geldof & The Happy Club: Too Late God. Spinal Tap: Infinity / The Majesties Of Rock. Guns n' Roses: Paradise City / Knockin' On Heaven's Door. Mango Groove: Special Star (Dedicated to Freddie) live via satellite from an Aids awareness concert in Johannesburg, South Africa. Liz Taylor: Speech.

Part 2: Queen provide backing for:
Brian May, Joe Elliott and Slash: Tie Your Mother Down. Tony Iommi & Roger Daltrey: I Want It All. Zucchero: Las Parablas De Amor. Gary Cherone & Tony Iommi: Hammer To Fall. James Hetfield & Tony Iommi: Stone Cold Crazy. Robert Plant: Innuendo / Kashmir / Thank You / Crazy Little Thing Called Love. Brian May & Spike Edney: Too Much Love Will

Kill You. Paul Young: Radio Ga Ga. Seal: Who Wants To Live Forever. Lisa Stansfield: I Want To Break Free. Annie Lennox & David Bowie: Under Pressure. David Bowie, Ian Hunter & Mick Ronson: All The Young Dudes. David Bowie & Mick Ronson: Heroes. David Bowie: The Lord's Prayer. George Michael: '39. George Michael & Lisa Stansfield: These Are The Days Of Our Lives. George Michael: Somebody To Love. Elton John & Axl Rose: Bohemian Rhapsody. Elton John: The Show Must Go On. Axl Rose: We Will Rock You. Liza Minnelli: We Are The Champions. Backing vocalists are Maggie Ryder, Chris Thompson & Miriam Stockley.

The tribute concert was conceived on the night that Freddie lost his fight for life, on November 24, 1991. The three remaining members of Queen assembled at Roger Taylor's house in Surrey, and eventually decided to organise some kind of tribute to their colleague – though at the time they did not know exactly what form it should take. That was decided later.

Roger formally announced the event at the Brit Awards ceremony on February 12, after he and Brian collected an award on Queen's behalf for their Outstanding Contribution To Music. During his acceptance speech, Brian became very emotional and had to pause for a moment to compose himself. It was equally emotional for the many fans watching the event at home, as well as an immensely proud one. The award was presented to them in fond memory of Freddie. The two received a standing ovation.

The show was co-ordinated from the London based Queen Offices in Pembridge Road. Gerry Stickells and promoter Harvey Goldsmith conducted meetings with television and radio

representatives, lighting and sound technicians, merchandising personnel, stage hands, crew members and roadies. Roger, Brian and John were present at many of the meetings, and were involved in every stage of the arrangements, especially those relating to the artists who would appear, all of whom they selected themselves. Every artist approached accepted their invitation to perform.

Among the first to be confirmed for the concert were Guns n'Roses. Axl Rose contacted the Queen office immediately after hearing of Freddie's death, and offered the services of his band for *any* event which might be organised. He was a huge Queen fan, and later went on to host an American television tribute documentary entitled *These Are The Days Of Our Lives*.

Rehearsals commenced in mid-March at a studio near Shepherds Bush in London. The three Queen members spent the first week sifting through and playing material, deciding which tracks to perform themselves and which to offer to the other acts on the bill. When the set list is established, the other performers attend to rehearse alongside Queen. Each arrival is eagerly observed by the world's press.

As April 20 loomed closer, the rehearsals moved on to Bray Studios near Windsor, Berkshire where the significantly larger sound stage provided a more realistic simulation of Wembley Stadium. The final soundchecks took place at Wembley on Sunday, the 19th.

"The concert however is looking tremendously exciting, with an unbelievable line up, and hopefully some real surprises. We are keeping much of it a secret to provide us with more flexibility up to the last minute and maximum entertainment and surprise factor on the day. Therefore please keep an open mind brothers and sisters!

"We see the concert as primarily a tribute to our friend and colleague, but also as a way of using the tragedy of his death to good effect, in bringing an awareness of the fact that AIDS AFFECTS ALL of us, to a wider range of people – by using a wide and weighty spectrum of the very best in serious contemporary popular music.

"This is such an important message, especially for the younger people of the world – and especially – NOW! If Freddie can posthumously help that awareness, it will be a major addition to the already wonderful achievements of his life.

"In advance, the band and myself, Jim Beach, Gerry & Sylvia Stickells – Julie & the staff, would like to thank all the brilliant people helping and participating in the event. Names will be named! See you April 20th – fingers crossed for a great day! Love Roger."

When Roger, Brian and John walked out on stage they were greeted by a deafening roar. Brian's first words are obscured by the din, but he continues anyway: "Good evening Wembley – and the world (it's daytime really). We are here today to celebrate the life, and work, and dreams, of one Freddie Mercury. We're gonna give him the biggest send off in history!"

Brian then made way for Roger: "Today is for Freddie, it's for you, it's to tell everybody around the world that Aids affects us all – that's what these red ribbons are all about... You can cry as much as you like! And John's got something to tell you..."

John: "Hello. First of all, Brian, Roger and myself would like to thank all the artists who we have performing here today, in London. They've given their time and energy to make this tribute to Freddie a reality, and to happen today. First of all – the show must go on – and we'll start with an American band, three times Grammy

Award winners – please welcome Metallica."

The section of the show which features U2 was recorded live on April 18, at the Oakland Coliseum, in California, as part of their Zoo TV Tour. During that show Bono dedicates 'Dancing Queen' and 'Satellite Of Love' to Freddie. He explains to the audience: "We're sending some of tonight's show down the wire to Freddie Aid in London. He was a very cool guy. He was exceptionally cool to me." Bono made numerous other references to Freddie during the show also. 'Until The End Of The World' was the song which was shown on the Wembley screens, on the day.

When Freddie himself suddenly appeared mid-way through the show on the huge 20 by 30 ft video screens addressing a concert audience from yesteryear, there was a stunned silence. "Are you ready?" he asks, as large as life. "YEAH," the masses respond. "Huh, are you ready brothers and sisters?" he asks again, courtesy of a recording of his voice from the June 1982 Milton Keynes gig. No one had expected Freddie to be present at his own tribute but, then again, he'd always been in his element before big crowds and this was Queen's biggest ever.

During the concert Neil James of Radio One spoke to Brian and Roger backstage...

Brian: "We thought it would be nice to do something which would give Freddie the proper send off, when the right time came. The concert came out of that really. But it was a long road from that point to this. At some points I think we almost decided that it couldn't be done. But I think we're extremely glad we pressed on, at this point - eh Rog?"

Roger: "Yes, there was a lot of work, and a lot of talking to be done, and a lot of logistics to overcome – from the fact of using a lot of people. We had a lot of encouragement in the early days, from I must say – to single out two people – Elton John and Guns n'Roses, who were behind the idea of doing something from the beginning, and offered their services from the beginning – along with everyone else.

"It's not a marathon and it's not a telethon, it's not even entirely about raising money. It's a celebration of Freddie's life and Freddie's work, and it's a raising of awareness about the fact that Aids affects all of us, and what a terrible hidden threat it is."

Brian: "We've had positive feelings from everybody – everybody's been great. Most people said do whatever you like. It might be worth saying that artistically this is different from your average sort of charity concert I think. In Live Aid for instance – which was a wonderful success – you had people coming on doing their thing, then they're off, then the next person comes on and does his thing. This, from the point where the three of us hit the stage, is a very co-operative thing – it's not Queen – it's the three of us combined with a lot of other people, in various capacities. It's almost like one band. Every song you see will be a one-off. You'll never see the likes of this happening again - well not this week anyway."

Neil James: "As far as Queen is concerned, is this the last show for Queen?"

Brian: "I think the last show for Queen was 1986. Truly. The Knebworth show on the end of the Magic tour was the last time you saw Queen as a band. I don't think it can ever exist, as such, again. The spirit is still alive – as you'll see. And I think the three of us definitely still work together great – there's no question about that. This is just my own personal view (Roger agrees), the last chapter has already been written, and I think we're very proud of the whole book. It has a beginning, and a lot of good stuff in the middle - a good catalogue - and it has an ending, and I think that's where we are".

Q magazine's review of the show was headlined: YOU WERE WONDER-FUL, MY DEARS! "Bowie burst into prayer; Axl sang his 'buns' off; George & Lisa went for the Peters & Lee vote; Ian Hunter arose and appeared to many; while Brian, Roger and 'Deaky' played themselves sore. The Freddie Mercury Tribute Concert for Aids Awareness... they laughed, they cried, they hurled."

On a technical level, 1,000 people were involved in producing the show; 5,000 stage lights, thirty tons of scaffolding, one hundred and seventy-five microphones, four hundred miles of cable, thirteen satellite link-ups (including the first ever such link to South Africa) are used. A record breaking £600,000 worth of merchandising material was sold: £50,000 in programmes, £100,000 in T-shirts, £50,000 in badges, £40,000 in baseball caps and £40,000 in posters. Furthermore, 5,000 cans of beer and 2,000 bottles of wine were laid on by the Hard Rock Café for the performing artists, while the audience drank and ate their way through 26,000 pints of lager, 64,000 Cokes, 20,000 burgers, 15,000 hot dogs, a quarter of a ton of chips and 3,000 boxes of popcorn. 100,000 red ribbons and 40,000 red scarves were given away free at the turnstiles on the day, as a symbol of Aids awareness. Ultimately £12 million is raised for Aids research.

Of all the many images that day, the ones I recall most vividly were two home made banners. The first featured a huge black double posted flag, with the words "Freddie... Pure Genius" in gold stencilled letters, a concept lifted from the Guinness television commercials. The other was more poignant: "How I loved you – how I cried", it read. The line from Brian May's 'Save Me' seemed to summarise the mood of most of us Queen aficionados, as we shuffled expectantly towards Entrance gate 'C'.

The atmosphere outside the stadium was electric, the sense of camaraderie fantastic. In whichever direction you chose to look, there was a British, or American, or Dutch, or Canadian fan sharing sandwiches, crisps and pork pies with fellow Japanese or Australian fans, who only hours beforehand had been total strangers. When Roger invited us all to cry as much as we liked, it struck me that for many fans the advice had probably come too late.

UK Singles

Love Of My Life (Live) /
Now I'm Here (Live)
EMI 2959 (29/06/79)

Crazy Little Thing Called Love /
We Will Rock You (Live)
EMI 5001 (05/10/79)

Save Me / Let Me Entertain
You (Live)
EMI 5022 (25/01/80)

The Miracle / Stone Cold Crazy
(Live)
QUEEN 15 (7") (27/11/89)

The Miracle / Stone Cold Crazy
(Live) / My Melancholy Blues (Live)
12 QUEEN 15 (12") (27/11/89)

The Miracle / Stone Cold Crazy
(Live) / My Melancholy Blues (Live)
CD QUEEN 15 (CD Single) (27/11/89)

Somebody To Love / Killer / Papa
Was A Rollin' Stone / These Are
The Days Of Are Lives / Calling You
PARCO 8 805502 (1993)

Japanese Singles

Love Of My Life (Live) /
Now I'm Here (Live)
P-423E (05/79)

We Will Rock You (Live) /
Let Me Entertain You (Live)
P-486E (10/79)

Crazy Little Thing Called Love /
Spread Your Wings (Live)
P-529E (01/80)

Save Me / Sheer Heart
Attack (Live)
P-550E (04/80)

American Singles

We Will Rock You (Live) /
Let Me Entertain You (Live)
E46532 (24/08/79)

Crazy Little Thing Called Love /
Spread Your Wings (Live)
E46579 (07/12/79)

Dutch Single

Live At Wembley '86
We Will Rock You (Live) / We Are
The Champions (Live) / We Will
Rock You (Studio Version) / We Are
The Champions (Studio Version)
Issued only in Holland (1992)

Albums:
Worldwide Releases

Live Killers
Double LP/CD
UK LP
EMSP 330
Released (22/06/79)
Reached No.3

UK CD
CDS 7 462118
Running time: 47.11/43.12

US LP
BB 702
Released (26/06/79)
Reached No.16

US CD
HR 61066 2
Running time: 47.11/43.10

Japanese LP
Elektra P5567E 1/4
Green/red vinyl

Japanese CD
Elektra CP28 5316/7
Running time: 47.11/43.10

Side 1: We Will Rock You (3.18) /
Let Me Entertain You (3.15) / Death On
Two Legs (3.31) / Killer Queen (1.59) /
Bicycle Race (1.28) / I'm In Love With
My Car (2.01) / Get Down Make Love
(4.31) / You're My Best Friend (2.08)

Side 2: Now I'm Here (8.42) / Dreamers
Ball (3.44) / Love Of My Life (4.57) / '39
(3.26) / Keep Yourself Alive (4.02)

Side 3: Don't Stop Me Now (4.28) /
Spread Your Wings (5.22) / Brighton
Rock (12.13)

Side 4: Bohemian Rhapsody (6.02) /
Tie Your Mother Down (3.40) / Sheer
Heart Attack (3.35) / We Will Rock You
(2.48) / We Are The Champions (3.27) /
God Save The Queen (1.31)

Queen Live
Japanese single album
Elektra P13117E
Edited version of Live Killers

Side 1: We Will Rock You (3.23) /
Let Me Entertain You (3.17) / Killer
Queen (2.00) / Bicycle Race (1.13) /
You're My Best Friend (2.05) / Spread
Your Wings (5.29) / Keep Yourself
Alive (4.00)

Side 2: Don't Stop Me Now (4.26) /
Bohemian Rhapsody (6.03) / Tie Your
Mother Down (3.40) / Sheer Heart
Attack (3.33) / We Are The Champions
(3.34)

Live Killers
South African single album
EMI EXTRA5
Edited version of Live Killers

Marketed and distributed by EMI
Music South Africa (PTY) Limited.
Issued after the six Sun City shows in
October 1985. It contains an edited
tracklisting and different front cover
sleeve to the 1979 UK counterpart.
All proceeds were donated to charity.
It was also issued on audio cassette.

Side 1: We Will Rock You (3.23) /
Let Me Entertain You (3.17) / Killer
Queen (2.00) / Bicycle Race (1.13) /
You're My Best Friend (2.05) / Spread
Your Wings (5.29) / Keep Yourself
Alive (4.00)

Side 2: Don't Stop Me Now (4.26) /
Bohemian Rhapsody (6.03) / Tie Your
Mother Down (3.40) / Sheer Heart
Attack (3.33) / We Are The Champions
(3.34)

Queen Live
Australian single album
Elektra 60343/1
Edited version of Live Killers

Side 1: We Will Rock You (3.23) /
Let Me Entertain You (3.17) / Killer
Queen (2.00) / Bicycle Race (1.13) /
You're My Best Friend (2.05) / Spread
Your Wings (5.29) / Keep Yourself
Alive (4.00)

Side 2: Don't Stop Me Now (4.26) /
Bohemian Rhapsody (6.03) / Tie Your
Mother Down (3.40) / Sheer Heart
Attack (3.33) / We Are The Champions
(3.34)

Live In Concert
New Zealand single album
Elektra 60343/1
Edited version of Live Killers ·

Side 1: We Will Rock You (3.23) /
Let Me Entertain You (3.17) / Killer
Queen (2.00) / Bicycle Race (1.13) /
You're My Best Friend (2.05) / Spread
Your Wings (5.29) / Keep Yourself
Alive (4.00)

Side 2: Don't Stop Me Now (4.26) /
Bohemian Rhapsody (6.03) / Tie Your
Mother Down (3.40) / Sheer Heart
Attack (3.33) / We Are The Champions
(3.34)

Queen Live: Rock In Rio
Brazilian single album
4047224
Released in 1985

This material does not relate to the
January 1985 Brazilian Rock In Rio
Festival, as the title suggests. It was
merely issued at the time of the Festival.
It is actually an edited version of Live
Killers, although the album sleeve is
different.

Side 1: We Will Rock You (3.23) /
Let Me Entertain You (3.17) / Killer
Queen (2.00) / Bicycle Race (1.13) /
You're My Best Friend (2.05) / Spread
Your Wings (5.29) / Keep Yourself
Alive (4.00)

Side 2: Don't Stop Me Now (4.26) /
Bohemian Rhapsody (6.03) / Tie Your
Mother Down (3.40) / Sheer Heart
Attack (3.33) / We Are The Champions
(3.34)

Live Magic
UK LP
EMC 3519
Released (01/12/86)
Reached No.3

UK CD
CDP 746413 2
Running time: 49.22

Japanese CD
CP32 5173
Running time: 49.22

Not issued in USA, on either format

Side 1: One Vision (5.09) / Tie Your
Mother Down (2.59) / Seven Seas Of
Rhye (1.21) / A Kind Of Magic (5.30) /
Under Pressure (3.49) / Another One
Bites The Dust (5.50)

Side 2: I Want To Break Free (2.40) /
Is This The World We Created (1.31) /
Bohemian Rhapsody (4.42) / Hammer
To Fall (5.20) / Radio Ga Ga (4.27) /
We Will Rock You (1.33) / Friends
Will Be Friends (1.09) / We Are The
Champions (2.01) / God Save The
Queen (1.19)

Live At Wembley '86
Double LP/CD
UK LP
799594 1
Released (26/05/92)
Reached No.2

UK CD
CDPCSP 725
Running time: 60.34/50.28

US CD
HR 61104 2
Released (26/05/92)
Reached No. 53
Running time: 60.32/50.27

Side 1: One Vision (5.50) / Tie Your
Mother Down (3.52) / In The Lap Of
The Gods (2.44) / Seven Seas Of Rhye
(1.19) / Tear It Up (2.12) / A Kind
Of Magic (8.41) / Under Pressure (3.41) /
Another One Bites The Dust (4.54)

Side 2: Who Wants To Live Forever
(5.16) / I Want To Break Free (3.34) /
Impromptu (2.55) / Brighton Rock
Solo (9.11) / Now I'm Here (6.19)

Side 3: Love Of My Life (4.47) /
Is This The World We Created (2.59) /
(You're So Square) Baby I Don't Care
(1.34) / Hello Mary Lou (Goodbye
Heart) (1.24) / Tutti Frutti (3.23) /
Gimme Some Lovin' (0.55) / Bohemian
Rhapsody (5.50) / Hammer To Fall (5.36)

Side 4: Crazy Little Thing Called
Love (6.27) / Big Spender (1.07) /
Radio Ga Ga (5.57) / We Will Rock
You (2.46) / Friends Will Be Friends
(2.08) / We Are The Champions (4.05) /
God Save The Queen (1.27)

Queen At The Beeb
LP
Band Of Joy Records BOJ 001
Released (04/12/89)

CD
BOJCD 001
Running time: 37.43

Not issued in USA at time of going
to press

Side 1: My Fairy King (4.06) / Keep
Yourself Alive (3.47) / Doing Alright
(4.11) / Liar (6.28)

Side 2: Ogre Battle (3.56) / Great King
Rat (5.57) / Modern Times Rock'n'Roll
(2.00) / Son And Daughter (7.08)

Side 1 relates to Session 1. Side 2 to
session 3. Both sessions were recorded
at Langham 1 studio, London.
Produced by Bernie Andrews.

The album reached No.67 in the
UK album charts. It was not issued
elsewhere. The possibility of issuing
an At The Beeb sequel album is under
consideration.

Queen At The Beeb has since been
issued in america, on the Holliwood
Record label, retitled Queen At The BBC.
It Is Also Available As A 12" promo
Picture disc limited edition.

Videos

Greatest Flix: Volume I
MVP 99 1011 2
Released (19/10/81)

Essentially a collection of promotional videos which accompanied the band's singles up to 'Flash', though it also includes live footage of 'We Will Rock You' (fast version) and 'Love Of My Life'.

Live In Japan
APVG-4004
Released in Japan only in 1983
(on Japanese video system)
Watanabe Music Publishing 1983
Produced by Raincloud Productions
Recorded at the Seibu Lions Stadium,
Tokyo, Japan (03/11/82)

Flash's Theme; The Hero / Now I'm Here; Put Out The Fire; Dragon Attack; Now I'm Here / Love Of My Life / Save Me / Guitar Solo / Under Pressure / Crazy Little Thing Called Love / Bohemian Rhapsody / Tie Your Mother Down / Teo Torriatte / We Will Rock You / We Are The Champions

We Will Rock You
PVM 6122
Released September 10, 1984
Reissued October 1989 MC 2032
Recorded at the Forum, Montreal,
Canada (24-25/11/81)

We Will Rock You / Let Me Entertain You / Play The Game / Somebody To Love / Killer Queen / I'm In Love With My Car / Get Down Make Love / Save Me / Now I'm Here / Dragon Attack / Love Of My Life / Under Pressure / Keep Yourself Alive / Crazy Little Thing Called Love / Bohemian Rhapsody / Tie Your Mother Down / Another One Bites The Dust / Sheer Heart Attack / We Will Rock You / We Are The Champions / God Save The Queen

Live In Rio
MVP 99 1079 2
Released (13/05/85)
Recorded at the Rock In Rio Festival,
Rio De Janeiro, Brazil (19/01/85)

Tie Your Mother Down / Seven Seas Of Rhye / Keep Yourself Alive / Liar / It's A Hard Life / Now I'm Here / Is This The World We Created / Love Of My Life / Brighton Rock / Hammer To Fall / Bohemian Rhapsody / Radio Ga Ga / I Want To Break Free / We Will Rock You / We Are The Champions / God Save The Queen

Live In Budapest
MVN 99 1146 2
Released (16/02/87)
Recorded at the Nepstadion, Budapest,
Hungary (27/07/86)

Tavaszi Szel Vizet Araszi / One Vision / Tie Your Mother Down / In The Lap Of The Gods... Revisited / Seven Seas Of Rhye / Tear It Up / A Kind Of Magic / Tavaszi Szel Vizet Araszi / Under Pressure / Who Wants To Live Forever / I Want To Break Free / Now I'm Here / Love Of My Life / Tavaszi Szel Vizet Araszi / Is This The World We Created / Tutti Frutti / Bohemian Rhapsody / Hammer To Fall / Crazy Little Thing Called Love / Radio Ga Ga / We Will Rock You / Friends Will Be Friends / We Are The Champions / God Save The Queen

The Magic Years
MVB 991157 2
Released (30/11/87)

Sold as a three video boxed set and individually:
Volume I: The Foundations
Volume II: Live Killers In The Making
Volume III: Crowned In Glory

As the title suggests, the second collection contains numerous snippets of live performances. It covers the progression of Queen's live concerts from 1974 to 1984.

Rare Live: A Concert Through Time And Space
MVP 9911893
Released (21/08/89)

I Want It All (Title track / credits, 1989) / Crazy Little Thing Called Love (Osaka, Japan, 1982) / Liar (Rehearsal in London, 1973 & Rainbow Theatre, London, 1974) / Another One Bites The Dust (Buenos Aires, Argentina, 1981 & Vienna, Austria 1982) / Big Spender (Hammersmith Odeon, London 1975) / Jailhouse Rock (Hammersmith Odeon, London, 1975) / Stupid Cupid (Hammersmith Odeon, London, 1975) / My Melancholy Blues (Houston, Texas, USA, 1977) / Hammer To Fall (Wembley Stadium, London, 1986) / Killer Queen (Earls Court, London, 1977) / We Will Rock You (Live Aid, London, 1985) / Somebody To Love (Milton Keynes Bowl, 1982) / Tie Your Mother Down (Paris, France, 1979 & Rio De Janeiro, Brazil, 1985) / Keep Yourself Alive (Hammersmith Odeon, London, 1975 & Tokyo, Japan, 1985) / Love Of My Life (Sao Paulo, Brazil, 1981) / Stone Cold Crazy (Rainbow Theatre, London, 1974) / Radio Ga Ga (Sydney, Australia, 1985) / You Take My Breath Away (Earls Court, London, 1977) / Sheer Heart Attack (Houston, Texas, USA, 1977) / We Are The Champions (Knebworth Park, Stevenage, 1986 & Frankfurt, Germany, 1982)

Additional excerpts from Tokyo 1985, Hyde Park 1976, Hammersmith Odeon 1979, Montreal, Canada 1980, Newcastle 1986 and Budapest, Hungary 1986.

NB: Notes on the video sleeve relating to the date and venue of some tracks are incorrect.

Queen Live At Wembley
MVP 9912593
Released (03/12/90)

Brighton Rock / One Vision / Tie Your Mother Down / In The Lap Of The Gods... Revisited / Seven Seas Of Rhye / A Kind Of Magic / Under Pressure / Another One Bites The Dust / Who Wants To Live Forever / I Want To Break Free / Is This The World We Created / Tutti Frutti / Bohemian Rhapsody / Hammer To Fall / Crazy Little Thing Called Love / Radio Ga Ga / We Will Rock You / Friends Will Be Friends / We Are The Champions / God Save The Queen

For reasons best known to Queen and Picture Music International, this video is considerably shorter in length than its CD and LP counterparts. The following tracks appear on the disc formats but not on this video: Tear It Up / Impromptu, Brighton Rock / Now I'm Here / Love Of My Life / You're So Square / Hello Mary Lou / Big Spender / Gimme Some Lovin.

Note: Brighton Rock appears here in its studio recorded form (not as a live version). It provides the background music to the opening credits, and footage of the speeded up stage construction. Recorded at Wembley Stadium, London, July 12, 1986.

Live At The Rainbow
Released May 1992 as part of the Box Of Tricks boxed set
(The video has no catalogue no.)
Recorded at the Rainbow Theatre, London (20/12/74)

Procession / Now I'm Here / Ogre Battle / White Queen / In The Lap Of The Gods / Killer Queen / March Of The Black Queen / Bring Back That Leroy Brown / Son & Daughter / Father To Son / Keep Yourself Alive / Liar / Son & Daughter / Stone Cold Crazy / In The Lap Of The Gods... Revisited / Jailhouse Rock / God Save The Queen.

Freddie Mercury Tribute Concert
Double Video
MVB 4910623
Released (23/11/92)
Recorded at Wembley Stadium, London (20/04/92)
Running time: Video 1: 90 mins
Video 2: 117 mins
Produced by Queen and Jim Beach
Directed and re-edited by David Mallet
Remixed by David Richards

Some artists who took part in the concert declined permission for their performances to be included on this edited double video. Most, however, did give their permission. The majority of fans recorded the show directly from television, and so have the missing performances anyway.

Queen's BBC Sessions

Session 1:
My Fairy King / Keep Yourself Alive / Doing Alright / Liar
Recorded at Langham 1 Studio, London (05/02/73)
Producer: Bernie Andrews
Engineer: John Etchells
Broadcast: John Peel (Radio One) (15/02/73)
Released as Side One of 'Queen At The Beeb' (4/12/89)

Session 2:
See What A Fool I've Been / Liar / Son And Daughter / Keep Yourself Alive
Recorded at Langham 1 Studio, London (25/07/73)
Producer: Jeff Griffin/Chris Lycett
Engineer: John Etchells
Broadcast: Bob Harris (Radio One) (13/08/73)
'Keep Yourself Alive' was broadcast (24/09/73)

Session 3:
Ogre Battle / Great King Rat / Modern Times Rock'n'Roll / Son And Daughter
Recorded at Langham 1 Studio, London: (03/12/73)
Producer: Bernie Andrews
Engineer: Nick Griffiths/Mike Franks
Broadcast: John Peel (Radio One) (06/12/73)
Released as Side Two of 'Queen At The Beeb' (04/12/89)

Session 4:
Modern Times Rock'n'Roll / March Of The Black Queen / Nevermore / White Queen
Recorded at Langham 1 Studio, London 03/04/74
Producer: Pete Ritzema
Engineer: Unknown
Broadcast: Bob Harris (Radio One) (15/04/74)

Session 5:
Now I'm Here / Stone Cold Crazy / Flick Of The Wrist / Tenement Funster
Recorded at Maida Vale 4 Studio, London (16/10/74)
Producer/Engineer: Jeff Griffin
Broadcast: Bob Harris (Radio One) (04/11/74)

Session 6:
Spread Your Wings / It's Late / My Melancholy Blues / We Will Rock You
Recorded at Maida Vale 4 Studio, London (28/10/77)
Producer: Jeff Griffin
Engineer: Mike Robinson
Broadcast: John Peel (Radio One) (14/11/77)

Queen CD Bootlegs

Queen's live performances were always widely bootlegged, and since Freddie's death the number of unauthorised compact discs has grown dramatically. Prior to 1991 there were perhaps a dozen bootleg CDs on the market but in the two years that followed, that figure has increased almost tenfold, with 1993/94 releases pushing the number into treble figures.

What follows is a summary of all the discs known to me which are currently available, or which have at one time been in circulation around the world. The vast majority are not worth seeking out, for reasons detailed below. Many unofficial compact discs are purchased purely as additions to collections, and in many cases remain unplayed or even removed from their packaging; in which case the content is immaterial.

Very few discs are worth the generally exorbitant price, but the good ones are very good and should be regarded as a must for collectors.

The location and date of each recording, as advised immediately before each disc's tracklist, is exactly as it appears on the sleeve notes. Many are inaccurate. Additional notes have been added by the author (in italics beneath each set list), to clarify any particularly misleading, inaccurate, humorous or plainly absurd points of interest. The numerous spelling inaccuracies which invariably accompany bootleg releases have been corrected.

Queen Live Bootlegs

A Day At The Stadium
KTS 039
Kiss The Stone Records, Italy, 1992
Recorded live in London, Summer, 1985
Running time: 77.05

One Vision (4.47) / Tie Your Mother
Down (3.57) / Hammer To Fall (5.45) /
Seven Seas Of Rhye (1.51) / Tear It
Up (2.22) / A Kind Of Magic (6.37) /
Under Pressure (3.54) / Another One
Bites The Dust (4.48) / I Want To Break
Free (3.37) / Instrumental Jam (3.01) /
Now I'm Here (6.42) / Love Of
My Life (4.55) / Is This The World We
Created (2.59) / Baby I Don't Care /
Hello Mary Lou / Tutti Frutti (6.38) /
Bohemian Rhapsody (6.02) / Crazy Little
Thing Called Love (4.46) / We Are The
Champions (4.21)

*Queen played only one show in the
Summer of 1985 – Live Aid on July 13.
The material on this disc is actually from
the Magic tour of 1986.*

A Night At The Court
Double CD
TNT 007/008
Tarantula Records, 1991
Tracks 1-26 Earls Court, London,
June 6, 1977
Tracks 27-32 Town Hall, Birmingham,
November 21, 1973
Running times: 73.29/59.53

Disc 1: Procession / Tie Your Mother
Down / Ogre Battle / White Queen /
Somebody To Love / Killer Queen /
Good Old Fashioned Lover Boy /
The Millionaire Waltz / You're My Best
Friend / Bring Back That Leroy Brown /
Death On Two Legs / Brighton Rock /
'39 / You Take My Breath Away /
White Man / The Prophet's Song

Disc 2: Bohemian Rhapsody / Stone
Cold Crazy / In The Lap Of The Gods...
Revisited / Now I'm Here / Liar / Lucille /
Jailhouse Rock / Stupid Cupid / Be Bop
A Lula / God Save The Queen /
Procession / Father To Son / Son And
Daughter / Ogre Battle / Hangman /
Keep Yourself Alive

*Queen did not play Birmingham Town Hall
on the date indicated on the sleeve notes.
They played that venue on November 27,
1973, and Preston Guildhall on the 21st.
While the sleeve notes advise that both discs
contain sixteen tracks each, in fact they
both feature only eleven. A number of songs
on each disc are grouped together as one
complete medley. Curiously no recording
from the second night at this venue, has ever
materialised.*

A Tribute To Freddie Mercury
P910012
Dicid Records, Germany, 1992
Wembley Stadium, London (20/04/92)
Running time: 58.00

More Than Words (Extreme) (2.08) /
Now I'm Here (Def Leppard &
Brian May) (5.07) / Paradise City
(Guns n'Roses) (6.09) / Pinball Wizard
(Roger Daltrey) (0.29) / I Want It All
(Roger Daltrey) (2.48) / Innuendo
(Robert Plant) (6.02) / '39 (George
Michael) (1.56) / I Want To Break Free
(Lisa Stansfield) (3.40) / Under Pressure
(Annie Lennox & David Bowie) (4.24) /
All The Young Dudes (Ian Hunter,
David Bowie & Mick Ronson) (3.47) /
Bohemian Rhapsody (Elton John & Axl
Rose) (5.22) / Too Much Love Will Kill
You (Brian May) (4.29) / Radio Ga Ga
(Paul Young) (4.09) / We Are The
Champions (Liza Minelli) (5.49) /
The Lord's Prayer (David Bowie) (0.35)

*Tracks 4-14 feature Brian, John and
Roger providing back up.*

Absolutely Perfect
MNS 0292
Make Me Smile Records, Italy, 1992
Live in Brussels
Running time: 77.07

Under Pressure / Somebody To Love /
Killer Queen / Seven Seas Of Rhye /
Keep Yourself Alive / Liar / Instrumental
Tune / It's A Hard Life / Dragon Attack /
Now I'm Here / Is This The World We
Created / Love Of My Life / Another
One Bites The Dust / Hammer To Fall /
Crazy Little Thing Called Love /
Bohemian Rhapsody / Radio Ga Ga /
I Want To Break Free / Jailhouse Rock /
We Are The Champions

*This disc actually contains material
recorded in Japan, and not Belgium as the
sleeve notes claim. It is yet another variation
of the May 11, 1985 Yogishi Swimming
Pool Auditorium gig. The double CD set
'Le Fleur Du Mal' is by far a superior and
more sensible alternative, not least as it
offers four more tracks.*

Absolutely Rare
Double CD
QUCD 9202
1992
Various shows
Running times: 59.29/59.16

Disc 1: Imagine / You're So Square /
Hello Mary Lou / Tutti Frutti /
The Millionaire Waltz / Rock In Rio
Blues - America / Take Me Home / Teo
Torriatte / Tenement Funster / Last
Horizon / Mannish Boy / See What
A Fool I've Been / Cool Cat / Jailhouse
Rock / Flick Of The Wrist / It's Late /
Mustapha / Death On Two Legs

Disc 2: Rock In Rio Blues - Europe /
Immigrant Song / Fat Bottomed Girls /
Doing Alright / Lazing On A Sunday
Afternoon / Back Chat / I Can Hear
Music (Larry Lurex) / Need Your Loving
Tonight / Modern Times Rock'n'Roll /
Not Fade Away / Life Is Real /
Rip It Up (The Cross) / Saturday Night's
Alright For Fighting / Everybody Happy
(Freddie Mercury) / Goin' Back
(Larry Lurex) / Lucille / In My Defence
(Freddie Mercury) / Ogre Battle
(Forgotten Intro) / Hangman / Hello
And Goodbye

*Yet another disc which doesn't contain
all the material it purports to. Track 14 on
Disc 2 is not a rare unissued song, as
unfamiliar fans might be forgiven for
presuming, but merely Freddie's recorded
message for the 1987 fan club convention.
Each member of the band would record a
message which would be played in their
absence at the beginning of the convention.
This track is such an example.*

All Your Love Tonight
RC 2106
Rock Calender Records,
Luxembourg, 1993
Live in Milwaukee Arena,
September 10, 1980
Running time: 67.15

Jailhouse Rock (1.54) / We Will Rock
You (2.34) / Let Me Entertain You (2.37) /
Play The Game (3.39) / Mustapha (2.23) /
Death On Two Legs (3.32) / Killer
Queen (1.57) / I'm In Love With My
Car (1.59) / Get Down Make Love
(5.17) / You're My Best Friend (1.56) /
Save Me (3.44) / Fat Bottomed Girls
(3.10) / Love Of My Life (3.26) / Crazy
Little Thing Called Love (3.32) /
Bohemian Rhapsody (5.07) / Tie Your
Mother Down (3.32) / Another One
Bites The Dust (3.16) / Sheer Heart
Attack (3.20) / We Will Rock You (2.24) /
We Are The Champions (2.06)

*The writing credits for track 3 are very
curiously attributed to J. Styne & S. Sondheim
instead of Freddie; Julie Styne & Steven
Sondheim presumably. The disc title comes
from a line from Brian May's 'Tie Your
Mother Down'.*

Best Selection
VC 3024
Echo Industry Co Limited, Japan, 1992
Various shows
Running time: 66.21

Killer Queen (3.00) / Keep Yourself
Alive (3.47) / My Fairy King (4.06) /
Modern Times Rock'n'Roll (1.48) /
White Queen (4.33) / Seven Seas Of
Rhye (2.48) / Now I'm
Here (4.13) / Bohemian Rhapsody (5.59) /
You're My Best Friend (2.50) / Sweet
Lady (4.02) / Love Of My Life (3.34) /
Somebody To Love (4.56) / Good Old
Fashioned Lover Boy (2.53) / You And I
(3.25) / Who Needs You (3.07) / It's Late
(6.27) / We Are The Champions (2.59)

*Collectors need not get too excited at
the apparent inclusion of live versions of
'Nevermore', 'You And I' and 'Who Needs
You'. They are not what they purport to be.
Regrettably all are merely the familiar
'Queen II', 'Races' and 'N.O.T.W' album cuts,
as can be seen by their running times.
I made the same mistake as did many
collectors who purchased this disc, by
assuming that the set offered predominately
live renditions – it does not.*

Big In Japan
Double CD
NRG 010/11
Energy Records, Italy, 1994
Recorded live in Japan in May 1985
Extra tracks from 13-17 recorded
live in UK in 1985
Running times: 68.18/71.39

Disc 1: Tear It Up / Tie Your Mother
Down / Under Pressure / Somebody to
Love / Killer Queen / Seven Seas Of
Rhye / Keep Yourself Alive / Liar

Disc 2: Who Wants To Live Forever /
One Vision / A Kind Of Magic /
Instrumental / Radio Ga Ga / I Want To
Break Free / Jailhouse Rock / Baby I
Don't Care / Hello Mary Lou / We Will
Rock You / We Are The Champions /
God Save The Queen / I Can Hear
Music / Going Back / Under Pressure /
Another One Bites The Dust / I Want To
Break Free / Tie Your Mother Down /
Hammer To Fall

*Tracks 13, 14, 15, 16 and 17 actually
originate from the July 1986 Wembley
Stadium shows. Tracks 11 and 12 relate to
the June 1973 Phil Spector inspired Larry
Lurex single, for which Freddie sang lead
vocals (EMI 2030).*

**By Request: The Ultimate
Collection (Volume II)**
Double CD
RM002/003
Royalty Music, 1991
Running times: 73.24/73.55

Disc 1: Hammer To Fall (5.03) (Live in
Rio 1984) / Spread Your Wings (5.21)
(John Peel Session 1977) / I Wanna Testify
(3.48) (Rare Roger Taylor A-Side 1977) /
Bohemian Rhapsody (5.25) (Live in
London 1977) / Killer Queen (3.07)
(Demo 1974) / The Invisible Man (5.38)
(12" Version 1989) / Hijack My Heart
(4.12) (B-Side 1989) / Doing Alright
(3.54) (Rare Track 1970) / Blag (3.14)
(Rare Track 1970) / Back Chat (6.51)
(12" Version 1982) / Staying Power (4.20)
(12" Version 1982) / Flick Of The Wrist
(4.01) (Live in USA 1975) / In The Lap
Of The Gods (3.31) (Live in USA 1975) /
Killer Queen (1.26) (Live in USA 1975) /
Black Queen (0.40) (Live in USA 1975) /
Turn On The TV (3.28) (Rare Roger
Taylor B-Side 1977) / The World We
Created (3.29) (Live Aid - London 1985) /
Crazy Little Thing (4.31) (Live Aid -
London 1985)

Disc 2: A Kind Of Magic (5.34) (Live
in Zurich 1986) / Thank God It's
Christmas (4.20) (12" Version 1984) /
Man On The Prowl (6.05) (12" Extended
Mix 1984) / Keep Passing The Open
(6.50) (12" Extended Mix 1984) / Merry
Xmas (War Is Over) (3.39) (The
Cross) / I Want To Break Free (7.21)
(12" Extended Mix) / Machines (Back To
Humans) (5.07) (12" Version) / April Lady
(2.42) (Rare Smile Track 1970) / Polar
Bear (4.00) (Rare Smile Track 1970) /
Keep Yourself Alive (3.47) (Bob Harris
Session 1973) / Lost Opportunity (3.49)
(Rare 12" B-side 1991) Let Me Entertain
You (2.57) (live in USA 1980) / I'm In
Love With My Car (2.09) (live in USA
1980) / You Take My Breath Away (4.12)
(Demo 1976) / Friends Will Be Friends
(6.17) (Extended 12" Version) / Tie Your
Mother Down (5.02) (Live in USA 1993)

*The details in brackets are as they appear
on the sleeve notes. This double set is yet
another example of the packaging and
sleeve notes not living up to expectations.
For example: only one version of 'Thank God
It's Christmas' is available, so to suggest that
this CD contains the "twelve inch version",
is absurd.*

160

Coverin'
COW 100
Ugly Records, Italy, 1994
Various shows
Running time: 58.37

Be Bop A Lula (1.50) / Lucille (2.01) /
Mannish Boy (3.10) / Not Fade Away
(1.56) / Imagine (2.10) / Saturday Night's
Alright For Fighting (2.53) / Jailhouse
Rock (2.41) / Medley: You're So Square /
Hello Mary Lou / Tutti Frutti (6.40) /
Gimme Some Lovin' (1.55) / Big Spender
(1.49) / Immigrant Song (1.56) / Tavaszi
szel (3.47) / Everybody Happy (1.50) /
Can Hear Music (3.19) / Going Back
(3.22) / The Night Comes Down (4.33) /
Great King Rat (5.54) / My Fairy King
(4.15) / Misfire (1.54) / Tenement Funster
(2.43) / Cool Cat (3.29) / God Save The
Queen (1.49)

Origin of recordings: 1. Seattle Arena
(13/3/77) / 2. Earls Court (7/7/77) /
3. Glasgow Apollo (30/5/77) / 4. London
(4/9/80) / 5. Frankfurt (14/12/80) / 6. USA
(1982) / 7, 8, 9. Tokyo, Japan (11/5/85) /
10. Seattle Arena (13/3/77) / 11. Berlin
(26/6/86) / 12. Budapest (27/7/86) /
13. Fan Club Song / 14, 15. Larry Lurex /
16, 17, 18. BBC Session (1973) / 19, 20.
Voice Reduced Album Versions / 21. David
Bowie Vocal / 22. Unknown Source.

With the exception of track 4
(September 4) in fact relating to 1984, not
1980, the remaining date and venue details
are correct.

Crowning Glory
KTS 071
Kiss The Stone Records, Italy, 1992
Recorded live in Europe, 1986
Running time: 78.06

One Vision / Tie Your Mother Down /
You're So Square / Hello Mary Lou /
Tutti Frutti / In The Lap Of The Gods /
Seven Seas Of Rhye / Tear It Up / A Kind
Of Magic / Under Pressure / Another
One Bites The Dust / Who Wants
One Live Forever / I Want To Break Free /
Improvised Jam / Now I'm Here /
Love Of My Life / Bohemian Rhapsody /
Hammer To Fall / Crazy Little Thing
Called Love / We Are The Champions

This set is actually that of July 11, 1986 –
the first of the Wembley Stadium shows.
Curiously, the sleeve notes advise that all
tracks are written by Freddie, unless
otherwise stated. In fact only four tracks on
the disc are Freddie compositions, the other
fourteen are made up of cover versions,
other band member songs, or were written
by Queen collectively. Nothing is 'otherwise
stated' anyway.

Cry Argentina
Double CD
OH BOY 2-9145
Oh Boy Records, Streamway Limited,
France, 1992
Recorded live in Buenos Aires,
Argentina, 1981, except tracks 9-12
(Disc 2), recorded in London 1973
Running times: 59.29/52.48

Disc 1: We Will Rock You (4.30) /
Let Me Entertain You (2.53) / Play The
Game (3.51) / Somebody To Love (7.17) /
Killer Queen (1.54) / I'm In Love With
My Car (3.52) / Get Down Make Love
(4.42) / Save Me (3.55) / Now I'm Here
(4.51) / Dragon Attack (5.02) / Love Of
My Life (3.39) / Under Pressure (3.28) /
Keep Yourself Alive (11.29)

Disc 2: Crazy Little Thing Called Love
(4.33) / Bohemian Rhapsody (5.18) /
Tie Your Mother Down (3.45) / Another
One Bites The Dust (3.53) / Sheer Heart
Attack (3.45) / We Will Rock You (2.05) /
We Are The Champions (3.22) / God
Save The Queen (1.07) / Father To Son
(6.15) / Son And Daughter (7.39) / Ogre
Battle (3.57) / Liar (7.09)

All the material purporting to have been
recorded in Argentina has actually been
lifted straight from the September 1984
home video release 'We Will Rock You'
(PVM 6122). The video consists of a mixture
of two shows, recorded in Montreal,
Canada, on November 24 & 25, 1981.

Domo Arigato
Double CD
A 2157
Aulica Records, Italy, 1993
Recorded at Nishinoimiya Stadium,
Osaka, October 24, 1982
Running times: 48.30/58.08

Disc 1: Flash (4.04) / We Will Rock You
(3.21) / Action This Day (5.08) /
Somebody To Love (7.52) / Calling All
Girls (4.24) / Now I'm Here (12.30) /
Love Of My Life (4.05) / Save Me (6.02)

Disc 2: Get Down Make Love (5.02) /
Guitar Solo (9.04) / Body Language
(3.09) / Under Pressure (4.28) / Fat
Bottomed Girls (5.28) / Crazy Little
Thing Called Love (5.31) / Spread Your
Wings (2.54) / Saturday Night's Alright
For Fighting (2.13) / Bohemian Rhapsody
(3.13) / Tie Your Mother Down (3.56) /
Another One Bites The Dust (2.30) /
Jailhouse Rock (4.45) / We Are
The Champions (3.50) / God Save The
Queen (1.57)

The inclusion of some rare 'Hot Space'
material makes this disc a welcome addition
to any live CD collection. While the date
of this show is accurate, the spelling of the
venue is not.

Done Under Pressure
Double CD
LCD 115-2
Leopard Records, Italy, 1992
Live in Germany, 1986
Running times: 50.13/49.15

Disc 1: One Vision / Tie Your Mother
Down / In The Lap Of The Gods / A Kind
Of Magic / Under Pressure / Another
One Bites The Dust / Who Wants To Live
Forever / I Want To Break Free /
Guitar Solo

Disc 2: Now I'm Here / Love Of My
Life / Is This The World We Created /
You're So Square / Tutti Frutti / Bohemian
Rhapsody / Hammer To Fall / Crazy Little
Thing Called Love / Radio Ga Ga / We
Will Rock You / Friends Will Be Friends /
We Are The Champions / God Save
The Queen

There are so many excellent quality
audio tape copies of this show currently in
circulation, all of them easily accessible, that
there seems little point in paying out the
best part of £15 just for a compact disc
alternative. An attractive and neatly
assembled eight page booklet, is perhaps
the only reason many people seek out this
set. The audio and vinyl sister products
remain much more sought after.

**18 Greatest Hits Live
From Queen**
STEN 91.005
Stentor Records, Germany, 1991
Recorded live in Zurich '82/86 Hallen
Stadium
Running time: 70.54

Killer Queen (2.02) / Now I'm
Here (4.20) / In The Lap Of The Gods...
Revisited (3.15) / Bohemian Rhapsody
(5.05) / Love Of My Life (4.30) /
Somebody To Love (3.44) / We Will
Rock You (2.20) / We Are The Champions
(3.42) / Crazy Little Thing Called Love
(4.26) / Another One Bites The Dust
(3.30) / Play The Game (3.49) / Save Me
(3.40) / Under Pressure (3.16) / Radio
Ga Ga (5.40) / I Want To Break Free
(3.29) / One Vision (3.49) / A Kind Of
Magic (5.40) / Who Wants To Live
Forever (3.27)

In typical bootleg fashion, the writing
credits for tracks 14 and 17 are attributed
to a Mr 'Tawler'!

Eve Of Christmas
TR 256
Turtle Records, Australia, 1992
Live at the Hammersmith Odeon,
December 24, 1975
Running time: 55.53

Now I'm Here / Ogre Battle / White
Queen / Bohemian Rhapsody / Killer
Queen / March Of The Black Queen /
Bring Back That Leroy Brown / Keep
Yourself Alive / Brighton Rock / Liar /
In The Lap Of The Gods / See What A
Fool I've Been

Flash Freddie
Double CD
BM 051/052
Beech Marten Records, Italy, 1992
Recorded live at Wembley Arena,
London (UK) July 5, 1986
Running times: 42.28/43.48

Disc 1: One Vision (4.38) / Tie Your
Mother Down (3.50) / Hammer To Fall
(5.31) / Seven Seas Of Rhye (3.37) /
A Kind Of Magic (6.26) / Under Pressure
(3.45) / Another One Bites The Dust
(4.37) / I Want To Break Free (3.35) /
It's Late (6.37)

Disc 2: Spread Your Wings (5.18) /
Ready Freddie (3.11) / Now I'm Here
(6.14) / Love Of My Life (4.46) / Is This
The World We Created (2.52) / You're So
Square (1.46) / Mary Lou (1.53) / Tutti
Frutti (3.27) / Bohemian Rhapsody
(5.50) / Crazy Little Thing Called Love
(5.05) / We Are The Champions (4.41)

Apart from the venue actually being
Wembley Stadium, and not the Arena, and
the fact that Queen played Slane Castle,
Dublin on July 5, 1986, the other glaring
error on the sleeve notes, is that all
the tracks are attributed to Freddie and
Brian only.

Freddie Mercury Is Alive
Double CD
WR CD 001/2
World Records, Italy, 1994
Various shows
Running times: 68.49/30.35

Disc 1: It's Late (6.41) / My Melancholy
Blues (3.11) / Spread Your Wings (5.24) /
Now I'm Here (4.41) / Ogre Battle
(5.14) / White Queen (5.27) / Killer
Queen (2.10) / March Of The Black
Queen (2.33) / Bring Back That Leroy
Brown (1.51) / Keep Yourself Alive
(4.32) / Brighton Rock (8.53) / Son &
Daughter (1.52) / Liar (8.39) / In The Lap
Of The Gods (3.38) / See What A Fool
I've Been (4.18)

Disc 2: Flash (2.45) / We Will Rock
You (2.40) / Play The Game (4.02) /
Seven Seas Of Rhye (3.07) / Under
Pressure (3.22) / Bohemian Rhapsody
(5.16) / Another One Bites The Dust
(3.31) / We Are The Champions (2.48) /
God Save The Queen (1.31)

This provocative title warrants no
comment from me.

From The Beeb To Tokyo
CD 17
RS Records, France, 1990
Live studio sessions for The Sound
Of The 70's BBC radio show
Tracks 1-4 from '73, 5-8 from '77,
9-12 Tokyo, Japan '75
Running time: 69.46

See What A Fool I've Been / Keep
Yourself Alive / Liar / Son And Daughter /
Spread Your Wings / It's Late / My
Melancholy Blues / We Will Rock You /
Father To Son / Ogre Battle / Son And
Daughter / Brighton Rock

The first four tracks relate to Queen's first
BBC session, recorded February 5, 1973, and
the latter material would seem to originate
from other vinyl bootleg sources. As far as
the session material is concerned, the 1989
'At The Beeb' collection (BOJCD 001) is a
far more sensible alternative. It is an official
release, and so offers a sound quality which
befits the work.

God Save The Queen
OS CD 4
Onstage Records, Italy 1992
Recorded live during '80
Running time: 44.48

Love Of My Life / Crazy Little Thing
Called Love / Now I'm Here / Under
Pressure / Who Wants To Live Forever /
Tie Your Mother Down / In The Lap
Of The Gods... Revisited / Bohemian
Rhapsody / Tutti Frutti / We Are The
Champions / We Will Rock You / Radio
Ga Ga

This disc offers only the second half of a
(1986 London) show. Why this isn't a double
CD is absurd and typical of bootlegs.

Golden Demos 1973/76
STECK 001
Steck Records, Germany, 1993
Various oddities
Running time: 61.28

See What A Fool I've Been (4.22) /
Keep Yourself Alive (3.55) / The Night
Comes Down (4.36) / Great King Rat
(5.56) / My Fairy King (4.16) / Ogre
Battle (1.16) / Father To Son (6.28) /
Killer Queen (3.09) / Misfire (1.54) /
Tenement Funster (2.47) / Flick Of The
Wrist (3.18) / Lazing On A Sunday
Afternoon (1.12) / Bohemian Rhapsody
(6.06) / The Millionaire Waltz (4.37) /
You Take My Breath Away (4.04) / You
And I (3.32)

*Collectors will not be entirely surprised
to learn that with only one exception, not
one track on this deliberately misleading
titled compilation is actually a Queen demo.
The only reason that even one is included
is because the version of 'The Night Comes
Down' from the band's 1973 début album,
was lifted straight from a De Lane Lea
Studios demo tape. As the track could not
not be bettered in the time available during
recording sessions at Trident Studios, it
appeared in this form. For that reason
alone, it is the only true demo track on this
bootleg, but obviously not a rare one.*

*The remaining fifteen tracks on the disc
are made up of either BBC session material,
a brief live snippet ('Ogre Battle'), or more
often, simply the regular album cuts recorded
without the output to one speaker, thus
effectively bypassing the stereo effect and
muting the main vocals – an experiment
which most school boy music enthusiasts
will have attempted at some stage.*

*This insultingly transparent ploy is most
evident on 'Misfire', 'Father To Son', 'Killer
Queen', 'Sunday Afternoon' and 'Bo Rhap'.
Every track in this category is further
given away by the fact that the running
times are all but exactly the same as their
respective mother album versions.*

Goodbye
Double Disc
Limited edition anniversary
CD in presentation folder
NE2211
Never End Records By Abraxas,
Italy, 1992
Disc 1: Tracks 1 and 2 live in London
(05/02/73) 3-5 and 6-17 (25/12/75)
Disc 2: live in Tokyo (05/11/85)
Running times: 75.20/61.03

Disc 1: My Fairy King (4.06) / Doing
Alright (4.11) / Great King Rat (5.57) /
Modern Times Rock'n'Roll (2.00) / Son
And Daughter (7.08) / Now I'm Here
(3.22) / Ogre Battle (4.46) / Bohemian
Rhapsody (2.11) / Killer Queen (2.10) /
March Of The Black Queen (2.25) /
Brighton Rock (10.35) / Keep Yourself
Alive (4.23) / Liar (8.20) / In The Lap Of
The Gods (3.06) / Seven Seas Of Rhye
(2.55) / See What A Fool I've Been
(4.13) / God Save The Queen (1.09)

Disc 2: Tear It Up (1.55) / Tie Your
Mother Down (3.32) / Under Pressure
(3.16) / Somebody To Love (4.02) /
Instrumental Inferno (4.08) / It's A Hard
Life (4.05) / Dragon Attack (3.57) /
Love Of My Life (3.11) / Another One
Bites The Dust (3.44) / Hammer To Fall
(4.57) / Crazy Little Thing Called Love
(4.54) / Radio Ga Ga (5.29) / I Want
To Break Free (3.16) / Jailhouse Rock
(2.35) / We Will Rock You (2.33) /
We Are The Champions (3.43)

*Tracks 1 and 2 (disc 1) were not recorded
live in London, but are in fact two cuts from
the début album. Queen were however,
in London on February 5, 1973, recording
their first session for the BBC. As well as
'My Fairy King' and 'Doing Alright' they also
recorded alternative takes of 'Keep Yourself
Alive' and 'Liar'.*

*The third, fourth and fifth tracks also
relate to a BBC session – their third.
The band also recorded 'Ogre Battle' during
that session, which is curiously absent here.*

*While the remaining material on the first
disc was recorded in London, in December
1975, it was in fact performed on the 24th,
not the 25th.*

*Queen did not play any shows at all after
Live Aid in 1985, and the material on the
second disc relates to Japanese shows from
May 1985 – of which there were six.*

*The writing credits to tracks 10, 11, 14
and 16 (disc 1), are incorrectly attributed to
Queen collectively, instead of the individual
songwriters. On the second disc, Brian's
'Dragon Attack' is credited to Freddie.*

Greatest Hits USA
GH 1826
Mikasa & Tsusho Limited, Japan, 1992
Various shows
Running time: 46.30

Bohemian Rhapsody (5.55) / Killer
Queen (3.00) / Good Old Fashioned
Lover Boy (2.52) / Somebody To Love
(4.55) / Now I'm Here (4.15) / Teo
Torriatte (5.00) / You're My Best Friend
(2.50) / We Will Rock You (2.00) /
We Are The Champions (2.59) / Seven
Seas Of Rhye (2.49) / Sheer Heart
Attack (3.25) / Brighton Rock (5.10)

*No details relating to venue or dates
are contained on this set. Not all the
material originates from American shows
(as the title implies) – especially track six,
which was only ever performed in Japan.*

I Want To Break Free
CD/ON 2223
On Stage Records, 1994
Recorded September 14, 1984,
Palazzo Dello Sport, & July 26, 1986,
Nep Stadium, Budapest
Running time: 51.14

Under Pressure / Killer Queen /
Another One Bites The Dust / Who
Wants To Live Forever / I Want To Break
Free / Guitar Solo / Now I'm Here /
Bohemian Rhapsody / Hammer To Fall /
Radio Ga Ga / We Will Rock You /
Friends Will Be Friends / We Are The
Champions / God Save The Queen

*Only tracks 1-3 and 14 relate to the
Milan show. The remaining material has been
recorded directly from the 'Live In Budapest'
video.*

I'm In Love With Freddie
MLP 2
Music Lovers Production, Italy, 1992
Running time: 65.22
Recorded live in Chicago, USA (19/09/80)

Let Me Entertain You (2.59) / Play
The Game (4.40) / Mustapha (3.03) /
Death On Two Legs (3.12) / Killer Queen
(1.57) / I'm In Love With My Car (2.10) /
Get Down Make Love (6.52) / Save
Me (4.01) / Now I'm Here (7.29) /
Dragon Attack (4.53) / Fat Bottomed
Girls (4.29) / Love Of My Life (3.54) /
Bohemian Rhapsody (5.10) / Tie Your
Mother Down (3.36) / Another One Bites
The Dust (3.18) / Sheer Heart Attack
(3.37)

*As numerous good quality bootleg
alternatives already exist from this show,
this miserably titled set is hardly worth
parting with hard earned cash for.*

Immortal
G53203
NCB Records, 1993
Country of origin: unknown
Various shows
Running time: 48.44

Seven Seas Of Rhye / White Queen /
Bohemian Rhapsody / Under Pressure /
I Want To Break Free / Now I'm Here /
Tear It Up / One Vision / We Are
The Champions / Radio Ga Ga / We
Will Rock You / Who Wants To Live
Forever

*Tracks 1 and 2 recorded in London
(24/12/75), tracks 3-7 in Tokyo, Japan
(11/05/85) and tracks 8-12
in London (11/07/86)*

*The notes on the sleeve laughably advise:
'This is a professional digital remixed and
remastered recording which was originally
realized by a member of the audience.'*

*Since this is obviously a live performance,
one wonders what material it was necessary
to 'remix' and 'remaster', and why. The notes
conclude with the contradictory point:
"Possible variations in audio quality are not
due to the performance of the artist."*

In The Lap Of The Gods
SCM 01
Splat Cat Records, 1994
Recorded at the Rainbow Theatre,
London (20/12/74)
Running time: 50.38

Procession (0.27) / Now I'm Here
(4.51) / Ogre Battle (5.16) / White Queen
(5.43) / Medley: In The Lap Of
The Gods / Killer Queen / March Of
The Black Queen / Bring Back That
Leroy Brown (7.39) / Son And Daughter
(7.00) / Medley: Father To Son / Keep
Yourself Alive / Liar (10.41) / Stone Cold
Crazy (2.18) / In The Lap Of The Gods
(4.00) / Jailhouse Rock (2.41)

*Since this material has obviously been
recorded directly from the 'Live At The
Rainbow' video, from May 1992's 'Box Of
Tricks' boxed set, it is that collection, and
not this, that should be recommended,
albeit significantly higher in price.*

In The Lap Of The Queen
CO 25153
Chapter One Digital Recordings,
Germany, 1991
Recorded live in Seattle, USA (17/03/77)
Track 9: unreleased Queen/Bowie
song, 1981
Running time: 48.03

Somebody To Love / '39 (3.20) / You
Take My Breath Away (2.56) / Bohemian
Rhapsody (5.10) / In The Lap Of The
Gods... Revisited (3.12) / Now I'm Here
(4.38) / Medley: Big Spender / Jailhouse
Rock / Saturday Night's Alright For
Fighting / Stupid Cupid / Be Bop A Lula
(10.45) / Liar (5.32) / Cool Cat (3.26)

*Queen played Seattle Arena on
March 13, not the 17th as stated on the
sleeve notes. Track 9 is the 'Hot Space'
album track, in an early form which was not
released. It features an ad-libbed vocal
from David Bowie and occasional backing
from Freddie. My guess is, that Queen were
working on the track during the sessions
which spawned 'Under Pressure', and played
the backing track to Bowie, who ended up
recording a crude version himself, though
probably only for fun.*

Japan 1985 Highlights
TCS CD 001
The Concert Series, Luxembourg, 1991
Running time: 70.36

One Vision (4.43) / Tie Your Mother
Down (3.48) / In The Lap Of The Gods
(2.17) / Seven seas Of Rhye (1.14) /
A Kind Of Magic (5.26) / Under Pressure
(3.23) / Is This The World We Created
(2.40) / Tutti Frutti (3.16) / Bohemian
Rhapsody (5.11) / Hammer To Fall
(5.07) / Crazy Little Thing Called Love
(4.14) / Radio Ga Ga (5.11) / Another
One Bites The Dust (3.30) / Who Wants
To Live Forever (4.00) / I Want To Break
Free (3.03) / We Will Rock You (2.53) /
Friends Will Be Friends (2.03) / We Are
The Champions (4.01) / God Save The
Queen (1.05)

*Queen performed six shows in Japan
between May 7 and 15, 1985. It is unlikely
that this disc represents material from any
of them. Although it is not – as might be
expected – yet another copy of the May 11
Yogishi Swimming Pool Auditorium show,
much of the material has been lifted straight
from the official 'Live At Wembley '86'
release. This would obviously account for the
excellent sound quality, which the sleeve
notes have the gall to attribute to: A Sonic
Solutions Nonoise System, apparently used
by a fan to record the show from a live
American radio station broadcast.*

*An identical CD bearing a very similar
name (Japan '85 Highlights) and identical
catalogue number, but packaged differently,
is also available. The disc predictably offers
the same sound quality as its counterpart.*

Killers
FLASH 09.90.0130
Flashback World Products,
Luxembourg, 1990
All songs recorded live in London 1973,
1974 and 1975
Running time: 46.25

See What A Fool I've Been (4.24) /
Keep Yourself Alive (3.49) / Liar (6.27) /
Son And Daughter (6.04) / Procession /
Father To Son (7.06) / Ogre Battle
(5.06) / Son And Daughter (Reprise)
(7.36) / White Queen (5.42)

*This is yet another European bootleg
which refers to 'Ogre Battle' as 'Orge Battle'.
At least four separate discs include the
same error - proving conclusively that the
manufacturers of such material rely on
previous issues for sleeve note information,
instead of conducting their own research,
or indeed, consulting any number of books.
As a consequence they repeat some, or all,
the errors which appear time and
time again.*

Le Fleur Du Mal
Double CD
WORK 5538.2
Men At Work Records, Italy, 1992
Distributed by Vox Populi, issued in
gatefold sleeve
Recorded live in Tokyo Swimming Pool
Auditorium (11/05/85)
Running Times: 48.06/40.10

Disc 1: Tear It Up (1.54) / Tie Your
Mother Down (3.41) / Under Pressure
(3.31) / Somebody To Love (4.04) /
The Medley - Play The Hits: Killer Queen
(2.08) / Seven Seas Of Rhye (1.48) /
Keep Yourself Alive (2.36) / Liar (2.53) /
Tokyo Blues (4.17) / It's A Hard Life
(5.34) / Dragon Attack (3.37) / Now I'm
Here (5.37) / Is This The World We
Created (2.29) / Love Of My Life (4.13)

Disc 2: Another One Bites The Dust
(4.17) / Hammer To Fall (5.03) /
Crazy Little Thing Called Love (5.21) /
Bohemian Rhapsody (5.26) / Radio Ga Ga
(5.41) / I Want To Break Free (3.16) /
Jailhouse Rock (2.43) / We Will Rock You
(3.16) / We Are The champions (3.47) /
God Save The Queen (2.09)

*'Now I'm Here' is incorrectly credited as
a Freddie Mercury composition. In fact
Brian wrote it – from his bed, during a spell
of recuperation from hepatitis and an ulcer
in 1975. The song was inspired by Mott
The Hoople, hence the reference to them
in the lyrics.*

*The nearest translation of the title, is
'The Flower Of Evil'. The name is borrowed
from the classic French novel Les Fleurs
Du Mal.*

Live Dates: Volume 17
STONED 012
Stoned Records, 1992
Xmas 1975
Running time: 52.40

Now I'm Here (3.52) / Ogre Battle
(5.13) / Bohemian Rhapsody (2.15) /
Killer Queen (2.11) / March Of The
Black Queen (2.11) / Brighton Rock
(10.41) / Keep Yourself Alive (4.30) / Liar
(8.44) / In The Lap Of The Gods (4.13) /
Seven Seas Of Rhye (3.13) / See What
A Fool I've Been (4.24) / God Save The
Queen (1.13)

Live In Cologne
PRCD 1033
Golden Stars Records, Italy, 1990
Live in Cologne, (01/02/79)
Running time: 79.24

We Will Rock You (3.31) / Let Me
Entertain You (3.11) / Somebody To Love
(6.56) / If You Can't Beat Them (5.34) /
Death On Two Legs / Killer Queen /
Bicycle Race (9.40) / Get Down Make
Love (5.26) / Now I'm Here (8.21) /
Don't Stop Me Now (4.59) / Spread Your
Wings (5.42) / Love Of My Life (3.37) /
'39 (4.30) / Brighton Rock (12.39) /
Keep Yourself Alive (5.16)

*This was Queen's seventh concert in
Germany in 1979. They played 13 in all, but
just the one in Cologne. This disc is one of
the best representations available – in
any bootleg format. It is a pity that so much
of the show was overlooked. A double disc
would have been far better.*

*The writing credits for '39 are incorrectly
attributed to John Deacon, instead of Brian.*

Live In Montreal
Double CD
CS CD 10006
Continental Sounds, Italy, 1993
Montreal (01/12/78)
Running times: 73.31/48.49

Disc 1: We Will Rock You / Let Me
Entertain You / Somebody To Love /
If You Can't Beat Them / Death On Two
Legs / Killer Queen / Bicycle Race /
I'm In Love With My Car / Get Down
Make Love / You're My Best Friend / Now
I'm Here / Spread Your Wings / Dreamers
Ball / Love Of My Life / It's Late

Disc 2: Brighton Rock / Fat Bottomed
Girls / Keep Yourself Alive / Bohemian
Rhapsody / Tie Your Mother Down /
Sheer Heart Attack / We Will Rock You /
We Are The Champions / God Save
The Queen

*This disc offers a tracklist which again,
closely resembles that of the 'Live Killers'
album. It also contains four popular tracks
of the period which were not included
on the album – 'Somebody To Love',
'If You Can't Beat Them', 'It's Late' and 'Fat
Bottomed Girls', and for that reason is
popular with fans and collectors alike.*

*An unrelated front cover picture (from 1981)
spoils it somewhat.*

Live In USA 1977
HL CD014
Headliner Records, Germany, 1993
Running time: 48.03

Somebody To Love / '39 (3.20) / You
Take My Breath Away (2.56) / Bohemian
Rhapsody (5.10) / In The Lap Of The
Gods.. Revisited (3.12) / Now I'm Here
(4.38) / Medley - Big Spender / Jailhouse
Rock / Saturday Night's Alright For
Fighting / Stupid Cupid / Be Bop A Lula
(10.45) / Liar (5.32) / Cool Cat (3.26)

*This is a copy of 'In The Lap Of The
Queen'. While the original disc featured
sleeve pictures of the band with Elizabeth II
lookalike Jeanette Charles, and a portrait
photograph from 1976 (available through
the fan club at the time), this one features
a decidedly dull sleeve.*

*The incorrect date advice which
accompanied the first disc has been rectified
for this issue. The material was recorded on
March 13, 1977, in Seattle, USA.*

Live USA
IMT 900.076
Imtrat Records, Germany, 1992
Recorded live in USA in 1977 and 1982
Running time: 50.29

White Queen (5.11) / Tie Your Mother
Down (4.24) / Ogre Battle (8.05) / Brian
May Guitar Solo (12.00) / Action This Day
(9.15) / Action This Day (4.16) / '39
(3.23) / You Take My Breath Away (3.00)

*Six other tracks appear on this disc, but
are ignored on the sleeve notes. 'Father To
Son' follows the first track, a four song
medley ('Killer Queen', 'Millionaire Waltz',
'Best Friend', 'Leroy Brown') follows track 2,
and 'White Man' merges with 'The
Prophet's Song'.*

*While 'Calling All Girls' makes an
uncredited appearance on this disc, 'Action
This Day' is not featured at all.*

*For some unfathomable reason, tracks
1, 3, 6 and 7 are incorrectly credited to
Mercury/Taylor/May collectively. In fact they
were written individually by May,
Mercury, Taylor and May respectively.*

Live USA
Triple CD
IMT 920.076/083/084
Imtrat Records, Germany, 1992
Recorded live in USA in 1977 and 1982
Recorded live in USA in 1982
Recorded live in USA in 1982
Running times: 50.34/41.21/42.02

Disc 1: White Queen (5.11) / Tie
Your Mother Down (4.24) / Ogre Battle
(8.05) / Brian May Guitar Solo (12.00) /
White Man (9.15) / Action This Day
(4.16) / '39 (3.23) / You Take My Breath
Away (3.00)

Disc 2: Flash (2.44) / We Will Rock You
(2.39) / Play The Game (4.01) / Calling
All Girls (4.16) / Body Language (2.51) /
Under Pressure (3.21) / Bohemian
Rhapsody (5.16) / Another One Bites
The Dust (3.30) / We Are The Champions
(3.21) / God Save The Queen (0.55) /
Somebody To Love (7.06)

Disc 3: Now I'm Here (6.24) / Put
Out The Fire (1.52) / Dragon Attack
(3.42) / Love Of My Life (3.45) / Save Me
(3.48) / Back Chat (5.08) / Fat Bottomed
Girls (4.50) / Crazy Little Thing Called
Love (4.58) / Saturday Night's Alright For
Fighting (2.44) / Tie Your Mother
Down (3.30)

*A lack of continuity in catalogue
numbering here suggests that discs two and
three were probably intended to be issued
on their own, as a double set only (they
are packaged in identical sleeves). The third
disc is not only packaged entirely differently,
but its catalogue number is inconsistent too.
I can find no good explanation, however,
as to why all three actual discs are similar
in appearance. If a triple CD set was always
the intended proposition, why weren't all
three packaged the same?*

*To sequence any track after 'God Save
The Queen' – widely known as the one
which for so long concluded Queen's
concerts – demonstrates gross ignorance on
the part of the manufacturer.*

London 1975
FBCD 1146
Golden Stars Records, EEC, 1991
Recorded live at Hammersmith Odeon,
(24/12/75)
Running time: 59.37

Now I'm Here / Ogre Battle / White
Queen / Medley: Bohemian Rhapsody /
Killer Queen / March Of The Black
Queen / Bring Back That Leroy Brown /
Keep Yourself Alive / Brighton Rock / Son
And Daughter / Liar / In The Lap Of
The Gods (Revisited) / Seven Seas Of
Rhye / See What A Fool I've Been

*Yet another disc which offers a variation
of the legendary Christmas Eve concert of
1975. An unusual pencil drawing on the front
cover sleeve, makes this disc fractionally
more attractive to collectors than it might
otherwise have been.*

London 1986
PSCD 1170
Red Line Records, EEC, 1992
Recorded live at Wembley Arena during
the European tour
Running time: 73.05

One Vision / Tie Your Mother Down /
Hammer To Fall / Seven Seas Of Rhye /
Tear It Up / A Kind Of Magic / Under
Pressure / Another One Bites The Dust /
I Want To Break Free / Ready Freddie /
Now I'm Here / Love Of My Life /
Is This The World We Created / You're So
Square / Hello Mary Lou / Tutti Frutti /
Bohemian Rhapsody / Crazy Little Thing
Called Love / We Are The Champions.

*Track 9 is another of Freddie's piano
improvisation interludes.*

*The manufacturers have once again made
the mistake of confusing London's Wembley
Stadium with the much smaller Arena venue,
on the sleeve advise notes.*

Made In Heaven
P&L 1992
Peace & Love Music, EEC, 1992
Alternative demo versions of the classic
Queen songs
Running time: 57.41

Keep Yourself Alive (3.54) / The Night
Comes Down (4.32) / Great King Rat
(5.55) / My Fairy King (4.16) / March Of
The Black Queen (6.19) / Father To Son
(6.25) / Killer Queen (3.05) / Misfire
(1.54) / Lazing On A Sunday Afternoon
(1.11) / Bohemian Rhapsody (6.05) /
You Take My Breath Away (4.02) / You
And I (3.32) / Who Needs You (3.12) /
Mustapha (2.43)

*These tracks are most definitely not
alternative demo versions of classic Queen
songs, but just the standard album takes
with Freddie's lead vocals somewhat muted.
This is one of many discs that was
hastily issued soon after Freddie's death –
hence the pretentious title and much
over-used front cover illustration (Freddie
on stage with regal cloak and crown).*

*An extremely collectable cassette version
of this bootleg is also available, although
strangely it's titled 'Exposed For Now'.
The material featured is the same as this
CD. 'Who Needs You' is incorrectly attributed
to Freddie, instead of John Deacon.*

*'Made In Heaven' was also one of the
many proposed titles for the forthcoming
final Queen studio album for which Freddie
recorded lead and backing vocals and to
which the three remaining band members
subsequently laid down instrumental
tracks. The title was discarded and Fan Club
members were invited to suggest
alternatives.*

Made In Japan
RS 9210
Rarities Special, Italy, 1992
Live in Japan, 1985
Running time: 70.31

One Vision (4.43) / Tie Your Mother
Down (3.48) / In The Lap Of The Gods
(2.17) / Seven seas Of Rhye (1.14) /
A Kind Of Magic (5.37) / Under Pressure
(3.35) / Is This The World We Created
(3.04) / Tutti Frutti (3.27) / Bohemian
Rhapsody (5.19) / Hammer To Fall
(5.27) / Crazy Little Thing Called Love
(4.42) / Radio Ga Ga (5.58) / Another
One Bites The Dust (3.48) / Who Wants
To Live Forever (4.04) / I Want To Break
Free (3.05) / We Will Rock You (2.47) /
Friends Will Be Friends (2.06) / We
Are The Champions (4.04) / God Save
The Queen (1.20)

*This is yet another variation of the
'Japan 1985/'85 Highlights' CD's, but is
again packaged differently, and the track
timings are slightly different.*

*A reference to Roger 'Tailor' mars the
otherwise error free sleeve notes.*

Merry Christmas
GDR CD 9108
Great Dane Records, Italy, 1991
Recorded Christmas 1975,
Hammersmith Odeon, London, England
Running time: 53.12

Now I'm Here (3.47) / Ogre Battle
(5.06) / Bohemian Rhapsody (2.26) /
Killer Queen (2.11) / March Of The Black
Queen (2.42) / Brighton Rock (10.41) /
Keep Yourself Alive (4.30) / Liar (8.44) /
In The Lap Of The Gods (4.12) / Seven
Seas Of Rhye (3.13) / See What A Fool
I've Been (4.25) / God Save The Queen
(1.13)

*This is by far the most common bootleg,
though not necessarily in this form.
The same show has cropped up under
several names and in several formats over
the years with varying sound quality and
tracklistings.*

*Other compact disc bootlegs related to this
show include: 'Eve Of Christmas', 'London
1975', 'Rhapsody In Red', 'Command
Performance', 'X'Mas 1975', 'Live Dates
Volume I 7', 'Christmas At The Beeb' and
'Unauthorised'. In addition to discs which
offer this show exclusively, many others
contain segments of it alongside material
recorded elsewhere. 'Goodbye', 'Thanks' and
'Noblesse Oblige' are three such examples.*

My Favourite Dance Tracks
MMS 0892
Make Me Smile, Italy, 1992
Recorded Buenos Aires, 1981
Running time: 68.03

We Will Rock You (3.35) / Let Me
Entertain You (2.42) / Play The Game
(3.51) / Rock It (4.08) / Love Of My Life
(3.42) / Keep Yourself Alive (5.21) /
Another One Bites The Dust (3.18) /
Now I'm Here (7.43) / Dragon Attack
(3.35) / Sheer Heart Attack (2.30) /
Mustapha (2.54) / Crazy Little Thing
Called Love (3.35) / Need Your Loving
Tonight (2.51) / Save Me (3.55) / Tie
Your Mother Down (3.23) / Brighton
Rock (6.04) / Flash (3.27)

*Queen played the Velez Sarfield, Buenos
Aires, on February 28 and March 1, 1981.
The two shows were their first, and only,
gigs in Argentina.*

*According to the sleeve notes, 'Let Me
Entertain You' was written not by Freddie
Mercury, but by J. Styne and S. Sondheim, a
mistake which is not uncommon. 'All Your
Love Tonight' includes an identical oversight.*

Nihon
Double CD
NSCD 0014/15
Record label: unknown, made in
Italy, 1993
Running Times: 47.47/55.03

Disc 1: Tear It Up (3.46) / Tie Your
Mother Down (3.57) / Under Pressure
(3.22) / Somebody To Love (4.08) /
Killer Queen (2.10) / Seven Seas Of Rhye
(1.51) / Keep Yourself Alive (2.32) / Liar
(2.54) / It's A Hard Life (10.17) / Now
I'm Here (5.58) / Is This The World We
Created (3.10) / Love Of My Life (4.09)

Disc 2: Another One Bites The Dust
(4.20) / Hammer To Fall (5.16) /
Crazy Little Thing Called Love (5.32) /
Bohemian Rhapsody (5.45) / Radio Ga
(5.39) / I Want To Break Free (3.18) /
Jailhouse Rock (2.51) / We Will Rock You
(3.17) / We Are The Champions (4.00) /
God Save The Queen / Who Wants To
Live Forever (4.00) / One Vision (4.11) /
A Kind Of Magic (5.30)

*Although the sleeve notes contain no
details of where this material was recorded,
it is evident that disc one and most of
the second revisits the Tokyo show (May 11,
1985), and the remainder originates from
London, July 1986.*

Nikon
Double CD
LSCD 5250051/2
Live Storm Records, Italy, 1994
Tracklisting: as 'Nihon' above
Running times: 47.48/55.03

*This is a reissue of the above CD, but in
a repackaged form. Perhaps it was put out
as a result of the Italian manufacturers
discovering the date and venue information,
which is included here but was absent
from the first release.*

*Although this disc was issued through
the so called 'Live Storm' label, it does not
necessarily follow that the 'Nihon' disc was
distributed by the same people.*

*The catalogue number prefix however,
would seem to point to that being likely.*

*Instead of Roger Taylor, the writing credits
for 'A Kind Of Magic' are wrongly attributed
to Freddie, although it is generally excepted
that Freddie took a shine to the song in
its early stages, and contributed substantially
to the arrangement.*

No More Heroes
POET 9212
Poetry In Motion Records, Italy, 1992
Date and venue unknown, though
probably various
Running time: 57.28

Somebody To Love (5.06) / '39 (3.24) /
Bohemian Rhapsody (5.25) / Father To
Son (4.36) / Son And Daughter (6.42) /
Ogre Battle (4.37) / Keep Yourself Alive
(3.48) / Liar (7.01) / Now I'm Here
(4.29) / Big Spender (1.46) / Jailhouse
Rock (2.35) / Saturday Night's Alright For
Fighting (4.24) / Be Bop A Lula (2.06)

*Despite the sleeve notes advising this to
be a thirteen track disc, there are only ten.
Tracks 10-13 are all recognised as one
track – hence a ten and a half minute
running time.*

Noblesse Oblige
LLRCD 149
Living Legend Records, Italy, 1992
Recorded live in concert 1973-86
Running Time: 74.42

We Will Rock You (5.00) / White
Queen (5.50) / In The Lap Of The Gods
(Revisited) (2.20) / Seven Seas Of Rhye
(1.18) / Tear It Up (2.18) / Who Wants
To Live Forever (4.22) / I Want To
Break Free (2.58) / Coming Out (13.28) /
Now I'm Here (4.42) / One Vision
(4.35) / Under Pressure (3.35) /
Is This The World We Created (2.55) /
Bohemian Rhapsody (5.17) / Radio Ga
Ga (5.35) / We Will Rock You (2.46) /
Friends Will Be Friends (2.05) / We Are
The Champions (4.02) / God Save The
Queen (1.18)

*Some of the material here relates to the
Christmas Eve 1975 show (yet again), and
the Wembley Stadium July 11th, 1986
show (yet again). The first track however, is
a strange mixture of 'Rock You' album cut,
mixed with the 'Live Killers' rendition!*

*Although track 8 might seem to be a
misspelled and extremely rare live version
of 'Coming Soon' from 'The Game'
album – indeed, it would have been the only
live version in existence – sadly it is not.
It is another semi-improvised instrumental
piece featuring Freddie's wonderful
nonsense vocal ad-libbing, with guitar
support from Brian.*

On Fire
1018
New Keruac Line, Italy, 1993
Limited Edition CD (issued in 5"
round tin with numbered certificate)
Running time: 70.07

We Are The Champions (4.11) /
A Kind Of Magic (6.31) / Under Pressure
(3.27) / Seven Seas Of Rhye / Tear It Up
(3.42) / Another One Bites The Dust
(4.36) / I Want To Break Free (3.38) /
Hello Mary Lou / Tutti Frutti (5.05) /
Bohemian Rhapsody (5.39) / Crazy Little
Thing Called Love (5.39) / Tie Your
Mother Down (3.54) / Hammer To Fall
(5.32) / Now I'm Here (6.41) / Is This The
World We Created (2.57) / Who Wants
To Live Forever (4.01) / Love Of My Life
(4.44)

*Recorded: July 11, 1986 Wembley
Stadium. The tracklist sequence is erratic to
say the least. An extremely attractive round
tin (similar to the 1989 Rolling Stones
'Almost Hear You Sigh' release) makes this
disc more collectable than it would otherwise
have been, since the musical content is
far from exciting.*

Opera Omnia
4 CD Boxed Set
RPBX 012/13/14/15
Red Phantom Records, Italy, 1992
Limited edition of 2,000
Running times: 79.20/75.56/78.33/72.20
Various shows, dates and venues
unknown

Disc 1: Keep Yourself Alive (2.34) /
Liar (2.55) / Doing Alright (5.07) / Son
And Daughter (7.32) / Modern Times
Rock'n'Roll (2.43) / Seven Seas Of Rhye
(1.51) / See What A Fool I've Been
(4.16) / White Queen (5.13) / March Of
The Black Queen (2.30) / Procession
(1.46) / Father To Son (5.15) / Ogre
Battle (5.02) / Killer Queen (2.13) /
Now I'm Here (7.11) / In The Lap Of The
Gods (2.32) / Stone Cold Crazy (2.14) /
Brighton Rock (13.15) / Bring Back That
Leroy Brown (2.15) / Flick Of The Wrist
(3.18)

Disc 2: Bohemian Rhapsody (5.38) /
Love Of My Life (4.20) / I'm In Love
With My Car (2.21) / You're My Best
Friend (2.18) / '39 (3.28) / Death On
Two Legs (3.20) / Sweet Lady (3.51) /
Lazing On A Sunday Afternoon (1.52) /
The Prophet's Song (5.46) / White Man
(2.56) / Somebody To Love (4.11) /
Tie Your Mother Down (3.32) / You Take
My Breath Away (1.46) / The Millionaire
Waltz (1.47) / Good Old Fashioned Lover
Boy (2.27) / Teo Torriatte (4.26) / We
Will Rock You (Speed) (2.57) / We Will
Rock You (Slow) (3.21) / We Are The
Champions (3.55) / Get Down Make
Love (6.34) / Spread Your Wings (5.40)

Disc 3: My Melancholy Blues (2.55) /
Sheer Heart Attack (2.33) / It's Late
(7.11) / Fat Bottomed Girls (4.35) /
Bicycle Race (1.46) / Let Me Entertain
You (3.05) / If You Can't Beat Them
(5.00) / Dreamers Ball (4.13) / Don't
Stop Me Now (4.42) / Mustapha (2.46) /
Crazy Little Thing Called Love (5.13) /
Another One Bites The Dust (3.55) /
Play The Game (4.10) / Dragon Attack
(3.52) / Save Me (3.58) / Need Your
Loving Tonight (2.56) / Rock It (Prime
Jive) (4.13) / Flash (2.02) / The Hero
(2.07) / Under Pressure (3.26) / Staying
Power (3.48)

Disc 4: Body Language (3.00) / Calling
All Girls (4.24) / Put Out The Fire
(2.05) / Back Chat (5.16) / Action This
Day (5.08) / Life Is Real (3.32) / Radio
Ga Ga (5.44) / I Want To Break Free
(3.22) / Machines (1.46) / Tear It Up
(1.52) / It's A Hard Life (4.22) / Is This
The World We Created (2.47) / Hammer
To Fall (5.08) / One Vision (4.17) / A Kind
Of Magic (5.53) / Who Wants To Live
Forever (3.59) / Friends Will Be Friends
(2.00) / Tutti Frutti (3.39) / Jailhouse Rock
(2.45) / God Save The Queen (1.51)

*Although it is impossible to say for
certain when and where each track was
recorded, much of the material (like most
bootlegs) is instantly recognisable. Some of
the better known shows represented on
this set include: Earls Court (June 6, 1977),
Milton Keynes Bowl (June 5, 1982), Tokyo
(May 11, 1982) and the two Buenos Aires
shows in Feb/Mar 1981.*

*The sound quality of some of the material
featured on this set is absolutely superb,
and must surely have been compiled using
original mixing desk tapes. Furthermore,
much of the music is extremely rare.
'Love Of My Life' (disc 2) is truly outstanding.
'White Man' (on disc 2) does not appear as
a whole song, instead it is the conclusion
of the preceding song, 'The Prophet's Song'.
This is without doubt the creme de la creme
of all compact disc bootlegs.*

Over The Best Or Worst (The Greatest Tribute)
Double CD
5556 2/1
Men At Work Records, Italy, 1992
Various shows
Running times: 65.52/68.52

Now I'm Here (01/05/75 Tokyo, Japan) / Love Of My Life (26/08/80 Providence, USA) / Tie Your Mother Down (03/11/82 Tokyo, Japan) / Hammer To Fall (14/09/84 Milan, Italy) / Stone Cold Crazy (12/05/77 Copenhagen, Denmark) / Crazy Little Thing Called Love (24/10/82 Osaka, Japan) / Radio Ga Ga (08/09/84 Wembley Stadium, London) / Who Wants To Live Forever (30/07/86 Frejus, France) / Want To Break Free (30/07/86 Frejus, France) / Under Pressure (05/06/82 Milton Keynes, England) / '39 (12/05/77 Copenhagen, Denmark) / Somebody To Love (08/03/81 Buenos Aires, Argentina) / Bohemian Rhapsody (08/03/81 Buenos Aires, Argentina) / We Will Rock You (21/09/84 Brussels, Belgium) / We Are The Champions (21/09/84 Brussels, Belgium) / God Save The Queen (21/09/84 Brussels, Belgium)

This extremely lavish double CD package is let down by disappointing musical content, all of which is available elsewhere. The attractive sleeve design is similar to the 'Le Fleur Du Mal' set, which is not entirely surprising, as each was issued by the Italian 'Men At Work' record label. The overall package is marred by tasteless illustrations of a syringe and an identification label tied to the toe of a human corpse.

Pearly Queen
BGS 018
Future Music, Italy, 1994
Recorded live in Rio De Janeiro, Brazil, (12/02/85)
Running time: 59.26

Tie Your Mother Down (4.56) / Seven Seas Of Rhye (1.53) / Keep Yourself Alive (2.47) / Liar (1.54) / It's A Hard Life (4.22) / Now I'm Here (5.12) / Is This The World We Created (3.03) / Love Of My Life (4.25) / Brighton Rock (7.08) / Hammer To Fall (4.56) / Bohemian Rhapsody (5.16) / Radio Ga Ga (6.12) / Want To Break Free (3.23) / We Will Rock You (2.29) / We Are The Champions (4.07) / God Save The Queen (1.57)

This disc is an exact copy of 'Regina De Ipanema', though packaged differently. 'Regina' was issued in January 1994, and this followed it only two months later. So clichéd is the title, it could only have come from a non-English source!

Queen
Double CD
NE1122
Never End Records, Italy, 1992
Running times: 75.20/61.03

This double CD set is an extremely rare advance copy of 'Goodbye'. It is housed in a lilac and white cardboard sleeve, and sports a printed sticker. The tracklisting and running times are obviously the same.

Queentessance:
In Memoriam Of Frederick Bulsara
LL CD 9214
Live Life Records, Luxembourg, 1992
Tracks and 2 recorded on (13/09/73) (London) tracks 3 and 4 on (31/03/74) (London) tracks 8, 9 and 10 on (12/05/77) (Denmark), tracks 11 and 12 on (08/12/80) (London), tracks 13, 14 and 15 on (16/04/82) (Switzerland), tracks 16 and 17 on (15/05/85) (Japan) and tracks 18, 19, 20 and 21 recorded on (13/08/86) (London)
Running time: 75.14

Procession (1.32) / Father To Son (4.43) / Keep Yourself Alive (4.10) / Seven Seas Of Rhye (2.59) / In The Lap Of The Gods... Revisited (3.51) / Now I'm Here (4.23) / Jailhouse Rock (5.09) / Somebody To Love (5.43) / '39 (3.33) / Good Old Fashioned Lover Boy (2.02) / Mustapha (2.47) / Bohemian Rhapsody (5.21) / Love Of My Life (4.04) / Back Chat - Improvisation (1.33) / Save Me (3.39) / Crazy Little Thing Called Love (5.24) / Saturday Night's Alright For Fighting (3.12) / You're So Square (1.30) / Hello Mary Lou (1.25) / Tutti Frutti (3.40) / We Are The Champions (4.01)

The details of where and when each recording was made, as outlined above (from the disc notes), are riddled with inaccuracies — too numerous to note.

An introduction to this disc on the back sleeve, begins: "We wants to eat Hamburgers every day when variety is the spice of life", and continues in an equally nonsensical vane. Thankfully, such sleeve notes are uncommon.

Queen Reigns The World
Double CD
TCC 028/029
Three Cool Cats, 1991
Exact country of origin is unknown
Recorded live in concert 1986
Running times: 55.34/47.11

Disc 1: One Vision (9.04) / In The Lap Of The Gods (2.23) / Seven Seas Of Rhye (1.21) / Tear It Up (2.45) / A Kind Of Magic (5.32) / Under Pressure (3.40) / Another One Bites The Dust (4.35) / Who Wants To Live Forever (4.43) / I Want To Break Free (3.09) / Instrumental (13.34) / Now I'm Here (4.46)

Disc 2: Love Of My Life (3.55) / Is This The World We Created (2.50) / You're So Square (1.29) / Hello Mary Lou (1.24) / Tutti Frutti (3.22) / Bohemian Rhapsody (5.57) / Hammer To Fall (4.59) / Crazy Little Thing Called Love (6.45) / Radio Ga Ga (6.24) / We Will Rock You (2.56) / Friends Will Be Friends (1.58) / We Are The Champions (3.46) / God Save The Queen (1.24)

Amazingly, the sleeve notes have 'Robert' Taylor credited with drums and vocals, and neglect to mention track 9 on disc 1 at all. Of less interest, perhaps, is the failure of the disc manufacturer to correctly spell the name of their own record label. While the discs themselves carry the Three Cool Cats reference, the sleeve notes conflict with Three 'Cole' Cats.

Radio Ga Ga
HS 29104
Hotshot Records, Germany, 1992
Live in Japan '85
Running time: 70.33

One Vision (4.43) / Tie Your Mother Down (3.48) / In The Lap Of The Gods (2.17) / Seven Seas Of Rhye (1.14) / A Kind Of Magic (5.37) / Under Pressure (3.35) / Is This The World We Created (3.04) / Tutti Frutti (3.27) / Bohemian Rhapsody (5.19) / Hammer To Fall (5.27) / Crazy Little Thing Called Love (4.42) / Radio Ga Ga (5.58) / Another One Bites The Dust (3.48) / Who Wants To Live Forever (4.04) / I Want To Break Free (3.05) / We Will Rock You (2.47) / Friends Will Be Friends (2.06) / We Are The Champions (4.04) / God Save The Queen (1.20)

Well, surprise of surprises, this is not a Japanese show at all, but the umpteenth visit to London's Wembley Stadium, July 11, 1986.

Regina Versus Freddie And The Boys
Double CD
OTR 75517/18
Off The Record, Italy, 1994
Recorded Seattle Arena (13/03/77), Brussels, Vorst National (20/09/84)
Running times: 57.28/77.07

Disc 1: Somebody To Love (5.06) / '39 (3.24) / Bohemian Rhapsody (5.25) / Father To Son (4.36) / Son And Daughter (6.42) / Ogre Battle (4.37) / Keep Yourself Alive (3.48) / Liar (7.01) / Now I'm Here (4.29) / Big Spender (1.46) / Jailhouse Rock (2.35) / Saturday Night's Alright For Fighting (4.24) / Be Bop A Lula (2.06)

Disc 2: Under Pressure / Somebody To Love / Killer Queen / Seven Seas Of Rhye / Keep Yourself Alive / Liar / Instrumental Tune / It's A Hard Life / Dragon Attack / Now I'm Here / Is This The World We Created / Love Of My Life / Another One Bites The Dust / Hammer To Fall / Crazy Little Thing Called Love / Bohemian Rhapsody / Radio Ga Ga / I Want To Break Free / Jailhouse Rock / We Are The Champions

This rather expensive and dubiously titled double set merely brings together two already available CDs — 'Saturday Night's Alright For Fighting' (Disc 1) and 'Absolutely Perfect' (Disc 2). Issued this time as a limited edition of 1000, it was probably a final attempt at promoting sales.

Regina De Ipanema
BC 008
Future Music, Italy, 1994
Recorded live in Rio De Janeiro, Brazil (11/01/85)
Running time: 59.26

Tie Your Mother Down (4.56) / Seven Seas Of Rhye (1.53) / Liar (1.54) / It's A Hard Life (4.22) / Now I'm Here (5.12) / Is This The World We Created (3.03) / Love Of My Life (4.25) / Brighton Rock (7.08) / Hammer To Fall (4.56) / Bohemian Rhapsody (5.16) / Radio Ga Ga (6.12) / I Want To Break Free (3.23) / We Will Rock You (2.29) / We Are The Champions (4.07) / God Save The Queen (1.57)

Identical musical content to 'Pearly Queen' disc. Sorry, I have no idea as to how the title translates.

Rhapsody In Gold
Double CD
LIMES 3001
Limited edition of 300
Record label: unknown, made in Italy, 1993
Running times: 68.03/77.03

Disc 1: We Will Rock You (3.35) / Let Me Entertain You (2.42) / Play The Game (3.51) / Rock It (4.08) / Love Of My Life (3.42) / Keep Yourself Alive (5.21) / Another One Bites The Dust (3.18) / Now I'm Here (7.43) / Dragon Attack (3.35) / Sheer Heart Attack (2.30) / Mustapha (2.45) / Crazy Little Thing Called Love (3.35) / Need Your Loving Tonight (2.51) / Save Me (3.55) / Tie Your Mother Down (3.23) / Brighton Rock (6.01) / Flash (3.27)

Disc 2: Under Pressure (3.16) / Somebody To Love (4.03) / Killer Queen (2.07) / Seven Seas Of Rhye (2.14) / Keep Yourself Alive (2.30) / Liar (2.40) / Instrumental Tune (4.13) / It's A Hard Life (4.04) / Dragon Attack (5.15) / Now I'm Here (5.34) / Is This The World We Created (2.17) / Love Of My Life (3.57) / Another One Bites The Dust (3.42) / Hammer To Fall (5.23) / Crazy Little Thing Called Love (4.51) / Bohemian Rhapsody (5.17) / Radio Ga Ga (5.30) / I Want To Break Free (3.15) / Jailhouse Rock (2.35) / We Are The Champions (3.44)

Recorded in Buenos Aires, Argentina (March 1, 1981) and Brussels, Belgium (September 21, 1984). Another bootleg which attributes the writing credits for 'Let Me Entertain You' to J. Styne and S. Sondheim, instead of F. Mercury. Track 7 (Disc 2) incidentally, is credited to all four members, as is probably fair. Both discs are packaged in an unusual triangular box, which also contains a T-shirt and numbered authentication card.

Rhapsody In Red
BUC 033
Buccaneer Records, Italy, 1991
Tracks 1-4 recorded live in Middlesex, UK (10/76), tracks 5-17 recorded at Hammersmith Odeon '76 (Christmas Concert)
Running time: 75.04

We Will Rock You (4.32) / It's Late (6.41) / My Melancholy Blues (3.12) / Spread Your Wings (5.24) / Now I'm Here (4.42) / Ogre Battle (5.14) / White Queen (5.27) / Bohemian Rhapsody (2.10) / Killer Queen (2.10) / The March Of The Black Queen (2.32) / Bring Back That Leroy Brown (1.48) / Keep Yourself Alive (4.32) / Brighton Rock (8.53) / Son And Daughter (1.50) / Liar (8.38) / In The Lap Of The Gods (3.37) / See What A Fool I've Been (4.18)

Tracks 1-4 feature Queen's final BBC session, as recorded in October 1977. It includes the fabricated audience overdubs. Queen did not play the Hammersmith Odeon in 1976, hence tracks 5-17 in fact relate to the 1975 Christmas Eve show — yet again.

Rock In Japan
Double CD
FLASH 07.91.0156/1/2
Flashback World Productions, Luxembourg, 1991
Tracks 1-13 (Disc 1) and 1-11 (Disc 2) recorded live in Osaka (15/05/85), tracks 12-15 recorded live in San Diego, 1977
Running times: 42.36/63.22

Disc 1: Tear It Up (1.50) / Tie Your Mother Down (3.33) / Under Pressure (3.20) / Somebody To Love (4.03) / Killer Queen (2.08) / Seven Seas Of Rhye (1.14) / Keep Yourself Alive (2.27) / Liar (1.57) / Instrumental Inferno (4.18) / It's A Hard Life (5.34) / Dragon Attack (3.59) / Now I'm Here (5.38) / Is This The World We Created (2.29)

Disc 2: Love Of My Life (4.11) / Another One Bites The Dust (3.46) / Hammer To Fall (5.28) / Crazy Little Thing Called Love (5.09) / Bohemian Rhapsody (5.33) / Radio Ga Ga (5.35) / I Want To Break Free (3.19) / Jailhouse Rock (2.41) / We Will Rock You (2.59) / We Are The Champions (3.49) / God Save The Queen (1.15) / We Will Rock You (4.24) / It's Late (6.35) / My Melancholy Blues (3.11) / Spread Your Wings (5.20)

Contrary to the sleeve notes, tracks 12-15 (Disc 2) were not recorded in San Diego, in 1977, but are once again the tracks Queen recorded for the BBC in October 1977.

Rocking Osaka In 1982
BIG 067
Big Music Records, Italy, 1993
Recorded live at the Tiger Stadium, Osaka, Japan (25/10/82) (second night)
Running time: 57.35

Now I'm Here (6.56) / Medley: Put Out The Fire/ Dragon Attack/ Now I'm Here (Reprise) (6.18) / Love Of My Life (4.01) / Save Me (4.10) / Brian May Guitar Solo (5.07) / Under Pressure (3.36) / Crazy Little Thing Called Love (5.04) / Bohemian Rhapsody (5.32) / Tie Your Mother Down (3.59) / Teo Torriatte (4.26) / We Will Rock You (2.23) / We Are The Champions (3.10) / God Save The Queen (1.48)

Although Queen were in Japan during late October 1982, they did not play any show on the 25th. They were in fact en route to Nagoya on that day, having performed a show in Osaka on the 24th, which was not at the Tiger Stadium. In fact Queen have never played at a venue of that name, if indeed it exists. As a matter of interest, the only occasion which saw the band play two consecutive nights at an Osaka venue (as the sleeve notes suggest is the case here), was on April 19 and 20, 1979.

Saturday Night's Alright For Fighting
BOD CD 214
Buy Or Die Records, Italy, 1991
Recorded live during the 1977 tour
Running time: 57.28

Somebody To Love (5.06) / '39 (3.24) / Bohemian Rhapsody (5.25) / Father To Son (4.36) / Son And Daughter (6.42) / Ogre Battle (4.37) / Keep Yourself Alive (3.48) / Liar (7.01) / Now I'm Here (4.29) / Big Spender (1.46) / Jailhouse Rock (2.35) / Saturday Night's Alright For Fighting (4.24) / Be Bop A Lula (2.06)

Most of this material (tracks 1-3 and 9-13) relates to the March 13 Seattle Arena show of 1977. The remaining tracks (4-8) come from the March 31, 1974 Rainbow Theatre show. Although thirteen tracks are listed on the sleeve notes, the disc actually comprises only ten. The four rock'n'roll medley songs which conclude the set are recognised as one track, as is frequently the case on unauthorised discs.

Shivers Down My Spine
XXI
Luhjaa Records, Germany, 1992
Live Munich, Olympia Hall (29/06/86)
Running time: 63.52

One Flash Of Light (5.28) / I'm Just A Peace Loving Guy (3.57) / No Meaning In My Pretending (2.20) / Naked To The Eyes / Give Me Your Body (3.30) / There Can Be Only One (6.27) / Touch My Tears With Your Lips (4.38) / It's Strange But It's True (3.23) / Play The Rock In Rio Blues Baby (3.52) / Don't Take It Away From Me (5.00) / If There's A God In The Sky (2.38) / I Wanted You For Evermore (1.19) / We Never Part (1.37) / Awuppabeelooda Awuppbammboom (3.00) / Send Shivers Down My Spine (5.39) / KYA / History Won't Care At All (5.44) / Here We Go / Tired Of All This Visual (5.53) / Mud On Your Face (2.54) / Hold Out Your Hands (1.52) / I Thank You All (3.42) / God Didn't Do That... (1.16)

This is perhaps the most intriguing of all the bootleg compact discs currently in circulation. Each song has been retitled using a line from its lyrics, a practice commonly used on vinyl bootlegs of The Beatles which appeared during the Seventies. Although the example on track 13 displays a sense of humour on the part of whoever produced the disc, it's a pity he did not have the foresight to have the sleeve notes printed after the actual disc production. He would have realised that tracks 18-21 (as described on the notes) do not actually appear on the disc. Apparently there wasn't room for them.

For those unfamiliar with Queen's lyrics, the 17 tracks on this disc are as follows:

One Vision / Tie Your Mother Down / In The Lap Of The Gods / Seven Seas Of Rhye / A Kind Of Magic / Who Wants To Live Forever / I Want To Break Free / Rock In Rio Blues / Love Of My Life / Is This The World We Created / You're So Square / Hello Mary Lou / Tutti Frutti / Bohemian Rhapsody / Keep Yourself Alive / Here We Go / Radio Ga Ga.

Having never before come across the so called 'Here We Go' track, and bearing in mind its absence from the disc, there is no clue as to what it is. At only 22 seconds though, it is almost certainly another of Freddie's pre-song improvisations.

Tavaszi Szel
Double CD
LCD 109-2
Leopard Records, Italy, 1992
Live in Europe (27/07/86)
Running times: 44.36/37.27

Disc 1: One Vision (5.04) / Tie Your Mother Down (2.00) / In The Lap Of The Gods (2.30) / Seven Seas Of Rhye (2.19) / Tear It Up (2.54) / A Kind Of Magic (5.40) / Under Pressure (3.38) / Who Wants To Live Forever (3.08) / I Want To Break Free (3.05) / Now I'm Here (11.48) / Love Of My Life (2.39)

Disc 2: Tavaszi Szel (2.43) / Is This The World We Created (2.42) / Tutti Frutti (3.47) / Bohemian Rhapsody (5.17) / Hammer To Fall (4.12) / Crazy Little Thing Called Love (3.30) / Radio Ga Ga (7.04) / We Will Rock You (3.03) / Friends Will Be Friends (2.01) / We Are The Champions (3.57) / God Save The Queen (3.07)

This disc is merely a copy of the 'Live In Budapest' video, but with the various interludes taken out.

Thanks!!!
Triple CD
9320.23
Aulica Records, Italy,1993
Limited edition CD of 1000 presented in silk box
Running times: 75.20/61.03/20.41
Various shows

Disc 1: My Fairy King / Doing Alright / Great King Rat / Modern Times Rock'n'Roll / Son And Daughter / Now I'm Here / Ogre Battle / Bohemian Rhapsody / Killer Queen / March Of The Black Queen / Brighton Rock / Keep Yourself Alive / Liar / In The Lap Of The Gods / Seven Seas Of Rhye / See What A Fool I've Been / God Save The Queen

Disc 2: Tear It Up / Tie Your Mother Down / Under Pressure / Somebody To Love / Instrumental Inferno / It's A Hard Life / Dragon Attack / Love Of My Life / Another One Bites The Dust / Hammer To Fall / Crazy Little Thing Called Love / Radio Ga Ga / I Want To Break Free / Jailhouse Rock / We Will Rock You / We Are The Champions

Disc 3: One Vision / A Kind Of Magic / Is This The World We Created / Who Wants To Live Forever / Friends Will Be Friends

This uninspiring set contains Queen's first and third BBC sessions (probably lifted directly from 1989's 'At The Beeb' album) on Disc 1, the May 1985 Yogishi Swimming Pool show on Discs 2 & 3, and, tediously, the Christmas Eve 1975 gig again, which makes its umpteenth live CD appearance on Disc 1.

Thank You Freddie
Triple CD
PWCD 101/1/2/3
Power Records, Italy, 1993
Recorded live in London (20/04/92)
Running times: 61.11/60.20/66.08

Disc 1: 1/2/3. Metallica: Enter Sandman (6.30) / Sad But True (5.22) / Nothing Else Metal (6.41) / 4-12. Extreme: Mustapha (1.54) / Keep Yourself Alive (2.03) / I Want To Break Free (2.01) / Bicycle Race (1.57) / Another One Bites The Dust (2.04) / Stone Cold Crazy (2.01) / Radio Ga Ga (3.37) / Love Of My Life (4.03) / More Than Words (2.26) / 13/14/15. Def Leppard: Animal (4.59) / Let's Get Rocked (5.45) / Now I'm Here (5.06) / 16. Bob Geldof: Too Late God (2.49) / 17. Spinal Tap: The Majesty Of Rock (3.43)

Disc 2: 1. U2: Until The End Of The World (4.35) / 2/3. Guns n'Roses: Paradise City (6.15) / Knockin' On Heaven's Door (8.33) / 4. Queen & Joe Elliott: Tie Your Mother Down (4.28) / 5. Queen & Roger Daltrey: I Want It All (6.21) / 6. Queen & Sugar: Las Parablas De Amor (5.02) / 7. Queen & Gary Cherone: Hammer To Fall (4.46) / 8. Queen & James Hetfield: Stone Cold Crazy (3.01) / 9/10/11. Queen & Robert Plant: Innuendo (6.13) / Thank You (1.58) / Crazy Little Thing Called Love (4.34) / 12. Queen & Spike Edney: Too Much Love Will Kill You (4.50)

Disc 3: 1. Queen & Paul Young: Radio Ga Ga (5.57) / 2. Queen & Seal: Who Wants To Live Forever (4.11) / 3. Queen & Lisa Stansfield: I Want To Break Free (4.29) / 4. Queen, Annie Lennox & David Bowie: Under Pressure (4.08) / 5. Queen, Ian Hunter & David Bowie: All The Young Dudes (5.25) / 6. Queen & David Bowie: Heroes (5.27) / 7. Queen & George Michael: '39 (2.36) / 8. Queen, George Michael & Lisa Stansfield: These Are The Days Of Our Lives (5.09) / 9. Queen & George Michael: Somebody To Love (6.37) / 10. Queen, Elton John & Axl Rose: Bohemian Rhapsody (6.18) / 11. Queen & Elton John: The Show Must Go On (4.17) / 12. Queen & Axl Rose: We Will Rock You (2.38) / 13. Queen & Liza Minelli: We Are The Champions (6.59) / 14. Queen: God Save The Queen (1.58)

This set includes oversights which are strange even by bootleg standards. Not only do the sleeve notes advise that track 3 on Disc 1 is 'Nothing Else Metal', instead of Matters, but it also states that Queen perform track 6 on disc 2 with an artist called Sugar. I cannot begin to imagine how Italian rock star Zucchero could be confused with sugar. Spike Edney accompanied only Brian May on 'Too Much Love', not Queen. The discs are packaged in a 12" x 12" box – usually associated with vinyl boxed sets – which contains a beautifully presented 24-page book of colour photographs from the concert.

The Carriage Of Mystery
REX DISCS
Royal Amusement Records, Germany, 1993
Recorded at St. Pauls, London, 1986
Running time: 69.13

One Vision / Tie Your Mother Down / In The Lap Of The Gods / Seven Seas Of Rhye / Under Pressure / Another One Bites The Dust / Who Wants To Live Forever / Love Of My Life / Bohemian Rhapsody / Crazy Little Thing Called Love / We Will Rock You / Friends Will Be Friends / We Are The Champions / Tear It Up / A Kind Of Magic / I Want To Break Free / Hammer To Fall / God Save The Queen

Never in their career did Queen perform live at St. Pauls, London. This disc relates to the Mannheim, Germany, show of June 21, 1986.

The Freddie Mercury Tribute
Triple CD
TFKRL 9204-3 CD
TFKRL Records, Germany, 1993
Recorded Easter Monday (20/04/92), Wembley Stadium
Concert for AIDS Awareness
Running times: 69.45/48.17/44.06

Disc 1: Sad But True / Nothing Else Matters / Medley / Love Of My Life / Animal / Let's Get Rocked / Now I'm Here / Too Late God / The Majesty Of Rock / Til The End Of The World / Paradise City / Knockin' On Heaven's Door

Disc 2: Tie Your Mother Down / I Want It All / Pinball Wizard / Hammer To Fall / Stone Cold Crazy / Innuendo / Kashmir / Too Much Love Will Kill You / Radio Ga Ga / Who Wants To Live Forever

Disc 3: I Want To Break Free /
Under Pressure / All The Young Dudes /
Heroes / '39 / These Are The Days Of
Our Lives / Somebody To Love /
Bohemian Rhapsody / The Show Must
Go On / We Will Rock You / We Are
The Champions

*The musical content here differs slightly
from the Italian 'Thank You Freddie' triple
set: while that set offers 43 tracks
collectively, this one offers 33. The packaging
is similar to that of the official tribute video
release (MVB 4910623). The failure to
issue a proper CD of this, one of the most
important Queen related live performances
ever, ensured the inevitable arrival of this
bootleg, and others like it, though some
would no doubt have emerged regardless.*

The Jewels
Double CD
IST 31/32
Insect Records, Italy, 1994
Running times: 61.50/44.27

Disc 1: Tear It Up / Tie Your Mother
Down / Under Pressure / Somebody To
Love / Killer Queen / Seven Seas Of
Rhye / Keep Yourself Alive / Liar /
Mustapha / It's A Hard Life / Staying
Power / Dragon Attack / Now I'm Here /
Is This The World We Created / Love
Of My Life / Stone Cold Crazy / Great
King Rat / Brighton Rock

Disc 2: Another One Bites The
Dust / Hammer To Fall / Crazy Little
Thing Called Love / Bohemian Rhapsody /
Radio Ga Ga / I Want To Break Free /
Jailhouse Rock / We Will Rock You /
We Are The Champions / God Save The
Queen

*It could have been worse. I imagine that
'The Crown Jewels' must have at some point
been toyed with as the title.*

The Mercury Is Rising
ARC 003
Alternative Recording Company,
Germany, 1993
Limited edition of 1500
Recorded live in London, Earls Court,
(14/06/74) except for tracks 8, 9 and
10, Santa Monica Auditorium (22/03/74)
and tracks 11, 12, 13, 14 and 15, Seattle
Arena (13/03/77)
Running time: 74.45

Procession / Father To Son (6.50) /
Ogre Battle (5.10) / Son And Daughter
(7.30) / Keep Yourself Alive (4.00) / Seven
Seas Of Rhye (3.15) / Modern Times
Rock'n'Roll (2.45) / Liar (7.50) / Flick
Of The Wrist (3.40) / Medley - Killer
Queen / March Of The Black Queen /
Bring Back That Leroy Brown (4.10) /
Stone Cold Crazy (2.20) / Somebody To
Love (5.00) / '39 (3.41) / You Take My
Breath Away (2.55) / Bohemian Rhapsody
(5.10) / Medley - Big Spender / Jailhouse
Rock / Saturday Night's Alright For
Fighting / Be Bop A Lula (10.45)

*While the inner sleeve notes offer the
information given above, the outer notes
contradict them. They advise instead that
tracks 1-7 relate to an American Cleveland
Arena show (June 14). In fact Queen did
not perform any show at all on June 14,
1974, nor on March 22, 1975. They did,
however, play the Seattle Arena show on
March 13, 1977, as stated. The individual
track timings displayed on the sleeve notes
are also inaccurate. Again, such glaring
oversights are common on bootleg releases.*

**The Ultimate Collection:
Rarities, Oddities and Cover
Versions**
Double CD
RMCD 001
Royalty Music, Germany, 1992
Various shows
Running times: 65.07/68.30

Disc 1: Imagine (live: 14/12/80) /
You're So Square / Hello Mary Lou /
Tutti Frutti (all live: 26/06/86) /
The Millionaires Waltz (Instrumental
Mix-Demo 1976) / Rock In Rio Blues-
America (live: 15/01/85) / Take Me
Home / Teo Torriatte (live: 29/10/82) /
Tenement Funster (Alternate Version
Demo 1974) / Last Horizon (Brian May:
live British TV 1991) / Mannish Boy
(live: 30/05/77) / See What A Fool I've
Been (live: 13/09/73) / Cool Cat (first
take with David Bowie) / Jailhouse
Rock (live: 15/05/85) / Flick Of The Wrist
(John Peel session 1974) / It's Late (live:
(04/02/78) / Mustapha (full live version) /
Death On Two Legs - Instrumental
(live: 08/12/80) / Earth (Smile) / Step On
Me (Smile)

Disc 2: Rock In Rio Blues - Europe /
Immigrant Song (live: 26/06/86) /
Fat Bottomed Girls (first take 1979) /
Doing Alright (live) / Lazing On A Sunday
Afternoon (live: 29/03/76) / Back Chat
(full live version: 05/06/82) / I Can
Hear Music (Larry Lurex) / Need Your
Loving Tonight (live: 08/12/80) / Modern
Times Rock'n'Roll (John Peel session
1974) / Not Fade Away (live: 04/09/80) /
Life Is Real (live: 09/08/82) / Rip It
Up (The Cross: live in Germany) /
Saturday Night's Alright For Fighting
(live: 15/05/85) / Everybody Happy
(Freddie - Special Fan Club song) /
Going Back (Larry Lurex) / Lucille (live:
Earls Court, London 1977) / In My
Defence (rare track from *Time*) / Ogre
Battle (forgotten intro – demo 1973) /
Hangman (live: 01/05/75) / Hello And
Goodbye / No Turning Back (Joy Stick
Mix) / No Turning Back (Chocs Away
Mix - Rare Immortals 12" with John
Deacon)

*Note: The details in brackets are as they
appear on the sleeve notes. At first glance
this CD would seem to be the most exciting
collectors' set ever. However, as much of the
material on it is not what it purports to be,
it is a huge disappointment. Tracks described
as first takes, alternate versions, forgotten
intro's and demos, are labelled as such
purely to deceive collectors into buying the
discs. Needless to say, many of the date and
venue references are incorrect. The set does
at least offer an idea as to what rare live
and pre-Queen tracks do exist, and when
they were recorded, though the fan club
biography provides that information in far
greater detail. In typical bootleg fashion, the
compact disc catalogue numbers and main
title are different to those which appear
on the accompanying sleeve notes. It is most
likely that what was originally intended to
be a predominately pre-Queen rarities set –
Larry Lurex is the credited artist on each
CD – was later changed into this curious
mishmash compilation.*

Back Catalogue: Volume 1
No catalogue number or year of
release details are contained on the
disc or sleeve
Running time: 76.20

Doing Alright (May / Staffell) 3.43,
1969 / Blag (Smile) 3.13, 1969 / April Lady
(Lucas) 2.43, 1969 / Polar Bear (Smile)
3.58, 1969 / Earth (Staffell) 4.00, 1970 /
Step On Me (May/Staffell) 3.12, 1970 / I
Can Hear Music (Spector/
Greenwich) 3.21, 1973 / Goin' Back
(Goffin/King) 3.21, 1973 / Mad The Swine
(Mercury) 3.21, 1973 / See What A
Fool I've Been (May) 4.32, 1974 / Misfire
(Deacon) 1.56, 1974 / A Human Body
(Taylor) 3.40, 1980 / Soul Brother
(Queen) 3.37, 1981 / I Go Crazy (May)
3.43, 1984 / Thank God It's Christmas
(Taylor / May) 4.18, 1984 / Man On The
Prowl (Mercury) Extended Version 5.57,
1984 / Keep Passing The Windows
(Mercury) Extended Version 6.45, 1984 /
One Vision (Queen) Extended Version
6.22, 1985 / Blurred Vision (Queen)
4.38, 1985

*The Smile, Larry Lurex and non-album
B-side material here offer newcomers to the
band's music a welcome introduction to
some rare songs, many of which are still
awaiting an official release. It is increasingly
likely that Freddie's superb vocal
performance as Larry lurex will be released
at some point as part of a long overdue
rarities set, but nothing could be confirmed
at the time of writing. 'I Can Hear Music'/
'Going Back' is a vastly underrated pairing,
one of Freddie's finest recorded moments.
All in all, this disc is a sensible investment.*

**The Ultimate Queen Back
Catalogue: Volume 2**
ODY 022
Record label unknown, Italy, 1994
Running time: 77.01

Back Chat (12" Version) 1982 / Staying
Power (12" Version) 1982 / Man On
The Prowl (12" Version) 1984 / Keep
Passing The Open Windows (12" Version)
1984 / I Want To Break Free (12" Version)
1984 / Machines (Or Back To Humans)
(12" Version) 1984 / A Dozen Red Roses
For My Darling (B-side) 1986 / Friends
Will Be Friends (12" Version) 1986 / Pain
Is So Close To Pleasure (12" Version)
1986 / Stealin (B-side) 1989 / Breakthru
(12" Version) 1989 / We Will Rock
You (Rick Rubin Mix) 1991 / Ruined
Instrumental (of above track) 1991 /
We Are The Champions (Rick Rubin Mix)
1991 / Big Beat A Capella (mix of We Will
Rock You) 1991 / Zulu Scratch A Capella
(mix of We Will Rock You) 1991

*Though this disc (and Volume 1) clearly
do not offer live material, it is included here
for its informative and interest value.
Following the success of Queen's penultimate
studio album 'The Miracle' in 1989, a follow
up set containing non-album B-side material
and the augmented cuts of 'Breakthru'
(track 11), 'Scandal' and 'The Invisible Man'
was considered. Tentatively titled 'Another
Miracle', the idea was shelved and later
cancelled – like numerous other Queen
related projects. Had it emerged, however,
it would have contained the other two
non-album B-sides ('My Life Has Been
Saved' and 'Hijack My Heart'), in addition to
'Stealin' (track 10). While tracks 1 and 2
have still not been made officially available
on CD, tracks 3, 4, 5, 6, 9 and 11 were all
included on the 1992 'Box of Tricks' 12-track
compilation CD 'The 12" Collection'
(CDQTEL 0001).*

Tokyo 1985
TKCD 1120
Golden Stars Records, EEC, 1991
Recorded live in Tokyo (05/11/85)
Running time: 72.00

Tear It Up / Tie Your Mother Down (5.39) / Under Pressure (3.27) / Somebody To Love / Killer Queen (6.12) / Seven Seas Of Rhye / Keep Yourself Alive / Liar (6.43) / Instrumental Inferno (4.08) / It's A Hard Life (4.10) / Dragon Attack (3.57) / Now I'm Here (6.22) / Love Of My Life (2.43) / Another One Bites The Dust (3.51) / Hammer To Fall (4.59) / Crazy Little Thing Called Love (5.07) / Radio Ga Ga (5.34) / I Want To Break Free (3.16) / Jailhouse Rock (3.20) / We Will Rock You (2.38) / We Are The Champions (3.50)

Not to be confused with the above disc (as some collectors seem to do) for this 17 track set is the better option. Although both offer material already available in various forms elsewhere, this one does at least include a two page booklet. We must once again disregard the sleeve notes.

Queen did not play any live shows in November 1985. In fact they performed no shows at all that year after Live Aid. It would seem that whoever set out the sleeve artwork for this disc mistook 11/5/85 to mean the fifth day of the eleventh month, instead of the eleventh day of the fifth month, which is the correct date. This set comprises material recorded at the Yogishi Swimming Pool, Tokyo, Japan.

Unauthorised:
Live: Volume 1
JOK 015-A
Joker Records, Australia, 1993
Running time: 55.53

Now I'm Here / Ogre Battle / White Queen / Bohemian Rhapsody / Killer Queen / March Of The Black Queen / Bring Back That Leroy Brown / Keep Yourself Alive / Brighton Rock / Son And Daughter / Liar / In The Lap Of The Gods / Seven Seas Of Rhye / See What A Fool I've Been

If it's originality you're looking for, you won't find it here. This disc merely covers well trodden ground in offering the festive 1975 performance. This limited edition disc (of 1500) is the only one I have come across that originates from Australia. There no doubt are other examples, but none as yet seem to have found their way onto the European market, though that is certain to change.

Two other similarly titled discs exist, with the addition of a 'We Will Rock You' sub-title, but because both discs offer yet again the Christmas Eve 1975 and Yoshigi, Tokyo, May 1985, shows, full details are unnecessary.

Catalogue No's:
Volume 1: BAN 037 A
Volume 2: BAN 037 B

Unforgettable Music
Double CD
10201
Red Line Records, Italy, 1993
Running Times: 50.19/53.19

Disc 1: Tie Your Mother Down / I Want It All / Las Parablas De Amor / Hammer To Fall / Stone Cold Crazy / Innuendo / Thank You / Crazy Little Thing Called Love / Too Much Love Will Kill You / Radio Ga Ga / Who Wants To Live Forever

Disc 2: I Want To Break Free / Under Pressure / All The Young Dudes / Heroes / '39 / These Are The Days Of Our Lives / Somebody To Love / Bohemian Rhapsody / The Show Must Go On / We Will Rock You / God Save The Queen

Because 'Crazy Little Thing Called Love' was not performed by anyone at the concert, I can offer no explanation as to how it came to be included here – bootlegs gremlins at work presumably.

This is one of the most difficult Queen CD bootlegs to locate – and one of the most expensive. It is presented in 10" x 10" box and includes a 12-page booklet, numbered certificate of authentication and – what no Queen fan should be without – a medallion! The significance of the rather tacky medallion remains a mystery.

I would suggest that it is the untypical packaging that attracts the attention of collectors, because it can't be the music which has been lifted straight from Discs 2 and 3 of the German 'Freddie Mercury Tribute' bootleg CD (TFKRL 9204-3 CD), as already outlined. The set is limited to 3000.

Waiting On A Death Trip
TGP 137
Grand Pick Records, Italy, 1991
Live in Argentina, 1981
Running time: 68.03

We Will Rock You / Let Me Entertain You / Play The Game / Rock It / Love Of My Life / Keep Yourself Alive / Another One Bites The Dust / Now I'm Here / Dragon Attack / Sheer Heart Attack / Mustapha / Crazy Little Thing Called Love / Need Your Loving Tonight / Save Me / Tie Your Mother Down / Brighton Rock / Flash

This set offers an extremely good representation of 1981's infamous South American tour. Recorded in Buenos Aires on March 1, it contains most of the material that Queen chose to perform there. Only the familiar concluding few songs are absent.

We Still Rock You
ROLA 009
Rockland Records, Germany, 1993
Live in Europe, 1986
Running time: 73.52

Now I'm Here / Love Of My Life / Is This The World We Created / You're So Square / Hello Mary Lou / Tutti Frutti / Bohemian Rhapsody / Hammer To Fall / Crazy Little Thing Called Love / Radio Ga Ga / Under Pressure / Another One Bites The Dust / Who Wants To Live Forever / I Want To Break Free / Mayday / We Will Rock You / We Are The Champions / God Save The Queen

Track 15 is a ten and a half minute semi-heavy improvisation, which mostly features Brian. Having only read the sleeve notes, but not actually heard the music, I cannot confirm that this featured in the show. It may well have been introduced onto the disc from an entirely unrelated gig.

As if the title of this disc wasn't guaranteed to arouse extreme prejudice, the two page accompanying booklet included the words "In Memory of Brian Mercury".

There are literally hundreds of errors on bootlegs but this takes the cake.

We Will Love You
Double CD
SKCD 2063
Skeleton Records, Italy, 1992
Recorded live at Palazzo Dello Sport, Milan (14/09/84) & Wembley Stadium, London (13/07/85)
Running times: 69.52 / 59.25

Disc 1: Tear It Up / Tie Your Mother Down / Under Pressure / Somebody To Love / Killer Queen / Seven Seas Of Rhye / Keep Yourself Alive / Liar / It's A Hard Life / Dragon Attack / Now I'm Here / Is This The World We Created / Love Of My Life / Stone Cold Crazy / Another One Bites The Dust / Hammer To Fall

Disc 2: Crazy Little Thing Called Love / Bohemian Rhapsody / Radio Ga Ga / I Want To Break Free / Jailhouse Rock / We Will Rock You / We Are The Champions / God Save The Queen / Hammer To Fall / Is This The World We Created

Although it would be reasonable to assume that Queen's illustrious Live Aid performance would have made copious bootleg appearances, curiously it has made surprisingly few. Tracks 9-15 on Disc 2 offer not only the main six song set, but also Brian and Freddie's finale. The inclusion of the Italian material is also uncommon.

We Will Rock You
CD 12018
On Stage Records, EEC, 1992
Date and venue (of tracks 5-14) unknown
Running time: 65.10

We Will Rock You (4.27) / It's Late (6.42) / My Melancholy Blues (3.12) / Spread Your Wings (5.22) / Now I'm Here (8.29) / Love Of My Life (3.41) / Keep Yourself Alive (4.09) / Bohemian Rhapsody (5.43) / Brighton Rock (9.06) / Son And Daughter (1.40) / Don't Stop Me Now (4.30) / Tie Your Mother Down (3.56) / We Are The Champions (3.33) / God Save The Queen (0.40)

Tracks 2, 3 and 10 are incorrectly credited to Mercury/May jointly. Brian wrote 'It's Late' and 'Son & Daughter', while Freddie wrote 'My Melancholy Blues'.

There are two identical CDs with this title, both issued by the On Stage label with the same catalogue number. Only the front cover pictures differ. Unsuspecting collectors invariably end up with a copy of each.

Who Wants To Live Forever
PLR CD 9201
Pluto Records, Italy, 1992
Recorded live in Paris, France
Hippodrome De Vincennes (14/06/86)
Running time: 76.14

Brighton Rock / One Vision / Tie Your Mother Down / In The Lap Of The Gods / Seven Seas Of Rhye / A Kind Of Magic / Under Pressure / Another One Bites The Dust / Who Wants To Live Forever / I Want To Break Free / Is This The World We Created / Tutti Frutti / Bohemian Rhapsody / Hammer To Fall / Crazy Little Thing Called Love / Radio Ga Ga / We Will Rock You / Friends Will Be Friends / We Are The Champions / God Save The Queen

Though Queen did perform at this venue on the day indicated, this disc does not relate to it. Instead it features the July 12 Wembley Stadium show. When the concert was televised on ITV, the show opened with speeded up footage of the stage being constructed. The track which accompanied the film was the studio version of 'Brighton Rock'. Had the producers of this disc been aware of that, and omitted it, the deception might not have been discovered quite so quickly.

X-mas 1975
SR 012
Stoned Records, Korea, 1989
Queen – X-Mas 1975
Running time: 53.11

Now I'm Here / Ogre Battle / Bohemian Rhapsody / Killer Queen / March Of The Black Queen / Brighton Rock / Keep Yourself Alive / Liar / In The Lap Of The Gods / Seven Seas Of Rhye / See What A Fool I've Been / God Save The Queen

The sleeve notes claim that this was the first ever Queen CD bootleg release. An advanced copy (packaged in a black sleeve) also exists, though neither one is as early an issue as it purports to be.

Year Of The Opera
AAF 014
All About Fame Records, Germany, 1993
Various shows
Running time: unknown

In The Lap Of The Gods / Killer Queen / The March Of The Black Queen / Bring Back That Leroy Brown / Stone Cold Crazy / Liar / Bohemian Rhapsody / Flick Of The Wrist / Hangman / Brighton Rock / Seven Seas Of Rhye / Father To Son / Lazing On A Sunday Afternoon / Keep Yourself Alive / Now I'm Here / See What A Fool I've Been

You're My Best Friend
CD 12030
On Stage Records, EEC, 1992
Recorded live between 1975 and 1979 on the European Tour
Running time: 60.01

Sheer Heart Attack (3.36) / I'm In Love With My Car (2.02) / Get Down Make Love (4.32) / Let Me Entertain You (3.14) / Death On Two Legs (3.26) / Killer Queen (1.58) / Bicycle Race (1.35) / You're My Best Friend (2.09) / Dreamers Ball (3.46) / '39 (3.26) / Ogre Battle (4.59) / White Queen (5.21) / See What A Fool I've Been (4.22) / Seven Seas Of Rhye (3.07) / Liar (8.35) / In The Lap Of The Gods (3.53)

As the sleeve notes correctly observe, the first ten tracks do indeed originate from the European tour of 1979. Whoever compiled this disc need only to have looked at the 'Live Killers' sleeve notes to establish this... all ten tracks are the versions contained on that album. They appear in a different running order to the album, probably in an attempt to deceive fans. This song sequence, however, would never have been performed.

This bootleg does offer one of Roger Taylor's finest recorded moments – 'I'm In Love With My Car' – which he sings himself while simultaneously drumming. Other than the writing credits of 'Killer Queen' being attributed to Freddie, all the rest are incorrectly credited to Queen collectively. Nonspecific venue and date details - as presented here – usually indicate that the material featured, originates from numerous other bootleg recordings. They are essentially cocktails of various shows mixed together.

Live Bootleg LPs

Prior to the advent of compact discs, there was a thriving trade in vinyl bootlegs. Most collectors now consider these obsolete but there will always be a number of fans who will continue to collect vinyl, though the choice on offer to them is steadily decreasing.

What follows is as comprehensive a list as is possible to provide. As with all bootleg formats, it is constantly being updated, and will be out of date almost immediately.

A Day In Munich
QMU
(26/06/86)

Absolutely Enthusiastic
Double Album
TFKRL 9002-2
(11/05/85)

Absolutely Rare
Double Album
TFKRL 9201
Various Shows

Black & White Queen
EEN 98
(24/12/75)

Cardiac Arrest
HIP 001
Various Shows

Command Performance
TAKRL 1997
(24/12/75)

Crazy Duck
DR 481
(26/12/79)

Crazy Tour
Double Album
26Q
(26/12/79)

Crowning Glory
FLAT 8218
(04/04/76)

Dear Friend Goodbye
TFMML 001
(07/05/75)

Done Under Pressure
Double Album
(21/06/86)

Don't Stop Us Live
(02/02/79)

Duck Soup
SLA 007
(13/03/77)
Also available as 'Somebody To Love'
RRL 6900
Part 2 issued as PNW
ODD 3

Dynasty
Double Album
QN 1-6
(27/09/84)

Elizabeth II
(14/09/84)

En Viva Pueblo
(16/10/81)
Also available as 'No More Mananas'

Flash Alive
Double Album
Q 80128
(08/12/80)

Falklands Are Rocking
STQ 231082
(03/81)

Falklands II - The Sequel
KQ001
(03/81)

Freddie's Boys At The Beeb
JOKE 40 HO
BBC sessions
(see note below:)

Freddie's Last Journey
Double Album
(24-25/11/81)
Copy of 'We Will Rock You' video
PAN 648-09

Free In The Park
MARC
(18/09/76)

Ga Ga
Double Album
ETS 2563/64
(01/09/84)

Geisha Boys
SLA 001
(04/04/76)
Copy of Japanese bootleg/'Lazing On A Sunday Afternoon'

Get Down
Double Album
LR 140RC
(24/10/82)

Gonna Rock
Side 1 is first side of
'No News Is Good News' and
Side 2 is first side of 'Sheetkickers'
QLS 1957

Halfpence
EEN 98 (24/12/75)
Same as 'Black & White Queen'
Same catalogue no. also

Her Majesties Secret Service
Double Album
TFKRL 9001
Unknown venue and date

High Voltage
Double Album
SR 25 703
(24/12/75)
Re-release of 'Sheetkickers' and
'Command Performance'

Hot Space Tour '82
Triple Album
ETS 2511
(14/09/82)

I've Just Got To Have It Now
Unknown venue, date and catalogue no.

Kimono My Place Live
MARC 75122
(01/05/75)

King's Favourite
Double Album
141RC
(20/09/84)

Lazing On A Sunday Evening
MARC TQ-76042
(04/04/76)

Live
OG-860
(19/04/75)

Live At Budokan
TAB 001
(24/12/75)
Recorded in London, not Japan
Copy of 'Royal Rock Us'

Live In Japan
Double Album
S3004
(Japan 1982)

Long Life To The Queen
Triple Album
(April 1982)

Magic At Knebworth
Double Album
RSR 250
(09/08/86)

Mania
EGF 1200 (13/03/77)

Mercury Poisoning
IMP 1118
(31/04/76)

Moet & Chandon
TFKRL 9101
Unknown venue and date

No More Mananas
SLA 0009
Reissued as KWIN 101
1981 tour
Unknown catalogue no.

No News Is Good News
BBC session and live material

Queen At St. James' Park
Double Album
(09/07/86)
Extremely Limited Edition

Queen Elizabeth II
(14/09/84)

Queen Invite You To A Night At The Budokan
MARC TQ-76059
(31/04/76)

Queen Invite You To A Night At The Warehouse
STONED 5
Double Album
(12/05/77)
Reissued as QUO 012

Queen Reigns The World
Double Album
Miles Records
(21/06/86)

Queen's Last Stand
Double Album
ETS 2583/84
(15/05/85)

Rogues And Scoundrels
AFTERMATH 8
Usually advertised as Rogues And Scandals
Various shows

Royal American Tour
WRMB 307
(22/03/75)

Royal Rock Us
TAKRL 927
(24/12/75)

Save Me
Double Album
(01/02/79)

Sheetkickers
2 sleeves
TAKRL 1957
Various Shows from 1974
Includes 'Ballroom Blitz'
by Sweet!

Stunning
BRR 006
(01/05/75)
Copy of 'Kimono My Place Live' reiss by Rodan Records in a colour cover

Tie Your Mother Down
KQ 001
(28/02/81)

Tokyo Rampage
TKRWM 1801
Various Shows

Tornado In The Far East (Part 1) TFKRL 9002 2
Unknown venue and date
Part 2 - same catalogue no.)

Zoom Queen
Double Album
LLX 314
(Japan 1976)

There seems to be much confusion about an album called 'Freddie's Boys At The Beeb'. As the catalogue number implies (Bulsara: Freddie's real surname), it is a bootleg disc which features session material recorded for the BBC on both sides. The eight track disc was issued in three different coloured vinyls (yellow, blue and red), though I have yet to see a red copy. The material on Side 1 relates to Queen's second BBC session (25/7/73), and Side 2 to the final one (28/10/77). See the Live discography section for tracklist details.

Mercury Poisoning (IMP 1118): Some copies of this album were mispressed, and contained Side 2 of Paul McCartney's Wings From The Wings album, on the B-side (IMP 1117-1119).

Crazy Little Thing Called Love / Hammer To Fall (IMC CMS 847): a seven inch vinyl bootleg disc is also available. Both tracks are live performances and are believed to originate from the Mannheim, Germany show on June 21, 1986. The same A-side was also issued later, but this time featured a live cut of 'Tutti Frutti' as the B-side.

Like their compact disc equivalents, many vinyl bootlegs contain sleeve note errors and incorrect date and venue advice. 'Dear Friend Goodbye' is a good example. Queen did not play a concert on May 7, 1975. The eight shows they performed in Japan that year concluded on May 1.

The following list is an at-a-glance summary of the information outlined above. It contains only those discs which relate to one specific show, not those which feature material from various sources.

Vinyl Album Bootlegs originating from one concert only

A Day In Munich (26/6/86)
Absolutely Enthusiastic (11/5/85)
Black & White Queen (24/12/75)
Command Performance (24/12/75)
Crazy Duck (26/12/79)
Crowning Glory (04/04/76)
Dear Friend Goodbye (07/05/75)
Done Under Pressure (21/06/86)
Don't Stop Us Live (02/02/79)
Duck Soup (13/03/77)
Dynasty (27/09/84)
Elizabeth II (14/09/84)
En Viva Pueblo (16/10/81)
Flash Alive (08/12/80)
Falklands Are Rocking (03/81)
Falklands II - The Sequel (03/81)
Free In The Park (18/09/76)
Ga Ga (01/09/84)
Geisha Boys (04/04/76)
Get Down (24/10/82)
Halfpence (24/12/75)
Hot Space Tour '82 (14/09/82)
High Voltage (24/12/75)
Kimono My Place Live (01/05/75)

King's Favourite (20/09/84)
Lazing On A Sunday Evening (04/04/76)
Live (19/04/75)
Live At Budokan (24/12/75)
Magic At Knebworth (09/08/86)
Mania (13/03/77)
Queen At St. James' Park (09/07/86)
Queen Elizabeth II (14/09/84)
Queen Invite You To A Night At The Warehouse (12/05/77)
Queen Reigns The World (21/06/86)
Queen's Last Stand (15/05/85)
Royal American Tour (22/03/75)
Royal Rock Us (24/12/75)
Save Me (01/02/79)
Stunning (01/05/75)
Tie Your Mother Down (28/02/81)

Audio Cassette Recordings

The most effective way new fans can familiarise themselves with Queen's live performances is to respond to fan club or *Record Collector* advertisements.

Most collectors who start, and built up, their collections in that way (myself included), prefer not to sell copies of shows they have, but instead swap them for shows they do not have.

In addition to live recordings, fans also exchange Queen related press conference, biography, documentary, American radio show, tribute and interview tapes. There are well over a thousand of these, and it would be impossible and impractical to summarise them all here.

Although Queen performed a total of 704 documented shows in their career, almost exactly a quarter of that number (approximately 150), have at some stage emerged in audio cassette form.

The following chronological list details only the tapes which most frequently appear on sale and swap lists.

Marquee
Marquee Club, London, England (20/12/72)

Queen On The Green
Golders Green Hippodrome, London, England (13/09/73)

Paris Theatre
London, England (20/10/73)

Oxford New Theatre
Oxford, England (20/11/73)

Opera House
Manchester, England (26/11/73)

Birmingham Town Hall
Birmingham, England (27/11/73)

Bristol Colston
Colston Hall, Bristol, England (29/11/73)

Rainbow Theatre
London, England (31/03/74)

Mott Tour
Uris Theatre, New York, USA (07/05/74)

At The Palace
Manchester, England (30/10/74)

St Georges Hall
Bradford, England (06/11/74)

Live At The Rainbow
Rainbow Theatre, London, England (20/11/74)

Sheetkickers
Various shows from 1974 (originally known as 'Shitkickers')

Rogues And Scoundrels
Various shows from 1974

Cardiac Arrest
Various shows from 1974/75

Tokyo Rampage
Various shows from 1974/75

Royal American Tour
Santa Monica Civic Auditorium, USA (29/03/75)

Kimono My Place Live
Budokan Hall, Tokyo, Japan (01/05/75)

Stunning Live In Tokyo
Various shows in Tokyo, Japan (19-30/04/75)

Budokan
Budokan Hall, Tokyo, Japan (19/04/75)

Liverpool Empire
Liverpool, England (15/11/75)

Coventry Theatre
Coventry, England (16/11/75)

Manchester
Manchester, England (26/11/75)

Halfpence
Hammersmith Odeon, London (24/12/75)

Command Performance
Hammersmith Odeon, London (24/12/75)

Christmas At The Beeb
Hammersmith Odeon, London (24/12/75)

Merry Christmas
Hammersmith Odeon, London (24/12/75)

Los Angeles
Santa Monica Civic Auditorium, USA (03/76)

Fukuoka
Kyden Gymnasium, Fukuoka, Japan (26/03/76)

Kosei Nenkin
Osaka, Japan (29/03/76)

Mercury Poisoning
Budokan, Tokyo, Japan (01/04/76)

Geisha Boys
Nichidai Kodo, Tokyo, Japan (04/04/76)

Crowning Glory
Nichidai Kodo, Tokyo, Japan (04/04/76)

Lazing On A Sunday Afternoon
European copy of above

Adelaide
Apollo Stadium, Adelaide, Australia (15/04/76)

Playhouse Theatre
Edinburgh, Scotland (02/09/76)

Free In The Park
Hyde Park, London, England (18/09/76)

Queen At The Races
College Park, Maryland, USA (04/02/77)

Vancouver
PNE Coliseum, Vancouver, Canada (11/03/77)

Pacific North Western
Seattle Arena, USA (13/03/77) (aka PNW)

Duck Soup
Seattle Arena, USA (13/03/77)

Queen Mania
Seattle Arena, USA (13/03/77) (similar to above – different listing)

Stockholm
Ice Stadium, Stockholm, Sweden (08/05/77)

Sheer Bloody Poetry
Scandanavium, Gothenburg, Sweden (10/05/77)

Queen Invite You To A Night At The Warehouse
Broendby Hall, Copenhagen, Denmark (12/05/77)

Bristol Hippodrome
Bristol, England (24/05/77)

Glasgow
Glasgow Apollo, Scotland (30/05/77)

Glasgow Apollo
Glasgow, Scotland (30/05/77)

Apollo II
Glasgow, Scotland (31/05/77)

Empire Theatre
Liverpool, England (03/06/77)

Earls Court
London, England (06/06/77)

Copenhagen
Falkoner Theatre, Copenhagen, Denmark (13/04/78)

Rotterdam
Ahoy Hall, Rotterdam, Holland (19/04/78)

Paris Pavillion
Paris, France (23/04/78)

Vienna
Stadhalle, Vienna, Austria (02/05/78)

Bingley Hall
Stafford, England (06/05/78)

Dallas
Convention Centre, Dallas, USA
(28/10/78)

Queen Play The Square
Madison Square Garden, New York, USA
(17/11/78)

The Forum
Montreal, Canada (01/12/78)

Deutchlandhalle
Berlin, Germany (24/01/79)

Back On The Road Again
Sportshalle, Cologne, Germany (01/02/79)

Don't Stop Us Live
Festhalle, Frankfurt, Germany (02/02/79)

Zurich
Hallenstadium, Zurich, Switzerland
(04/02/79)

Basketball Halle
Munich, Germany (11/02/79)

Pavillion De Paris
Paris, France (28/02/79)

Pavillion De Paris II
Paris, France (01/03/79)

Tokyo Budokan
Budokan Hall, Tokyo, Japan (23/04/79)

Budokan
Budokan Hall, Tokyo, Japan (24/04/79)

Saarbruken
Ludwigsparkstadion, Saarbruken,
Germany (18/08/79)

City Hall
Newcastle, England (03/12/79)

Mack Attack
Newcastle, England (04/12/79)

Queen Go Crazy
Hammersmith Odeon, London, England
(26/12/79)

A Silent Night At The Odeon
Hammersmith Odeon, London, England
(26/12/79)

Crazy Tour
Various shows from European leg of
the Crazy Tour 1979

LA Forum
Los Angeles, USA (11/07/80)

Oakland
Oakland Coliseum, USA (14/07/80)

Rhode Island
Civic Centre, Providence, USA (26/08/80)

Mecca
Milwaukee, USA (10/09/80)

Chicago Plays The Game
Horizon Theatre, Chicago, USA
(19/09/80)

Paris
Le Bourget La Retonde, Paris, France
(25/11/80)

Leiden
Groenoordhalle, Leiden, Germany
(27/11/80)

Essen Germany
Grudhalle, Essen, Germany (29/11/80)

Berlin
Deutchlandhalle, Berlin, Germany
(30/11/80)

NEC Birmingham
National Exhibition Centre, Birmingham,
England (05/12/80)

NEC Revisited
National Exhibition Centre, Birmingham,
England (06/12/80)

Flash Alive
Wembley Arena, London, England
(08/12/80)

Wembley Arena
London, England (09/12/80)

Flash Bites The Big One
Wembley Arena, London, England
(10/12/80)

Frankfurt
Festhalle, Germany (14/12/80)

Falklands Are Rocking
Various South American shows
(Feb-Mar 81)

Falklands II (The Sequel)
Buenos Aires, Argentina (28/02-01/03/81)

Gluttons For Punishment
Sarfield Stadium, Buenos Aires, Argentina
(08/03/81)

Buenos Aires Revisited
Sarfield Stadium, Buenos Aires, Argentina
(08/03/81)

Save Us
Morumbi Stadium, Sao Paulo, Brazil
(20/03/81)

Puebla Mexico
Estadion Cuahtermoc, Puebla (17/10/81)

Stockholm
Isstadion, Stockholm, Sweden (10/04/82)

Long Life To The Queen
Hallenstadion, Zurich, Switzerland
(17/04/82)

Forest Nationale
Brussels, Belgium (23/04/82)

Frankfurt
Feathalle, Frankfurt, Germany (28/04/82)

Dortmund
Westallenhalle, Dortmund, Germany
(01/05/82)

Hamburg
Ernst-Mercke Halle, Hamburg, Germany
(16/05/82)

Kassel
Eisspdorthalle, Kassel, Germany
(18/05/82)

Elland Road
Football Ground, Leeds, England
(29/05/82)

Edinburgh
Ingliston Showground, Edinburgh, Scotland
(01/06/82)

Live At The Bowl
Milton Keynes Bowl, Buckinghamshire,
England (05/06/82)

Montreal
Forum, Montreal, Canada (21/06/82)

Queen Rock The Square
Madison Square Garden, New York, USA
(28/06/82)

Rock It Over America
Madison Square Garden, New York, USA
(28/06/82)

New Jersey
Brendon Burn Coliseum, New Jersey, USA
(09/08/82)

The Forum
Los Angeles, California, USA (15/09/82)

Get Down
Hankyu Nishinomiyakyujo, Osaka, Japan
(24/10/82)

Seibu
Seibu Lions Stadium, Tokyo, Japan
(03/11/82)

Dublin Eire
Royal Dublin Society Hall, Dublin, Eire
(28/08/84)

Live At The NEC
National Exhibition Centre, Birmingham,
England (31/08/84)

NEC Revisited
National Exhibition Centre, Birmingham,
England (01/09/84)

Break Free At Birmingham
National Exhibition Centre, Birmingham,
England (02/09/84)

Queen Give Em The Works
Wembley Arena, London, England
(04/09/84)

Wembley London
Wembley Arena, London, England
(05/09/84)

Wembley London
Wembley Arena, London, England
(07/09/84)

Wembley London
Wembley Arena, London, England
(08/09/84)

Queen Elizabeth II
Sportspalace, Milan, Italy (14/09/84)

Queen Elizabeth II – Second Night
Sportspalace, Milan, Italy (15/09/84)

Paris
Omnisports, Paris, France (18/09/84)

Kings Favourite
Forest Nationale, Brussels, Belgium
(21/09/84)

Let Us Entertain You
Forest Nationale, Brussels, Belgium
(21/09/84)

Stuttgart
Schleyerhalle, Stuttgart, Germany
(27/09/84)

Rock In Rio Festival
Roi De Janeiro, Brazil (12-19/01/85)

Melbourne
Sports & Entertainment Centre,
Melbourne, Australia (19/04/85)

Melbourne (Last Night)
Sports & Entertainment Centre,
Melbourne, Australia (20/04/85)

Sydney Australia
Entertainments Centre, Sydney, Australia
(26/04/85)

Twisting By The Pool
Yogishi Swimming Pool Auditorium, Tokyo,
Japan (11/05/85)

In A Sticky Situation
Yogishi Swimming Pool Auditorium, Tokyo,
Japan (11/05/85)

Jo Hall
Osaka, Japan (15/05/85)

Live Aid
Wembley Stadium, London, England
(13/07/85)

There Can Be Only One
Stockholm, Sweden (07/06/86)

Leiden
Groenoordhalle, Leiden, Germany
(12/06/86)

Done Under Pressure
Mannhiem, Germany (21/06/86)

Queen Reign The World
Mannhiem, Germany (21/06/86)

Berlin
Waldbuehne, Berlin, Germany (26/06/86)

Slane Castle
Dublin, Eire (05/07/86)

Magic Moments
St James Park, Newcastle, England
(09/07/86)

A Night Of Summer Magic
Wembley Stadium, London, England
(12/07/86) (aka Real Magic)

Don't Lose Your Seat
(USA Radio Broadcast - As Above)
Superstar Concert (Westwood One)
(12/07/86)

Maine Road Magic
Maine Road, Manchester, England
(16/07/86)

Vienna
Stadhalle, Vienna, Austria (21/07/86)

Vienna (2nd Night)
Stadhalle, Vienna, Austria (22/07/86)

Live In Budapest
Nepstadion, Budapest, Hungary (27/07/86)

Amphitheatre France
Frejus, France (30/07/86)

Magic At Knebworth
Knebworth Park, Hertfordshire, England
(09/09/86)

Summary of most common Queen Audio Bootleg Recordings which relate to one show only - not various shows

Marquee (20/12/72)
Queen On The Green (13/09/73)
Paris Theatre (20/10/73)
Oxford New Theatre (20/11/73)
Opera House (26/11/73)
Birmingham Town Hall (27/11/73)
Bristol Colston (29/11/73)
Rainbow Theatre (31/03/74)
Mott Tour (07/05/74)
At The Palace (30/10/74)
St Georges Hall (06/11/74)
Live At The Rainbow (20/11/74)
Royal American Tour (29/03/75)
Budokan (19/04/75)
Kimono My Place Live (01/05/75)
Liverpool Empire (15/11/75)
Coventry Theatre (16/11/75)
Manchester (26/11/75)
Halfpence (24/12/75)
Command Performance (24/12/75)
Christmas At The Beeb (24/12/75)
Merry Christmas (24/12/75)
Fukuoka (26/03/76)
Kosei Nenkin (29/03/76)
Mercury Poisoning (01/04/76)
Geisha Boys (04/04/76)
Crowning Glory (04/04/76)
Lazing On A Sunday Afternoon
   (04/04/76)
Adelaide (15/04/76)
Playhouse Theatre (02/09/76)
Free In The Park (18/09/76)
Queen At The Races (04/02/77)
Vancouver (11/03/77)
Pacific North Western (13/03/77)
PNW (13/03/77)
Duck Soup (13/03/77)
Queen Mania (13/03/77)
Stockholm (08/05/77)

Sheer Bloody Poetry (10/05/77)
Queen Invite You To A Night
   At The Warehouse (12/05/77)
Bristol Hippodrome (24/05/77)
Glasgow (30/05/77)
Glasgow Apollo (30/05/77)
Apollo II (31/05/77)
Empire Theatre (03/06/77)
Earls Court (06/06/77)
Copenhagen (13/04/78)
Rotterdam (19/04/78)
Paris Pavillion (23/04/78)
Vienna (03/05/78)
Bingley Hall (06/05/78)
Dallas (28/10/78)
Queen Play The Square (17/11/78)
The Forum (01/12/78)
Deutchlandhalle (01/01/79)
Back On The Road Again (01/02/79)
Don't Stop Us Live (02/02/79)
Zurich (04/02/79)
Basketball Halle (11/02/79)
Pavillion De Paris (28/02/79)
Pavillion De Paris II (01/03/79)
Tokyo Budokan (23/04/79)
Budokan (24/04/79)
Saarbruken (18/08/79)
City Hall (03/12/79)
Mack Attack (04/12/79)
Queen Go Crazy (26/12/79)
A Silent Night At The Odeon
   (26/12/79)
LA Forum (11/07/80)
Oakland (14/07/80)
Rhode Island (26/08/80)
Mecca (10/09/80)
Chicago Plays The Game (19/09/80)
Paris (25/11/80)
Leiden (27/11/80)
Essen Germany (29/11/80)
Berlin (30/11/80)
NEC Birmingham (05/12/80)
NEC Revisited (06/12/80)
Flash Alive (08/12/80)
Wembley Arena (09/12/80)
Flash Bites The Big One (10/12/80)
Frankfurt (14/12/80)
Gluttons For Punishment (08/03/81)
Buenos Aires Revisited (08/03/81)
Save Us (20/03/81)
Puebla Mexico (17/11/81)
Stockholm (10/04/82)
Long Life To The Queen (17/04/82)
Forest Nationale (23/04/82)
Frankfurt (28/04/82)
Dortmund (01/05/82)
Hamburg (16/05/82)
Kassel (18/05/82)
Elland Road (29/05/82)
Edinburgh (01/06/82)
Live At The Bowl (05/06/82)
Montreal (21/07/82)
Queen Rock The Square (28/07/82)
Rock It Over America (28/07/82
New Jersey (09/08/82)
The Forum (15/09/82)
Get Down (24/10/82)
Seibu (03/11/82)
Dublin Eire (28/08/84)
Live At The NEC (31/08/84)
NEC Revisited (01/09/84)
Break Free At Birmingham
   (02/09/84)
Queen Give Em The Works
   (04/09/84)
Wembley London (05/09/84)
Wembley London (07/09/84)
Wembley London (08/09/84)
Queen Elizabeth II (14/09/84)
Queen Elizabeth II - Second Night
   (15/09/84)
Paris (18/09/84)
Kings Favourite (21/09/84)
Let Us Entertain You (21/09/84)
Stuttgart (27/09/84)
Melbourne (19/04/85)
Melbourne (Last Night) (20/04/85)

Sydney Australia (26/04/85)
Twisting By The Pool (11/05/85)
In A Sticky Situation (11/05/85)
Jo Hall (15/05/85)
Live Aid (13/07/85)
There Can Be Only One (07/06/86)
Leiden (12/06/86)
Done Under Pressure (21/06/86)
Queen Reign The World (21/06/86)
Berlin (26/06/86)
Slane Castle (05/07/86)
Magic Moments (09/07/86)
A Night Of Summer Magic
   (12/07/86)
Don't Lose Your Seat (12/07/86)
Maine Road Magic (16/07/86)
Vienna (21/07/86)
Vienna (2nd Night) (22/07/86)
Live In Budapest (27/07/86)
Amphitheatre France (30/07/86)
Magic At Knebworth (09/08/86)

Books

Predictably, there is a dearth of written matter relating to Queen's live performances The few which have emerged through the years offer brief details and summaries. Unofficial publications generally offer fans and collectors most information, and the following summary is made up of both official and unofficial books.

Gluttons For Punishment
Published in 1982 (by Peter Lubin), this 82 page souvenir book tells the story of the 1981 South American tour, from the view point of the tour organisers and crew members. An amusing text (by Mike Reynolds) details many of the behind the scenes mishaps which plagued almost the entire tour.

A Magic Tour
Published in 1987 (by Sidgwick & Jackson), this 98 page book provides technical and logistic information relating to the Magic tour of 1986. The book commences with several pages of text, but is made up for the most part of on and off stage photographs. The text is provided by Peter Hillmore, and the photography by Denis O'Regan.

Live Aid
Published in 1985 (by Sidgewick & Jackson), almost 200 pages of text and photographs detail every artist who performed on the day, and in the order in which they appeared. The main text is courtesy of Peter Hillmore, and Bob Geldof provides the introduction. Four pages relate to Queen (Freddie mostly), and one to Brian and Freddie's acoustic finale.

The First Ten Years/ The First Twelve Years
First published in 1981 (by Babylon Books), an entirely reworked and updated edition appeared later in 1984. Compiled by Mike West, the original book contained 112 pages of factual band history, discography and bootleg information. By 1984 however, the retitled work had been condensed down to only 90 pages, and sported a different cover.

To my knowledge, this was the very first publication of its kind. It is certainly the earliest documentation I have come across which relates to Queen bootlegs. It is unauthorised and fan club members were politely asked not to buy it, nor others like it. Inevitably the request inspired the reverse. Curious fans who were previously unaware of this book went straight out in search of it.

The quality of photographic reproduction in the amended edition is vastly superior to the first edition, as is the binding.

The earlier edition fell to pieces within a month of buying it. Both books are recommended to serious collectors.

The Bootleg CDs
Not so much published, as compiled and independently issued, this A4 size booklet was originally made available in March 1994, but was updated and issued again in October the same year.

No one person is credited as its creator, though its copyright (if one is appropriate) is attributed to Johnny The Limiter. The book originates from Holland, and is most definitely worth seeking out. It is concise, informative and has been meticulously researched. The grammar leaves much to be desired, often making little or no sense at all, but you get the general idea of what the Dutch author is driving at.

As the title suggests, the book concentrates solely upon the many Queen related bootleg compact discs. It also includes details of four Brian May band discs, and 'The Cross' May 29, 1990 and December 22, 1992 shows.

Having heard almost every disc the book mentions, a few minor discrepancies are apparent. In fairness, most are due to the editor's unfamiliarity with the finer points of the English language, but others are the result of poor research. The book includes a guide to prices as well as an illustration of each one.

As It Began
First published in 1985 (by Sidgewick & Jackson) and reprinted in paperback form in 1993 (by Pan Books). Co-written by Jim Jenkins and Jacky Gunn (now Smith).

Authorised by Queen, and written with their full cooperation, this book offers a great deal of previously unpublished information and anecdotes, and concludes with full Uk (non live) single, album and video discographies, all of which have been meticulously researched by Jim.

As outlined in the opening Preface to this book, 'As It Began' is the perfect example of a book from which seemingly every other music journalist has borrowed material for their own projects. The text reappears almost word for word in some cases.

Collectors should extend their search to the original hard back edition, which is already proving troublesome to locate.

Non album material

The following were all issued as single A or B-side tracks, but do not appear on any album, nor were they ever featured in any concert.

A Human Body
B-side of Play The Game, 1980.

Soul Brother
B-side of Under Pressure, 1981.

I Go Crazy
B-side of Radio Ga Ga, 1984.

Thank God It's Christmas
Single A-side, 1984.

Blurred Vision
B-side of One Vision, 1985.

A Dozen Red Roses For My Darling
B-side of A Kind Of Magic, 1986.

Mad The Swine
Extra track on Headlong CD and 12" singles. Originally recorded for the debut album but ultimately not included, 1991.

Note: Blurred Vision and A Dozen Red Roses are instrumental tracks.

Groups that have played as support act to Queen

After The Fire / The Alarm / Airrace / Angel Child / The B52's / Bangles / Belouis Some / Big Country / The Blasters / Bow Wow Wow / Bullitt / Cate Brothers / Cheap Trick / The Commodores / Craaft / Dakota / Kiki Dee / The Exploited / Andy Fairweather-Low / Fountainhead / Rory Gallagher / General Public / The Go Go's / Molly Hatchet / Head East / Heart / Steve Hillage / Hustler / INXS / Joan Jett & The Blackhearts / Kansas / Alvin Lee and Ten Years After / Lucifer / Mahogany Rush / Manfred Manns Earth Band / Marillion / Frankie Miller's Full House / Mr Big / Gary Moore / Nutz / Chris Rea / Red Baron / The Royal Dragoon Guards / Bob Segar / Billy Squier / Solution / Straight Eight / Status Quo / Styx / Supercharge / The Teardrop Explodes / Thin Lizzy / Tombstone / Voyager / Yesterday and Today / Z'Zi Labor

Once they were signed to a major label, Queen played support for only one band - Mott The Hoople.

Summary of where Queen have performed and in which years they did so

Listed Alphabetically (except that UK is always listed first)

* Denotes Queen played their first show in that country in this year. (excluding the Freddie Mercury Tribute Concert)

YEAR	COUNTRY	NO. OF SHOWS	SHOWS TOTAL
1970	UK	12	12
1971	UK	20	20
1972	UK	5	5
1973	UK	34	36
	Germany *	1	
	Luxembourg *	1	
1974	UK	41	71
	Australia *	1	
	Belgium *	1	
	Finland *	1	
	Germany	5	
	Holland *	1	
	Spain *	1	
	Sweden *	1	
	USA *	19	
1975	UK	25	71
	Canada *	2	
	Japan *	8	
	USA	36	
1976	UK	4	56
	Australia	8	
	Japan	11	
	USA	33	
1977	UK	12	87
	Canada	8	
	Denmark *	1	
	Germany	3	
	Holland	1	
	Sweden	2	
	Switzerland *	1	
	USA	59	
1978	UK	5	55
	Austria *	1	
	Belgium	3	
	Canada	5	
	Denmark	1	
	France *	2	
	Germany	4	
	Holland	2	
	Sweden	1	
	Switzerland	1	
	USA	30	
1979	UK	19	64
	Belgium	2	
	Eire *	1	
	France	5	
	Germany	13	
	Holland	2	
	Japan	15	
	Spain	4	
	Switzerland	1	
	Yugoslavia *	2	
1980	UK	5	63
	Belgium	2	
	Canada	3	
	France	1	
	Germany	8	
	Switzerland	1	
	USA	43	
1981	Argentina *	5	20
	Brazil *	2	
	Canada	2	
	Japan	5	
	Mexico *	3	
	Venezuela *	3	
1982	UK	4	
	Austria	2	
	Belgium	2	
	Canada	4	
	France	3	
	Germany	12	
	Holland	2	
	Japan	6	
	Norway *	1	
	Sweden	2	
	Switzerland	2	
	USA	30	
1983	No Shows		
1984	UK	7	
	Austria	2	
	Belgium	2	
	Eire	2	
	France	1	
	Germany	7	
	Italy *	2	
	South Africa *	7	
1985	UK	1	
	Australia	8	
	Brazil	2	
	Japan	6	
	New Zealand *	1	
1986	UK	5	
	Austria	2	
	Belgium	1	
	Eire	1	
	France	2	
	Germany	5	
	Holland	3	
	Hungary *	1	
	Spain	3	
	Sweden	1	
	Switerland	2	
Total			

Live songs/album breakdown

A: *No of tracks on album.*
B: *No of tracks performed live.*
C: *No of tracks not performed live.*
D: *Percentage played live/not played.*

Queen's 12 studio recorded albums contain 137 tracks. 79 of those were performed in concert, and 58 were not. Queen performed 58% of their entire album catalogue.

ALBUM	A	B	C	D
A Night At The Opera	12	10	2	83/17
Hot Space	11	8	3	73/27
A Day At The Races	10	7	3	70/30
The Game	10	7	3	70/30
The Works	9	6	3	67/33
News Of The World	11	7	4	64/36
Sheer Heart Attack	13	8	5	62/38
Queen	10	6	4	60/40
Queen II	11	6	5	55/45
Jazz	13	7	6	54/46
A Kind Of Magic	9	4	5	44/56
Flash Gordon	18	3	15	17/83
Total	137	79	58	58/42

Songs Queen have not performed live

Throughout the fifteen years in which Queen toured, a significant volume of album material and single issue B-sides did not feature in the live set. While many were included repeatedly and remained in the repertoire for numerous tours, others did not appear even once.

It is especially noticable that the ballads – many and varied as they are – seem to have fared the worst. Although several were deemed suitable for the concert environment:

My Melancholy Blues
White Queen
Love Of My Life
You're My Best Friend
Teo Torriatte
Life Is Real
Is This The World We Created
Who Wants To Live Forever

A significant number were not it seems:

The Night Comes Down
Someday One Day
Funny How Love Is
Nevermore
Lily Of The Valley
Dear Friends
You And I
She Makes Me
All Dead All Dead
Who Needs You
Jealousy
In Only Seven Days
Leaving Home Ain't Easy
Las Parablas De Amor
Sail Away Sweet Sister
One Year Of Love

Songs Queen performed live (original material)

The following tracks were all performed by Queen during their fifteen years of touring. The number in brackets relates to the album on which each track can be found.

1. **Queen** (1973)
2. **Queen II** (1974)
3. **Sheer Heart Attack** (1974)
4. **A Night At The Opera** (1975)
5. **A Day At The Races** (1976)
6. **News Of The World** (1977)
7. **Jazz** (1978)
8. **The Game** (1980)
9. **Flash Gordon** (1980)
10. **Hot Space** (1982)
11. **The Works** (1984)
12. **A Kind Of Magic** (1986)

NA *Does not appear on any album*
* *Denotes an Instrumental track*
+ *See Below*

A Kind Of Magic (Taylor) (12)
Action This Day (Taylor) (10)
Another One Bites The Dust (Deacon) (8)
Back Chat (Deacon) (10)
Battle Theme (May) (9)
Bicycle Race (Mercury) (7)
Body Language (Mercury) (10)
Bohemian Rhapsody (Mercury) (4)
Brighton Rock (May)(3)
Bring Back That Leroy Brown (Mercury) (3)
Calling All Girls (Taylor) (10)
Crazy Little Thing Called Love (Mercury) (8)
Death On Two Legs (Mercury) (4)
Doing All Right (May Staffel) (1)
Don't Stop Me Now (Mercury) (7)
Dragon Attack (May) (8)
Dreamer's Ball (May) (7)
Fat Bottomed Girls (May) (7)
Father To Son (May) (2)
Flash (May) (9)
Flick Of The Wrist (Mercury) (3)
Friends Will Be Friends (FM & JD) (12)
Get Down Make Love (Mercury) (6)
God Save The Queen (Arr. May) (4)
Good Old Fashioned Lover Boy (Mercury) (5)
Great King Rat (Mercury) (1)
Hammer To Fall (May) (11)
Hangman (unknown) (NA) +
The Hero (May) (9)
I Want To Break Free (Deacon) (11)
If You Can't Beat Them (Deacon) (7)
Impromptu (Queen) (NA) +
Improvisation (Queen) (NA) +
I'm In Love With My Car (Taylor) (4)
In The Lap Of The Gods (Mercury) (3)
In The Lap Of The Gods... Revisited (Mercury) (3)
Instrumental Inferno (Queen) (NA) +
Is This The World We Created (FM & BM) (11)
It's A Hard Life (Mercury) (11)
It's Late (May) (6)
Keep Yourself Alive (May) (1)
Killer Queen (Mercury) (3)
Lazing On A Sunday Afternoon (Mercury) (4)
Let Me Entertain You (Mercury) (7)
Liar (Mercury) (1)
Life Is Real (Mercury) (10)
Love Of My Life (Mercury) (4)
Machines (Or Back To Humans) (BM & RT) (11) *
The March Of The Black Queen (Mercury) (2)
The Millionaire Waltz (Mercury) (5)
Modern Times Rock'n'Roll (Taylor) (2)
Mustapha (Mercury) (7)
My Melancholy Blues (Mercury)(6)
Need Your Loving Tonight (Deacon) (8)
Now I'm Here (May) (3)

Ogre Battle (Mercury) (2)
One Vision (Queen) (12)
Play The Game (Mercury) (8)
Procession (May) (2) *
The Prophet's Song (May) (4)
Put Out The Fire (May) (10)
Radio Ga Ga (Taylor) (11)
Rock In Rio Blues (Queen) (NA) +
Rock It (Prime Jive) (Taylor) (8)
Save Me (May) (8)
See What A Fool I've Been (May) (NA)
Seven Seas Of Rhye (Mercury) (2)
Shag Out (?) (NA) +
Sheer Heart Attack (Taylor) (6)
Somebody To Love (Mercury) (5)
Son & Daughter (May) (1)
Spread Your Wings (Deacon) (6)
Staying Power (Mercury) (10)
Stone Cold Crazy (Queen) (3)
Sweet Lady (May) (4)
Tear It Up (May) (11)
Tie Your Mother Down (May) (5)
Teo Torriatte (May) (5)
39 (May) (4)
Tokyo Blues (Queen) (NA) +
Under Pressure (Q & DB) (10)
We Are The Champions (Mercury) (6)
We Will Rock You (May) (6)
White Man (May) (5)
White Queen (As It Began) (May) (2)
Who Wants To Live Forever (May) (12)
You're My Best Friend (Deacon) (4)
You Take My Breath Away (Mercury) (5)

See What A Fool I've Been
Single B-side. Played live, but not on any album.

Hangman
Played live, and it was possibly recorded, but has never been released.

Shag Out
No such track. It is part of above track.

Rock In Rio Blues
Jamming type Improvisation, not recorded and not on any album.

Tokyo Blues
Jamming type Improvisation, not recorded and not on any album.

Impromptu
Jamming type Improvisation. not on any studio album, but on 'Live At Wembley 86' album.

Improvisation
Jamming type Improvisation, not recorded and not on any album. Usually a vocal or guitar (or both) ad-libbed piece.

Instrumental Inferno
Jam type Improvisation, not recorded and not on any album.

Date of début show
in each country

(Number in bracket denotes
total amount of shows performed
in that country)

Argentina . . . . . . 28 February 1981 (5)
Austria . . . . 2 May 1978 (7)
Australia . . . . 2 February 1974 (17)
Belgium . . . . 1 December 1974 (13)
Brazil. . . . . 20 March 1981 (4)
Canada . . . . 2 April 1975 (24)
Denmark. . . . . 12 May 1977 (2)
Eire. . . . . 22 November 1979 (4)
Finland . . . . 25 November 1974 (1)
France . . . . 23 April 1978 (14)
Germany . . . . . . 13 October 1973 (58)
Holland. . . . . . . 8 December 1974 (11)
Hungary. . . . . 27 July 1986 (1)
Italy . . . . 14 September 1984 (2)
Japan . . . . 19 April 1975 (51)
Luxembourg. . . . . 14 October 1973 (1)
Mexico . . . . 9 October 1981 (3)
New Zealand. . . . . . 13 April 1985 (1)
Norway . . . . 12 April 1982 (1)
South Africa. . . . . . 5 October 1984 (7)
Spain. . . . . 10 December 1974 (8)
Sweden. . . . . . 23 November 1974 (7)
Switzerland . . . . 19 May 1977 (8)
UK . . . . 27 June 1970 (199)
USA. . . . . 16 April 1974 (250)
Venezuela . . . . . 25 September 1981 (3)
Yugoslavia . . . . . . 6 February 1979 (2)

Total   704

*Queen's first ever public live performance
(UK - 27/6/70) is the first recorded show.*

Album tracks which
never featured in any
Queen live show

Queen (1973)
My Fairy King (Mercury) / The Night
Comes Down* (May) / Jesus (Mercury)

Queen II (1974)
Someday One Day (May) / The Loser
In The End (Taylor) / The Fairy Feller's
Master Stroke* (Mercury) / Nevermore
(Mercury) / Funny How Love Is (Mercury)

Sheer Heart Attack (1974)
Tenement Funster (Taylor) / Lily Of The
Valley (Mercury) / Dear Friends (May) /
Misfire (Deacon) / She Makes Me (May)

A Night At The Opera (1975)
Seaside Rendezvous (Mercury) / Good
Company (May)

A Day At The Races (1976)
Long Away (May) / You And I (Deacon) /
Drowse (Taylor)

News Of The World (1977)
All Dead All Dead (May) / Fight From
The Inside (Taylor) / Sleeping On
The Sidewalk* (May) / Who Needs You
(Deacon)

Jazz (1978)
Jealousy (Mercury) / Dead On Time
(May) / In Only Seven Days (Deacon) /
Fun It (Taylor) / Leaving Home Ain't Easy
(May) / More Of That Jazz (Taylor)

The Game (1980)
Don't Try Suicide (Mercury) / Sail Away
Sweet Sister (May) / Coming Soon
(Taylor)

Flash Gordon (Soundtrack) (1980)
With the exception of Flash's theme,
The Battle Theme and The Hero, no
other material from the album was
considered appropriate for inclusion in
the live set - it is after all a soundtrack
project.

Hot Space (1982)
Dancer (May) / Las Parablas De Amor
(May) / Cool Cat (Deacon/Mercury)

The Works (1984)
Man On The Prowl (Mercury) / Machines
(Or Back To Humans) (Album Vocal
Version) (Taylor/May) / Keep Passing The
Open Windows (Mercury)

A Kind Of Magic (1986)
One Year Of Love (Deacon) / Pain Is So
Close To Pleasure (Mercury/Deacon) /
Gimme The Prize (May) / Don't Lose Your
Head (Taylor) / Princes Of The Universe
(Mercury)

* These three tracks were played only
once, as far as can be determined.

Songs Queen
have performed live -
but did not write

Bama Lama Bama Loo
Reached No. 37 in July 1977 for
Little Richard. Written by
Penniman (Little Richard) and Collins.

Be Bop A Lula
Reached No. 30 in July 1956 for
Gene Vincent. Re-entered the charts
on two more occasions. Written by
G. Vincent and T. Davis.

Big Spender
Reached No. 21 in October 1967 for
Shirley Bassey. Written by
C. Coleman and D. Fields.

Danny Boy
Written in 1913 by Fred Weatherly;
original recording by Madame Schumann.
Has become an Irish favourite.

Gimme Some Lovin
Reached No. 2 in November 1966 for
Spencer Davis Group. Written by
Steve Winwood, Muff Winwood and
Spencer Davis.

Hello Mary Lou (Goodbye Heart)
Reached No. 2 in June 1961 for
Rick Nelson. Written by Gene Pitney.

I'm A Man
Reached No. 9 in January 1967 for
Spencer Davis Group. Written by
Steve Winwood and Jimmy Miller.

Imagine
Reached No. 6 in November 1975
and No. 1 in December 1980 for
John Lennon. Written by John Lennon.

Immigrant Song
Recorded by Led Zeppelin for the
Led Zeppelin III album in 1970.
Not issued as a single. Written by
Jimmy Page and Robert Plant.

Jailhouse Rock
Reached No. 1 in January 1958 for
Elvis Presley. Reissued in December 1971,
September 1977 and February 1983.
Written by Jerry Leiber and Mike Stoller.

Lucille
Reached No. 10 in June 1957 for
Little Richard. Written by
Penniman (Little Richard) and Collins.

Mannish Boy
Reached No. 51 in July 1988 for
Muddy Waters. Written by
Muddy Morganfield (Muddy Waters),
E. McDaniel and M. London.

Mull Of Kintyre
Reached No. 1 in 1977 for Wings.
Written by Paul McCartney.

Not Fade Away
Reached No. 3 in February 1964 for
The Rolling Stones. Written by
Buddy Holly.

**Saturday Night's Alright
For Fighting**
Reached No. 7 in July 1973 for
Elton John. Written by
Elton John and Bernie Taupin.

Shake, Rattle & Roll
Originally recorded by Big Joe Turner.
Reached No. 4 in December 1954 for
Bill Haley And His Comets. Also covered
by Elvis Presley, Buddy Holly, Carl Perkins
and Cliff Richard, amongst others. Written
by Jessie (Charlie Calhoun) Stone.

Silent Night
Reached No. 8 in December 1952
for Bing Crosby, No. 47 in 1978 for
The Dickies, and No. 2 in 1988 for Bros.
Originally a German hymn. Written by
Joseph Mohr.

Stupid Cupid
Reached No. 1 (B-side of Carolina Moon)
in August 1958 for Connie Francis.
Written by Sedaka and Greenfield.

Take Me Home
Essentially a Brian guitar ad-lib, it crops
up on numerous bootleg compilations.

Tavaszi Szel Vizet Araszt
Hungarian folk song. Composer unknown.

Tutti Frutti
Reached No. 29 in February 1957 for
Little Richard. Also covered by
Elvis Presley. Written by Lubin,
LaBostrie and Penniman (Little Richard).

White Christmas
A hit for numerous artists between
1952 and 1985, most familiarly
Bing Crosby - No. 5 in December 1977.
Reissued in December 1985 (No. 69).
Written by Irving Berlin.

**You're So Square
(Baby I Don't Care)**
Originally recorded by Elvis Presley for
his movie Jailhouse Rock. Reached No. 12
in July 1961 for Buddy Holly. Written by
Jerry Leiber and Mike Stoller.

A Concert Documentary

"Freddie had great strength of
will, and actually used the effort of
getting to work in the last three
years or so, as a kind of focus to help
him through all the pain he was
going through.

"We felt that just by being
involved with him – working closely
together in the studio, we were
actually helping him as much as we
could.

"In fact, I think the rest of
the band feel that his best vocal
performances – in terms of range,
power and emotion, were on the last
album.

"He was warm, and generous
to a fault, and work was always fun.
We were honoured to work with
him, and we'll never forget him."

Roger Taylor, November 1991

Queen Live